Out of the Gobi

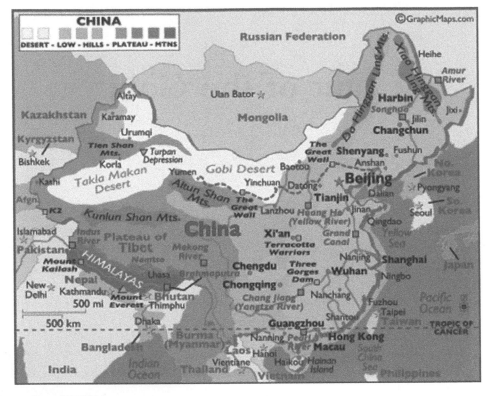

Source: WorldAtlas.com

Note: China, with a landmass of approximately 9.6 square kilometers (3.7 million square miles), is about the same size as the United States (with its landmass of 9.8 million square kilometers, or 3.8 million square miles). China's population of about 1.4 billion (in 2016) is more than four times that of the United States (325 million). The shape of the country reminds one of a rooster. The Gobi Desert is located on the back of the rooster, in the north. The Great Wall, shown as a dotted line, stretches from the throat of the rooster near Beijing all the way to the west, roughly parallel to the rest of the Gobi Desert for 6,259 kilometers (3,889 miles), but its total length, including all its branches, is 21,196 kilometers (13,171 miles). The Yellow River, part of which flows close to the southern edge of the Gobi Desert, is the second-longest river in China and the sixth-longest in the world, with an estimated length of 5,464 kilometers (3,395 miles).

Out of the Gobi

*My Story of China
and America*

Weijian Shan

WILEY

Published by John Wiley & Sons, Inc., Hoboken, New Jersey.

Published simultaneously in Canada.

For general information on our other products and services or for technical support, please contact our Customer Care Department within the United States at (800) 762-2974, outside the United States at (317) 572-3993, or fax (317) 572-4002.

Wiley publishes in a variety of print and electronic formats and by print-on-demand. Some material included with standard print versions of this book may not be included in e-books or in print-on-demand. If this book refers to media such as a CD or DVD that is not included in the version you purchased, you may download this material at http://booksupport.wiley.com. For more information about Wiley products, visit www.wiley.com.

Library of Congress Cataloging-in-Publication Data:
Name: Shan, Weijian, 1953–, author.
Title: Out of the Gobi : my story of China and America / Weijian Shan.
Description: Hoboken, New Jersey : John Wiley & Sons, Inc., [2019] | Includes index. |
Identifiers: LCCN 2018046912 (print) | LCCN 2018049208 (ebook) |
ISBN 978-1-119-52956-9 (Adobe PDF) | ISBN 978-1-119-52955-2 (ePub) |
ISBN 978-1-119-52949-1 (hardcover)
Subjects: LCSH: Shan, Weijian, 1953– | Businesspeople—China—Biography. | Chinese—United States—Biography. | China—History—1949– | United States—History—1945–
Classification: LCC HC426.5.S43 (ebook) | LCC HC426.5.S43 A3 2019 (print) |
DDC 338.092 [B] —dc23
LC record available at https://lccn.loc.gov/2018046912

Printed in the United States of America

V10008919_031819

*To my wife, Bin Shi, and to our son,
Bo, and daughter, LeeAnn*

Contents

Foreword

The manuscript of Weijian Shan's book arrived on my desk at a hectic time: I had commitments for weeks to come. But when I finally picked up the manuscript, I was so gripped by his stories that I could hardly put it down.

I have known Shan for 36 years, since he first showed up in my office on a sunny September day in 1982. He struck me as a charming young man, full of smiles, but in need of a good meal and a new haircut. He had arrived at Berkeley to start his Ph.D. program, and I was his academic advisor. I was stunned to discover that he had no formal math training. All the math he knew he had learned by himself, by candlelight. Over time, I learned a bit about Shan's unique and extraordinary background growing up in China, where he was denied an education for 10 years after elementary school.

Yet I was fascinated to read his detailed account of a China gone mad during the 1966–1976 Cultural Revolution, of the severe hardship he and his generation had endured, of his relentless pursuit of an education through reading whatever books he could find while serving as a hard laborer in China's Gobi Desert at a time when almost all books were banned, and of how, against all odds, he was able to get out of the Gobi and eventually find his way to America to attend graduate school.

He recounts a contemporary history of China rarely told in the English literature from a personal perspective, a history that paralleled our own tumultuous period in the 1960s and 1970s in America. His keen observation of the United States from the viewpoint of someone with a totally different cultural, political, and economic background is unique, insightful, heartwarming, and often funny. He recounts his stories with vivid clarity, short, punchy sentences, and light and dark humor. They captivate the reader, who feels as if he is watching a movie, anxious to know how the plot will unfold and where it will all end.

After earning his doctoral degree, Shan received offers of professorships from some of the most renowned American universities, including MIT and the Wharton School of the University of Pennsylvania. I remember him calling me for advice, asking which school he should choose for his academic career. I told him he couldn't go wrong at any of these top schools. As I remarked to one of my Berkeley colleagues at a celebration party on the occasion of Shan's graduation in 1987, I found it mind-boggling how far he had journeyed—from working as a hard laborer without a secondary education and with no command of English to becoming a professor at one of America's most prestigious universities, all in about ten years.

Shan's story shows the crucial role that education plays in the success of individuals and society as a whole. Moreover, Shan's life provides a demonstration of what is possible when China and the United States come together, even by happenstance. It is not only Shan's personal history that makes this book so interesting but also how the stories of China and America merge in just one moment in time to create an inspired individual so unique and driven, and so representative of the true spirits of both countries.

Particularly now, the people of both nations have much to learn from and teach one another. I hope that Shan's book will serve as a cornerstone in that ongoing conversation.

Janet Yellen
Federal Reserve Chair (2014–2018)
Eugene E. and Catherine
M. Trefethen Professor of Business and
Professor of Economics Emeritus,
University of California, Berkeley

Acknowledgments

This book is a memoir, not an autobiography. The distinction may be blurred at times, but my idea has always been to tell stories that I consider reflective of history as I lived it, both in China and in America.

By coincidence, the release of this book will mark the fiftieth anniversary of the start of my life in the Gobi Desert in China's Inner Mongolia. My generation in China is truly a lost generation, because for 10 long years the vast majority of us were deprived of a formal education and many were unable to make up for the lost years later in life. I dedicate this book to my friends of the Gobi days and to the people of my generation who shared similar ordeals.

I am immensely grateful to Dr. Janet Yellen for providing the foreword for this book.

I began to write this book in 1990, and after a few months I completed about 100 pages, which included my recollections covered in Chapters 5 through 7, 9 through 13, and 15. Dr. Judy Shapiro at the University of Pennsylvania helped me edit those pages. Before I was able to finish them, I became extremely busy, and by good fortune I remained so for the next 26 years. On New Year's Day 2017, at my son's home in California with our family, I decided to pick it back up again.

I wish to thank Bill Falloon, my editor at Wiley, who, in addition to his editing work, made good suggestions from which the book benefited immensely. It is based on his suggestion that I include a prologue for each chapter, to provide historical background and context for the ensuing story. I also thank the Wiley teams in copyediting, design, production, and marketing for an excellent job in turning the book into a beautiful product.

I owe my gratitude to my other editors, Mark Clifford, Jill Baker, and Tim Morrison, for their encouragement and their essential help editing, fact-checking, and suggesting numerous good ideas to improve the quality of the manuscript. I thank my assistant Rachel Kwok for helping me in countless ways related to this project.

The stories in the book are based on recollections of my own experiences, and on rare occasions those of others, woven together into a coherent narrative. I have incorporated materials and data from historical research, but do not otherwise provide sources and citations as you might find in a more formal work of history. I have made an effort to check multiple sources to determine the accuracy and reliability of the data included here. I along with my editors have made our best efforts to fact-check all material information in the book. The responsibility for any errors is mine alone.

My good friend Liu Xiaotong, a self-taught photographer who owned a rare 135mm camera, took many of the photographs of us in the Gobi, including the photograph on the cover showing me running in the Gobi. He would have been an accomplished musician and multi-talented artist if not for the Cultural Revolution.

I am deeply indebted to my wife, Bin Shi, for her support and sacrifice as I devoted almost all my spare time to this project, and to my children, Bo and LeeAnn, whose fascination with the stories of my past strongly motivated me to write and complete this book, and whose critiques helped improve it greatly.

Weijian Shan
October 17, 2018
Hong Kong

Author's Note

Chinese names are written and spoken with the surname or family name first, followed by the given name. Take, for example, the most famous Chinese names of the twentieth century: Mao Zedong, Zhou Enlai, Deng Xiaoping, Chiang Kai-shek—all are written with the family name first.

Western-educated Chinese tend to adopt the European way to write their names in English (i.e., putting the given name first and family name last). My name as presented in Chinese is Shan Weijian. In English, it is Weijian Shan. In mainland China today, a woman does not adopt the family name of her husband, so there is no distinction between a "maiden" and a "married" name as in the United States or Europe. Some Chinese women living outside mainland China, such as Hong Kong and Taiwan, adopt their husbands' family names. My wife's given name is Bin and her family name is Shi. In China, it is written as Shi Bin, but in America her name is written as either Bin Shi or Bin Shi Shan, the latter adopting my family name.

In this book, all Chinese names are presented in the order of family name first, followed by the given name, and are indexed in this way as well.

I refer to some characters in the book by their given names and others by their family names, with or without an honorific or professional title (Mr., Mrs., Dr., or Professor). This largely depends on how I would greet them in real life, as such references come naturally to mind when I write. It should be noted that it is common in Chinese culture to greet someone by putting either "lao (Old)," which is a form of respect, or "xiao (Little)," which is a form of endearment, in front of their family name. In this book, I use this in referring to Old Yi, Old Cui, Old Huang, and so on, because this is how they were addressed by the people around them.

China uses a traditional system of measurement as well as the metric system. The Chinese system can be easily translated into the metric system in whole numbers. For example, one kilometer is exactly two Chinese *li*, one meter is exactly 3 Chinese *chi*, one kilogram is exactly two Chinese *jin*, one hectare is exactly 15 *mu*. In the book, I provide the imperial equivalent when a unit of measurement is presented in the metric system or Chinese system, for example, 100 kilometers (~62 miles) or 100 kilograms (~220 pounds).

I make an effort to minimize the use of acronyms, abbreviations, or untranslated Chinese terms to make it easier for the reader to understand. For example, I use the "Nationalist" Party or the "Nationalist" government to refer to Chiang Kai-shek's organization, instead of "Kuomintang" or "KMT," which are loanwords based on Chinese phonetics often seen in the English literature of Chinese studies.

Prologue

On September 13, 1950, UN forces commanded by General Douglas MacArthur made an amphibious landing at the port of Incheon, on the west coast of Korea, about 40 kilometers from Seoul. The operation involved more than 260 naval vessels, including 6 aircraft carriers, and 75,000 troops, the largest deployment of firepower since the D-Day landing at Normandy. North Korean forces had squeezed the opposing UN troops to a toehold around Pusan, in the southeastern corner of the Korean Peninsula, and threatened to push them into the Pacific Ocean. For the North Koreans, victory was in sight. The Incheon landing, however, was a complete success: It put MacArthur's troops well behind the North Koreans' front lines and turned the tide of the Korean War. By October, UN forces crossed the 38th parallel dividing North and South Korea. By the end of the month they were within striking distance of the Yalu River, which demarcates the border between North Korea and China. General MacArthur declared that the war would be over by Christmas.

On November 1, advancing US troops were halted at the Battle of Unsan some 200 kilometers from the Chinese border and repelled by Chinese forces, which eventually pushed all the way back across the 38th parallel and recaptured Seoul, the capital of South Korea.

As his troops lost ground, US president Harry Truman declared that he would take whatever steps necessary to win the war in Korea, including the use of nuclear weapons. In April 1951, he sent nine nuclear bombs with fissile cores to Okinawa, along with nuclear-capable B-29 bombers. In October, Operation Hudson Harbor conducted mock nuclear bombing runs across the war zone, preparing to rain fire on a huge swath of northeast Asia, including parts of China and Russia if necessary. Fortunately, they never had to. By that summer the war had largely devolved into skirmishes in a narrow zone around the 38th parallel, and armistice talks were under way.

I was born in October 1953 in China's Shandong Province, one of the two primary target areas for the planned nuclear strike. I was lucky to have been born.

★ ★ ★

My parents' generation, and the generation before theirs, had lived through numerous wars, each more devastating than the last, with almost no respite or peace in between. Tens of millions of people died in China in those wars and in famines during the century before my birth.

The last Chinese dynasty, the Qing, was overthrown in October 1911. Prior to this, the country had been repeatedly ravaged by foreign invasions and peasant uprisings.

In the First Opium War of 1840, Britain invaded and defeated China for refusing to allow British merchants to sell opium to China. The Second Opium War followed, from 1856 to 1860, during which the joint forces of the British and French empires marched all the way to Beijing to force China to legalize the opium trade and open its ports to foreigners. They burned down the magnificent Old Summer Palace, said to be many times larger and grander than its replacement, which itself is still considered one of the greatest imperial palaces in the world.

Between 1851 and 1864, there was a massive peasant uprising known as Taiping Rebellion. About 20 million people perished in the seesaw battles between the peasants and government forces before the rebellion was brutally crushed. The Boxer Rebellion (1899–1901) led to another invasion of China and the occupation of Beijing by the joint forces of eight foreign powers, which included European countries, the United States, and Japan. In 1894, Japanese warships obliterated the newly formed Chinese navy off China's northeast coast, clearing the way for Japan's colonial occupation of Korea. The ground battle of the Russo-Japanese war (1904–1905) was fought in the Chinese port city of Lushun, known at that time as Port Arthur, and resulted in hundreds of thousands of Chinese civilian deaths.

By the beginning of twentieth century, the Qing dynasty was rotten to the core, and the country was on the verge of being torn apart by foreign powers. The 1911 Revolution marked an end to the imperial era and gave birth to the Republic of China. But it did not bring either peace or a stronger nation. The country soon fractured into many different territories, controlled by warlords who relentlessly waged bloody wars against each other, causing numerous deaths and much misery.

In 1927, a Northern Expedition Force led by Chiang Kai-shek marched from the southern city of Guangzhou, fought its way north against the warlords, and eventually brought the country under one flag, albeit extremely tenuously. Along the way, Chiang carried out a purge of Communists, his former allies in the fight against the warlords. Thousands were massacred by Chiang's Nationalist troops, and the rest either went underground or led uprisings against the new regime. In August 1927, Zhou Enlai, who later became the first premier of the People's Republic of China, led an armed uprising in the southern city of Nanchang, which marked the founding of the People's Liberation Army. In autumn 1927, Mao Zedong led what became known as the Autumn Harvest Uprising, establishing the first Communist base in the mountainous areas of Jiangxi Province. This began the first civil war between the Nationalists and the Communists; it would last for the next 10 years.

In 1931, Japanese troops invaded northeast China and captured a territory about twice the size of France, turning it into a puppet state they called Manchukuo. In 1937, Japan launched an all-out war against China and occupied all the coastal cities and some inland provinces. By various estimates, Chinese casualties from the time of Japan's invasion to its surrender in 1945 numbered between 20 and 30 million, the vast majority of which were civilian deaths.

The Nationalists and the Communists cooperated in the war against Japan, but as soon as hostilities were ended, their own conflict was rekindled. In the ensuing war, Communist forces led by Mao Zedong rapidly grew in strength to rival and eventually overwhelm the Nationalist troops. Between 1947 and 1949, the Communists won three decisive battles, each of which eliminated about half a million Nationalist troops, sealing the fate of Chiang Kai-shek's Old China. Chiang fled to Taiwan with what was left of his troops and his government, taking with him tons of gold and all movable treasures from Beijing's Forbidden City.

Mao Zedong proclaimed the founding of the People's Republic of China on October 1, 1949. This was to be the New China: finally unified, free of the yoke of imperial and colonial aggression, marching forward into a promising future.

★ ★ ★

I was born into this New China, a country that had finally begun a period of sustained nation-building after a hundred years of tragic upheaval and war. It is for this reason my parents named me Weijian. The Chinese character *wei* means "great," and *jian* means "build" or "construct." They certainly had great hopes for nation-building, for peace, and for a better life for their children.

But it was not to be. Not, at least, as they had hoped.

Chapter 1

Man-Made Famine

On March 10, 1945, President Franklin D. Roosevelt wrote a letter to Mao Zedong, the leader of Chinese Communist forces in the war against Japan. "My Dear Mr. Mao," Roosevelt wrote, "I received your letter of November 10, 1944 upon my return from the Yalta Conference and appreciate very much receiving your personal views on developments in China." Roosevelt noted Mao's emphasis on the unity of the Chinese people and expressed his hope that Mao and the Nationalist leader, Chiang Kai-shek, could find a way to work together to defeat the Japanese. Roosevelt concluded by saying: "The friendship of the Chinese people and the people of the United States is, as you say, traditional and deep-rooted, and I am confident that the cooperation of the Chinese and American peoples will greatly contribute to the achievement of victory and lasting peace."

It was rather extraordinary that Roosevelt should have written to Mao at all. At the time, Mao was mainly known as a Communist guerrilla leader with a force far smaller and worse equipped than that of Chiang's Nationalist government; few would have predicted that he would seize national power only four years later. But Mao went out of his way to make overtures to the US president. In 1945, months before the Japanese surrender, Mao offered to visit Roosevelt in Washington, but the offer was spurned by the US ambassador at the time, Patrick J. Hurley, who never delivered Mao's offer to the president.

After the founding of the People's Republic of China (PRC) on October 1, 1949, Chiang Kai-shek's remaining forces fled to the island of Taiwan. Although the United States continued to recognize Chiang's government as the legitimate government of all of China, it seemed that it was not prepared to throw its lot in with the defeated Nationalist government altogether. On January 5, 1950, President Harry Truman announced that the United States would not intervene in the event of an attack on Taiwan by the PRC, indicating that while it remained wary, the United States had not entirely ruled out a relationship with the Communists, who had cooperated effectively with the Americans in the war against Japan.

But if Mao had cherished any hope of a good relationship between his New China and the United States, it was dashed six months later with the outbreak of the Korean War. On June 27, Truman ordered the Seventh Fleet into the Taiwan Strait, declaring that a Communist takeover of the island would constitute a "direct threat to the security of the Pacific area." The United States also imposed a total trade embargo on China. From that point on, Mao's China leaned inexorably into the camp of the Soviet Union. But that friendship proved to be short-lived as well.

In the United States, the political discourse in the 1950s became focused on "who lost China"—as if the US had ever owned it. In an era when McCarthyism dominated the US scene and all the "China hands" in the State Department saw their careers trashed or worse, any relationship with "Red China" was out of the question. The "Red scare" with respect to China would persist long after Senator Joseph McCarthy was discredited and disgraced. It would take 20 years, and a staunch anti-communist Republican president, to break the ice in the US relationship with China.

Meanwhile, the China Mao had conquered remained a country in dire poverty. Outside the major urban areas, it was largely a preindustrial society; by the estimates of British economist Angus Maddison, China's per capita GDP in 1950 was about $450, less than 20 percent that of the United States in 1870 (in 1990 dollars). Mao's New China began economic reconstruction in earnest when peace finally came after the end of the Korean War in 1953. That same year, China adopted its first five-year economic development plan and began a process of rapid industrialization, with the help of the Soviet Union. Between 1953 and 1957, China's GDP grew by about 50 percent, or more than 9 percent a year.

But Mao still thought the pace of growth was too slow. In 1958, he launched the "Great Leap Forward," a social and economic campaign to mobilize the entire nation to massively increase industrial and agricultural production in an effort to catch up with the more developed countries. I turned five in October of that year, and so began my earliest recollections and memories as a young child in China.

★ ★ ★

When I first met my late mother-in-law, who was a dentist in a military hospital, she could not find anything good about me except my teeth. To this day, I cannot truly explain why I was blessed with such nice teeth and the smile of an optimist, or why that was my one redeeming feature in her eyes.

I suffered my fair share of malnutrition, occasional starvation, and poor oral hygiene in my formative years, so it is a little bit of a mystery where I got my unusually good teeth. The only reason I can think of is all the vitamin D I got from being exposed to sunlight in the little one-room home in Beijing where I spent my infant years. The window faced south, and filled the room with sunlight and brightness. My first memory is of my mother bringing my newborn brother home from the hospital in 1957, when I was about three and a half years old.

My parents had come to Beijing from Shandong Province when I was about a year old, and we lived in that sun-drenched room until just before my fifth birthday. That year, 1958, we moved to a new home in a walled residential compound located approximately a mile east of Beijing's Tiananmen Square. There were a few residential buildings of different vintages and styles in the compound where, I would guess, 50 to 60 households resided. Our family shared our dwelling with more than 20 households under one tiled roof of a dilapidated, probably 100-year old Chinese-style house that used to be the office of Old China's customs administration. Each household occupied one or two rooms and all the families shared the only two toilets located on each side of the building. There was a relatively new, gray-colored, four- or five-story apartment building on one side of the compound, and there were some buildings that looked like military barracks on the other. At the very far end of the compound was an auditorium, no doubt built for the official function of the old customs administration but now used for occasional movie showings. In the center of the dwellings was an open, irregular-shaped space the size of about three tennis courts with a few old trees growing here and there.

The year 1958 turned out to be eventful and pivotal in the history of the New China. Even though I hardly remember anything of our personal life at home, I vividly remember taking part in what was happening around us. Those episodes and activities were so unusual and so tantalizingly exciting to a child that they left an indelible impression on me.

The Great Leap Forward, a campaign launched that year by China's charismatic leader, Mao Zedong, became a mass movement that touched everyone in the country. The policies of the Great Leap Forward were designed to mobilize China's masses and resources to drastically accelerate China's economic growth, to increase agricultural and industrial production, and to propel China quickly into the ranks of more developed economies. This would pave the way for China to move from the "stage of socialism" to the "stage of communism"—the classless, materially abundant utopia that was Karl Marx's ultimate vision.

Mao effectively aimed to accomplish in a few years what it had taken Europe more than a century to develop. But he was confident. After all, the Communist Party had grown from nothing to become the masters of the world's most populous nation and had won victory after victory against overwhelming odds. China could achieve anything by mobilizing and motivating its masses. His Great Leap Forward would be a people's war to accelerate China's economic development and drastically increase its production of all things. His goal? "To surpass Britain in 15 years and to catch up with America in 20 years" in steel production, considered the main barometer of industrialization.

In 1957, China produced less than a quarter of the steel that Britain did, and less than half as much iron. Surpassing Britain in 15 years was a colossal task. But as a 1958 publication of Beijing's foreign-language press put it, "To the emancipated Chinese people nothing is impossible."

Some people believed that making iron and steel was not so hard. It was suggested that iron and steel could be made anywhere with simple homemade tools and methods. It required no more than a small blast furnace made of bricks and clay, fired by coal and fed with scrap metal.

The small blast furnace I saw, built in the open space of our residential compound, was only a couple of meters tall, in size and shape very much like the smallest camping tents in today's sporting goods stores. Soon there was a frenzied effort to build such homemade blast furnaces everywhere throughout China, in the backyards of homes, in schools and in villages. It was later reported that at least 60 million such blast furnaces had been built. The nationwide campaign, known as "mass steel-making," became so feverish that people toiled at their furnaces day and night as fire and smoke bellowed out of the small chimneys. All families were expected to contribute to steel production. To demonstrate their enthusiastic support, people donated whatever metal they had in their possession, eventually including their cooking pots and pans. I followed some activist adults in our compound and went door-to-door to collect anything made of iron or steel.

The only iron we had at home was our stove, which was stripped of its ornamentation; children helped adults carry the metal parts to the blast furnace to be melted. The fire, the smoke, the piles of scrap, the busy crowd carrying pieces of metal or doing this and that—and above all the noise—were all very exciting. Children ran around the makeshift blast furnaces more excited than on Chinese New Year. I do not know how many days or weeks this went on, but it must have gone on for a long time to leave a lasting impression on me. I do not know how much iron and steel the blast furnace in our yard produced. In the end, as I later learned, the steel production campaign was a total failure. Well, it was a big joke: Anyone with any knowledge of metallurgy would know that you can't just toss scrap metal into a backyard furnace and expect it to produce durable, high-quality steel. People destroyed or damaged useful metal things and burned tons of wood and coal to produce only waste, as the output from the small blast furnaces was completely useless.

In the end, China only produced about 10 percent more steel in 1958 than in 1957, but nobody knew how much of that increased production was usable. An estimated 100 million farmers, government employees, schoolteachers, and students went into the backyard steel production in that year, diverting resources and manpower from the production of other goods (including food). As a result, there was a shortage of farm labor and 15 percent of the grain crop rotted in the fields because there was no farm labor available to harvest it, which directly contributed to the Great Famine that engulfed the country.

★ ★ ★

To boost agricultural production and to improve health, another campaign was waged in 1958 simultaneously with the Great Leap Forward. It was called "Eradicate the Four Pests"—mosquitoes, flies, rats, and sparrows.

The whole country was mobilized to kill the four pests. Beijing used to have many flies and mosquitoes. Our home was sprayed with pesticides and fumigated from time to time. When this happened, we would stay outside, running and horsing around. Our building was very old and in need of repairs, and there were rats in the roof. I could sometimes hear them rustling around at night. Rat traps and poison were used to kill them. Sometimes we were warned to stay indoors as the entire city was blanketed by insect-killing smoke. We also used ingenious flytraps made with a see-through screen stretched over a pyramid-shaped frame with an opening at the bottom. We put a piece of rotten fish head in the bottom to attract flies. They had no trouble getting into the pyramid, but when they took off they were trapped; flies do not know how to fly sideways.

But the most exciting and memorable thing to a child was the campaign to capture and kill sparrows. The alleged crime of sparrows was the theft of grain. For this offense, Mao decided to condemn them all to heaven. Between March 14 and 19, 1958, a national "Coordination Conference for the Great Leap Forward to Eradicate Four Pests" was held in Beijing. For the purpose of killing off sparrows, Beijing established a command center, and a vice mayor, Wang Kunlun, was appointed the commander-in-chief of the effort. On the day of the action, April 19, 1958, it seemed that the entire population of the city came into the streets. Some people carried long sticks with colorful rags tied on the tips, or held flags on long poles. People beat drums, gongs, and pans so loudly the noise was deafening. Initially, startled birds were flying everywhere. Whenever a bird flew over our heads, people would make even louder noises and wave their flags more wildly to prevent the bird from landing.

Sparrows are short-distance fliers. Big as the city is, there was no place for the birds to hide or land as there were multitudes of people everywhere, making loud noises and waving flags. The commotion sent birds into a panic and they flew like shooting arrows here and there in search of safety. Sometimes a bird would land on a roof corner, exhausted. But there were people on the roof, and under the roof, and the crowds would rush toward the bird or throw stones at it, forcing it to take off again. After a while, exhausted birds began to drop from the sky, one after another. Whenever a bird fell, crowds would cheer and swell forward to capture it. I have never seen anything like this before or after. I had a great time with other children running around, yelling, and throwing stones at the birds.

Poor birds. This was a doomsday they had never dreamed of. For all I knew at the time, the campaign was successful. The *People's Daily* reported on April 20, 1958, that three million people in the capital participated in the operation on April 19, and by 10 p.m., 83,000 sparrows perished in the waves of the people's war. In three days, the residents of Beijing killed more than 400,000 sparrows.

Birds basically disappeared from Beijing from that time on. This was a nationwide campaign, so similar operations were carried out in other population centers in China. I don't know what they did in China's rural areas where there was more land than people. But later I saw posters depicting farmers and their children laying traps on their threshing ground to capture sparrows. Indeed, there was no escape.

It was soon learned that sparrows and other birds were actually "good" birds, not pests, because they do not eat only grain but also crop-eating insects such as locusts. When the birds were killed off, the insects lost their natural enemies and their population exploded, causing damage to crops.

When presented with reports to that effect by researchers from China's Academy of Sciences, Mao ordered that sparrows be struck off the list of the Four Pests and replaced with bedbugs instead.

At least in Beijing, the population of birds never fully recovered. When I was small, swarms of swallows visited the city every spring. They flew everywhere. Historic buildings such as the Imperial Palace had to be protected with wire mesh to prevent swallows from building nests under their eaves. Today, swallows are rarely seen in Beijing. Neither are bats. Beijing used to see numerous bats in the summer, flying around at dusk and into the night. There were also many dragonflies that flew around in small clouds when it was about to rain. Swallows, bats, and dragonflies have all disappeared from Beijing. I think flies and mosquitoes have largely disappeared as well, but nobody misses them.

★ ★ ★

In 1957, the Soviet Union became the first nation to successfully launch a satellite into orbit. China celebrated this achievement by its socialist brothers and henceforth labeled every major achievement as having "launched a satellite." The Great Leap Forward produced numerous "satellites" in the form of record-breaking feats of production. The numbers stretched credulity. A mu of land, about the size of three tennis courts, typically produced at most 400 kilograms (~880 lbs) of grain. But some places were reporting 5,000 kilograms (~11,000 lbs) per mu or more. It appeared that the productivity of the masses had been unleashed on an unimaginable scale. All the provinces, counties, and villages reported record harvests and agricultural output. These reports poured into Beijing, leading Mao to worry about too much food. "What do we do if there is too much grain?" he wondered aloud.

Mao's confidence was boosted. He said, "Now it seems it will not need to take 15 years to surpass Britain and 20 years to catch up with America." He declared in meetings with senior leaders that it looked as if China would transition into the true communist society that Marx had envisioned much sooner than thought, and even ahead of the Soviet Union. But Mao wanted to be humble: "Even if we entered communism sooner than the Soviet Union, we shouldn't announce it," lest China should embarrass the USSR, the big brother in the camp of socialist countries.

Since food was thought to be plentiful, communes in the country-side throughout China set up mass dining halls where farmers and their families ate for free. Farmers who had previously only been able to eat what they could grow now consumed with abandon. China doubled its grain exports. During a visit by the Soviet leader Nikita Khrushchev, Mao asked him if the Soviet Union had had experience in dealing with a huge food surplus. Khrushchev answered that his country had never had such a problem.

It turned out that almost all these claims to have "launched a satellite" were made up or vastly exaggerated. Instead of a huge surplus, there was a food shortage in China. Officials at different levels falsified their numbers to show the success of the Great Leap Forward and to please their superiors. Since peasants were required to sell a proportion of their harvest to the government at proscribed prices, which was a form of taxation, this falsified reporting led to overcollection and overexporting of grain. Local officials sometimes resorted to coercion, forcing peasants to sell their grain even if there was not enough left to feed their families. In extreme cases, they were forced to sell the seeds held back for the next growing season.

At the time, the severe food shortage was not obvious to a child like myself. Although I did not experience hunger, I knew there was not enough food at home. I could see it in the patterns of our daily lives. My mother was always the last to eat. Although I did not realize it, she was famished. I could see my mother's face and legs gradually turn puffy and her skin translucent. She showed me that if she sank the tip of her finger into the flesh of her leg, the dent would stay there for a long time, as if her flesh was made of dough. Now I know she was suffering from edema, an inflammation and swelling sometimes associated with severe malnutrition. She never complained of hunger, however, not even once. So out of curiosity, I would push the tip of my finger into her flesh to see the dent, the likes of which I could not create on myself.

I did help my mother to get more food, however, always sensing it was needed. There were a few elm trees in our compound. We learned that elm seeds could be eaten. I picked up the seeds shaken down by bigger children and brought them home. My mother would mix them with flour and cook them. I probably got a bite or two, but I do not remember really eating them. I also went around to find edible wild plants in every corner to collect them and bring them home. I am sure that those elm seeds and wild plants helped my mother, although I did not fully understand or quite appreciate it at the time. I also remember when her relatives from her home village in Shandong asked someone to bring her a bag of dried turnip strips. Every little bit of food helped.

One day, my father came home with a pair of small gray-colored rabbits. I loved them. We built an enclosure against the wall where the covered walkway ended and kept the rabbits there. My father and I went out to all the corners of the compound where wild grass grew and brought the grass back to feed the rabbits. From then on, every day I helped my father pull and collect grass, hay, and other vegetation to feed the rabbits.

Soon the rabbits were grown. Before long, the female gave birth to a litter. When the litter was grown, my father would slaughter one rabbit on a Sunday and my mother would cook it for us. So we had meat to eat from time to time during the Great Famine. My father loathed slaughtering animals as he had a tender heart. He had no choice. But he refused to eat rabbit meat and never shared in the feast.

I don't know how other families in Beijing coped, but I knew many friends later told me their parents suffered from edema as well. If food was in such short supply in the nation's capital, I can only imagine how bad it became in the rest of the country.

When senior leaders finally learned the truth about the Great Famine, most were reluctant to share the news with Mao for fear of appearing critical of his policies. The only one to speak out was Peng Dehuai, the defense minister, who had commanded the Chinese troops during the Korean War. He told Mao the truth, in a long letter of more than 10,000 characters. He criticized the Great Leap Forward as "more losses than gains," although he was careful to only blame overly zealous local government officials. Mao, who had heard some troubling reports through his own channels, was already considering changing course. But he was furious with Peng's criticism. He fired Peng from his position, along with those senior government officials sympathetic to Peng's views, and doubled down on his radical policies. Peng was first allowed a low-level job in a province in southwest China, but in the next political campaign, which took place about seven years later, he was severely beaten by mobs and eventually died in prison.

The famine continued unabated, then got worse. Before 1958 was out, there were already widespread food shortages in vast swaths of

China's countryside. Millions of people would die of starvation in the next few years. Reliable studies estimate that 20 million to 36 million people, 3 to 5 percent of the Chinese population, died during between 1958 and 1962.

As a child, I was oblivious to most of this. My parents must have cut down on their own meals to make sure there was enough for us children. But there was not enough to go around. Once my mother pulled me aside and snuck a boiled egg into my hands, telling me to eat it immediately without letting others know.

★ ★ ★

The children in our compound often played together. I don't remember toys of any kind but there were sticks, pig knuckles that we could roll like dice and play games with, and cigarette boxes that opened up and folded into triangular shapes. We chased one another around in the compound, playing hide and seek and war games with little sticks, pretending they were guns or swords. I remember rolling around in a pile of "rock cotton," which felt like cotton and had shiny fibers, near a building site. Now I know it was a pile of asbestos, a commonly used construction material at that time. Maybe I have tough lungs, or maybe I was lucky. In any case, I am not aware of any harmful health effects to me from playing in asbestos.

My parents were both born to poor peasant families in Shandong Province, on the east coast of China. My father received some basic education, probably no more than elementary school. Still, he was proficient in Chinese language and literature. He was an avid reader of Chinese classics and history books from different Chinese dynasties. He wrote well, and his calligraphy was excellent.

Shandong was a dirt-poor province. In the Old China, it was frequently struck by famine, and each outbreak launched a mass migration of people from Shandong into the less populated northeast of China in search of food and work. Many people went all the way into Korea, about 400 kilometers away by sea. When I first visited South Korea in 1987, I was surprised to hear restaurant owners speak the same dialect of Chinese as my parents. My father left Shandong during one of these mass migrations in the late 1930s or early 1940s; I do not know how old he was at the time. But the war had come to China's northeast by that time, and my father joined the Communist anti-Japanese forces in 1944, one year before Japan's surrender.

My father worked in the Customs Administration, a department of the Ministry of Foreign Trade, as a deputy division chief.

My father had no hobbies that I know of, other than reading Chinese classics, such as the official histories of the 24 dynasties. I think I owe my interest in reading to him. I still have some of his history books on my shelf.

He read us some books when we were small, which I enjoyed immensely. But that didn't happen often. He was a chain smoker. He often lit a new cigarette with the butt of the one he had just smoked. When he read us stories, he would smoke continuously. I often fell asleep engulfed in the thick smoke from his cigarettes as he sat next to me.

He was a man of few words. Once as a teenager, while telling him something I had experienced, he asked me if anyone had told me I was verbose. From then on, I have tried not to waste words, although I have not always been successful at it. I always had a strong desire to please him and to make him feel proud of me. I could sense that he was pleased with every little achievement I made, although I don't recall any personal praise from him that he shared with me.

My mother also grew up in a poor village in Shandong. She never told us why she left home, although I think she ran away to escape an arranged marriage. In 1947, at a young age, she joined the Communist forces, which were active in the areas surrounding her home. My mother was about 10 years younger than my father; she told us he might have understated his age by a couple of years when he asked her to marry him. She also worked in the Ministry of Foreign Trade, as a secretary.

My mother was the gentlest woman I have ever known. She was kind and literally would not harm an insect—and would not let me, either. She had a strong sense of right and wrong, which influenced me greatly and made a lasting impression on those around her. She always worked hard, both at work and at home. At every meal, she would eat very slowly, using her chopsticks to put food into our bowls and waiting for her children and my father to stop eating before she finished up what was left on the table. I learned to wash clothes and to cook at a young age to help her because I felt bad watching her always work so hard.

Like my father, my mother probably received the equivalent of an elementary school education. But she writes well, and her handwriting is unusually beautiful. At that time the weekend consisted of only Sunday, and on that day she would handwash the clothes of the entire family, often in cold water, summer or winter. She also cooked for the family. So she did not have time to take us children on outings. I remember only once in our childhood, when I was about nine, she took my little brother and me to Beijing's Beihai Park on a Sunday and we had a picture taken of the three of us in front of a lake.

★ ★ ★

Because of the size of our family we were given an extra room, for a grand total of two. Both of our two rooms faced south, so sunlight came in through the glass especially in wintertime. There was one bare 25-watt bulb in each room and a reading lamp on the desk in the larger room.

My parents, my brother, and I shared the bigger room. The other room was half the size and was partitioned with a curtain. My paternal grandfather, who had moved in with us from his home village in Shandong, slept behind the curtain. In front of it was the family dining table, surrounded by a few wooden stools and a wooden food storage cabinet about 4 feet tall, 2 feet wide, and 1 foot deep. This room would also hold my older sister's bed after she joined us in 1960 from my mother's home village in Shandong.

There was no kitchen. My mother cut vegetables and prepared food on the dining table and then took everything out to the covered exterior walkway to be cooked on the small coal stove that each family had outside its door. Cooking outdoors in winter was unpleasant, so you wanted to get it done as soon as possible. The top of the stove could fit one cooking pan or pot. Waiting in that freezing walkway for the pot to boil felt like watching grass grow—a slow, painful ordeal. If you ducked back inside for warmth, as I sometimes did when I learned to cook, the rice might burn or the soup might boil over, not only spoiling the family dinner, but also possibly extinguishing the fire, either of which would be quite disastrous.

The food cabinet and the dining table were always infested with roaches, too many to kill. I imagine that since we applied roach poison everywhere, on the table and in the food cabinet, we probably consumed a fair amount of it ourselves. In retrospect, the roaches probably were less harmful than the poisons we inadvertently absorbed. But what did we know at the time, and what else could we do?

Our small coal stove burned round coal cakes honeycombed with small, circular holes; we called these briquettes "beehive coal." Two or three coal cakes were stacked in the stove with the holes aligned so that air could pass through. When a cake was about to burn out, a new coal cake would be placed on top, again with holes perfectly aligned, so the fire would continue to burn.

China started a rationing system for rice, wheat flour, edible oil, and cloth around the time I was born. Each person was issued coupons every month; these entitled the bearer to purchase (with money) a fixed amount of the item listed on the coupon. Sometimes meat was rationed as well, but few could afford buy much of it anyway. Nobody could buy rice, wheat flour, or cotton clothes without coupons, even if he or she had the money.

We grew up not knowing there was such a thing as a refrigerator. We had to buy fresh vegetables every few days, as there was no place to keep them cool. Fresh meat is impossible to keep at room temperature for long, but it can be kept for a few days if cooked. My mother would store the cooked meat in a jar kept in the food cabinet to be taken out a little at a time, to put into the wok and stir-fried together with some vegetables. Sometimes, especially in summer, meat would go bad and change flavor if kept too long. But I don't remember ever throwing any meat away.

There was no running water inside homes. About a dozen families shared one outdoor water spigot where residents fetched water for all their needs. Winter in Beijing can be harsh, with temperatures frequently dropping below freezing. The exposed water pipe connecting the spigot had to be wrapped with thick layers of straw rope to keep it from freezing. Otherwise the pipe would burst. To fetch water in wintertime, we had to carry a kettle of hot water to pour on the spigot to unfreeze it before water would come out.

The same dozen or so families also shared an outside, one-hole public outhouse. In winter, the call of nature had to be resisted until it became more unbearable than the punishing cold in the toilet. When the weather was too rough, children were allowed the privilege of using a chamber pot indoors.

Without running water at home, we fetched water from the public spigot, boiled it on the stove, and washed ourselves using a washbasin filled with a mixture of hot and cold water. My parents bathed my brother and me at home when we were small. When we grew older, we would go with them to a public bath.

I would be amiss not to mention the history of our neighborhood, which is unique and interesting even for an old city like Beijing, although growing up there, I was oblivious of its history. The narrow lane in front of our compound used to be named Rue Hart, after Sir Robert Hart, a British diplomat who had served the Chinese imperial government of the Qing dynasty as head of its customs service for an incredible half century, from about 1861 until his death in 1911. The sign for Rue Hart is still visible today, engraved into a wall on the northwest corner of the lane.

It was no accident we lived there. My father worked for the customs administration and the old building where our home was used to be part of Old China's customs administration, where Sir Robert Hart probably had worked. In the nineteenth century, during Hart's time, the neighborhood became known as the Quarter of Foreign Legations, where the first foreign embassies were located. This was the place besieged by the Boxers during the Boxer Rebellion (1899–1901), which led to the invasion of Beijing by the joint forces of eight foreign powers.

★ ★ ★

China's Great Famine of 1959–1962 claimed millions of lives, more than any war in memory. In the summer of 1962, Liu Shaoqi, China's president (Mao was the chairman of the Communist Party), said to Mao, in a rare moment of fluster: "So many were starved to death; history will record you and me [as being responsible]. Man eating man, it will be recorded in the annals of history." His disagreements with Mao would eventually prove to be his undoing, leading to his downfall and tragic death about seven years later.

Chapter 2

School Cut Short

Reports of widespread famine and death finally filtered through to China's top leadership, and the Great Leap Forward was brought to a halt around the end of 1960. It was the year when I reached school age. The severe food shortages the Great Leap Forward created continued until after 1962. The failure and futility of Mao's radical policies dealt a blow to his reputation within the Communist Party; some senior colleagues began to question Mao's "mistakes," which he himself ultimately acknowledged as well. But there was never a serious challenge to his supreme authority. In January 1962, the Chinese leadership held a meeting in Beijing attended by more than 7,000 government officials from around the country. The Meeting of 7,000, as it became known, lasted for more than a month, as the party leadership reflected on their policy failures and the attendees "vented their anger," in the words of Mao, over the man-made disaster of the Great Leap Forward. After the meeting, Mao, who was chairman of the Communist Party but otherwise held no official government position, took a step back from running the country. He left the job to a trio of his senior comrades: Liu Shaoqi, China's president, Zhou Enlai, the premier, and Deng Xiaoping, the general secretary of the Communist Party. The three adopted moderate policies beginning in 1961 to normalize the economic affairs of the country. After a couple of years, the food shortage gradually eased.

From the founding of the People's Republic of China (PRC) in 1949 until the end of the 1950s, China maintained a friendly relationship with the Soviet Union and the countries of the Eastern Europe part of the Soviet bloc. But around 1959, ties with the Soviets began to fray. Soviet leader Nikita Khrushchev spoke critically of Mao's policies during the Great Leap Forward, including the large-scale collectivization of farming—known as the people's commune system—that eliminated farmers' private ownership of land. Mao also suspected that Khrushchev was trying to bring China into the Soviet Union's sphere of influence, as it had with the rest of the Eastern Bloc countries. During a state visit to Beijing, Khrushchev proposed that China and the Soviet Union establish a joint navy fleet, a proposal Mao considered a disguised means of Soviet control of China. He thought that Khrushchev and the Soviet leadership had betrayed the doctrines of Marxism and Leninism by denouncing Joseph Stalin and by promoting "peaceful coexistence" with the West. In 1960, to put pressure on Beijing to toe the Soviet line in international affairs, the Soviet Union abruptly canceled all economic aid programs to China, withdrew all its technical personnel, and demanded the immediate repayment of the debts incurred by China during the Korean War. All these moves dealt a heavy blow to China's development and exacerbated its economic woes just as the country was struggling to cope with the disasters of the Great Leap Forward.

After 1960, the split between China and the USSR was complete. Beijing officially labeled the Soviets "revisionists" who had betrayed the true tenets of Marxism and Leninism. The relationship between the two countries grew ever more hostile. After its split with the USSR, China became almost completely isolated, with its only ally the tiny Balkan country of Albania, which unequivocally sided with China in the ideological fight within the socialist camp.

Mao despised Khrushchev for his efforts to reduce tensions with the West, especially the United States. After an American U-2 spy plane was shot down in Soviet airspace, Khrushchev's attempts to improve relations with the United States suffered a severe setback. In 1962, as the United States and the Soviet Union almost turned the Cold War into a hot one during the Cuban Missile Crisis, Mao remained scornful of Khrushchev's conduct. He was an "opportunist" for stationing nuclear missiles in Cuba in the first place, Mao declared, and a "capitulationist" for withdrawing the missiles under US threat. (At the time the quid pro quo, in which President John F. Kennedy agreed to withdraw US nuclear arms from Turkey, was not disclosed; Khrushchev had gotten something from the United States after all.)

★ ★ ★

I started school in autumn 1960, when I was about to turn seven years old. On the first day of school, my mother put some nice clothes on me and gave me a multicolored cloth schoolbag, which she had probably sewn together herself, as a real schoolbag would have been quite expensive. I thought the bag was too girlish and was afraid I would be laughed at. I made a fuss, refused to take it, and asked instead for a real, green-colored schoolbag like everyone else was carrying. My mother insisted I take the one she made until I threatened to throw it away as soon as she was out of sight. I did not really mean it, but I also knew she feared I might follow through on my threat. She gave in and got me a real schoolbag.

The Elementary School for Children of the Ministry of Foreign Trade was located in the western suburbs of Beijing, about 40 minutes away from our home by bus. The schoolyard was very big to my eyes. There was a redbrick two-story building in the center, a soccer field and playground to the south side of the building, and a canteen on the north side separated from the main building by a road and an open space.

The elementary school was relatively new, built in 1955. It was a boarding school, so we spent the week at the school, going home only for Sundays.

My sister, Weimin, who is one year older than me and whom my parents had left in the care of our maternal grandmother, arrived from Shandong to live with us. She ended up going to a day school two blocks away from our home.

In many ways, the children who went to boarding schools like ours were privileged. The school was well funded by the ministry to make sure that we received a first-rate education, and we were well taken care of. During the day, we had regular teachers for classes ranging from mathematics and Chinese to arts, music, and physical education. In our spare time and in the evenings, "daily-life" teachers took over to make sure that we washed ourselves, changed our clothes, and went to bed at specific hours. They even came around every night with a chamber pot to help those who still wet their beds. Other than studying, we never worried about anything at all.

Every week, we went home by school bus on Saturday after lunch and returned to school on Sunday before dinner. Every Saturday I was excited to go home. I was just as reluctant to return to school on Sundays.

The school bus dropped us off inside the entrance of the ministry. Every Saturday, after getting off the bus, I went to the office of either my mother or father to wait for them to finish work and take me home.

My father had a modest-size office, but he had a swivel chair. I twirled around and around in one direction until it would go no further. Then I would twirl in the other direction. My father's desk drawer was usually messy, but I enjoyed finding something in it to play with, like a lighter or even an invitation card for certain events. When my parents finished their work, they would often take me to the canteen to have dinner or buy food before we went home together. I loved the ice cream there.

★ ★ ★

I was assigned to classroom no. 1. There were about 30 pupils in the class, half boys and half girls. The classrooms and dormitories were in the main building, classrooms on the first floor and dormitories on the second. All the boys in my class slept in one big room with 15 or 16 beds. There was a big common washroom and a common bathroom on each side of the floor, one on the boys' side and one on the girls' side.

Most of my classmates were several months older than me; we were all six or seven years of age. It did not feel hard to live away from home, even at that young age, and soon I became quite used to the routine of living together with other children. The daily-life caretaker I remember most clearly was Zhou Xiuchun. Adults called her Ah Chun. We called her Auntie Zhou. Short and hunchbacked, she always looked severe. I never saw her smile, not even once. All of us thought she was scary. She would punish in her own way whoever got into trouble with her. I managed to avoid her wrath and never got into trouble with her, thankfully.

Once she got angry with all of us, probably because she caught some of us being naughty for something I don't remember. That night in the study room after dinner, she announced she would punish us all by requiring us to copy one chapter in our language-study textbook 100 times. Nobody could leave the classroom to go to bed before finishing.

She sat in a chair at the door to check our work and would not allow us to leave the classroom until she was satisfied with our work. One chapter in the elementary textbook was probably one or two pages long in big characters. To write 100 pages would be a lot of work. It was unbearably tedious. We collectively moaned but we had no choice. I was writing as fast as I could but there seemed no end to it. Finally, I decided to take a shortcut. I knew she would not read more than a few characters. So I began to copy only the first and last few sentences of the text each time and soon I was done. She took a quick look at my neat writing and her facial muscles relaxed. She praised my work and let me out. My classmates all raised their heads to watch me leave. They were astonished I could write so fast. I enjoyed a good evening to myself as my classmates labored away. I didn't consider what I did cheating because I thought she was unjust and unfair, and she deserved to be tricked even though I loved her in general. I have defied authorities from time to time in my life when I thought the authority was stupidly unfair with its demands.

Auntie Zhou was also in charge of our personal hygiene. She was strict and never wavered in her requests. We were required to wash our face, hands, and feet every day before bed. There was no hot water in the washroom, but the rumor in the boys' dormitory was that the girls were provided hot water in their washbasins to wash their butts. All the boys hated washing, especially in wintertime when the water was stingingly cold.

Auntie Zhou would sit at the entrance of the washroom to check our hands and feet to make sure we had cleaned ourselves well. She would send us back to rewash ourselves if we did not pass her test. But she would only check one hand and one foot. Therefore, I often washed only one hand and one foot to pass her examination and to save myself the unpleasantness of the freezing water.

For all her sternness, Auntie Zhou took good care of us. Some boys still wet their beds. So every night, during the wee hours, she would come into our room with a chamber pot and a flashlight, repeatedly calling the likely offenders in a loud voice in her Shanghai dialect, to wake them up to pee one by one.

There was a public bath in the back of the schoolyard. We were required to take a bath every week. All the boys would line up naked to go through a pool of steaming hot water. Auntie Zhou stood on the side of the pool and washed each of us one by one thoroughly with a towel soaked with soap. After she was done, we each looked like a cooked prawn (I did not know there was such a thing as lobster at that time). We would proceed to the next pool to rinse ourselves off.

We had our three meals a day in the school canteen. Despite the famine in the country and the food shortage in Beijing, we always had enough to eat. Though I knew food was rationed, I only became aware of the catastrophic scope of the Great Famine later in life. Even though I was not picky about food, I knew the menu was simple and rarely changed from week to week. I still do not like ribbonfish, seaweed, or carrots, because these were served so often in those years I became literally fed up with them.

I later learned we owed our food supply to Principal Li, who worked tirelessly and went out of her way to use her connections at high levels to ensure there was enough food for her pupils. From time to time, we were each given some vegetables and other kinds of food to bring home on Saturdays, because every family in the school was short of food.

At one time, the school canteen served the meat of "yellow goat," or wild Mongolian gazelle. The gazelles used to roam, in great numbers, throughout the grasslands on the Loess Plateau, which extends from Gansu Province in the west through Ningxia, Shanxi, and Shaanxi Provinces into Inner Mongolia. During the Great Famine, the gazelles were hunted for their meat. Many organizations in Beijing sent special teams to Inner Mongolia to join the hunt. They were armed with rifles and rode in jeeps equipped with spotlights for night hunting. Trucks brought gazelle carcasses back some 700 kilometers (~430 miles) to Beijing. I saw truckloads of the stocky, fawn-colored animals arriving in the compound where we lived and at our school.

The organized hunt was a catastrophe for the animals, as they were slaughtered by the thousands. I think the hunt made these animals almost extinct and it stopped only because they could not be found anymore. As this hunt took place on the Chinese side of the border with Mongolia, the gazelles were able to maintain their range in Mongolia, and their numbers have gradually recovered.

★ ★ ★

The head teacher of my class was Ma Yaxian, a tall and elegant woman with smooth skin and dark hair. She was from Shanghai and spoke the same Shanghainese dialect as Auntie Zhou. She stayed with us from the day we started until we left elementary school. She taught us all subjects, except physical education and music. Teacher Ma was always patient and kind to students. Every day she taught us how to read and write and, in later grades, more advanced language and calligraphy. She would put a red circle on each of the characters we wrote if she approved of the calligraphy. I tried to get as many red circles as possible on my character worksheet.

Each day, there were classes in the morning. We studied Chinese language, including classical Chinese, writing and brush calligraphy, arithmetic, and geography. We all went to the canteen for lunch. After lunch, there was one hour of nap time back in the dormitory. Auntie Zhou walked around to make sure we were quiet and sleeping before sitting down by the door to do her knitting. In the tall trees outside the windows of our dormitory floor, cicadas chirped loudly, especially when the sun was bright. In summertime we napped with the loud and constant choir of cicadas droning in the background.

Afternoons were devoted to less important subjects, such as arts and music. Classes ended with physical education. Boys frequently played soccer in the full-size soccer field. The girls did something else, but whatever it was I wasn't paying attention.

There was a school clinic on the first floor of the main building, which was attended by a nurse. I was frail as a child and was frequently sick, typically with a headache for no particular reason I, or any doctor, could ascertain. So I occasionally spent time lying on the bed of the clinic chatting with the nurse. She asked me what I aspired to do when I grew up. I told her my ambition was to become a zookeeper, so I could see and take care of all kinds of animals. Alas, my ambition remains unfulfilled.

★ ★ ★

Elementary school was a breeze. I never felt learning was difficult and I was a good student. I usually received full marks. All the marks and grades were published for all the students to see, so everyone knew who was a good student and who wasn't. I do not remember anyone being bothered by that system of transparency or no privacy, maybe because I didn't have anything to worry about. Not until I went to graduate school did I notice that US schools do not publicly disclose all grades for all students. In the Old China, the results of imperial exams were also published for all to see. I suppose it was the same tradition when it came to our school. Those students who did not do well were frequently required to do make-up homework. I was quick with my schoolwork, so I was usually among the first ones to finish and go out to play.

There was not much effort to teach the kids to be creative at our school. I don't remember doing creative projects or making anything, with the exception of art classes. For drawing, we went to the nearby Beijing Zoo and painted animals. I remember painting a tiger together with one of my classmates, Liu Wanyi. I had no sense of three dimensions or perspectives. So my tiger looked like a squashed omelet whereas his looked like, well, a tiger, with its head and tail in the right proportions.

During summer and winter breaks, we would be sent home. Summer vacation was about one-and-a-half months. Winter break was much shorter, just a couple of weeks long. We would be assigned daily homework covering the whole summer. I would finish all my assign-ments within the first three or four days, so I did not have to worry about it for the rest of the summer. My parents never supervised or helped with my homework. It was not necessary, but it also seemed to me that in those days teachers did not expect parents to help their children with teaching and homework as they do today.

After I had learned enough characters, my parents bought or borrowed small illustrated storybooks. They were no bigger than the size of my two palms and the best ones told stories with characters from Chinese classics such as the Monkey King and General Yue Fei fighting invaders from the kingdom of Jin. Each page was a picture vividly depicting a scene from the story with captioned words below. I loved them. I would be absorbed in these stories throughout the summer. I suppose kids today get the same satisfaction by watching television dramas, but in my opinion, they don't read enough. Nothing ignites the imagination more than good stories complemented with illustrations that bring characters and events vividly to life.

My friends and I also went to public swimming pools to escape Beijing's summer heat. They were usually packed. My parents bought me a life preserver, a flotation device like a thick rubber belt, which was a big expenditure for them. I was proud to own it and learned how to swim with it.

A lake called Yuyuantan was located not far away from our school, and I went there with some friends to swim. There was a wooden platform in the middle of the lake and people swam back and forth between the beach and the platform. I had just learned to swim but I could not swim well, or for long. I swam with friends, with the life preserver around my waist, to the platform. Then someone took my life preserver and left for the shore.

I was stranded on the platform with only one friend, a boy named Gao Jianjing, and I did not think I could make it back to the shore without my life preserver. We waited and waited until it was getting late. So I decided to try to swim back without the preserver. Halfway to the shore, I was completely exhausted and I began to sink. I only had strength left to yell "help!" Gao swimming next to me was yelling for someone to help me as well. But as I still managed to keep my head above water, people around us at first did not think there was an emergency. Fortunately, a strong swimmer came to my rescue just when I was about to drown, and soon a boat came alongside us. That, I suppose, was my rite of passage for swimming; after that I did not need my life preserver anymore.

★ ★ ★

My love of reading continued as I grew older, and I began to read more extracurricular stuff. I particularly loved popular science books written for children. There was a series titled *One Hundred Thousand Whys* that was like an encyclopedia. I learned why daytime was long in summer but short in winter, why there were seasons, why airplanes could fly, why ice was slippery, and why water pipes might burst in cold weather. I learned most of my science at an early age from those books. I also remember another book, *Scientists Talk About the 21st Century*. It was a collection of articles written for children by well-known scientists who envisioned the world of the next hundred years. It talked about wireless communication, supersonic jet travel, nuclear energy, semiconductors, electronics, and agriculture without soil. I was also fascinated by popular books on astronomy, man-made satellites, and space travel.

I enjoyed science fiction, too. I was particularly fond of the translated works of the French author Jules Verne. I was mesmerized by his *Twenty Thousand Leagues Under the Sea* and my mind followed Captain Nemo in the depths of the sea in his submarine, the *Nautilus*, all over the world.

I dipped my toes into applied science by joining the Children's Palace of Science and Technology when I was in the fourth or fifth grade. This was a permanent establishment, but it functioned like a camp. It offered activities in science and technology for a couple of hours per week to a select group of a few hundred students, mostly teenagers. I was accepted even though I was an elementary school student, probably with a recommendation from my school. I think they made exceptions for some younger students considered to have potential in science. Each of us joined one of the specialized groups in the camp, such as physics, chemistry, astronomy, telecommunications, and wireless control (which built models of wirelessly controlled boats and airplanes, now called drones). I joined the wireless communication group.

The camp was located in Beihai Park. Beihai means "North Sea." The beginning of the park traced back to the Jin dynasty rulers in 1179. It was progressively built up over the centuries by various ruling dynasties as part of the imperial park. It occupies an area of about 70 hectares (~170 acres), half of which was a man-made lake. There is a tall hill in the middle of the lake with many ancient temples, palaces, pavilions, and buildings scattered around its slopes.

On the very top of the hill, overlooking the city, stands a very large white Tibetan Buddhist pagoda.

On the north bank of the lake, there are five large pavilions by the water, collectively known as the Five Dragon Pavilions. Next to the pavilions but standing in the middle of nothing is Nine Dragons Wall, a large wall of green- and blue-glazed tiles with the pattern of nine yellow dragons on it. Behind the Five Dragon Pavilions there are stone stairs leading up to what used to be a temple by the name of Chanfusi, or Enlightened Happiness Temple. The temple occupied a large area with many buildings, some of which were burned down or collapsed long ago, but a few remained standing. That was the site of the science camp and all camp activities took place inside what used to be the temple. It was secluded, spacious, and beautiful. Not only was there much open space outside the buildings, but also it was right by the lake where the remote-control group would sail their model boats and fly their model planes. There was even a small hydropower plant built by the students near there.

The membership card for the science camp allowed us to go in and out of Beihai Park freely, without having to pay the two-fen entrance fee. On camp days, I would take a trolley bus from our school to Beihai. Past the entrance, there was a long but pleasant walk along the lake to get to the camp. The lake bank was lined with willow trees whose long, thin, hanging branches provided shade for visitors. Under the willows, people sat by the lake with fishing rods. The lake was stocked with fat carp, and for a fee people could fish there.

I learned to build a radio in science camp. We started with a simple crystal radio. It required only a small crystal encased in a tiny glass tube with two wires sticking out and some simple connectors and an ear-phone. It received broadcast signals without the need for any power. Once we mastered the crystal radio, we advanced to building radios with diodes. Finally, we began to build radios with transistors. There were no integrated circuit boards at that time, so all the transistors, diodes, and batteries had to be connected with wires and resistors that we soldered together ourselves.

It gave me a feeling of accomplishment once my hand-built radio worked. At the time, the best commercially sold radios I knew of had eight transistors. The most sophisticated one I attempted to build, with the help of a friend, was a six-transistor radio. In 1971, the first-generation Intel processor had 2,300 transistors. Today, a single microchip can have a transistor count in the billions. This kind of processing power was beyond imagination when I soldered my first single transistor on a board.

★ ★ ★

Back in school, I got into trouble for the first time in my life. I was walking one day in the hallway of the main building, and I passed some girls jumping rope. The girl jumping swung her thick wool scarf around her neck and it hit me in the eye. I was startled and annoyed, so I pushed her and walked by. It turned out she was a tattletale and soon I was hauled into the office of the director of school affairs, Mr. Huang Liqun.

Mr. Huang would not listen to my explanation and suspended me from class. I became upset and poured ink onto his desk. The next thing I knew, my mother showed up. She had been summoned by phone by Mr. Huang and she had to find someone with a motorcycle equipped with a sidecar to take her to our school. She collected me and took me home by bus. I was afraid I was in big trouble. If my father heard of this, he probably would spank me.

Instead of punishing me, my mother took me to a Shanghai-style restaurant close to our home. It was the first time in my memory I ever ate in a restaurant. I don't think my parents could afford to eat in restaurants. I thought the food was delicious, like nothing I had tasted before.

To this day, I don't know why my mother did not punish me. I could only guess she knew that by personality I would not yield to punishment, but I would give in to a soft approach. Indeed, I felt so guilty to have brought shame to my mother that I was determined not to repeat silly behaviors like this.

The school, however, disciplined me with one demerit in my record. I thought Mr. Huang was unfair because he refused to hear my side of the story. I decided to be defiant. During one class, I stood up while the teacher was lecturing and left the classroom by jumping out of the window (as I mentioned, the classrooms were on the first floor). My classmates were shocked that I pulled such a stunt. The school, however, did not punish me further. I think the school authorities must have calculated that another demerit so immediately after the first one would only demonstrate such penalties were ineffective or counter-productive. I ended my resistance movement and went back to class the next day.

Other than this incident, I was a good student, consistently earning top grades. I loved school and most of my teachers. Probably for these reasons, the school authority let me off the hook lightly and ignored my defiance after giving me that one demerit. But I was worried that the demerit in my record would affect my chances for the best middle school I was aspiring to attend. It turned out that my worry was unnecessary, because soon my entire school record would become completely irrelevant and would never be referred to again in my life.

Chapter 3

Storm of Revolution

At the founding of the People's Republic of China in 1949, Mao envisioned a new and inclusive government for the country. Its representatives would be two-thirds "Communists and progressives" and one third "independents and rightists." Mao became president and Zhou Enlai the premier. Two of the four vice premiers and 14 of the 34 cabinet members were non-Communists, including a few left-leaning Nationalists and members of other political parties, many of whom had sided clandestinely with the Communist cause during the civil war out of disgust with the corruption endemic to the old regime.

But this honeymoon did not last long. In 1957, the leadership of the Communist Party launched a "self-rectification campaign" aimed at cleansing itself of "bureaucrat-ism, faction-ism and subjectivism." While the campaign was supposed to be internal to the Party, leading intellectuals and the general public were invited to help the Party by criticizing it. Mao, in his characteristic way, described the policy as "Let a hundred flowers bloom and a hundred schools of thought contend."

For a while, government-controlled newspapers came as close as they would ever get to becoming forums of free speech, as prominent figures inside and outside the Communist Party were encouraged to express their views, ranging from mild advocacy for democracy and inclusiveness to harsh criticisms of one-party rule and the Party's failed policies.

To Mao, the chorus of criticism went too far. Concerned it would threaten the rule of the Party, he and his comrades swiftly launched a counterattack, known as the "Anti-Rightist Movement," to purge those they perceived as hostile to their rule. At the end of the campaign, more than one million people, including many prominent scholars, writers, scientists, and social activists, were tarred as "rightist" counterrevolutionaries or enemies of the people. They were demoted, exiled, or, in some cases, jailed. They would not be officially rehabilitated until 20 years later, after Mao's death. By then their lives and those of their families had already been ruined.

The Anti-Rightist Movement silenced dissenting voices outside of the Communist Party, but it could not eliminate dissent entirely. In 1959, Mao purged the defense minister Peng Dehuai for criticizing his policies of the Great Leap Forward. After that, hardly anyone among the Party's senior leadership dared to disagree with Mao.

But not everyone agreed with him either. The failure of the Great Leap Forward was a wake-up call for those within the Party who might have thought Mao could do no wrong.

In 1962, Mao handed the task of running the country to Liu Shaoqi, his no. 2 and chosen successor. Liu was a Mao loyalist and a pragmatic leader. He stabilized the economy and helped it recover, but as his stature grew, Mao must have felt his own authority was being challenged—not only by Liu but also by the rest of the leadership and the entire government, which had fallen in line with Liu's policies.

According to the principles of Marxism, the Communist-led revolution was a struggle by the working class against the capitalist and landowning classes. For Mao, however, this struggle did not end with the triumph of socialism. Not only did the members of the old ruling class still exist, but the capitalist ideas still pervaded traditions and culture. Khrushchev, Mao believed, had abandoned the principles of Marxism; Russia had become a "revisionist" country in which capitalist ideas persisted in the Soviet leadership. Capitalist ideas could corrupt anyone in the leadership, Mao believed; even senior leaders could become agents of class enemies within the Party. Therefore, he was ever vigilant that a Chinese Khrushchev, whose name was now synonymous with revisionism, would emerge within the Chinese Communist Party. He suspected, in fact, that such a leader already existed.

Mao was an accomplished student of history. In 1959, before the beginning of the Anti-Rightist Campaign, he spoke admiringly of a historical figure, a sixteenth-century official named Hai Rui, who he suggested could serve as a role model in daring to tell the truth in defiance of authorities. Hai Rui was unflinchingly loyal to the Ming emperor, but he was also willing to sharply criticize the emperor for his misdeeds. In doing so, he provoked the emperor's rage and faced almost certain death and was spared only by the emperor's own unexpected but timely demise. Heeding Mao's call, a vice mayor of Beijing named Wu Han, who was also an acclaimed historian of the Ming dynasty, wrote an opera in 1960 titled *The Firing of Hai Rui* in tribute to his daring deeds.

Initially, Mao liked the opera. But a few years later, as the political winds changed, he smelled a conspiracy—or perhaps he simply needed an excuse to launch a political campaign against those the spirit of Hai Rui represented. Mao came to see the opera as an indictment of his own firing of Peng Dehuai. Mao's genius had always been his ability to rally public opinion to his side, even before he moved against his political opponents. Mao's wife, Jiang Qing, secretly got a young Shanghainese writer named Yao Wenyuan to pen a critique of the opera, in which he condemned the play as a "poisonous weed," not a flower, and as a plot to overturn the verdict on Peng.

The publication of Yao's article at the end of 1965 was the opening act of a political movement of unprecedented scale in human history that would engulf the nation. The purpose of the Cultural Revolution, as it was called, was ostensibly to carry on a class struggle to rid China of "old thought, old culture, old tradition and old customs," and to purge class enemies from within the Party and the government. The movement was marked by a groundswell of millions of ordinary people who responded to Mao's call to attack and overthrow almost anything or anyone in a position of authority: leaders in government, the judicial system, cultural circles, academic fields, and economic affairs became targets. The movement would plunge the country into a state of anarchy for years to come and by some estimates would result in the deaths of more than a million people, including Liu Shaoqi himself and some of the best talents China ever had.

But all still seemed calm and blissful in the spring of 1966 when I was preparing to finish elementary school.

★ ★ ★

It was early summer 1966. All through the broiling summer days, the cicadas continued their unrelenting chorus. The Beijing habit of napping on summer days must have something to do with the heat and the cicadas. The hot, still air and the constant noise of cicadas enervate people and lull them to sleep.

Not me. I spent the afternoons studying. I was 12 years old and about to graduate from elementary school. We had already taken the elementary school graduation exams and were preparing to take the all-important middle school entrance examination. Middle school in China was roughly the same secondary education program as junior high and high school in the United States. I would attend junior middle school until about age 15, followed by senior middle school from age 15 to 18. Thus, getting into a good middle school was critical. If I did not perform well on my entrance exams, I risked ending up in a mediocre program, with no chance of getting into a good college.

In fact, I was determined to score top grades in the two major subjects: mathematics and Chinese language composition. I had more confidence in mathematics than in Chinese. I usually received the highest grade in mathematics, but in composition I had received only 98 percent on the elementary graduating exam, and I was disappointed. (Composition was always too tricky a subject: the teacher might not have liked your style, and you could easily misuse a Chinese character.) But I had to get a double hundred to be accepted into Middle School No. 101, one of the best in Beijing.

I had been too busy studying to notice that some of my classmates were missing. They came back at dinnertime to tell us what had happened to them that day. Gao Jianjing, the Young Pioneers leader of our class, had led a group of our classmates to Beijing City Hall to watch "revolution" in action.

We had heard earlier that in some schools, particularly middle schools and universities, students had rebelled against their teachers and refused to take final exams. This rebellion was spreading in Beijing; but until that day, our school had not been affected.

Having heard that there was a lot of activity at city hall, Gao and some other classmates went there to watch the excitement. They went in the name of revolution, so none of our teachers or principals dared stop them.

City hall was close to my home, but about 15 kilometers (~10 miles) away from our school. To a group of 12- and 13-year-olds, it was a long distance. Yet they walked all the way to city hall and saw everything.

They saw crowds of people haranguing the mayor and vice mayors. They saw people giving speeches about the necessity of revolution. They saw Ma Lianliang, one of the best-known opera actors, being beaten up by a group of "revolutionaries." His leg was broken and he passed out. His crime was having played a lead role in Wu Han's opera, *The Firing of Hai Rui*, now regarded as a "poisonous weed." He was then labeled a "capitalist-reactionary authority" in the arts. Ma, one of the most accomplished performing artists in China, would die a physically broken man before the end of the year. The revolutionaries shouting slogans, making speeches, and beating people up, Gao and the others told me, were Red Guards. It was the first time I had heard the name.

It was all much more exciting than studying for the final exam. It was even more exciting that the school authorities did not do anything to prevent my classmates from going to city hall. They even had to send a school bus to pick them up and bring them back. Who would dare not to support revolution, especially one led by Young Pioneers?

Over the past few months, we had heard stories about how a girl "rebelled" against her parents because they promised to give her a bicycle as a gift if she did well on the final exam. She said that her parents were trying to motivate her with "materialistic incentives," which, by definition, were capitalistic. She was praised in the newspaper for upholding revolutionary principles.

In a document my father showed me, I read some remarks made by Chairman Mao excoriating the current educational system. Mao said teachers treated students like enemies and exams were like "surprise attacks." He said that such a system discouraged creativity. Mao cited examples showing that the most accomplished emperors in Chinese history were usually not well educated, whereas the most educated ones turned out to be disasters or losers. He also said that students should be allowed to whisper to each other, exchange notes, and check their textbooks during exams.

Well, those remarks were pleasing to the ears of impressionable students swept up in conversations of revolution, not to mention those who do not like to study for exams.

Even though Mao's remarks had been made a couple of years earlier, the decision was made in 1966 that the college entrance exams would be scrapped, to be replaced by a new system of recommendations yet to be worked out. Consequently, the college entrance date was postponed—at first for half a year, then indefinitely. There would be no more entrance exams for middle schools either.

I was a little disappointed that I would not have the opportunity to go to the best middle school of my choice. I had no idea that I would never attend middle school.

Soon after this trip by my classmates to city hall, the Cultural Revolution came to our campus in earnest. The oldest of us were 13 years old, but we felt quite grown-up. We were filled with revolutionary energy and zeal. The exciting times gave us adult authority before we were even mature enough to develop our independent viewpoints to understand what was happening around us.

A few teachers were said by their colleagues to be "bad elements." They were criticized and humiliated in public mass meetings attended by both teachers and students. We were happy to see some unpopular teachers in trouble. Huang Liqun, the director of student affairs, who had earlier given me a demerit, was among the most unpopular teachers. He wore a severe expression on his face and he would stare at you with his slightly bulging eyes behind a pair of thick glasses that looked like the bottom of a beer bottle. His glare could scare the wits out of you. I thought he resembled a toad. His surname, Huang, means "yellow" in Chinese, so we nicknamed him "Yellow Toad." We learned that he had some dirt in his personal history. We wanted to find him to confront him. He got wind of it and vanished. I posted a "Most Wanted" note on the school's door naming Yellow Toad a fugitive. But we never bothered to find him. He remains at large to this day, and I hope he has forgiven me, as I have him.

Some popular teachers were also in trouble. We did not quite under-stand what problems they had. Overnight, someone might become a bad person. A cook in our dining service was said to be a "bad element." His crime was possessing a set of playing cards, brought back from overseas when he worked as a chef at a Chinese embassy, with pictures of naked women.

Soon the school was in chaos. Not one day passed without some teacher being "dug out" by his or her colleagues or students as a bad element. So-called big-character posters appeared on walls all over the campus, written by the students and by teachers themselves to target and attack some person or another. We learned that many of our respected teachers were suddenly considered bad people. The school nurse, whom we all loved, was found to have worked as a nurse in the Nationalist army during the civil war. Therefore, she was a class enemy.

The movement was sweeping elementary schools, middle schools, and universities all over the city. Middle-school students formed Red Guard squads. Many teachers became targets. They were paraded in dunce caps and even tortured by Red Guards in front of students for crimes ranging from being "historical counterrevolutionaries" to "bourgeois reactionary academic authorities."

We were not content with watching all the action around us. We wanted to join the revolution as well.

A group of us broke into the dormitory room of a young art teacher, Teacher Cai. Good-looking and young, in her twenties, Teacher Cai was a popular teacher. Students loved her and what she taught. She had graduated from an art college. But she had, we knew, a small statue of a half-naked woman on the table in her room. (Now I know it was a replica of the Venus de Milo.) That had to be a capitalist object.

We stormed into her room and broke the Venus statue. She dared not utter a word of objection, in spite of her usual authority as a teacher. Times had changed. We were revolutionaries. We all felt excited and proud. But I also felt a pang of sympathy for Teacher Cai when I saw the tears in her eyes.

★ ★ ★

On August 18, 1966, Mao reviewed masses of Red Guards assembled in Tiananmen Square from atop Tiananmen Gate, waving to over a million of them below. The Red Guards responded with loud cries of "long live Chairman Mao" while jumping up and down, laughing and crying.

A teenage girl named Song Binbin put a red armband around Mao's left arm. Her name, Binbin, meant "courteous" in Chinese. After asking her for her name, Mao remarked in his quick-witted way that "militant" would suit her better. She became an instant nationwide celebrity and changed her name to Yaowu, meaning to "be militant." In 2014, 48 years later, Song would publicly admit to, and apologize for participating in, a Red Guard torture session that resulted in the death of the principal of her school.

Between August and November 1966, Mao reviewed Red Guards in Tiananmen Square eight times. According to official reports, a total of 13 million Red Guards participated in these events. Red Guards were heroes, endorsed by the Great Leader. Mao famously said, "To rebel is justified." Whatever the Red Guards did was justified.

The streets of Beijing that summer were swamped with Red Guards day and night. It was such a glorious thing to be a Red Guard that almost every young student put on a red armband with "Red Guard" printed on it. It became fashionable to wear red armbands, and green army caps and uniforms. The students unable to obtain green uniforms made do with dark-blue uniforms, known overseas as Mao suits. It was also cool to wear oversized armbands, so they were made bigger and bigger until some reached almost from the shoulder to the elbow.

The Red Guards had turned the city upside down. Teenagers in armbands would walk into a store and demand that random merchandise—perfume, for instance, or a toy bus that looked like the double-decker ones in British-controlled Hong Kong—be removed from the counter, because these were not things of consequence or importance for the proletariat. Anything that was deemed one of the "Four Olds" opposed by Mao—old thoughts, old culture, old traditions, and old customs—was smashed and destroyed. Beijing's main shopping thoroughfare, Wangfujing, a more crowded version of New York's Fifth Avenue, was about a block away from our home. Many revolutionary actions took place there. The signboards of century-old shops were pulled down because they too represented "Four Olds." I watched as people pulled down with a thick rope the signboard of Hengdeli Time Pieces Store, a brand name almost synonymous with watches and clocks in Beijing. As the board shook under the force of the pull, many people joined in to help. I did, too. Finally, it collapsed from its perch atop the building with an explosive sound. Everyone cheered, for having accomplished a great deed of revolution.

By the end of the summer, the entire judicial and law enforcement system in the 800-year-old city had ceased functioning. Policemen disappeared from traffic stands; pedestrians, as well as cyclists, cars, buses, and other vehicles could move freely, without anyone directing traffic. There was a serious proposal to change the traffic light system entirely. Why should people stop at a red light, the symbol of revolution? No. Red should signal go and green should signal stop. Some Red Guards went out to enforce this new, revolutionary system. Premier Zhou Enlai, the only sensible person in the leadership who had not yet had his authority challenged, had to personally intervene to stop the madness.

Zhou now was No. 2 in the top leadership, second only to Mao, after Liu Shaoqi was effectively removed from his position as the country's president. Zhou was pragmatic and careful in carrying out Mao's wishes without appearing to disobey them, even while minimizing their excesses. It was a great balancing act, and he, as a political survivor, was probably uniquely able and positioned to do it.

Meanwhile, no one dared challenge the ever-revolutionary acts of the Red Guards, no matter what they did. There were so many deaths in those months. Rumor had it that the city crematorium running at full capacity still could not handle the truckloads of bodies that continued to arrive, and the situation was so chaotic that it seemed nobody kept a count or record of how many people died in the violence unleashed by the Red Guards.

One day on Wangfujing, the busiest shopping street in Beijing, I saw a man and his wife paraded by a group of Red Guards through a crowd of onlookers. The man had blood all over his head, which was bent so low that it was impossible to see his face. The wife was in even worse shape. Her hair was gone, apparently cut with scissors. They were being beaten continuously, and forced to mutter, in faint voices: "I am a cow-ghost-snake-devil," a term used in the newspapers to label all class enemies. Nearby was their home. Two scrolls of characters hung on either side of the door. One scroll read: "Temple was small but devil spirit big"; and the other side read: "Pond was shallow but turtles many." Across the top of the door were the words: "A nest of bad eggs." In Chinese, turtle and bad egg are both curse words.

I doubted the couple survived the day.

Later that summer, a few friends and I went to the nearby No. 13 Girls Middle School to watch a mass meeting known as a "struggle session." Such meetings were held everywhere in Beijing every day, in almost all the middle schools, colleges, and other institutions, and conducted by student Red Guards or by a group called the Rebels. The purpose of these meetings was to haul the identified counterrevolutionaries, including school administrators and teachers, onto the stage to force them to confess their crimes and to publicly denounce them. There were also mass gatherings organized typically by college students on a much larger scale, sometimes involving tens of thousands of participants. In those meetings, the class enemies kneeling or bent low on the stage to be "struggled against" included such figures as Peng Dehuai, the former defense minister, Peng Zhen, the former mayor of Beijing, Luo Ruiqing, the former minister of public security, and other former prominent Communist Party leaders. Violence against the targets was commonplace. Often, after a long struggle session, these class enemies—wearing tall dunce hats, and with large cardboard plaques that listed their crimes hanging down from their necks—were paraded in open trucks with loudspeakers blaring their offenses through the streets of Beijing.

Beijing No. 13 Girls School was reputed to be a top-tier school. All schools were public schools, but their perceived qualities varied. Only the best and brightest students were chosen through exams to attend the top-ranked schools, and their teachers were presumed to be the best and brightest as well. As elementary school kids, we could wander into almost any mass meeting anywhere in the city to watch the proceedings.

The meeting was somewhat entertaining at first, when the Red Guards, with a serious look of justice on their young faces, hauled the "bad elements" up on stage. The bad elements included both men and women, some apparently senile. They had tall white paper dunce hats on their heads and wore heavy plaques around their necks. On the plaques were their names and alleged crimes written in big black-inked characters, with their names crossed out in red ink. The bad elements were forced to hold the "jet fighter" position, with their heads bent to their knees and their arms twisted high in the air behind their backs by Red Guards on each side. The crowd shouted slogans. The bad elements were all teachers and administrators of the school. One after another, students or rebelling teachers marched onto the stage, to make speeches shouting out and denouncing their crimes.

Before long, the action settled into a monotonous pattern and could no longer hold the attention of teenagers like myself. My friends and I snuck out of the crowd and walked around the campus. Night had fallen. It was dark, with just a few lightbulbs providing illumination here and there. In a corner of the sports field, there was an amorphous lump with cover on it. We were told that it was the body of the school's principal. Red Guards, in this case teenage schoolgirls (as this was a girls' school), had beaten her to death earlier in the day. The angry crowd was simply too busy to dispose of the corpse. We decided to leave the campus.

As we were passing by the gatekeeper's room, we heard shouts and commotion. Curious, we peeked through the window.

The room was dimly lit. Four or five teenage girls were standing in a circle, each swinging a heavy leather belt. In the center of the circle knelt an old woman who appeared to be in her sixties. Her head and body were covered in blood. She was moaning and crying in a weak voice, in great pain. The girls continued to beat her relentlessly with their belts, shouting all the while.

I knew the girls were Red Guards. They were supposed to be the good guys. I also knew that the old woman was a "class enemy." But, somehow, the whole thing looked to me so grotesque that I felt sick to my stomach. My friends and I quickly left. Later, I learned that the woman was the school's vice principal. She died later that night.

Nobody could stop or even stand in the way of the Red Guards. After all, they were answering the call of Chairman Mao to rise up against the "counterrevolutionary revisionists" who, Mao said, had infiltrated schools, universities, and the Communist Party itself. Almost all the "counterrevolutionary revisionists" were high-ranking government officials who were Communist Party members. Many of them were Mao's comrades in arms since the Red Army days. Like Russia's Joseph Stalin a few decades earlier, Mao now wanted to identify and purge the enemies of the people from within the Party, the government, and other establishments throughout the country.

Across the country, Red Guards sprang up to support Mao's Great Proletarian Cultural Revolution against anyone perceived to oppose him and his "proletariat headquarters." Red Guards were all students. The groups called the Revolutionary Rebels (hereafter I'll just call them "Rebels") arose outside the school system, in places like factories or offices. Just as there were organizations and factions of Red Guards, there were also organizations and factions of the Rebels.

Like Red Guards, Rebels also began to scour their villages, factories, and work units for potential revisionists and rightists. Anyone suspected of being a capitalist or from a bad family background (landlords, rich farmers, the bourgeoisie) was purged, imprisoned, or worse. There were numerous stories about well-known figures, high-ranking officials, ministers, artists, and intellectuals being beaten up or tortured to death. Many committed suicide.

Officials of any rank were in danger. In our neighborhood, someone was "exposed" almost every day as a "capitalist roader," or a spy, or a traitor, or a historical counterrevolutionary. Once declared a class enemy, these people became untouchables and were severely punished. Their homes were broken into and ransacked, and their property confiscated. Some were forced to leave their homes to live in so-called cattle stables, simple shelters that functioned like concentration camps. They were made to confess their crimes in front of Mao's portrait every morning and evening and to do the most menial labor, such as cleaning public toilets and sweeping the streets.

★ ★ ★

At the compound where we lived, the situation was chaotic as well. Any books not authored by the great leader himself, or by Marx, Engels, Lenin, or Stalin, could be considered poisonous weeds. Every family dumped all the books they owned. They were brought to a great bonfire built in the center of our courtyard and burned. I saved some of the books from the bonfire and brought them home to read. It was a big risk because I would be in serious trouble if caught.

At the time, the most difficult books to come by were European classics, including Russian ones. I don't quite remember when and where I picked up the titles and don't remember them all, but my reading included Leo Tolstoy's *War and Peace* and *Anna Karenina*, Maxim Gorky's *The Song of the Stormy Petrel*, Nikolai Ostrovsky's *How the Steel Was Tempered*, Hans Christian Andersen's fairy tales, Victor Hugo's *Ninety-Three* and *Les Misérables*, *Jane Eyre* by Charlotte Bronte, Herman Melville's *Moby-Dick*, novels by Charles Dickens, and books by Jules Verne, such as *Around the World in 80 Days* and *Journey to the Center of the Earth*, now considered precursors to science fiction.

People threw away anything considered to represent the "Four Olds." Since nobody knew precisely what one of the Four Olds might look like, and nobody wanted to risk being caught in possession of anything offensive, people just threw away or burned everything they were not sure of.

Many employees of the Ministry of Foreign Trade had been abroad and had brought home souvenirs from overseas. Now these had to be thrown away or destroyed. I saw Western-style clothing—including high-heeled shoes with the heels sawed off, and other articles that might indicate a bourgeois lifestyle—stuffed in the trash container.

My own family did not possess anything so bourgeois. My father only threw out some books. My mother forced me to get rid of my goldfish, which in their lazy and leisurely ways looked anything but proletarian.

The entire law enforcement system was paralyzed. Nobody dared to interfere with the revolution. The violence went on unabated. The Red Guards started a campaign to search and ransack homes. They stormed into the homes of those they considered or suspected of being class enemies, to search for evidence and to confiscate the inhabitants' property. Often, they beat up the owners. They were free to commandeer any vehicle on the streets of Beijing. They took away books, manuscripts, and documents, and household items from jewelry to furniture or anything else that caught their eye. Some people lost all their belongings and were kicked out of their own homes.

There was a Catholic church called St. Michael's located in our neighborhood. The French built it in 1901 for the foreigners who lived here. But all religious practices had stopped. The church was now used as a warehouse where the Red Guards stored their loot. I visited the church with my friends to see what was going on. Loaded carts and trucks were constantly arriving in front of the church's Gothic facade. Crowds helped unload confiscated articles from the vehicles and carried them into the nave, stacking up tables, desks, chairs, sofas, and all kinds of household items and valuables. When I got there, the big church was already half full. Someone pointed to a radio and said it was a wireless receiver that had belonged to a Nationalist spy. He said the radio was used to receive instructions and to transmit intelligence. Well, the radio looked quite innocuous to me, not much different from the vacuum-tube models found in any home. There was also a fruit knife placed on top of the radio. I was told that its owner tried to stab a Red Guard with it when his home was raided. I could only imagine what happened to the owner.

One day I went with friends to the residential compound for the employees of the Beijing municipal government. There was a big crowd gathered there. We watched as a man was being harangued, or "struggled against," on a balcony in front of the crowd. The man was Hu Yaobang, the secretary general of the Communist Youth League, an important training ground for young Communist Party members. He had been a "red kid," still a teenager during the Red Army's Long March, who had risen through the ranks to become one of the Communist Party's leaders. Hu would survive the Cultural Revolution and become the Communist Party's general secretary, the highest position in China's leadership, in the mid-1980s. In 1987 he would be purged again; his death in 1989 provided the spark for the nationwide protests that year that ended with the Tiananmen crackdown. All that was still decades away, however; that day, he was just a slight, middle-aged man submissively being yelled at by teenagers wearing armbands before being led off the balcony.

After the struggle session, the crowd was shown the decadent and capitalistic lifestyle of Hu Yaobang. We filed into his home, a three- or four-bedroom apartment probably on the second floor of the building. The apartment was not spacious so the crowd had to walk in single file.

I noticed a notebook on top of an upright piano. I opened it. It was a diary, probably kept by his young daughter. I read a couple of pages. One of the entries read: "Papa told us to always listen and follow Chairman Mao ..." I remember thinking to myself that these did not look like the words of a counterrevolutionary.

★ ★ ★

The beating on the door was gentle but rapid and persistent. It finally yanked me out of my dream. For a moment, I thought the noise came from a raging rainstorm outside, as thunderstorms occurred often in Beijing's summer. It took me a few seconds to realize someone was knocking on the door. It was only about 5 o'clock in the morning and my part of the room, which was separated by a curtain from my 13-year-old sister's bed, was still dark. I heard her getting up to open the front door of our parents' two-room home and let someone in. Then I heard some muffled chattering.

I got out of my bed and opened the partition curtain while rubbing my eyes to see what was going on. By the windowed door stood a girl, whom I recognized to be Hou Erman, a sixth-grade classmate of mine. Our parents both worked for the Ministry of Foreign Trade. Even though she was a good friend of ours, I was surprised to see her visiting so early. When she saw me, she stopped whispering.

"What happened?" I asked. Erman diverted her eyes away from me to look at my sister. Then she returned her gaze to me and said in a barely audible low voice, "My father is dead."

I was 12 years old in 1966 and had little experience with death, much less it happening to people I actually knew. I was shocked both by the news and by how calmly and unemotionally Erman uttered those words. It was as if she was wearing an emotionless mask. She was talking about her own father, and yet I felt she was talking about a distant stranger.

I quickly put on my clothes and ran out into the yard of our residential compound. Our home was in a flat building that housed dozens of families. Erman's family lived around the corner in the nicer, light gray building reserved for senior cadres; her father held the rank of bureau chief. There was a small crowd of people gathered in front of the door to the apartment building's staircase, and there was an ambulance.

I arrived just as a stretcher, on it a body covered with a sheet, was being brought down the stairs. I knew it was her father.

Erman stayed with my sister at our home and did not come out as her father's body was taken away.

Kang Li, Erman's father, had been accused of being a traitor by some of his own colleagues, I later learned, piecing together the story from Erman and my parents. Unable to clear his name, he chose to kill himself. He had gently kissed his children before they went to bed that night. The family woke up to find him in the bathroom, hanging from a rope. Fearing that any sign of sorrow would implicate other members of the family, her mother instructed the children to "draw a line" with their father. It was remarkable, as I think about it today, that a 12-year-old girl could remain so calm at the death of her father. But thank God she did not show any sign of emotion, or else she could have been in trouble herself for having feelings for a man who had betrayed the revolution. It became known later that some Red Guards beat a young girl to death for desecrating Mao's *Little Red Book*, because she had sat on it. They even forced her mother to join in the beating to prove her mother's own innocence.

★ ★ ★

Not everyone could become a Red Guard. To qualify, even as a student, one had to come from a "proletariat" family background, which included "revolutionary cadres," factory workers, or poor peasants. If one's parents did not belong to any of those "red categories," one was unlikely to be accepted. Many Red Guard leaders, especially at the middle school level, were children of high-ranking cadres. They had a strong sense of entitlement because their parents had taken part in the revolution. Ironically, during the Cultural Revolution, many of their parents would be labeled as capitalist roaders, and their children would become known as "children of the black gang." That label, however, didn't prevent many of them from continuing to wage revolution.

If the children of high-ranking cadres were often the most self-righteous and self-entitled members of the Red Guard, they could also be the most ferocious and brutal. What was most inexplicable to me was the cruelty of middle school students, both boys and girls, which I witnessed repeatedly. These youngsters usually dressed in yellowish green military uniforms, secured, infamously, by a leather belt with a big steel buckle. I had seen these belts in action. They could be used as a whip to flog their victims. The worst would use the buckle end of the belt to kill, as I had witnessed in the girls' middle school in 1966.

★ ★ ★

He Yuzhou was four years older than me. He was the big brother in our neighborhood, a good student and well read. I had just finished elementary school, but he had finished the first year of senior middle school at Beijing No. 5 Middle School, one of the best in the city. Bespectacled, tall, and athletic—it seemed there was no sport he did not excel in—Yuzhou was also good with his hands. While I struggled to assemble a diode radio, he could build an eight-transistor one. In my eyes, he was like an adult. I respected him and looked up to him as a role model and as our leader.

He Yuzhou invited me, along with some of my classmates, to move to Jingxinzhai, or Peaceful Heart Garden, within Beihai Park, where he and his Red Guard friends had taken up residence. I packed my sleeping quilt, a washbasin, and a few other essentials, and joined them.

I don't remember any particular purpose for our moving in there, other than that it was available and was a nice place. Jingxinzhai was indeed a large garden, about the size of a football field, on the north bank of Beihai Lake, a short walk from the science camp. The garden was built in 1757 as a place for the crown prince to read. Immediately beyond the garden gate, there was a large rectangle-shaped pond with a white marble walkway and railings around it. A few lotuses dotted the pond, although they were withering from lack of tending.

Behind the pond on each side was another gate. Inside there was a row of empty rooms with large windows under one roof. From the windows, one could see another large pond with man-made rock hills around it. The rocks were in many strange shapes with holes in them. They were shipped to Beijing from the southern part of China ages ago by the emperors. I remember one piece of the rock sticking out over the pond, an ideal place to fish. On the rocky hills was a small

covered walkway that zigzagged to the top of the hill. There was a row
of pavilion-type houses that we turned into our sleeping quarters.

This area had been the site of the Research Center for Culture and
History, established by Mao in 1951 and led by Mao's former teacher Fu
Dingyi. Mao's vision was for the center to provide a place for prominent
"leftovers" from the old regimes to gather, study, and write—mostly
memoirs, given that they had witnessed the making of China's modern
history. Premier Zhou himself appointed all the members, as a reflection
of their prominence and the center's importance; they included former
officials and socialites of the Qing dynasty and the Nationalist regime.
I had read many of these memoirs, including *The First Half of My Life*
by Puyi, the last emperor of the Qing dynasty, who was born in 1906
and ascended to the throne in 1908, just before he turned three. Puyi
was dethroned just about two years later, however, after the Revolution of 1911, although the formal abdication took place in 1912.
Beginning in 1935 he was declared the puppet emperor of Manchukuo
(a Japanese-occupied territory in northeast China) until Japan surrendered in 1945. I thought it was a fascinating story of how he lived.

By the time we moved in, the center had been completely vacated,
and the garden was quiet and peaceful, indeed a perfect place to study.
With so many attractions, we could wander around for a long time
without getting bored. I found the whole time exhilarating, an endless
camping trip inside the beautiful park. During the day, when it was
open to the public, we did little except enjoy our freedom. When it
closed at night, we would scour the park with flashlights, flushing out
lovers and stragglers from its many caves and corners.

For us, living this way was a carefree adventure, away from the visitors inside the park and turmoil outside it. We did not want to go home
other than for an occasional meal. I felt I could happily stay there for a
very long time. In some very real sense, I was one of many boys living
in an ideal bubble.

But not for long.

Chapter 4

Turmoil Under Heaven

The first fires of the Cultural Revolution were lit in Beijing in 1966. But when Yao Wenyuan's critique of *The Firing of Hai Rui* was published in Shanghai, it caused a sensation; none of Beijing's state-controlled papers would run it. For one thing, the city leaders thought it inappropriate to elevate a discussion of a literary work to the level of politics. For another, Wu Han, the author of the opera, was a vice mayor of Beijing. For this and other reasons, Mao became angry with the city government and called it "an independent kingdom that needles can't penetrate and water can't seep through," meaning that it was beyond his control as it would not follow his orders. The city government itself was now in his line of fire.

On May 16, 1966, the Communist Party Central Committee, under Mao's direction, issued a call for a nationwide "Cultural Revolution," although few understood what this revolution specifically involved. In late June 1966, the Party announced that it had discovered within its ranks a counterrevolutionary, anti-Party clique consisting of Peng Zhen, the mayor of Beijing; Luo Ruiqing, China's minister of public security; Lu Dingyi, the Party's propaganda chief; and Yang Shangkun, Mao's former chief of staff. All of them had been in the top echelon of the leadership and were stalwart members of the Party, having fought alongside Mao since the founding of the Red

Army. Accused of plotting a coup d'état, among other charges, they were stripped of their positions and freedom. Those regarded as followers of the four, Wu Han among them, were fired from their jobs or thrown into jail.

The fires of revolution spread. Students and some faculty members in Beijing's colleges had risen up against school authorities, following Mao's call for a Cultural Revolution. They verbally, and often physically, attacked university presidents, administrators, professors, and prominent academics, forcing them to submit to "struggle sessions" to confess their crimes against the Party and condemning them in "big-character posters" for allegedly following a capitalist or revisionist line. Classes were suspended and schools were shut. Confusion and chaos reigned.

While this was happening in the early summer of 1966, Mao was traveling outside Beijing. Liu Shaoqi was in charge of running the country on a day-to-day basis, along with Deng Xiaoping, the general secretary of the Party. Liu dispatched "work teams," which consisted of officials from various government agencies, to bring the situation at the colleges under control, or to "put out the fire," as he instructed them. Under orders to "rely on the Party leadership," the work teams would join forces with the schools' administration and restore order, calming or quashing the rebellious radical student groups.

When Mao returned to Beijing on July 18, 1966, he was furious. Liu and Deng had suppressed a revolution and a student movement, a treacherous move more befitting of the reactionary Nationalist government of the old regime. He published an open letter titled "Firing at the Command Center—My Big Character Poster," in which he identified, without mentioning any names, a "capitalist headquarters" within the Party. Obviously, he was referring to the leadership of Liu and Deng.

Praising the students for their revolutionary deeds, Mao ordered the withdrawal of all government-dispatched work teams. Liu and Deng were forced to admit their mistakes and their misunderstanding of the purpose of the Cultural Revolution.

Mao's words and actions strongly appealed to the students, especially those who had been suppressed at the hands of Liu and

Deng's work teams. From that point on, the Red Guard movement began in earnest and soon spread to all the colleges and middle schools in Beijing.

Mao's encouragement of the Red Guards had its intended effect. The personal cult of Mao had reached its zenith. Students were mad with happiness just to get a glimpse of him in the mass rallies. They worshipped him like a god and they followed his every word. They attacked whatever they considered to represent the Four Olds (old thought, old culture, old tradition, and old customs). The flames of the Cultural Revolution consumed Beijing.

The Cultural Revolution was slow to take hold in other parts of China's vast land. So Beijing's Red Guards took upon themselves a new mission: to bring the news of the Cultural Revolution to the country. They began, around August 1966, a Great Networking movement, traveling in great numbers to all parts of China to spread the revolution. Meanwhile Red Guards and Rebels from other cities and provinces journeyed to the capital to experience the revolutionary fervor for themselves, and to learn Beijing's revolutionary ways.

The Great Networking movement spread the Cultural Revolution like a wildfire and would soon touch the lives of all Chinese. The Red Guards and the Rebels attacked and "knocked down" the leadership at every level of government throughout the country. Anarchy reigned.

Mao was exuberant. "Everything under the heaven is in great turmoil; the situation is excellent," he declared. He watched with satisfaction as the Rebels blew the old order and his own government to pieces with revolutionary zeal. "The great chaos will lead to great rule," he predicted confidently.

In January 1967, the Rebels in Shanghai seized power and established a new city government, called the Revolutionary Committee. The action was sanctioned and supported by Mao and was hailed by the *People's Daily* as the "January Storm." This touched off a nationwide wave of disruption as Rebels seized power and established revolutionary committees throughout the country. In some places, some semblance of order was restored under the new regime; in others, the fighting between different factions of the Rebels only intensified. Mao's vision of "great chaos leading to great rule" was leading to ever-greater chaos.

★ ★ ★

Outside Beihai Park, events were becoming even more surreal. The central government announced on September 5, 1966, that "revolutionary little generals," or Red Guards, could travel and lodge anywhere in the country without having to pay for the purpose of spreading the revolution and of connecting with Red Guards elsewhere in the country. The movement soon became known as *da chuan lian*, or the "Great Networking." The all-consuming wildfire of the Cultural Revolution was now spreading rapidly to other parts of China.

He Yuzhou decided we should join the Great Networking to see the country. We were 12 or 13 years old and Yuzhou was about 17. My elementary-school friends Chen Jiamin and Qin Zhiqiang also joined us on the trip. So did several of my classmates, including my neighbor Hou Erman, who must have been still secretly mourning her father's suicide, although she was careful never to show it.

My parents did not stop me. My mother gave me 20 yuan for spending money. I don't know how they felt at the time, but I suppose they did not want to appear to oppose the revolution. I cannot imagine today letting my own kids do such a thing at a similar age, without knowing where they would go, with whom they would stay, or how they would find food. But in 1966 in China, so many kids were doing it. We embarked on our journey in such a hurry that I did not have time to go back to Jingxinzhai to collect my belongings. For a long time, I regretted it because my mother lived so frugally that she would have been upset with my waste.

We left Beijing by train for Shanghai in late September 1966. It was the first time I had ever left the city and it was my first long train ride. Our train was so crowded with students that there was not much room to wiggle. Young students were packed in everywhere. Some stood on the backs of the seats, others slept under the seats.

Since I was quite small at the time, I climbed onto the baggage rack and sat there. The train was overcrowded and overloaded, and it moved at a snail's pace. Normally it took 24 hours to travel from Beijing to Shanghai. Our journey took three days. When our train crossed the Yangtze River in Nanjing, it moved particularly slowly, apparently because the engineer was worried that the bridge might collapse under so much weight. We were never hungry because all of us were provided by the kitchen of the train with lunchboxes for every meal, free. The challenge was going to the bathroom. I had to walk on the backs of seats to get there.

By the time we got to Shanghai, my feet had become swollen because I had sat with my legs hanging down from the baggage rack for too long. I could not walk. Yuzhou found a three-wheeler to wheel me to our destination while others in our group walked. Our lodging was the classroom of a school. The people from that school gave us bedding, and we pulled some desks together to make our beds.

The next day I woke to yelling outside. It was the voices of night soil collectors who were pulling carts with tanks into which people emptied their chamber pots. I had never seen anything like this in Beijing, which at least had flush toilets.

I didn't go out with the group that day because I still couldn't walk. It took two or three days for the swelling in my feet to finally subside. It felt great to walk normally again. And then it was time to leave Shanghai.

Our first stop after Shanghai was in Shang-rao, a small city about 500 kilometers (~300 miles) to the southeast. We visited an infamous Nationalist concentration camp there, where the captured Communist fighters had been imprisoned and tortured.

Our next destination was Fuzhou, the capital of Fujian Province. Yuzhou wanted to take us to Xiamen, a coastal city across from Taiwan. But we were not permitted to travel there because it was on the front line of hostilities; the Communists and Nationalists were still technically at war, and there was artillery shelling every other day.

Fuzhou was a much quieter city, and we stayed on the campus of Fuzhou University, which was almost deserted, with just a few students hanging around. We noticed that numerous wall posters were splattered everywhere, denouncing this or that person from the administrative or academic authorities. We wandered around the campus, reading the posters. We noticed that one organization was impressively prolific. Poster upon poster bore the signature of the United Rebellion Headquarters of Red Guards. This had to be the largest Red Guard organization in the university, we thought, and we decided to pay it a visit.

We traced the organization to a classroom. We went in and saw a man standing with his back to the door, brush in hand, writing with furious speed. Hearing us enter, the man turned around and greeted us. We asked him if we were at the United Rebellion Headquarters. He answered in the affirmative and invited us to sit down. He introduced himself as Zheng Lian.

Yuzhou said: "We are from Beijing. We are here to do the Great Networking. We read the wall posters of your organization and think there is a lot we could learn from you. Can we meet with the commander-in-chief of the United Rebellion Headquarters?"

"That's me," he said.

"Ah. How many people are under your command?"

"Oh, just myself," Zheng Lian replied.

We were surprised but also impressed, as Zheng Lian single-handedly had covered nearly the entire campus with his essays in big-character posters. What a singular revolutionary force.

Zheng Lian began telling us his grievances against the university authorities, most of which predated the Cultural Revolution. As a student, he said, administrative leaders persecuted him because he had criticized them for pursuing a capitalist path in education. To silence and punish him, the authorities refused to let him graduate and locked him in a mental hospital, where Zheng Lian fought back by going on a hunger strike. In response, the hospital staff force-fed him. Thanks to Chairman Mao, he said, he was freed at the start of the Cultural Revolution. Now he was going after the authorities in full force, fighting with his writing brush to expose the true counterrevolutionary color of the leadership of the university and the province.

That he was persecuted in such a cruel manner for his dissent sounded outrageous to us, and we offered him our sympathy. Yuzhou decided we should go to the mental hospital to investigate our new comrade's mistreatment. The next day, some of our team members and Zheng Lian went there, and came back saying that the nurses and Zheng Lian's doctor corroborated his story. Indeed, he had been a patient, and they did force-feed him. Yuzhou asked how they diagnosed him as mentally ill. The doctor told him Zheng Lian was delusional because on a group outing he was offered a bowl of water by a girl on the roadside, and he later insisted that the girl was in love with him. Then Yuzhou asked the doctor why Zheng Lian was released. The doctor said that he was considered cured because he admitted that he had a mental problem. In the doctor's view, if a mental patient admitted he was a nut case, he had already recovered, because mental patients never admitted they were sick.

★ ★ ★

We left Fuzhou by bus for Changting in Fujian Province. This area had been one of the earliest revolutionary bases of the Red Army, between 1929 and 1934. Yuzhou plotted a mini–Long March for our group. We would hike nearly 50 kilometers (~30 miles) from Gucheng in Fujian's Changting district, to Ruijin in neighboring Jiangxi Province. Our walk would take us through the Wuyi Mountains, retracing the footsteps of the Red Army. Ruijin was the capital of the short-lived Chinese Soviet Republic, also known as the Jiangxi Soviet. It was from here that Mao and his Red Army began the Long March to avoid annihilation by the Nationalist troops in 1934.

We set out late one afternoon when it was no longer hot. Since the trek was expected to be tough, Hou Erman and another girl took a bus and said they would meet us at the destination. The mountain road was reasonably good and the slope was quite gentle. There were trees on both sides of the road and covering the entire mountain. But the road was quite wide and open, so I did not feel like walking in the woods. From time to time, we encountered local farmers walking in the opposite direction carrying heavy loads on a big pole slung across their shoulders. We walked and walked until night fell and we did not see any other trekkers on the road. Then it became a little scary because we heard the howls of wild animals, but we could not see anything in the gathering darkness. Soon it was completely dark, and we could only pick our way forward in the moonlight. Just then, we heard some people shouting from behind us.

"Stop! Wait!" came the female voices.

We all stopped in our tracks, stiffened up, and turned around.

We could see only a few shadows of human figures running toward us. As they ran, they kept yelling, "Wait! Wait!"

They were four or five women, each with a pole on her shoulder. When they caught up with us, they told us in halting voices, as they were out of breath, that there were tigers in the mountains.

"Can we walk together with you?" they asked, clearly afraid.

Knowing about the tigers made us frightened and nervous, too, even though I doubted they were lurking in the woods around a road so close to people. As we walked together, I did not know if our company made them more comfortable or their company did us. But after a while, we reached their village on the side of the road. They thanked us and disappeared into the darkness.

Zheng Lian traveled with us. He told us he thought it was hopeless to win his case in Fujian Province. He was determined to go to Beijing and petition the central government personally. As our little group approached the border dividing Fujian and Jiangxi Provinces, Zheng Lian grew increasingly tense and nervous. Finally, he walked close to me and grabbed my arm.

"I fear I'll be assassinated," he whispered into my ear. "The Fujian government would never let me go to Beijing to petition against them. I think they will try to kill me before we reach the provincial border."

He was so deadly serious that I felt scared. Then he said, as he handed me his carrying bag, "These are my petition papers with important evidence that will expose the crimes of the Party organizations in Fuzhou University and Fujian Province. I want you to carry them. If I am assassinated, I ask you to take them to Beijing and deliver them to Chairman Mao personally. I want you to swear that you will do this for me."

No one in my young life had ever taken me so seriously or entrusted me with anything so important. I was touched by his trust and impressed by the gravity of the situation. I felt a great sense of revolutionary responsibility. I did not so much as consider my own safety. I think he chose me because I was the youngest, shortest, and smallest in our group, so his assassins might overlook me. I accepted his bag, slung its straps across my shoulders, and held it tightly with both my arms. Feeling the weight of the bag, and my duty, I solemnly promised that I would carry it to Beijing and personally hand it to Chairman Mao.

Satisfied, he walked away and kept a distance from me.

Soon we reached the provincial border. Along one side of the road was a wall surrounding a compound of houses that straddled the border. On the Fujian side, the wall was dark, but on the side of Jiangxi, a neighboring province, it was painted a bright white. The difference in color clearly marked the border between the two provinces.

We walked across that border line without being ambushed. After we crossed it, Zheng Lian came over to me. He said now he was out of danger, so I could give the bag back to him. I did, but I wondered why the bad guys would not simply follow him all the way, because after all, they could go where we could. It was then that I began to question his ability to reason and suspect maybe he really was a delusional lunatic as the doctors in the mental hospital diagnosed. In any case, my heroic willingness to help him in a situation of life and death seemed to be in vain.

By now, we were hungry. We walked into another small village by the roadside. We knocked on the door of a house and a man answered. We told him we wanted to find something to eat. He prepared a meal for us, and we left him some money for the food. We rarely had occasion to spend the money we carried with us, because everywhere we went, whether it was a school or a government reception station, lodging and food were provided for free. It was only in places like this, at private homes in the middle of nowhere, that we had a chance to spend some money.

This was the longest walk I had ever done. I became more and more tired as we walked. My legs felt like lead and every step was difficult. I sat down to rest and immediately fell asleep. My companions woke me up and pushed me to move forward.

Finally, in the wee hours of the morning, we reached Ruijin. There was a local government reception station where I fell asleep immediately after lying down on the straw-covered floor in a small room. The next morning, I was awakened by the laughter of children.

"You come to Ruijin to visit and to learn. What visit and learn? You sleep!"

Then they would laugh and repeat the taunt again and again. I suppose they did not see outside visitors often and, because of my size, I was an easy target for their jeering.

Ruijin was nestled in the middle of rice paddies surrounded by mountains. It felt more like a big village than a small town. There were still a few buildings from the days of the Jiangxi Soviet of the 1930s, including Mao's residence and Party meeting places.

Of particular interest to us was a nearby well that Mao had supposedly dug himself. There was a story in our elementary school textbook about it. According to the story, there was a village by the name of Shazhouba outside Ruijin. One day, Mao saw some farmers from Shazhouba carrying buckets of murky water. It turned out that the only source of water for everyone in the village was the village pond, where people also washed their clothes. So Mao had a well dug there to supply them with clean drinking water. There was a stone tablet at the head of the well erected by the villagers, and it read: "When drinking water do not forget the well digger; always miss Chairman Mao." We asked around and found the well with the stone tablet. We drank the water from the well.

The water was supposed to be sweet, but I could not taste any sweetness at all. Nobody, however, would say a word about it not being sweet, which would be disrespectful to Mao. We took a picture of ourselves standing on both sides of the inscribed stone tablet to memorialize this great moment of having visited the sacred well and drunk its water.

I was quite impressed by an octagonal auditorium the Red Army built in the village to hold big meetings. The building's shape echoed the shape of the caps worn by the Red Army soldiers. Edgar Snow's picture of Mao in an octagonal cap became the cover photo of his book *Red Star over China*. But the shape of the building was not just symbolic. Each side of the octagon had a big door. The local people explained there had been aerial bombings from time to time by Nationalist forces. The doors on all sides of the auditorium facilitated evacuation when there was an air raid. I thought the design was quite clever.

★ ★ ★

After Ruijin, we took a bus to Ganzhou, a major city in Jiangxi Province. The only impression I had of Ganzhou was its spices. It seemed all the food was spicy there. Even breakfast was spicy. I asked people if there was anything not spicy and I was told no. I could not eat such spicy food, so I ate only rice at every meal.

From Ganzhou, we went by bus to Jinggang Mountain, in Jiangxi Province, where Mao had established his first base after leading the Autumn Harvest Uprising in 1927. It was there that Mao's men joined forces with the men led by Zhu De to found the Red Army. Zhu became the chief commander and Mao the political commissar.

For Red Guards and those of us on the Great Networking, a visit to Jinggang Mountain was like a pilgrimage. We found it quite crowded there, and the local government had organized the place to accommodate a steady stream of visitors. There was a large dining hall where everyone ate. The menu was the same as what the Red Army supposedly ate about four decades earlier. There was a popular Red Army song that described the food:

> *Red rice, pumpkin soup,*
> *Autumn eggplant, taste so good,*
> *Every meal eaten up we could.*

We were served red rice and pumpkin soup for every meal to re-create the experience of Red Army soldiers. I found the rice coarse and the pumpkin soup somewhat tasteless, although I didn't dare to say that lest my friends laughed at me for not being as tough as a Red Army soldier.

★ ★ ★

The next day, we hiked to Huangyangjie, which was where the Red Army once defeated Nationalist troops. Our lodging place was about 800 meters (~2,600 feet) above sea level. Huangyangjie, at the top of the mountain, lies at about 1,300 meters (~4,300 feet) above sea level. There was a narrow, crowded trail leading there. I did not feel it was particularly difficult, although I saw many people resting along the trail's edge, huffing and puffing. On the mountaintop was a big stone monument with an inscription that read "the monument for the victory in the battle to defend Huangyangjie." The inscription was the calligraphy of Zhu De, the commander-in-chief of the Red Army. Mao wrote a poem in 1928 to commemorate the battle:

Below the hills fly our flags and banners,
Above the hilltops sound our bugles and drums.
Enemies encircle us thousands strong,
Steadfastly we stand our ground.
Already our defense is iron-clad,
Now our wills unite like a fortress.
From Huangyangjie roars the thunder of guns,
Word comes the enemy has fled into the night.

We looked around to see where the enemy might have attacked, but there was nothing to be seen. All around us were green mountains covered by trees and bamboo forests. The bamboo there was tall and thick. Local people used the bamboo for shoulder poles, water bottles, and all kinds of furniture. Each one of us was given a machete to cut a stalk of bamboo for our own use. I took my machete and went into the bamboo forest with my friends. I selected a nice, thick stalk, about as big around as the diameter of the mouth of a large rice bowl, and took a swing. I thought it would be quite easy to cut since bamboo trees were hollow. But I hacked and hacked without seeming to make much progress; the tough, fibrous outer wall of the trunk was nearly two centimeters thick. I worked with my machete for hours, until it started to get dark. The bamboo was so tall, and the forest so thick, that little sunlight shone through. Most people had already left. I had heard that there were tigers in this area, too, and was afraid that I would lose my way when night fell, so I stopped hacking and left in a hurry.

★ ★ ★

I think that in the mind of our friend Yuzhou, who had been the inspiration for the journey, the purpose of our trip was simply to see the country and have an adventure. There was no plan to spread any revolutionary ideas. Yuzhou and two of his older friends planned the entire trip. Because the government sanctioned the Great Networking, there was no need to book train or bus tickets in advance. You just showed up at the scheduled time and boarded the train. All the trains were overcrowded but we could always squeeze in. It did not matter that none of the trains were on time, as chaos was characteristic of the time and was normal, and we were not in a hurry anyhow.

★ ★ ★

We finished our Great Networking by the end of October 1966 and returned to Beijing after almost a month on the road. The situation there was as chaotic as when we had left, and the city was still filled with Red Guards from all over China. One day, I got wind of a big "struggle session" going on in the auditorium of the compound of our home. I went to check it out. There in front of a big crowd was Wang Enmao, who until then had been the Party Secretary of Xinjiang Province, in China's far west. I saw him on the stage, with his head bowed low, being held by two people on either side of him. One speaker after another jumped onto the stage to harangue and denounce him for his crimes.

"Down with the capitalist roader Wang Enmao!" one man shouted on the stage.

"Down with Wang Enmao," the crowd echoed in a roar.

"Long live the Great Proletariat Cultural Revolution! Long live Chairman Mao!"

The shouting of the slogans was so loud that the building seemed to shake.

Throughout, Wang did not utter a word, refusing to speak when his tormentors challenged him with this question or that. This old man was really tough, I thought.

Wang, 54 years old in 1966, was a veteran Red Army soldier who participated in the Red Army's Long March. At the founding of the PRC, he was made a lieutenant general. I later read in a memoir that in the end, Mao protected him, which spared him the worst of the Red Guards' excesses.

According to the story, in January 1967, a group of provincial governors and Party secretaries gathered in a hotel catering to senior officials in Beijing to attend a "study session," the real purpose of which was probably to hide themselves from the Red Guards and the Rebels. One day, Mao paid them a surprise visit. The memoir recounted:

Chairman Mao shook hands with those comrades standing in the front. Suddenly he spotted Wang Enmao who stood out in the crowd because of his height. Mao walked over to him to shake his hand and said: "I heard the Rebels of Xinjiang want to knock you down. How is it? Will you be knocked down?"

"Knock-down" was a commonly used revolutionary terminology of the time, meaning to bring down someone from his high position. A "knocked-down" senior official or an academic authority, publicly considered a counterrevolutionary bad person, was deprived of his previous job, disgraced, and subject to constant struggle sessions and humiliation.

Wang didn't know how to respond to Mao's enquiries and blurted out, "That depends on the Chairman's attitude [toward me]."
Chairman Mao smiled and said "I don't think you can be knocked down." As he was walking away, he turned his head and added, "Wang Enmao won't be knocked down."

But Wang lost his position and did not assume a similar position until 10 years later.

Soon after, we heard of more trouble in Xinjiang Province. In 1967, there was a fight brewing between different Rebel factions in the town of Shihezi, outside the provincial capital, Urumqi. Each faction had captured weapons, including guns. Ever adventurous, He Yuzhou wanted to organize a trip to go there. Shihezi would be a long journey from Beijing. It takes five and half hours to fly there from Beijing today, about the same time as flying from New York to San Francisco. By train back then, it would have taken days. This time, my parents put their foot down and would not let me go because they knew that Shihezi had become a war zone, and they were concerned about my safety. But I was already 13 years old, old enough to make my own decisions, and I was living in a time of rebellion. I insisted on going. I packed a few things and went to the train station on the day of departure to join Yuzhou and the others. I was already aboard the train when my father showed up.

Without a word, as he knew reasoning with me would have been futile and could get him into trouble if he said something politically incorrect within earshot of the Red Guards on the train, he just grabbed my bag and took me home. The revolutionary in me did not have the courage to challenge or knock down my father's authority in the family.

About a month later, Yuzhou and his friends came back from Xinjiang. They reported seeing armed conflicts between factions of the Rebels, involving guns, even tanks and rockets, which they had looted from the military troops stationed there. (The military was ordered not to fight back when attacked to avoid casualties or to take sides.) One student from Beijing was killed when a rocket pierced the tank he was sitting in and blew it up. Some young people who went to Shihezi were killed. My father may have saved my life.

★ ★ ★

Meanwhile on the political front, things were coming to a head. Public criticism of President Liu Shaoqi intensified in 1967. As the verbal and written attacks on Liu intensified in the public, Liu remained holed up in the Zhongnanhai leadership compound, formerly an imperial garden in the Forbidden City. Many Rebel organizations descended on Zhongnanhai to demand that he be dragged out. This became known as the "Outing Liu Movement." Numerous tents and people occupied the sidewalk across the streets from the gates of Zhongnanhai. They stayed there day and night, shouting slogans and making demands through megaphones and loudspeakers.

After returning from the Great Networking, my classmates and I did not have anything to do but go to the Wangfujing shopping street to buy Red Guard newspapers to read, or just wander around the city day after day. I do not remember whose idea it was, but we decided to join the Outing Liu Movement and set up a tent outside Zhongnanhai. We, like others, managed to build a makeshift shelter, out of cardboard cartons. We stayed there whenever we wanted, but mostly at night, because there nobody would tell us to go to bed. We would go home only to have meals. This festival atmosphere lasted for some weeks.

One day in the summer of 1967, I went home for a meal and then took a nap. I did not get much sleep in the tent, so I was exhausted.

I asked my mother to wake me up after an hour or two, so I could go back to the tent to join my friends. When I woke up, it was already the next morning. I was quite upset with my mother for not waking me, and I stalked out of our home. I suppose either I was too tired, or she did not really try, as I am sure she didn't approve of my revolutionary actions.

When I got back to the tent, I saw that Wang Yuanbo was missing. I assumed he had also gone home to sleep. No, that was not the case, my other classmate told me. The night before, a man representing Premier Zhou had come around, asking those in each tent to send a representative to the Great Hall of the People for a meeting with the premier himself. Yuanbo went but had not returned.

When Yuanbo finally came back, he reported that Zhou had spent all night, until early that morning, talking with the representatives of the Rebel groups camped outside Zhongnanhai. Zhou tried hard to persuade them all to leave. Many did not agree and argued with him. But Zhou patiently worked on everyone until they all finally agreed to comply with his request. Maybe it was due to Zhou's powers of persuasion, or maybe he just exhausted everyone with his stamina. In any case, by the morning, an agreement was reached that all the protesters would pull out. When I reflect upon this event, I still find it incredible that Zhou, in his position of power, would bother to spend so much time patiently persuading a bunch of mindless teenagers to get out of that place.

Liu Shaoqi soon lost his freedom, regardless. In October 1968, the central committee expelled him from the Party. By then more than 70 percent of the members of the Party Central Committee had been purged for various "crimes." Liu Shaoqi died, in degrading and cruel circumstances, in prison in 1969 in Kaifeng, Henan Province.

For me, as 1966 gave way to 1967, and throughout my first year as a teenager, there was little to do. Our indefinite "school vacation" felt great at first, but by now we were quite bored and restless. Not only were there no schools to attend, but every form of entertainment was shut down. Public parks like Beihai were off limits. Closing down ancient temples and parks was a decision Premier Zhou had made when the Red Guards were roaming the country smashing up or burning down everything of the old, including temples and religious statues. Libraries were closed, and cinemas and theaters were shuttered because every program of theirs was considered bourgeois or worse. Bookstores were closed, too, because nobody could tell anymore which books would be considered offensive or anti-socialist. In Beijing alone, there must have been hundreds of thousands of students my age who were out of school and without a job. Groups of students wandered around the city on foot or on bicycles, looking for trouble.

In 1968, my parents decided to send my sister and me to my mother's old home village in Shandong Province. We took a train to the port town of Tanggu, near the city of Tianjin, about two hours away from Beijing, where we boarded a passenger vessel. The big passenger boat sailed out of the Haihe River into the sea and then to Yantai, a port city in Shandong. We had third-class tickets, which entitled us to a bunk bed in the crowded bowels of the boat. The journey took several days. It was the first time I'd been on a big ship. I was seasick. I took with me a little duckling I had bought in Beijing in a small basket and tried to keep it alive by feeding it whatever I ate on the boat. Luckily, my duckling survived, and I raised it during my stay in my mother's village.

The village of Liushengyuan was in the Muping district of Yantai (the former colonial-era treaty port of Chefoo, briefly controlled by the Germans before World War I). My sister was already familiar with it because she was raised there until she was seven. The land was quite hilly, so farmland was all in small plots. We stayed with my mother's sister and her husband. They lived together with my maternal grandmother in a small brick house with two small bedrooms, each on one side of the home, and one common area in the middle for cooking and eating. Half of each bedroom was a *kang*, a raised platform made of mud bricks on which we slept. A mud-plastered wall circled the house, which had a small yard in front. At one side of the yard was the single-hole outhouse. There was also a backyard with a pigpen. I set my little duckling free in the front yard and fed him vegetables and chopped-up frogs that I caught in the river outside the village.

I worked during the day with the villagers, at their various tasks, now plowing a piece of land, now washing a relatively cheap sort of ginseng they grew there, now pushing a cart to move earth from one place to another, or digging ditches as needed. I also went with my sister into the hills to collect mushrooms after a rain. My aunt and grandma made noodle soup with the mushrooms we collected. The custom was for men to eat first, before women could eat, at every meal. Somehow my sister wasn't bothered by it, but it felt quite awkward for me to eat before my grandma, aunt, and sister.

The village had been organized into a production brigade, part of the "people's commune" of Wuning. People worked not for money but points. A strong laborer could get 10 points a day. A woman typically received 5 to 7 points. I forgot how many points I earned, but it was probably 3 to 5, considering my age, 14, and my small build. At harvest time, villagers were allocated grain and other things in accordance with the points they earned for the year.

There was a small shop in the village that sold staples like soy sauce, vinegar, salt, and soap. Many villagers did not have money to buy things. Instead, they bartered, bringing eggs laid by the hens they raised at home to the shop in exchange for food, soap, thread, needles, and the like.

My grandma and aunt cooked us steamed buns of wheat flour and occasionally noodles. Sometimes, my uncle would bring back a slice of meat when he went to the weekly barter market—like a flea market in the United States—a place farmers where gathered to sell some of their produce. It was some 10 kilometers (~6 miles) away. I knew wheat flour buns and noodles were a treat for us because we were guests. My relatives had a limited supply of wheat flour and instead they more often ate corn flour, which was considered inferior.

It was the first time I had tried my hand in farming, and I worked hard. I soon earned the respect of the men I was working with, although from time to time they teased me for my awkwardness. I enjoyed working with these men and talking with them. I also enjoyed catching grasshoppers in the fields and frogs and tiny fish in the river. There was not much of a river to speak of, and it only filled with water when it rained. Otherwise, it was just a tiny creek, with hardly any water flowing through. Occasionally I saw a snake. The villagers would not let me kill it because they thought killing a snake would bring bad luck.

One day I was digging a ditch with a relative of ours whom I had just gotten to know. He was talking with me about life in the village. Then he said, "Chairman Mao's leadership is not good."

I was shocked because criticizing Mao would be considered a crime in Beijing, and it could get someone in deep trouble. Besides, I had no idea why he thought Mao's leadership was not good. So I asked him why he would say such a thing. He answered, "We work very hard. But we don't have enough to eat."

I was speechless. This conversation made a deep impression on me because it was the first time in my life I had heard anyone question Mao. But I also knew that village life was hard, in comparison with our life in Beijing, and when he said there was not enough to eat, he was telling the truth.

★ ★ ★

In the autumn of 1968, word came that the schools were reopening. All of us would be assigned to a middle school near our home. My sister and I were both assigned to the Worker-Peasant-Soldier Middle School. The name of the school was brand new. In fact, it previously had been No. 13 Girls Middle School, where I had watched a group of teenage girls beat their principal to death two years earlier. I did not like the thought of going back there; I also did not like the idea of being assigned to a girls' school, even though it was co-ed now. But there was no choice, and all my classmates living in our neighborhood were assigned there as well, so at least I would have company.

There were no real classes at the Worker-Peasant-Soldier Middle School. There were no textbooks, and the few teachers around were too scared to teach anything. This being the case, I did not bother going to class very often, and only visited occasionally. They did try to teach us some English, although it was mostly repeating revolutionary slogans and the sayings of Chairman Mao. I remember one day in class the teacher wrote a sentence in English on the blackboard and asked us to repeat after her. The sentence was "Long live Chairman Mao." That was the first English sentence I ever learned. We repeated the sentence several times, and that was it.

That evening, two teachers came to our home after dinner. They sat down and began to interrogate me about what I had done at school that day. It turned out that after we had left school someone noticed some Chinese characters written in chalk on the blackboard. The pronunciation of the characters sounded like "Long live Chairman Mao." But in Chinese it read as "broken clothes Tiananmen cat," which made no sense at all, except that "cat" was pronounced the same way as "Mao." They thought "Tiananmen Cat" was a deliberate insult to Mao and they wanted to find the culprit. They knew my classmates and I had been the last to leave the classroom, so they suspected me of being one of the offenders.

I had not noticed anyone writing on the blackboard at all, so the teachers' effort to coerce a confession out of me failed. Eventually they found the perpetrator, who was indeed a close friend of mine and who had left school with me that day. His gaffe was of course unintentional—he was simply scribbling on the board to mimic the English pronunciation of what he had learned during the day. But in those days, such a mistake could have been considered a serious crime. Anyone caught saying anything critical or not respectful of Mao would land in deep trouble. Fortunately, the teachers of our school chose to believe my friend, but only after he repeatedly wrote self-criticisms was he let off the hook.

★ ★ ★

Since there was not much schooling going on, we were sent to help build Beijing's first subway line. It was being constructed where the old city walls and the moats were on the north side of the city. The ancient walls were torn down and a deep trench was dug, which was then covered over to make the subway tunnel. (Underground drilling is more common in today's construction.) We thought we were there to help, but the construction workers considered us a nuisance. They probably could not refuse to take us. I was fortunate to be able to add the building of a subway to my résumé, to no apparent use ever again in my life.

I worked with the construction workers to carry rails to their right positions. Today such work is done by heavy machinery. But in those days, rails had to be carried and moved about by hand. Otherwise, there really was not much a bunch of 15- and 16-year-olds could do in the tunnel. The workers had to find work for us. They came up with an ingenuous idea. They gave each of us a steel saw blade and told us to start cutting up portions of rail. Usually, a steel saw was made from a blade mounted on a bow-shaped frame. But we were only given the blade, not the bow. It was a narrow strip of steel with teeth on one side.

I could only hold it with two or three of my fingers and had no way to exert any pressure on what I was cutting. It would have taken a year at least to saw through a rail. That tool kept us busy for the remainder of our stay, but we did not make much of a dent in even one single rail.

We were not paid anything to do the work, so nobody cared how long we worked or if we were doing anything productive. I quite enjoyed just being there and seeing how the subway was built. We spent a long time in the subway, although I doubt if we made any real contribution.

★ ★ ★

A few months after his nighttime audience with Zhou Enlai, Wang Yuanbo came to my house with another surprise: He brought Zheng Lian, the self-styled Red Guard commander in chief and possible lunatic who had split with us partway through our Great Networking trip because he wanted to get to Beijing more quickly. I thought he had long ago gone home to Fuzhou. He looked haggard and dirty. I was sure he was wearing the same clothes he had on the last time I had seen him, about two years earlier, but they were tattered and soiled. He said he had been in Beijing for the past two years visiting the petition office of the central government almost every day. But he had not received the justice he was seeking. Now he had run out of money, so he came to ask for help. I gave him the little money and some grain coupons I had, as did Yuanbo. That was the last I saw him. I have no idea what eventually happened to him, as none of us heard anything about him again.

★ ★ ★

Elementary school never formally ended after my 1966 exams. We just kept going back to the campus whenever we wanted to hang around with friends. The school had become our playground. That was where we found ourselves on a summer day in 1967.

I was the first one to notice the man in the military uniform. Through the window of the gatekeeper's station where my friends and I were hanging around, I watched as he stepped out of a jeep parked in front of the school gate and walked toward us.

The uniformed man, who obviously was a military officer, walked into the gatekeeper's station and politely asked about the whereabouts of Li Lun, our principal. The gatekeeper told him to go to the school's main building where the principal's office was located, and he opened the gate to let in the officer's vehicle.

Sensing trouble and excitement, all of us children ran after the jeep, following it to the main building about a hundred yards away. This time, two officers got out of the vehicle and proceeded into the building, where they climbed the stairs to the second floor. They walked briskly, with a group of us following them. I thought they would shoo us away lest we interfere in their official business, but they were in a hurry and ignored us. We got bolder and ran ahead of them to lead them to the principal's office.

One of them swiftly turned the knob on the door without knocking and stepped in, followed by the other. A few of us children crowded into the office behind them. Principal Li looked startled and stood up from her chair. The first officer stepped forward and announced: "You are under arrest."

We were shocked. Principal Li was popular among students because she had always been kind to her pupils. Even though many teachers and administrators of the school were now in trouble, we all thought Li Lun was beyond reproach. She was an old revolutionary who personally knew Mao. In 1936, she had escaped from a Japanese-occupied city and journeyed to Yan'an, where Mao and his forces had holed up. She was traveling with Mao's nephew, and when they arrived, an aide mistakenly told Mao that his nephew and niece were arriving. Mao remarked that he didn't have a niece; when Li arrived, and forever after, he jokingly called her "niece." Now she was being arrested.

The first officer took out a piece of paper and showed it to Principal Li. It was an arrest warrant. She read it and calmly signed it. Then the two police officers took her away, one on each side of her, although she was not handcuffed. Her face showed no fear and betrayed no trace of emotion. As we later concluded, she was an old revolutionary, and probably nothing would surprise her anymore.

I did not hear of Li Lun's fate until after she was released from Beijing's Qincheng Prison eight years later. It was the same prison where Jiang Qing, Mao's wife, sent many high-profile political prisoners and her own personal enemies, and where she herself was ultimately incarcerated after her arrest in 1976, about one month after Mao's death, until, reportedly, her medical parole in 1984.

According to her son, Principal Li was prisoner number 6759, the fifty-ninth person sent to Qincheng in 1967. She was held in solitary confinement so strict that for six years she was not allowed to leave her cell. Her cell had just a tiny opening in the door through which her rations were passed each day. Only in the last two years of her eight-year incarceration was she allowed outside for fresh air. There she crossed paths with Wang Guangmei, the wife of President Liu Shaoqi. They had known each other but Li and Wang could only exchange a smile. The guards then changed her area so she would never bump into another person.

Li had been accused of being a Nationalist spy, apparently because she had attended Nanjing Women's University, a school known to be a recruiting ground for the Nationalists. This was despite her long record of working with the Communist Party. She was a tough revolutionary. After years of solitary confinement, she had lost her ability to speak, but she did not lose her mind, her son later told me.

Li was released in 1976, about nine years after she was taken away. She was exonerated only in 1979, after Deng Xiaoping had consolidated his power and taken the first tentative steps toward economic reforms.

Ordinary people, too, were caught up in the madness. Yu Zhuyun, our math teacher, joined the Red Guards in ransacking the home of my classmate Fu Heng, whose father was a vice minister of foreign trade suspected of being a spy or committing some other offense. Soon after, Yu himself was investigated at the elementary school by his own colleagues.

Fu Heng's father, Fu Shenglin, the vice minister, swallowed two dozen sleeping pills after their house had been raided. I had heard about Fu attempting to commit suicide, but many years later, Fu Heng told me that his father had not really wanted to kill himself. He was just too tired after being interrogated by the Red Guards for so long. He asked for some sleeping pills and took whatever remained in the bottle. Nobody would ever know if he was seeking temporary or permanent relief, but there was no question he wanted to escape from the torment.

Fu Shenglin was ultimately exonerated several years later, as were many of the officials who had been persecuted during the Cultural Revolution. He was in fact cleared at about the same time as Kang Li, the father of my classmate Hou Erman, who had hanged himself in the family bathroom in 1966. It turned out that Kang Li was not guilty of anything at all. The pressure of the investigation was just too much.

★ ★ ★

The revolution turned the country upside down. All the established systems and order were overthrown or trampled. What remained of the government simply disintegrated as the mass movement targeted nearly every public official, sparing few. Chaos and mob justice replaced law and order. So many people, including high-ranking officials and well-known scholars, were labeled as class enemies and ruthlessly persecuted, mostly by Red Guards and the Rebels in mobs. So many died violent, unnecessary deaths like Erman's father and the vice principal of No. 13 Girls Middle School. More were humiliated, beaten, or otherwise subject to inhumane treatment.

I considered myself lucky, however. My family was spared the worst, compared to some of my friends. And even as China convulsed, I was able to travel with my friends, at the tender age of 12, to see and experience life in many parts of the country, unfettered, unsupervised, and completely free from the watchful eyes of any adults. I came of age early, too early, as my childhood ended and my previously sheltered life became a thing of the past. I did not notice it and did not miss it, until I grew much older and realized what and how much I had missed and lost.

Chapter 5

Exiled to the Gobi

It was not long before the revolution began to consume itself. Factional violence broke out everywhere, including in Beijing, as Rebels disagreed sharply on who was or wasn't a bad element, hidden enemy, or capitalist roader. The Rebels were generally divided into two factions: the anti-establishment forces, or "true Rebels," and the pro-establishment conservatives, or "Loyalists." While the true Rebels attacked all establishment figures, the Loyalists considered some of these figures revolutionary in nature and sought to protect them. Soon these factions began to take up arms against each other, using weapons they had looted from the military, which had been ordered not to resist in the name of avoiding further bloodshed.

First, such fights were confined to particular institutions. But when like-minded organizations sought each other's support, they formed allies or unions, thereby substantially increasing the scope and scale of violent clashes. For this reason, Mao described the Cultural Revolution as another civil war. He did not do much to stop it, though. He only prohibited the military from getting involved.

The Cultural Revolution was supposed to be overseen by the "Leading Group," a committee of five or six members who reported to the central committee of the Party. In reality, the members were designated by Mao himself and included only those he trusted, one being his wife Jiang Qing. The Leading Group wielded enormous power, especially in passing judgment on who was a revolutionary and who was not.

In July 1967, during a visit by Mao Zedong, a large-scale armed clash broke out in the major industrial city of Wuhan in central China. Both of the feuding factions of industrial workers were more than a million strong. One faction was backed by General Chen Zaidao, chief commander of the Wuhan military region. The other was backed by certain members of the Leading Group. During the fighting, some members of General Chen's faction broke into the compound where Mao was staying, in the hope of petitioning him for his support. It was a major violation of Mao's security protocol. Although the intruders meant no harm, the situation in the city was so tense that his security guards feared for his safety. Zhou Enlai, the premier, flew into Wuhan to personally direct the evacuation of the chairman to Shanghai. But Zhou had to land at a military airport, because the civilian one was deemed to be no longer in safe hands.

Zhou was ultimately able to calm the situation in Wuhan. General Chen was relieved of his command and was brought to Beijing for punishment. Mao eventually pardoned him, because although the general had quarreled with the Leading Group, he did not mean disrespect for Mao. Still, the scale of the conflict, and the difficulty with which even China's most senior leaders were able to bring it under control, shocked the nation.

By September 1968, all the provinces and major cities had established "revolutionary committees," or new governments, consisting of a mixture of Rebels and former officials. The *People's Daily* declared, "The whole country has turned red." But the great rule and order envisioned by Mao still had not arrived and the turmoil continued, although it did abate somewhat. In part, the anarchy was caused by too many people in the cities having nothing to do. At this point the schools had been shut down for years; millions of jobless, schoolless youngsters roamed the streets.

Mao came up with an idea. He would send these idle students to the countryside, away from their home cities. It seemed a stone that would kill two birds, clearing the cities of troublemakers and putting them to productive use. Thus began yet another movement, the movement of young students "going up to the mountains and down to the countryside." This was necessary, Mao said, in order that the educated youth of the city be "re-educated" by the peasants to adopt a proletariat outlook. The peasants, in turn, needed the educated youth to help turn the countryside into a proletarian paradise with their labor. "The countryside had broad skies and vast land where great things can be accomplished," Mao pronounced.

It was 1969. Richard Nixon was inaugurated as US president, and US astronauts landed on the moon in July of that year. The war in Vietnam was escalating.

It was also the year I was supposed to have graduated from junior high school, although my schooling had been interrupted three years earlier. I turned 15 in October 1969. I was full of life, energy, ambition, hope, and an adventurous spirit. There was still no telling what the future promised. I was anxious for new ventures.

★ ★ ★

I had been looking forward to my departure for months, and the red flags and blasting revolutionary songs stirred me even more. September 5, 1969, seemed the most glorious day of my life. In the crowd of excited well-wishers, my father was standing next to my neighbor Cheng Yulin's father. I was glad that Yulin was going to Inner Mongolia, too, as were my friends Yuanbo and Zhiqiang. My mother did not come to the Beijing railway station because she was afraid she might cry.

It seemed strange to me that some people were embracing and crying. I was shocked to see a couple holding hands. The girl was weeping uncontrollably. I had never seen a couple touching each other so intimately in public. They must have lost all sense of shame.

When we boarded, I grabbed a window seat so I could stick out my head and talk to my father on the platform. Maybe he was resigned to the reality of my imminent departure, as he did not show any emotion, or perhaps he felt that it was better for me to be away from Beijing during those chaotic and dangerous times. Things were not going so well for us at home, although he had not told me why he had to stay up late and write long accounts of himself. Now he asked me to work hard, keep good relations with others, and take care of myself. I should send a letter to let them know I had safely arrived.

I knew, however, that my father was sad about one thing. I remember to this day what he had said to me just a few days before my departure. He and I were standing by the window of our home talking. At one point, half to himself and half to me, he said, "We joined the revolution for the purpose of being able to send our children to school, to college. We couldn't go to school. But I hadn't expected our children not to be able to go to school either." His voice was so sad that I was startled and did not know what to say. He had come from a poor peasant family and his schooling had ended prematurely because his parents could not afford it anymore. Like many poor people, he had joined the Communist cause in the hope of bringing a better future for the next generation. But now his hope dimmed.

Finally the whistle blew. As if waiting for this signal, the chorus of chatter and laughter turned into a thunder of cries. I was suddenly overcome with tears. It dawned on me that I was leaving my family for a long, long time. I could not even say goodbye. Through my tears, my father's face blurred. As the train picked up speed he became smaller and smaller, until I could not see him anymore.

The going-to-the-countryside movement had been officially kicked off a few months earlier. There had been a commotion in the streets, and one of my friends had rushed in to report some "good news." Chairman Mao had just issued one of his supreme edicts.

"It is necessary for the educated youth to go to the countryside to receive re-education from the poor and lower middle peasants. The countryside has a broad sky and a vast land where one can accomplish greatness."

Although no classes were being offered at my middle school now that Mao had issued the "supreme edict," the authorities would sometimes organize marches. We knew there would be a big rally to celebrate going to the countryside, so my friend and I hurried to school to parade and wave red flags in the streets.

Within a few days, the "mobilization" began. We studied Mao's words to understand their "great historical significance" and "immeasurably great implications for the Chinese and world revolution." We were told that Chairman Mao was charting the only way for China to avoid the tragedy of the revisionist, social-imperialist Soviet Union.

These study sessions made us eager to rush to the "broad sky and vast land" and contribute to the revolution. I wanted to help reform the backward countryside into a place as modern as Beijing.

Those who admitted that they were afraid to leave their parents were despised. At 15 or 16, we were surely old enough to venture into the world. After all, many of the old generation of revolutionaries had been even younger when they fought in the Red Army. If we were not capable of facing hardships as they had, how could we become their revolutionary successors?

Whether you wanted to go did not matter. In fact, you had little choice. Everyone was persuaded to "volunteer." Teams of teachers and representatives from revolutionary committees from your school, neighborhood committees, and parents' work units came to help you make up your mind. They came together and they came separately, again and again, day and night. They were patient. They said they did not want to pressure you. They merely wanted to help you. They would sit down and read you the "supreme edict." They would explain once again the historic significance of these instructions and their implications for the young people, for our motherland, and for world revolution. Of course, they didn't stop coming until you were convinced.

So everyone had to go.

My sister, one year older than I, also had to go. My mother wanted us to go to the northeast together so we could look after each other. Although young people were being sent all over China, those from Beijing would be assigned either to Inner Mongolia or to the northeast, both strategic areas because they were on the Soviet and Mongolian borders. My mother had heard that the climate in the northeast was not as harsh as that in Inner Mongolia. Besides, she was about to be sent to the northeast, too—to a "May 7 Cadre School," named for Mao's May 7, 1966, edict, which instructed that farms should be set up where cadres and intellectuals should learn to do agricultural labor and study revolutionary thought.

In the end, my sister was sent to the northeast, and I was assigned to Inner Mongolia. Although my mother begged the school authorities to send us to the same place, her efforts had been in vain and counterproductive. Sentiment toward family members was regarded as a bourgeois tendency to be suppressed.

I learned few details about my destination other than that I was to join the Construction Army Corps of Inner Mongolia. Along with my schoolmates—several of them also assigned to Inner Mongolia, known for the Gobi Desert—I attended a meeting where a regiment political instructor, an army man wearing a new green uniform, addressed us.

He told us that the land of Inner Mongolia was so vast that we would build a thoroughfare even wider and longer than Chang'an Boulevard in central Beijing. It never occurred to me, or apparently to anyone else, to wonder why anyone would need a boulevard in the middle of the desert. For transportation, we were promised helicopters. Most of us had never even seen one. We would eat white bread every day, he told us, and there would always be plenty of meat and fish. Each of us would get a brand-new uniform, "just like a soldier in the People's Liberation Army."

The backward countryside we were supposed to transform already sounded like a paradise. The presentation so boosted our enthusiasm that we could hardly wait to depart.

Each of us was given 30 yuan, a great sum of money that I was proud to bring home. We were also given some ration coupons for textiles. I went with my mother on a shopping spree. I bought enough fabric and cotton to make two quilts. We also bought mosquito nets, shoes, flashlights, work gloves, and two large wooden trunks. We bought two of everything, one for me and one for my sister.

★ ★ ★

The train ride took more than 30 hours, with numerous stops. I counted 65 tunnels. Whenever the train went through a long tunnel, black smoke from the locomotive would billow into the passenger cars and the soot would settle everywhere. Soon our faces were as dark as if we had come from a battlefield.

We were delighted to hear that our exact destination was a top military secret. We were also honored that our train was "special." But it was because of this designation that we had to stop to let other trains pass. The journey thus took twice as long as it should have.

On the second night, we arrived at a stop called Urat Qianqi or Wulate Qianqi. (*Urat* or *Urad* is the Mongolian pronunciation; *Wulate* is the Chinese name. *Qianqi* means "Front Banner," referring to a Mongolian tribe so designated by a Qing dynasty emperor.) We were told to get off the train. It was so dark that I could barely see the station. There were only a few dim bulbs. Still, I could sense that there were many hundreds of us on the platform.

I was surprised at how cold it was. It was only early September, and the nights were still warm in Beijing. Now I wished I had listened to my mother and carried a sweater with me.

None of us knew what to do. Then I noticed some people unloading trunks and suitcases, and I went over to help. Several people inside the cargo compartment would drag a wooden trunk to the door and throw it to the platform some two meters below. Many cracked open upon impact, spilling the contents across the platform. I sadly remembered how carefully my mother had packed my wooden case and how my father had bundled it tightly with straw ropes.

Someone directed us to carry the baggage toward a row of sturdy, open-backed Jiefang ("Liberation") trucks parked nearby. There was a steep slope from the train platform to the trucks, and it was hard to carry the heavy trunks downhill. Soon people started tossing the luggage cases here, too. Now more of them splintered open and their contents spilled out.

We were all summoned to an open space to hear our assignments. Each of us was given a regiment and a company. I was assigned to the Nineteenth Regiment, Fifth Company. To my dismay, my friends Yuanbo and Zhiqiang were assigned to Fourth Company. Only Cheng Yulin, my neighbor, was assigned to the same company as me.

A representative from the Fifth Company took charge of my group. He introduced himself as Liu Fengliang, a platoon leader, and directed us to find our baggage. After a long search in the dark, I found mine. By some miracle, my father's ropes had held. After we had loaded our belongings onto one of the trucks, we climbed on top. We had to help one another on, and it was difficult to find a secure seat amid the mountain of wooden cases and bags. I found a place toward the front, where I could hold on tight to a rope.

With a great shudder and squeal, the truck started to move. There were a few trucks ahead of us. In the glare of the headlights, I could see columns of dust rising behind them. The dust engulfed us. Now the trucks in the front were hardly visible. The road was so bumpy that a few times I felt I was surely going to be thrown off.

My thin body turned into an icicle on top of that truck. The truck jerked from one side to another, and I soon became nauseous. My grip on the rope grew weak. I feared that if I were thrown off, nobody would notice in the darkness. We rode for what felt like an eternity. One by one, the trucks in front turned in different directions and disappeared. Finally, ours was the only truck driving in the complete darkness. There was no sign of life other than the roar of the engine.

After four hours, just when I felt that I could not stand it any longer, the truck jerked to a stop. Opening my eyes, I saw some people coming toward us. Platoon Leader Liu emerged from the driver's cabin to announce that we were home.

We were in front of a long row of shacks with a door every few yards. A small kerosene lamp burned in each door. Cheng Yulin and I were assigned to the same room. It was about 4 meters (~12 feet) wide and 10 meters (~30 feet) deep. A neat pile of straw ran across the length of the room, and some boys appeared already to be asleep in it. This was to be the bed for seven of us.

Soon our squad leader, a man named Wang Lianfa, carried in a steaming bucket of noodle soup. Yulin and I dug out our tin bowls and helped ourselves. The soup tasted nice after the cold and bumpy journey. As we ate, we chatted with our new roommates to find out about each other.

Wang Lianfa was very warm to us, urging us to have more soup until we were full. We met Liu Xiaotong, who was also from Beijing. He and Wang had arrived a month or two earlier. Liu wanted to know if there was any news. He told me that here it was next to impossible to hear anything about the rest of the country, let alone the world.

Seeing that we could not finish the soup, the boys in bed got up to help themselves to the leftovers. We soon learned this "new arrivals soup" was rare to come by. They promised us the only reason we ate so little was that we still had "oil" in our stomachs.

We spread our quilts and blankets next to each other on the row of straw. Each of us had a territory less than half of a meter (~1.5 feet) wide and 3 meters (~9 feet) in length. Squad Leader Wang brought in a bucket of cold water, and Yulin and I poured some into our basins. The dirt on my sooty, coal-streaked face soon turned the water black. I asked where

I could get more, but Wang said that it was now too dark to go to the pond. We went to bed. Someone blew out the kerosene lamp.

Although I was exhausted, I could not sleep. I could not avoid leaning up against the boys on either side of me. Trying to keep some space to myself, I lay on my side with my legs out straight. Soon, my neighbor rolled over and occupied some of my territory. I tried to push him back without waking him. No sooner had I succeeded than he rolled over again. After several hours of this, I finally fell asleep.

The next morning, I awoke to find that we were in the middle of a sandy wasteland. Our shacks had apparently been built in great haste. The front wall was made of unbaked bricks. The rafters were rough-chopped tree branches, and the roof was a layer of straw covered by a thick layer of mud. The back wall was made of woven dried reeds, with mud that had caked off in many places.

There was no bathroom nearby, so people just did their business behind the shacks. One could smell the human waste from quite a distance. Behind our shelters was a small pond. My excitement at seeing water soon evaporated when I found it was stagnant and dirty. Other than a few reeds, it held no sign of life.

I learned that our shelters had indeed been recently put together because there was not enough housing to accommodate so many newcomers. There was another row of temporary housing adjacent to ours, intended for a girls' platoon. The Construction Army Corps was said to be building some better housing in the company compound so that we could move in before winter.

Our platoon leader, Liu Fengliang, had just retired from the army, where he had served four years without being promoted. He had been recruited from a village in the countryside somewhere in Hebei Province. Since he was from a peasant family, he knew quite a lot about farming. He was about 24 years old, well built and of medium height. He looked serious but friendly. He constantly smoked cigarettes that he rolled himself. When Platoon Leader Liu gave a whistle, we lined up in formation and marched toward the company compound. Soon, our whole column started to trot as the marching orders grew more rapid. I trotted along, maintaining my position in the column. I felt quite pleased with myself for being able to do that. When we reached the compound, I saw several columns like ours standing in front of a building. Some were boys and some were girls. As we ran up, they examined us curiously. We still looked like big-city students, with our white cotton shirts and pale skin. They looked more seasoned, tanned, and wiry; their clothes were all well patched.

After a brief announcement and a welcome speech by the company's political instructor, Zhang Songsen, and our commander, Zhang Yinghan, breakfast was served. Or rather, we served ourselves. Each column had a bucket and a washbasin. Two people from each column went up to a small window in the wall to collect the food, and they then ladled the food into our bowls. The meal consisted of porridge and steamed corn flour bread. There were also some salted vegetables. The porridge was made with some grain that looked like millet but had no taste. Later I learned that it was called *mizi*. It was to be the main staple for us for many years to come. It was such a coarse grain that we referred to it as "fake millet."

Breakfast was followed by a political study session. For several hours, Political Instructor Zhang droned on. He was telling us, as if we had not heard it hundreds of times, that Vice Commander-in-Chief Lin Biao (defense minister and Mao's designated successor after Liu Shaoqi was purged) had suggested forming the Inner Mongolia Construction Army Corps, and that the Great Leader himself had approved it. The significance of educated youth going to the countryside could not be overemphasized. It was the single most important measure to prevent the emergence of new revisionists and to prepare the next generation of revolutionary successors. We should be ready to "take root in the countryside."

I was shocked to hear someone muttering behind me, "A place that birds don't care to shit. Even trees don't take root here."

I looked back. It was Li Baoquan of our squad, a boy from Tianjin.

His words aroused laughter and the political instructor stopped. "What is it?" he demanded. Li Baoquan rose to report. "Someone just said that this is a place where birds don't care to shit and trees don't take root," he said.

Upon his words, there was another roar of laughter. His face was serious and his eyes were trained innocently toward the political instructor.

The political instructor praised Li Baoquan for "revealing a bad deed," and went on talking about how we would take root in the countryside. I began to wish someone would tell us more about the history of our farm, what we were going to do, and what kind of future there was for us. But I knew that political education had priority over practical matters. I felt tired and started to fidget on the small folding stool that I had brought from Beijing. Most of the others sat quietly on the cold ground with their legs crossed.

A deputy chief of staff of the Nineteenth Regiment was also there to deliver a war mobilization speech. He told us about the tense situation along the Sino-Mongolian border. A war with the Soviet "revisionist social-imperialists" was possible at any time. We should welcome war: The Soviet Union, the first socialist country, though it had changed color now, had been born after World War I. World War II brought the triumph of socialism in China, North Korea, and Eastern Europe. Another world war could easily turn the entire world socialist.

★ ★ ★

So, I now belonged to the Eleventh Squad of the Third Platoon of the Fifth Company of the Nineteenth Regiment of the Second Division of the Inner Mongolia Construction Army Corps. We were in a place called Wulate, a state farm. As I would soon learn, to call it a "farm" was a vast exaggeration. We were some 15 kilometers (~9 miles), from Lake Wuliangsu (Ulan su in Mongolian). Only four years earlier, I was told, this land we were on had been the bottom of the lake.

Our company was about 300 people strong, half boys and half girls. Most were students from big cities, like me. There were also a dozen or so adults, mostly old farmers who had founded the farm. Because of their "complicated" backgrounds, we were warned to watch out for them.

Most of the rest of the adults were veterans from the army, like Platoon Leader Liu. The company had six regular platoons and one logistics platoon, which included a cooking squad, a pig-raising squad, and a horse-drawn-cart squad. There was also a headquarters, with a support staff of messengers, medical personnel, and secretaries.

The army retirees held positions as platoon leaders or deputy platoon leaders for the male platoons. Because there were few women soldiers in the military, and none had retired to our farm, the leaders of the female platoons were appointed by the company leaders from among the girls themselves. The company leaders were army officers in active service. There were four of them. These were Company Commander Zhang Yinghan, Political Instructor Zhang Songsen, Deputy Company Commander Duan Dingshan (whom we called Lao Duan, or "Old Duan"), and Dr. Yu, the military doctor.

Of the six regular platoons, three were boys' platoons and three were girls'. Each platoon was divided into three squads, mostly led by students. The majority of those in our squad were from Beijing. A few, including Li Baoquan, were from Tianjin, an almost equally sophisticated northern port city close to Beijing.

The ages of the Army Corps "soldiers" in our company ranged from 15 to 21, with the average being 16 or 17. My group was referred to as 69ers, meaning that we would have graduated from junior high school in 1969 had it not been for the Cultural Revolution. There were also a few 66ers and senior 68ers. The senior 68ers were actually the oldest group, so named because they would have graduated from senior high school in 1968, not junior high, and would have been on their way to factories or universities. They were at least four years older than I was, and there were probably only three or four of them in the entire company. The 66ers and the senior 68ers were regarded as the most educated groups, because they had attended three years of junior high and one year of senior high, respectively, before the Cultural Revolution erupted. We 69ers had only completed elementary school.

Our regiment, the nineteenth, consisted of 10 companies scattered around Lake Wuliangsu, a big lake fed by the Yellow River when the rain was plentiful. In years of drought, the flow of water from the river to the lake was blocked off. Since there had been more drought than rain recently, the lake had shrunk. The lake was known for its carp and for the many square kilometers of high reeds growing in its shallow waters. Regiment headquarters was on the bank of the lake at a place called Batou.

Unfortunately, our company was not one of the lucky "fishing companies" and we would not have much opportunity to eat fish. As a farming company, we were to deal only with the land. Other companies included the tractor company and the construction company.

Regiments reported to a division. There were 20-odd regiments in the Second Division. Its headquarters was located in Urat Qianqi, the town on the rail line. The regiments were scattered across thousands of square kilometers of desert; the companies were stationed dozens of kilometers apart from each other and the regiments even more distant.

Army Corps headquarters was in Hohhot. I never found out how many divisions there were in the entire Army Corps. They occupied a territory that stretched all across the vastness of Inner Mongolia, a province that is twice the size of France and three times the size of Germany. Inner Mongolia represents about an eighth of China's total landmass, but only 2 percent of its population. Our regiment, with its 10 companies, was more than 3,000 people strong. The Second Division had more than 25,000 men and women. The entire Army Corps had a force of as many as 170,000 "soldiers."

Prior to our arrival, our farm had been called Wurat Farm, managed by just the dozen or so farmers who had founded it. The farm had been an effort by the government to provide these people with jobs and a living. They were managing quite well, producing enough to feed themselves and a substantial surplus to sell to the government. But the Cultural Revolution destroyed the old farm leadership when the Construction Army Corps arrived with us, the educated youth.

Much of the land around our company's compound was not cultivable, and stretched, quite barren, all the way to the distant Yin Mountains.

Because the land did not have much to offer, it was sparsely populated. The emptiness struck me when I walked a mile or two to a place where I could no longer see the company compound. Other than the mountains on the horizon, there was nothing to be seen anywhere. I could not help thinking that if I died in the middle of this wasteland, my body would rot and decompose for years without anyone finding it.

Where the ground was not covered by sand, one could see some hardy vegetation that was resistant to the soil's high saline and alkaline content and to the dry weather. It seemed unbelievable that they existed at all. There were some wild animals, too, though not many. The farmers had a saying that even rabbits did not care to pee or shit there, although you did see them once in a while. I had heard there were foxes, too, although they were rare.

Before I arrived, I had expected to see herds of cattle, sheep, and horses grazing on vast grasslands. I had an image of Inner Mongolia familiar to every Chinese elementary school child from an ancient Chinese poem: "The wind bends the grass low; cattle and sheep show." I was therefore quite disappointed. But wherever a few blades of grass could be found, there were also cattle and horses. The poem about Inner Mongolia was far more pastoral and romantic than the land itself. Around us, it was just the Gobi Desert.

In addition to us Han Chinese, there were, of course, some Mongolians. They had their own culture and language and belonged to the same ethnic group as the people in the country of Mongolia, which had broken off from China in the 1940s. Since the break in relations between China and the Soviet Union in the early 1960s, China's relations with Mongolia, a Soviet satellite, had become hostile as well. The Russians had about a million troops stationed along the Mongolia–China border.

The native Mongolians were nomads, following their herds across the grassland and living in yurts made of animal wool. They lived mostly to the north where there was more grass, so we rarely saw them.

Although the border was sealed and heavily patrolled, at least one kind of cross-border traffic got through, but only during the winter. When the harsh north wind blows down from Siberia, across Mongolia and China's Loess Plateau, it tosses up dust, sand, and snow. One can hardly see one's whereabouts in the middle of a sand- or snowstorm and can easily get lost and perish. The worst was a blinding "white-haired blizzard," a snow- and sandstorm combined. You could not venture to the outhouse for fear that you would not find your way back. But whenever the white-haired blizzard blew, herds of Mongolian horses and cattle would wander across the border into Inner Mongolia, driven by the wind. Traditionally, the horses were returned. Now that relations between the two countries were hostile, the horses were ours to keep.

As a farming company, our responsibilities were to grow crops on the several thousand hectares (1 hectare = ~2.5 acres) of land we had been assigned. Our main crops included wheat, potatoes, pumpkins, sorghum, and corn. The major portion of our work would be to "transform" the wasteland. It was a continuous job of digging irrigation canals and ditches. We also needed to collect manure to fertilize the fields and to stock as winter fuel. Then we had to transport sand to the fields to change the soil conditions. The high proportion of clay in the soil facilitated the seeping up of saline and alkaline to the surface, suffocating the crops. The sand was intended to change the soil composition.

It became very clear to us a few days after arriving that we would have none of the things that Army Corps representatives had promised us in Beijing. There was no white (wheat flour) bread. The major means of transportation was not a helicopter, but our legs. There was no plan to build a road as wide and straight as Chang'an Boulevard. Our monthly stipend would be five yuan, enough for two tin cans of pork. At that time, it cost 120 yuan, or my two-years' stipend, to buy a domestic-made Shanghai-brand watch.

I began to miss home and my parents. But I could not tell them what my living conditions were at the time, or they would have worried.

★ ★ ★

After the study sessions and two days of break, it was time to prepare the farmland. Tractors had already plowed the fields. Our job was to build ridges to segment the fields and ditches to channel water into the fields from the main irrigation canals. Although we lived in a desert, we were not too far from some canals that connected all the way to the Yellow River, the second largest river in China. We had plenty of water for irrigation in summertime.

The only tools we had were shovels. Usually, the whole platoon would work in a single field, then go on to another one. The farm could have used tractors and other types of machines, but the leaders believed that "people make trouble when they don't have enough to do." So they would retire the machinery for months. Tractors were only used to deep-plow the soil and to spread seeds.

Like almost everyone, I was not used to working all day with a shovel. My hands were soon covered with blisters. Even with a pair of work gloves, they still hurt. After a day in the fields I would pierce the blisters with a needle to let the fluid out. But after about a week, the blisters turned into calluses. The work did not feel as bad.

It was important to be able to carry things on one's shoulders, often the only means of transporting anything. In the beginning, it was extremely painful as my shoulders were tender. The first time I had to carry a heavy load was when Platoon Leader Liu ordered me to go back and fetch several shovels from our living quarters a few kilometers away. This was regarded as a good assignment since it involved walking empty-handed or with a "light" load for about an hour.

I picked up five shovels, put them on my shoulder and headed back to the fields. Almost as soon as I started, my shoulder began to hurt. I had to unload the shovels every 20 steps to catch my breath and allow the pain to ease. Eventually, my shoulder became too bruised to touch, and my destination was still not in sight. I had to carry the shovels in my arms or drag them along very slowly and painfully. When I finally rejoined my platoon, Platoon Leader Liu was annoyed and gave me a stern look. He thought I had stolen a break. I was too embarrassed to tell him that these few shovels were too heavy for my tender shoulders.

We were thirsty all the time we worked in the fields under the sun. Drinking water was scarce. Some old-timers carried canteens, but we newcomers had none. Each day, someone had to carry two buckets of water to the fields.

It required skill to fetch water. The hardest part was filling a bucket from a well. If you simply lowered the bucket, it would float. The trick was to pull the rope to one side and then very quickly and sharply to the other, so that the bucket would turn over and sink. Once you pulled two buckets up, you placed them on the ends of a shoulder pole. An experienced laborer could carry two buckets of water, weighing about 50 kilograms (~100 pounds), for up to 50 kilometers (~30 miles) in a single day.

At first, it took me forever to pull water from the well, and then the buckets were only half full. This was for the best; I could not carry more than two half-buckets. The narrow pole on my 15-year-old shoulders was pure torture. Besides, I could not balance to prevent water from spilling out. My pants and shoes were soaked when I arrived.

But I soon learned. I changed from a city boy to a farm laborer. Miraculously, although I was eating food with little in the way of nourishment and had come to the Gobi with a fairly weak constitution, I was in good health. I only wished that I could put a little weight on my 50-kilogram (~100-pound) body.

I had settled into the routines of life in the Gobi.

Chapter 6

Digging for Potatoes

Capitalism, which even before the founding of the People's Republic had been quite new and underdeveloped in China, had by the 1960s been systematically rooted out. In the cities, private ownership of the means of production—factories, businesses—had been expropriated, although usually with some compensation to the previous owners. What remained was either owned by the state or owned by collectives. The difference between the two was that the employees of a state-owned factory generally received a pay rate commensurate with their rank and seniority, and usually regardless of the performance of the business, whereas the compensation of a member of a collective varied greatly depending on the output of the business as well as the member's contribution.

The Communist Party had been carrying out a policy of land redistribution for decades, taking agricultural land from rich peasants and dividing it among the poor in areas it controlled during its war with the Nationalist government. This policy had only been suspended during the Anti-Japanese War in order to bring the big landowners into the war effort, but it resumed in earnest after the Japanese surrender and the establishment of the PRC.

By 1958, there was yet another major transformation in the rural areas, as the Party instituted a process of collectivization, resulting in a system known as the People's Commune. In the commune system, all the major means of production, including land, became collectively owned. Peasants worked for points and were allocated grain and other crops at harvest in accordance with the points they had earned in the year. Income levels for peasants varied greatly from one place to another, depending on how much their village produced, which in turn was determined by the fertility of the land (or lack thereof), the weather, and labor input.

There were state-owned farms, but only a small number of them, and they were generally located where there had not been much in the way of farming. Our farm in the Gobi was one. Whereas the peasants in a commune ate what they produced, more or less, we at a state-owned farm were paid regardless of our effort or output. But our pay was de minimis: Other than food rations and some basic clothing, we were paid only five yuan a month, not enough to buy a chicken.

Food and clothing had already been rationed before 1966. The turmoil of the Cultural Revolution had further hampered production, exacerbating the shortage. By 1969, just about everything, including basic necessities, was in short supply. All socialist economies are shortage economies, but China was probably the most extreme case in the late 1960s and 1970s as the Cultural Revolution took a heavy toll on the economy.

* * *

Three weeks after our arrival, the company leaders announced that the following day our platoon would march some 30 kilometers (~18 miles) to dig potatoes. Like soldiers, we were expected to be able to respond to any order without warning. They called this being "as fierce as thunder and as fast as wind" and told us we should consider it glorious that our platoon had been chosen for such an urgent and important task.

National Day, October 1, celebrated the founding of the People's Republic 20 years earlier. It was a holiday for the nation, but not for us. Each of us packed a quilt and some clothing into a small backpack and loaded it onto a horse-drawn wagon that would also transport shovels, food, and cookware. Then we set out on foot.

There was not much of a path. Platoon Leader Liu, who had been to the fields before, led the way. The autumn weather was great, dry and clear, with a refreshing snap in the air.

The land was virtually bare, with not a house or tree as far as I could see. Our view stretched to the Yin Mountains, at the horizon line. There was nothing between them and us but vast land. As the saying in Inner Mongolia went, "You could run a horse to death trying to reach the mountains." They appeared close, but they were far away.

The earth beneath our feet was sandy and barren and the few desert plants were all dead and dry. When the wind blew, they rolled around. Our feet broke through a crust of salt on the surface as we walked, and our shoes became heavy with salty dirt.

Occasionally we encountered long expanses of sand that could migrate with the wind. They could move unbelievably rapidly in a storm and were capable of engulfing a small house. All the houses in Inner Mongolia were built with doors and windows facing south, away from the northern Siberian wind. This way, there was less chance of being completely buried by the moving sand.

Small lizards darted from one hole in the dry ground to another. I spotted several larks, singing quite beautifully. I was always glad to see these little creatures. It made me feel like I was in a land with some life after all.

The sandy soil in some parts of Inner Mongolia was suitable for growing potatoes. Potatoes liked the sand, because they could grow large. In fact, any root vegetable grew well—even carrots grew to several kilos (~2 pounds per kilogram). But these enormous vegetables did not taste nearly as good as their small brethren, the kind that I used to eat in Beijing.

Each of us carried a canteen and some *wotou*, which is a type of steamed cornbread. I did not own a canteen, but Li Baoquan borrowed one for me from a friend of his. Li himself had also borrowed a canteen.

When I asked him what had happened to his own, he said, "I smashed it."

I was astonished. "Why?" I asked.

"To test its quality," he said, without smiling.

By the middle of the day, I had eaten the *wotou* and my canteen was empty. As I walked under the sun, I grew more and more thirsty. I noticed that the old-timers like Li Baoquan were still sipping water. Li told me that here you had to learn how to conserve your water, only using it when absolutely necessary. He was kind enough to share his canteen with me. I only moistened my lips and let some water trickle into my throat, for I did not want to drink too much of the little he had left. The journey ahead was still long.

Probably because we were thirsty, we started to talk about watermelon. Watermelons grew well in Inner Mongolia, especially in dry years, when they grew particularly sweet. Baoquan said that there had still been plenty of watermelons around at this time the year before. But they were difficult to come by this year.

He hoped there would be watermelon fields near the potatoes. I reminded him that none of us had any money, so that even if there were watermelons, it wouldn't make any difference. Baoquan said that only a fool would spend money on watermelons. He got his melons the direct way: by stealing them.

He told me how he would dress in dark colors before going to the melon fields. On a dark night, the guards could not see you in your "night-walking" clothes. Baoquan described how he would crawl out and pick the ripe melons, identifying the best ones by flicking them with his finger. I learned this skill from him. To this day, my wife is amazed how I can pick out the best watermelon in the supermarket by tapping my fingers on them.

He had had numerous adventures, but he had never been caught. Once he had to have a bowel movement halfway through his melon raid, because he was eating too much. The old man guarding the fields heard something and fired a shot with his bird gun. The pellets from the gun hit Baoquan in the rear end. He had to flee, pulling on his pants as he ran.

Baoquan told this story with such good humor that I could not help laughing. But I wondered if he felt bad about stealing. "Come on," he said. "A man eats from the mountain if he is next to the mountain and he eats from the water if he is next to the water. We contribute much more to socialism than our meager pay shows. Those turtle egg company leaders have a much better life than we do, and the girls give them cigarettes and candies as well. What's a few melons?"

I had to agree. And as I got to know him, I found that Baoquan was an upright and honorable man despite being a melon thief. He was always willing to help others, especially those he considered his friends.

When he stole from the melon fields or from the company kitchen, he shared his loot with everyone, although he was often the only one to take the risks. He was notorious for being "ideologically backward" in the company because he complained about everything. But the company leaders could not do much to him because they could not shame him by calling him "not progressive." He only cared about how he was perceived by his friends.

Baoquan continued, "Platoon Leader Liu loved the melons I gave him. So did his girlfriend." Liu's girlfriend was the leader of the Sixth Platoon. She came from Tianjin, same as Baoquan. "I wouldn't want to have a girlfriend from Tianjin," he added. "Tianjin wives make their husbands wash their feet for them. I would like to marry a Japanese woman. They take better care of their husbands." He said this loudly for everyone to hear. Nobody knew where he got the idea.

Wang Decai, who was also from Tianjin, was walking in front of us. He turned his head and sneered at Baoquan. "To find a mate," he said, quoting a Chinese saying, "a man needs to have talents or wealth and woman needs to have beauty. What do you have to offer?"

Without hesitation, Baoquan replied that he was good looking, with "big eyes and a high nose, not like you with disgustingly small eyes and a flat nose." The only shortcoming, he sighed, was his legs: they were somewhat O-shaped. But he said he had talents. He was good at soccer, wrestling, and doing tricks with a diabolo, a Chinese yo-yo. He also added that he liked to clean house. It was true; Baoquan always kept things tidy. "Anyway, I am much better qualified than you are, Big Decai."

Everyone laughed and Decai sniffed. This was how the conversation went on between them all the time. The boys from Tianjin were a funny bunch.

"Old Cui," Baoquan said, turning to Cui Xianchao. "What would you say I am worth?"

Old Cui was one of the oldest among us, so his words carried some weight. He frowned as if thinking seriously. "Baoquan, you are at least a four or four-plus out of five," he announced. "I have no doubt that you will find a beautiful Japanese wife."

Everyone laughed. We all knew that no one was really thinking about girlfriends or marriage. Even the oldest of us, like Old Cui and

Deputy Squad Leader Huang Shurong, were too young to get permission to marry. The only one in our platoon who was approaching that age was Platoon Leader Liu.

Old Cui said that he did not want to get married at all. In his opinion, marriage would be a prison. Old Cui often had strange and interesting theories. Once challenged, he would argue fervently.

Huang Shurong took the bait, saying that Old Cui would be among the first to get married because he was so messy that he could not take care of himself. It was true. Old Cui never made his bed and he was in the habit of losing things. "If I ever get married," Old Cui declared, "I will give you 50 cans of pork."

There was much cheering and laughter at this. Even Platoon Leader Liu slowed down to listen. Fifty cans of meat cost about 25 months of our pay. Besides, Old Cui was barely 19. Nobody was going to remember what he had said by the time he really got married.

But Old Huang, as we called him, made Old Cui swear that he would give him 50 cans of pork on his wedding day. Then Platoon Leader Liu observed that the deal was unfair. What would Huang give up if Cui really did not get married?

Huang said that he would give Cui 100 cans of pork if he did not marry by the age of 40. He was so serious that he wanted to put everything in writing once we found something to write with. Platoon Leader Liu made them both pledge that when either one won, all of us would be invited as guests.

Such conversations made the journey more bearable. But after many hours, our destination was still not in sight. My legs felt more and more heavy, and my thirst was getting worse. Nobody was talking anymore. We were all parched and dying of thirst.

After a few more kilometers, we stopped at a small inn used by drivers of horse-drawn wagons, where we had some water and took a rest. Still, we were exhausted by the time we reached our destination, which turned out to be a rather large potato field. As if by a miracle, an enormous crop was growing here in the middle of the barren land. We sat down by the edge of the field to recover from our journey and marveled.

The old farmers who reclaimed this field from wasteland had made it into a self-sufficient farm. Now it had been turned over to "people's ownership," another term for state ownership, and the dozen-odd farmers had become state employees with wages and grain rations. Looking at the obvious bumper harvest, I could not help but admire them. They must have known what they were doing to make the potatoes grow so well.

There were only a few hours left in the day and Platoon Leader Liu ordered us to start work with hardly any rest after the long walk. The job was not too difficult. The stems and leaves of the potato plants crawled on the ground. You had to lift them up to find the root, from which several potatoes grew. Then we put the shovel into the earth a foot or so away, so as not to cut into the potatoes. After loosening the earth, we pulled on the stem. Sometimes, all the potatoes attached to a root would come out together. More often, the root would break, and we had to dig the potatoes out one by one by hand.

These were gigantic white potatoes, larger than any I had ever seen. White potatoes are usually much smaller than sweet potatoes. But these were larger than the largest sweet potatoes in any market in Beijing. Very soon, there were large piles of potatoes in the fields. We were pleased to see the fruits of our labor.

At sunset, Platoon Leader Liu ordered us to stop digging and cover the piles with the stems and leaves. Although the temperature was about 25°C (about 77°F) during the day, at night it could fall below freezing. Once frozen, potatoes would rot quickly. We did not know if leaves would do much good to protect them from the cold.

After the potatoes were covered, the horse-drawn wagon arrived with some food and water. Cook Jin Jian from the cooking squad had gone to the horse-wagon inn to use their stove to prepare our meal. We ate right there in the open, sitting on the potato leaves.

Cook Jin also brought some letters, for the mail person had arrived just before we left our compound. There was a letter from my parents, the first I received since I left Beijing. They had received two of my letters. They told me that my sister left for the northeast the day after I had, and they had not yet heard anything from her. My mother would soon be sent to a farm, and she hoped she would not be too far from my sister. They told me to take care of myself and make new friends.

After dinner, Platoon Leader Liu announced that we had to spend the night in the open in the potato fields. There was no housing or shelter available, and we needed to guard the piles of potatoes, too. He said that we should each dig a hole in the ground large enough for ourselves and cover the opening with potato stems and leaves. We would sleep in the holes; the vegetation would be our shelter.

Nobody was happy about sleeping in the potato fields. But there was no alternative. We went to work.

The earth was soft and it was not too difficult to dig. I worked hard and soon there was a hole in the ground. The trick was not to dig too large a hole, for the opening had to be narrow enough to be covered with stems and leaves. I put a few stems and leaves across the bottom of mine, and then I covered the rest, leaving an opening big enough to squeeze through. When I looked at my finished project, I wondered if it had been worth digging in the first place. It did not look as if it would provide much protection against the cold.

I took a look at other people's foxholes. Li Baoquan had the best shelter. Old Cui's was like a hole left by some kind of explosion. There was no consistency in depth to the sides of his shallow hole.

A few people were examining the hole dug by Huang Shurong. It was huge already, but he was still working on it. Huang had been a weight lifter and gymnast on his high school team, so he was hefty. Everyone was telling him that his hole was already too big, but he would not listen. He then discovered, to his dismay, that the opening was too big to be covered by potato stems and leaves. But he had enough energy, so he started to dig another one.

I carefully unbundled my bedroll inside my hole. As I was doing so, sand and dirt fell off the wall. It was impossible to shake them off, since the quilt was larger than the hole. So I took the quilt out, shook it out, and put it back in. Again, it was covered by sand and dirt. It appeared that I had no choice but to sleep that way.

It was pitch dark by the time we finished building our nests and getting colder by the minute. There was nothing to do in the darkness, and besides, we were bone tired, having walked so long and worked so hard. Everyone climbed into his own foxhole. I wished that there was some water to wash off the sweat and dirt of the day, but there was only half a bucket of drinking water left.

I felt as if I were sleeping in a coffin. If I so much as adjusted my position, sand and dirt rained off the wall. I could not sleep. I lay there on my back, staring into the sky through the opening in the hole, wondering how many nights I would spend here. I figured that it would probably take 10 days to finish the field. I had heard that winter came early in this part of the country, and night temperatures could fall precipitously.

All of a sudden, there was a long howl that sounded like a wolf. As I was wondering where the sound came from, I heard Platoon Leader Liu shout: "Be quiet, Li Baoquan. Go to sleep." There was some muffled laughter. Then everything went quiet.

The air grew colder. The quilt simply could not keep me warm. I tried to curl up, but the hole was too small. I shivered with cold and stared at the stars. There were no clouds so all the stars were visible.

I missed home more than I had ever thought possible. I started to recite an ancient poem to myself, thinking especially of a single line: "One doubly misses his family on a festival day." Today was October 1, National Day. The skies of Beijing would be lit with fireworks. Were my parents and my younger brother out on the street? Were they talking about me or about my sister? My mother would soon be sent to the countryside herself. Could she still enjoy the National Day holiday? I tried to recall the sweet holidays that we had spent together and wished I had fully understood how valuable they were. Would the whole family ever be together again?

I slept fitfully in the cold and damp and was awakened by the songs of larks. There was a trace of red on the horizon, and the sky gradually became brighter and brighter. Then, almost suddenly, the sun jumped clear of the mountains. I crawled out of my hole and saw other people emerging from theirs. We walked around with our padded coats over our shoulders, trying to warm up. There were, of course, no toilets. So we walked some distance to relieve ourselves. Someone commented that it was too bad the potatoes did not need fertilizer anymore. But no one laughed in the freezing cold.

We started to work on an empty stomach. In about an hour, food arrived. There was good news, too: Cook Jin said that the horse-wagon inn might have enough space for us to sleep there. It would take us an hour to walk there, but an hour was nothing for us. Platoon Leader Liu must have had as tough a night as everyone else. He said he would go speak with the innkeeper.

Happy that we might sleep under a roof and wash ourselves, we worked doubly hard that day. We were not disappointed. Platoon Leader Liu had made arrangements for us to stay at the inn throughout our assignment, paying the innkeeper with potatoes.

That night, we saw that the inn was a mud house built with unbaked bricks. There was only one room, with two large *kang* on each side. A *kang* is a hollow brick platform, the standard bed in the northern Chinese countryside, where the winter is very harsh. A fire beneath it, fueled through a hole under a stove, keeps it warm. There is usually a cooking stove at one end that allows the bed to heat up while supper is prepared. I slept on a *kang* when I visited my mother's home village with my sister in 1968. Although now we slept on piles of straw, we had been promised *kang* when our new barracks were built.

Each of the inn's two *kang* could comfortably sleep about 10 people. Since there were 30 of us, 15 had to crowd into each one. It was so crowded that when one person wanted to turn over, the entire row had to turn with him. I tried to sleep motionless throughout the night. Some people complained that sleeping motionless was more tiring than staying awake. But nobody volunteered to get up.

Other than being crowded, the inn was infinitely better than our holes in the ground in the open air. The room did not have any windows, so it was dark inside even during broad daylight. On a pillar, there was a small container with kerosene oil and a wick, which burned with a column of dark smoke. Platoon Leader Liu slept right next to it, so he could light one cigarette after another. I was on the other side of the pillar, so that I could read the book that I had brought with me by its dim light. At the end of the *kang*, close to the door, there was a large pot on a stove. Unfortunately, the distribution of heat was by no means even. The area near the stove was so hot that the people sleeping there complained of being burned. Once, the boy nearest the pot had his quilt scorched when the cooking took longer than expected. Fortunately, the heat always dissipated a few hours after the cooking was done, so one could still sleep on that end of the *kang* at night.

There was a small room attached to the large one. This was the home of the innkeeper. He was an old single man. His job was not easy. If there were guests, he had to get up late at night several times to feed the horses. He also had to make sure that there was enough hay to feed the horses and fuel the stove.

There was a well in front of the inn, where we would brush our teeth and wash ourselves. Since there were no women around for miles, we could wash ourselves naked right in the open. Li Baoquan said he did not care to wash, as there was no need to be presentable if there were no girls around. "What for? To look good in the mirror?" he asked.

We settled in at the inn. During the day, we would go to work without a break for lunch. Cook Jin would prepare one meal for us before we departed and one meal after we came back. The meal was the same every day: steamed cornbread and "fake millet" porridge in the morning, and cornbread with boiled potatoes for dinner. Well, they were supposed to be stir-fried. But since we did not have much cooking oil, Cook Jin had to boil them.

There was a national shortage of matches. I had never realized that matches were so essential. We needed them to light the oil lamp at night, and to light a fire to cook meals. With the exception of myself and two or three others, everyone smoked cigarettes. Without matches, life would be impossible. But we soon ran out of matches.

It seemed silly to walk a whole day back to the company for a box of matches. So Platoon Leader Liu proposed to the old innkeeper that we exchange our potatoes for some matches. The innkeeper said he would swap half a box of matches for a full sack. Platoon Leader Liu protested that a sack of potatoes weighed about 50 kilos (~100 pounds) and was worth at least 10 yuan. An entire box of matches only cost 2 fen (Chinese cents). Well, the innkeeper said, take it or leave it: I would rather keep my matches. Liu grumbled, but he ordered someone to bring the innkeeper a full sack of potatoes. We had tons of potatoes and no matches.

We had versatile uses for our washbasins. We washed ourselves in them, of course. But also at night, when nobody was supposed to open the door to let in the cold air, we used the basins as chamber pots. Furthermore, at meals, each squad had to send a representative to the stove for their portion of the food. The only container that could hold enough food was our washbasins. Although we always made sure to wash our basins thoroughly, the thought of the other uses was not very appetizing. Li Baoquan was fond of a local saying that if you were used to eating the unclean stuff, you would not get sick easily. There might be some truth to this. Who knows? In any event, we had to eat.

It was still warm during the day when we arrived on October 1, 1969, but, as I had feared, the autumn weather quickly turned cold. A week after we arrived, water froze at night. We dug out piles and piles of potatoes. But for some reason the company did not send wagons to haul them back. Many potatoes froze. The stems and leaves we covered them with were not much protection. They started to rot and exude a bad smell. If good potatoes were piled on top of bad ones, they would all rot. So a large portion of our work now became separating the good potatoes from the bad, a procedure we had to repeat every day as long as they were left in the open. Our piles of good potatoes became smaller and smaller, while piles of the bad ones grew larger and larger.

Platoon Leader Liu complained that if he had known how little the company cared, he would have been more generous swapping potatoes for matches. He was a heavy smoker. With a shortage of matches, he had to smoke more than he usually did because he had to light up a new cigarette with the butt of an old one. Then his cigarette supply ran out. Our store of food was being depleted quickly, too, and as a result our daily diet was reduced to potatoes and more potatoes. In Beijing, I had loved potatoes. But after several days, the sight of boiled potatoes brought stomach acid into my throat, and I would feel the heartburn.

During the last few days at the potato field, we were not digging potatoes anymore. Everything had been dug up. But we spent hours sorting through the rotted potatoes for good ones. Platoon Leader Liu remarked bitterly that the best way to keep potatoes from being frozen was to bury them. It seemed that in a few days there would not be any good potatoes left.

Now that there was little left to do with the potatoes, our breaks were longer. Sometimes we filled them with wrestling matches. It turned out that boys from Tianjin were good wrestlers. Surprisingly, Li Baoquan was the best of them all even though he had a thin build. No wonder he commanded such respect among the boys from Tianjin.

Yan Chongjie was another Tianjin boy. He was shorter, but much stronger than Baoquan. He was also a good wrestler. In one out of three matches, he would win. Sometimes, when he was "in the right mood," he could maintain a winning streak for several matches. Whenever that happened, Li Baoquan would resort to his "psychological warfare." He would say that he lost because he was giving Yan Chongjie face, as Yan was the older of the two.

Yan would become a little agitated and challenge Li Baoquan to try again. Li Baoquan would dismiss such a challenge by saying that he did not want Yan to lose face in front of everyone.

"I will throw you around when nobody is around," he would say.

Yan would then drag him to the center of the circle for a match. But because he was upset, it was now easier for him to fall for Li Baoquan's leg tricks. In a few minutes, sure enough, Yan would be thrown to the ground. Knowing that he would jump up for another match, Li Baoquan would provoke him even further.

Cui Xianchao was even better than Yan, although no one would have guessed by looking at him. He wore a pair of thick, purple-rimmed glasses, and was sloppy with his clothes. His bookish look confirmed that he was much better educated than most of the other boys because he was a 66er. Despite that, he was well coordinated and had razor-sharp reflexes.

When Li Baoquan won a match against Old Cui, he would hurry to help Cui up, saying, "Old Cui, at your advanced age you should be very careful."

Usually, on the next try, Li Baoquan would be the loser. Then Cui would say:

"How about it, young man?"

Everyone would take turns to try his hand, even those like myself who had never wrestled before. When I first had a match with Li Baoquan, my body was in the air before I knew what was happening. The second time around, it took a little longer. But this time, Li Baoquan did not merely throw me off balance, but fell upon me as I fell to the ground, his weight almost crushing my ribs. Cui and Yan yelled at Li Baoquan for using such a "black hand" on a novice. Baoquan apologized and said he had gotten carried away.

From then on, I wrestled with Li Baoquan as often as I could. I wanted to be able to beat him some day. Cui was helpful, coaching me in how to do tricks and how to avoid being tricked.

There was, in fact, some practical use for learning how to wrestle. Fighting among boys was frequent in the platoons and, sometimes, between companies. Those without friends to stand up for them, or with no ability to fight, could be bullied. Many boys, especially those from Tianjin, had learned street fighting. Some of them were known for their fighting nicknames. Li Baoquan would not reveal his, but I later learned that it was "Hairless from East of the River." I was never able to find out how he had got that nickname as he had a full head of hair. The best wrestler from Tianjin was "Monkey Li" of the Second Platoon, and he was indeed quite agile.

Despite their wrestling skills the tough boys from Tianjin were not as good in real fights as the boys from Beijing. That's because the boys from Tianjin observed a certain code of conduct for street gangsters. Before they fought, they would agree on whether to "play boxing" or "play wrestling." The loser would graciously accept defeat. I heard that when they first came, they acted the same way with the toughs from Beijing, who played it rough with bricks, knives, and shovels, causing many injuries among the Tianjin boys. Then the Tianjin boys learned to use weapons, too.

Platoon Leader Liu liked to watch our matches, although he never participated. He would squat by the circle, smoking a cigarette, and smile broadly when a match was over. When challenged, he said that this was stuff for city boys—he only knew how to arm wrestle. Indeed, Huang Shurong, who was a former weight lifter, was the only boy in the platoon who could beat Platoon Leader Liu in arm wrestling.

Thus, we spent several days sorting potatoes and playing in the fields. When tractor-pulled wagons finally arrived, there were not many piles of edible potatoes left. The loading took but a few hours. I felt sorry that so many good potatoes had rotted. But perhaps it was just as well. The thought of having potatoes for dinner for the rest of the winter was unbearable.

For our last night at the inn, Platoon Leader Liu ordered Cook Jin Jian to empty the flour bag and make noodles. He was to use any cooking oil he had left. We all cheered. It had been some time since we had eaten anything made with wheat flour. Our squad took out two of the largest basins, and we washed them carefully several times. It was indeed a feast. Although the noodles were gone before I had had enough, I felt quite satisfied. For the first time in a long while, I did not feel heartburn. Strangely, I felt homesick. Not for Beijing, but for the barracks in the company compound.

The next morning, we packed our belongings and put them on a horse-drawn wagon. Platoon Leader Liu thanked the innkeeper and left him two sacks of potatoes, for we had no need of them. The old man was delighted. He had a better harvest than anyone else.

The return journey did not feel as long as when we came, probably because we were going home. The air was cool now even during the day. The mosquitoes were gone. I was walking with Cui Xianchao.

I heard from other people from his school that Old Cui had been a star student, known for composing essays and poems. He could memorize a poem after reading it only once. Doubtless he would have had a shot at attending one of the best universities in China. But the Cultural Revolution had changed his life forever.

Cui told me that he had not wanted to come to the Gobi. But he had no choice. His father had been labeled a rightist in 1957. Unable to understand how he had become an enemy of the people overnight, or perhaps to cope with the humiliation, he jumped into the Huangpu River in Shanghai and drowned himself when Cui was still very young. Cui's mother brought him to Beijing to live with his grown-up sister and her husband. With such a "black" family background, he had had no choice but come to the Gobi when many of his classmates were assigned jobs in the city.

I told him that in our class of 69ers, everyone had been assigned to the countryside, either in Inner Mongolia or the northeast. No one had a choice.

Cui said that we were being wasted here. "Chairman Mao said that we are here to receive re-education from the poor peasants, but we never see them. Besides, what can we learn from the peasants? Some of those who live at the foot of the mountains don't even know that Chairman Mao is the leader of the country. They still ask about the health of Fu Zouyi, the warlord of the old regime."

He said that with his family background he had no hope left of going to college. Even if the universities reopened, he would have no chance. He said I would have a better chance than he because I was not from a black family. He had seen that I liked to read and encouraged me to try to study systematically.

He also suggested that I should try to leave Inner Mongolia. A few people from our company whose parents were high-ranking cadres had already left to join the military, where the living conditions were much better. He told me that as far as he could see, none of the leaders here cared about farming. That was why they did not try to haul the potatoes back. They had fixed pay and generous rations of foods from the state. Why should they care about potatoes?

Cui made the bluntest and bleakest assessment of the Construction Army Corps I had heard. It depressed me to think that there was no future for us here and that there might be no chance to go anywhere else. I told him that I did not think my parents had any back-channel connections. But I would write to them and ask.

During the last part of the trip, Cui passed the time by telling me how some of his friends had escaped from the boredom of life in the Construction Army Corps of Yunnan, the southern province near Vietnam. They snuck across the border to join the North Vietnamese army and became officers because of their bravery in battles against the South Vietnamese and Americans. He said that it was easy to be promoted during war. However, he said, if one were caught trying to cross the border he would be executed, even if he said he wanted to fight the US imperialists.

The conversation made the return trip seem much shorter. We arrived at the company compound late in the afternoon. The new barracks that were supposed to have been completed still had no roofs. So we moved back into our old shacks.

That night I wrote a long letter to my parents. I explained why I had not written and reported the experience of the two weeks we had been away. Toward the end, I related my conversation with Cui and asked if they could see if there was any way they could get me out of the Gobi. With some hope, I sent the letter the next day.

For some reason, the leaders forgot about that potato field. During my entire stay in the Gobi, I did not set foot in it or even see it again. Nobody was sent to seed potatoes the next spring or the springs after, probably because the place was too far away, and the leaders did not want to be bothered. I wondered what became of it. Maybe it became a private plot for the innkeeper. Maybe the migrating sand buried it. Nobody seemed to care.

Chapter 7

War Is Coming

By 1969, China was in the rather unique position of having hostile relationships with both of the world's superpowers simultaneously. Its hostility toward the United States dated back to the Korean War, although with an ocean between the two countries there had not been any recent flare-ups. And following China's ideological split with the Soviet Union in the early 1960s, tensions from time to time erupted into clashes along the long border (4,350 kilometers or ~2,700 miles) between the two countries.

In March 1969, there was a major military clash between the two countries on Zhenbao Island (called Damansky by Russia) on the Wusuli (Ussuri) River in northeastern China. The Chinese side claimed that the Soviet casualties numbered 58 dead, 94 wounded, and 17 tanks and armored carriers destroyed or damaged, with the Chinese troops suffering 29 casualties. Russia claimed that at least 248 Chinese troops were killed, and of the Soviet border guards, 32 were dead and 14 wounded. The Chinese side shipped one of the crippled Soviet T-62 tanks to Beijing's Military Museum. In another incident, on August 13, Soviet troops ambushed a Chinese patrol in a region called Terekti, which straddles the border of China's Xinjiang Province and what is today the country of Kazakhstan. The Chinese side reported 35 military personnel and 3 reporters killed in the incident. There were no Russian casualties.

On March 21, a couple of days after the fighting on Zhenbao Island, Alexei Kosygin, the Soviet premier, placed an urgent call to Mao Zedong. The Chinese switchboard operator refused to make a connection for him, retorting, "You are the head of the Soviet revisionists. You don't deserve to speak with our great leader." Kosygin then requested to speak with Premier Zhou. The operator said, "Our premier is too busy to speak with you," and hung up the phone. Mao and Zhou later reprimanded the operator for hanging up before reporting the call to her superiors. The Soviet leader was almost in despair. The two premiers did not get to speak with each other until six months later.

It is well documented that the Soviet Union had considered a preemptive surgical strike against China's nuclear bases and certain border cities. According to various reports, the Soviet Union had asked the United States to stay neutral in the event of a nuclear attack on China, but the Nixon administration refused and leaked the information to the press, forcing the Soviets to abandon the plan. I have doubts whether the Russians had seriously considered such a nuclear strike, because by then China already possessed not only atomic but also hydrogen bombs, and the consequences of a nuclear conflict would have been unimaginable. It's possible the Soviets had suggested neutrality as a "trial balloon" for testing the US reaction.

In any case, the Politburo was reportedly terrified of a large-scale Chinese intrusion into Soviet territory. "A nightmare vision of invasion by millions of Chinese made the Soviet leaders almost frantic," wrote Arkady Shevchenko, a high-ranking Russian defector to the United States, in his memoir. "Despite our overwhelming superiority in weaponry, it would not be easy for the USSR to cope with an assault of this magnitude." In view of China's vast population and long experience in guerrilla warfare, Shevchenko wrote, the Soviets feared that an attack on China's nuclear program would leave them "mired in an endless war."

The name of the Construction Army Corps suggested dual purposes of our organization. One was to build and develop the border area; the other was to defend it when necessary. It was for the latter reason we were organized like an army, with leadership positions at the company level and above staffed by active-duty officers. While by and large we were not armed, we were always aware that we would have to fight if called to do so.

★ ★ ★

In mid-October 1969, the grain was brought in and a woeful accounting was made. Our company's harvest was only 70,000 kilograms (~140,000 pounds), for the year. Before we came, a mere dozen farmers had produced about 500,000 kilograms (~1 million pounds). And we were tending a much larger piece of land than they, because the 300 of us young people had greatly expanded the fields. Even worse was that we had sowed about 750,000 kilograms (~1.6 million pounds) of seeds. That meant that after a year of hard work, much fertilizer, and countless machine hours, not to mention the other costs of farming this land, our entire harvest equaled about one-tenth the weight of the seeds.

The leaders now organized political sessions to study next year's "economic plan." Initially, the plan had called for 900,000 kilograms (~2 million pounds) of grain. In view of the output by the old farm, this should have been well within reach. But having learned of our actual output, headquarters had scaled down the target to 90,000 kilograms (~20,000 pounds). They still allotted about 750,000 kilograms (~1.6 million pounds) of seeds. It did not take an expert to know that this made no economic sense.

Instructor Zhang tried to address our doubts at the company gathering. He explained that our task here in the Gobi was not only to farm the land but also to act as a deterrent against the aggressive Soviet-revisionist social imperialists. Moreover, we were here to remold our world outlook and reform our ideology to become true members of the working class. Therefore, although it appeared that we expended more resources than we produced, it was worth it if you considered that we were making ourselves socialist new men and defending our great motherland against Soviet aggression. Indeed, he said, we should feel grateful that the Party and the state were willing to spend so much on us.

The next session was to be a mobilization meeting. The political instructor and the commander would deliver speeches to pump up our morale. Representatives from each squad and platoon were to prepare notes to say how much they appreciated the concern of the Party and the state for the youth. We should show that we would uphold the motto "First, do not fear hardships and second, do not fear death," and "strive for even greater victory."

★ ★ ★

Now that the harvest was over, there was not much to do in the fields, and every morning we had political study sessions. The company commander or the political instructor would read us passages from *The Selected Works of Mao Zedong*. At first, we were grateful to be spared the backbreaking work. This was the longest break we had had and we badly needed it. Neither the company commander nor the political instructor had received much schooling, so there were many characters in the *Works* that they did not recognize. They mispronounced words constantly. It was amusing to hear them mangle these familiar words to us, and we were not reserved in our laughter. Instructor Zhang was the worse of the two. Whenever he read, people pricked their ears in anticipation of funny pronunciations.

But those study sessions soon grew dull. We heard the same articles every day. Besides, it was tiring to sit outside on the ground for hours on pieces of newspaper or bricks. My back often hurt, and it was getting colder each day. Nobody was allowed to go to the toilet during these sessions, so I could not even use that excuse to stretch. It was then I would wish that I were working in the fields.

Soon the leaders found something different for us to do.

Throughout 1969, there had been military clashes between China and the Soviet Union in border areas. As the border tensions rose, China began girding for all-out war. Lin Biao, the defense minister, issued an order known as Order Number One 1969 on October 18 to evacuate the top leaders from Beijing. The troops were mobilized. Mao issued a slogan, paraphrasing the advice given to the first Ming emperor: "Dig deep holes, store much grain and never seek hegemony"—in other words, China should prepare for an invasion by the Soviet Union.

The whole country went into a frenzy of constructing air-raid shelters and tunnels, spending millions of hours of manpower and much of the country's resources. Every work unit in China built air-raid shelters. This was not new to me; the Beijing subway, which I had helped work on, also furthered nuclear war preparation. The construction included lead-filled, radiation-proof gates that could separate one part of the subway from the rest, all part of the system's design to function as a fallout shelter if needed.

The leaders had told us that there were 70 divisions of Soviet troops on the Sino-Mongolian border ready to strike. This had been mentioned to us every so often, starting with the speech given by the official from regiment headquarters on our second day in the Gobi. But most of the time we had been too busy with farm work to think about the possibility of war.

One night, I was awakened by the sound of a bugle for an emergency gathering. I jumped out of bed to find that it was still completely dark outside. Nobody had a watch, so we did not know what time it was. Then Platoon Leader Liu told us to bundle a bedroll and come stand in formation. In about 10 minutes, the entire company was trotting in the direction of the Third Company.

There was an area nearby where, miraculously, a few trees stood. Trees were rare in the Gobi Desert. I was surprised to find that there was already a large crowd there. Every company for more than a dozen kilometers (~7.5 miles) had attended. Political Commissar Xuan of the regiment was there, too. He was known among us by his nickname "Xuan Junji," because whenever he introduced himself, he would say, "My family name is Xuan, Xuan like in Xuan Junji." Xuan Junji was the name of the North Korean ambassador to Beijing. Nobody remembered what the political commissar's name was.

By about five o'clock, every company that had been summoned had reported its arrival, with the exception of the Tenth Company. Xuan Junji started to speak. He first praised the companies that had arrived early as being "as fierce as thunder and as fast as wind." This was the same slogan they had used when they gave us our potato harvesting assignment earlier.

We were all proud that the Fifth Company was mentioned. Then he criticized the Fourth Company for arriving without their bedrolls. "It is possible that our regiment will move out of the area today. Can you survive a march of 1,000 *li* (300 miles) without supplies?" he bellowed. "No!" The crowd shouted in unison. I was wondering whether even with our "supplies" I could survive a march of 1,000 *li*. I had only a small quilt in my backpack.

Then he loudly instructed his messenger to order the Tenth Company, which was supposedly on its way, to change direction and go to Batou "to wait for further instructions." This was intended as punishment for their failure to show up.

Some people stuck their tongues out at this news. It was fortunate that we had been "as fast as wind." Batou, the regiment headquarters, was 25 kilometers (~16 miles) away. The poor guys of the Tenth Company would run themselves ragged getting there.

Then Xuan announced a strategy against the invasion by the Soviets. War, he said, was inevitable. But Chairman Mao had developed a grand scheme to defeat the aggressors. It was consistent with the strategic thinking contained in the *Selected Works*, which, therefore, we should now study especially hard. China would not fight with the Soviet Union on their terms—head on with troops and hardware—but on ours. We would lead them around by their noses. We would "lure the enemy deep into our territory" and "close the door to beat the dog."

In the vast land where our Inner Mongolia Army Corps was scattered, there were no natural barriers to stop an advancing army. Ours was the territory that Chinese troops should give up and sacrifice when the Soviets invaded. We would retreat to the mountains nearby. As the enemy marched into the country, we would come out of the mountains as guerrilla troops and strike at their supply lines. Of course, we would win the war, because it was to be a people's war.

★ ★ ★

I wasn't in the least afraid. On the contrary, like most of the boys, I was enthused and excited, even looking forward to the war. It never occurred to me that we might lose or die. Perhaps we hoped that a war would change our lot—the hard work in the fields, the endless political study sessions, and the terrible and insufficient food. Perhaps we could become heroes.

For days after that emergency gathering, we discussed what we would do when the Soviets invaded. The reaction from the boys of our platoon ranged from excitement to indifference. Li Baoquan declared that once he became a war hero, he would like to be a policeman in Taiwan.

Why in Taiwan? We were puzzled. "How handsome I will look standing under a big palm tree," he said.

One day, all the platoon leaders were summoned to the regiment headquarters for a meeting on strategy. When they came back three days later, Platoon Leader Liu told us that they had been taken deep into the Yin Mountains to survey the terrain and learn where each guerrilla division was to be based. He also said that some weapons would be distributed. But there were not enough to go around, so each company was to receive only 40 guns, sufficient to arm one platoon, which would be referred to as the armed platoon.

We all hoped that our platoon would be chosen. Platoon Leader Liu said that he would give it his best try, but we had to behave well these few days to show that we were the best-disciplined platoon.

We were quite disappointed when it was announced that the Second Platoon had been selected instead. Soon they all received submachine guns, which they showed off proudly. These turned out to be the same Russian-made submachine guns used by the Chinese army during the Korean War about 15 years earlier.

Like us, the company leaders were excited about the prospect of war. They seemed to think that their positions had been enhanced: They could claim to be military officers on active duty. The company political instructor walked around with a new air of importance now, his fat belly protruding. When he came to our platoon one day, Li Baoquan stepped forward, saluted, and greeted him, "General!"

Instructor Zhang grinned from ear to ear and reprimanded Li Baoquan in a fatherly tone: "You are being naughty again, Li Baoquan." But we could see that he was pleased with the salutation. We were all smiling, knowing that Baoquan was being sarcastic.

Baoquan said afterward that he would shoot the political instructor first if a war should really break out. "This dumb-head would have us all killed if he were to command us in a war," he explained. But whenever he saw the political instructor again, he would call him "General." The "General" would always grin, sticking out his belly even further.

The fact was that none of the company leaders had had any experience in battle. But they decided that they would lead us in rigorous training anyhow.

The training was not too difficult during the day. Those of us in platoons without weapons simply had to march and run in formation. The physical training sessions were mixed with sessions of political indoctrination because, according to Chairman Mao, the ultimate determinant of winning a war was political consciousness. We would be invincible if we possessed the "spiritual atom bomb."

A large portion of our physical training was devoted to crawling. We were supposed to learn how to move around under heavy gunfire. We would hit the ground and crawl rapidly forward, sideways, and backward, in whatever direction the leaders ordered. To train us to crawl under fire, they would take us to cow fields where the cow patties were still fresh and the earth was soaked with urine. We would be ordered to throw ourselves to the ground and crawl.

I would not have minded crawling on cow manure if there had been hot water to wash it off. But there was none, and winter was coming. Our platoon had recently moved out of temporary barracks and into new ones, but these were still damp because the mud on the walls was not dry. It was colder inside than outside. It became more and more difficult to rinse off the cow manure in the freezing water.

These training sessions were also hard on our clothes, of which we did not possess many. Each of us had been issued uniforms when we arrived, but they were of very poor quality. The cloth was so thin that some people joked that it should be used to make mosquito nets. These clothes quickly became rags. I had to mend my "mosquito-net uniform" often, putting patches upon patches. I never threw anything away because there were no substitutes. After a while, it was difficult to recognize the original fabric of the clothes.

Baoquan shared a room with me and four others. He was always fastidious about how he dressed. He would spend hours altering the uniforms himself to make them fit better. He washed his clothes more often than anybody else, explaining that he was old enough to have a girlfriend, so it was important to make himself look presentable. It should come as no surprise that he absolutely loathed crawling on cow manure. He would try to escape those training sessions as often as possible by hiding when the whistle blew.

Once, the company commander caught him and punished him. As we all stood in line and watched, Baoquan had to go through the crawl routine right on a steaming pile of fresh cow poop. We were all amused to see that even then he tried not to touch the ground with his clothes. He crawled quickly on his hands and feet, with his posterior raised high. It was a funny sight. The commander stepped forward and put one foot on his rear end, and he collapsed to the ground onto the manure. We all laughed. Nobody was sympathetic, because we were all covered with manure.

★ ★ ★

The worst part of these training sessions was that the drills came every other night, and sometimes several nights in a row. We had to be prepared for emergencies at any time, for it was unpredictable when the Soviets would invade. The Soviets were said to have air-dropped 21 spies, of whom 18 had been captured. But there were three still roaming around somewhere, and we had to be especially alert.

The bugle would usually blow at two or three o'clock in the morning, when most of us were in our deepest sleep. We would jump out of bed, bundle our bedding in the prescribed manner, and rush out to make a formation. In a few minutes, an order would come, and we would start a "rapid march" to an undisclosed location. Nobody knew where we were headed in the darkness. It was always a military secret.

Then, shortly before dawn, we would find ourselves back at the barracks. We would be told it had only been a drill, but that we should not relax our vigilance, because the next time might be real. We would then unload our bedrolls, wash our faces, and get ready for a day's work or military training. Usually the company leader on duty for that night would go back to his room to sleep.

One night, I remember, we were running toward an undisclosed location in formation. It was pitch dark. Suddenly, the person in front me just disappeared. I instinctively jumped out of the way. I thought he must have stumbled on something and would get up to follow the group, so I kept running. When we returned to our barracks, I learned that several boys had run onto the frozen surface of a cesspool and fallen through the ice. When they walked in later, they smelled so bad that we would not let them into the room. They had to go to the well and wash in the below-freezing night.

Each time there was a drill, the company leader would tell a different story to convince us that it was really an emergency. One night, for example, he announced that intelligence sources had reported that Soviet troops had been spotted in the vicinity. The next night, the "sources" would report the discovery of enemy spies. I never believed any of the stories and hated these exhausting emergency marches.

Soon enough, almost everyone grew used to the stories. Only a fool would have believed that there was a real threat. Li Baoquan did his best to dodge the marches, begging me to answer roll calls for him. Since it was dark, no one would find out if one person were missing. Soon, more and more people were doing the same thing. The company leader began going through our rooms after the bugle sounded to make sure that everyone was out. Even so, some people would leave the group and sneak back to bed in the middle of our marches.

Then one night, I was awakened by a burst of gunfire. I jumped out of bed with the others. Platoon Leader Liu's bed was in the outer room. He was already up, and sternly ordered us to hit the ground. The rapid gunfire outside continued. We were stunned. So after all, the Soviets had invaded! Despite all the training sessions, we didn't know what to do. It was completely dark. After a pause, Liu spoke softly. By the sound of the gunfire, he said, we were surrounded. Just then, an object with a burning fuse flew through the window.

"Grenade!" he shouted.

I instinctively covered my head with my hands. This is it, I thought. Then I heard the explosion. It was deafening. When it was over, I was surprised that I could still feel and think. I was still alive. I tried to feel if I was wounded but could not find anything wrong. Then I heard Zhou Wanling crying in a corner and Platoon Leader Liu saying, "Stop that. The enemy will hear us."

Liu called our names one by one in a low whisper. Miraculously, everyone was alive. There was no time to check if anyone was wounded. Liu said that we had to break out now. Otherwise, we would all be killed in here. Liu ordered us to crawl to the corner of the door to grab our shovels. Then he said that he was going to charge out. We should all follow him and then disperse in different directions. Nobody should stay in the room because the enemy would certainly bombard the house and kill anyone left behind.

There was no time to feel fear. Liu opened the door and ran out. Suddenly, through the open door, I could see gunfire coming rapidly toward him. He fell to the ground.

"Charge!" someone shouted.

"Charge!" we all shouted. Shovels in hand, we all rushed out of the room amid heavy gunfire.

I hit the ground as soon as I stepped out the door and crawled over to Platoon Leader Liu to check if he was still alive. He was, but he could no longer move. He urged me to go ahead and not to worry about him.

Just then, the gunfire stopped. Several flashlights shone from the source of the gunfire. I heard the voice of the company commander. "All right," he shouted, "the exercise is over!"

An exercise! I looked at Platoon Leader Liu. He was already on his feet. And he was smiling too. An exercise! I could not believe it. What about the gunfire and explosion? Did anyone get hurt?

It turned out that it had all been a setup. The grenade was a dummy grenade that only made a loud bang, very much like a powerful firecracker. The guns had been loaded with dummy ammunition, all blanks. Platoon Leader Liu, of course, had known this all along.

We went back into our room. It still smelled of gunpowder. Zhou Wanling was sitting in a corner. He looked at us incredulously, still sobbing. For a while, I did not know if I should laugh or cry. But I finally laughed, together with the rest. Platoon Leader Liu said he appreciated my coming to his rescue.

After this exercise, I knew that we would not care if the entire Soviet army attacked.

After the "gunfire exercise," things quieted down a little. There were still emergency drills, but they didn't take place as frequently.

Then the Army Corps leadership had a new idea. Each squad had to build two air-raid shelters. This time, even Platoon Leader Liu thought the idea was stupid. If the great leader's strategic thinking was to abandon this piece of land when the Soviets invaded, why should we spend our efforts and resources to build air-raid shelters? Why didn't we build more storage places for potatoes? Besides, who would care to stage an air raid on the Gobi, where you could go for miles without seeing a soul?

But an order was an order, and the deadline was strict. We started right away. Every inch we chiseled out of the frozen ground took many hours of effort. We had to collect dried grass and cow manure to build fires to warm the earth before we could dig. This process was grindingly slow. And the project became more difficult as the hole became deeper. The entrance was very small, allowing only one person to crawl in at a time. It was almost impossible to turn around once you were inside. We had to take turns crawling in, scratching at the earth with a sawed-off shovel, and passing a basket of dirt to the person behind. Inside, I felt like an ant digging tunnels in an ant colony.

Every day we would come back tired, our faces covered with dirt and sweat. We all wished that the Soviets would invade already. We would have felt better about fighting a war with the Russians than about digging this hole in the ground.

Finally, after several weeks of hard work, the project was completed. There lay our air-raid shelter, a deep hole in the ground. Ours was one among many that now dotted the land in front of our company compound. I thought it must have been a strange sight from the air to see all these holes. I wondered if the Soviet pilots would mistake them for storage places for secret weapons.

Once the air-raid shelters were finished, we were ordered to build trenches along one side of the company compound. We didn't know or care anymore if the Soviets would attack us from that particular direction. It was easier to build these trenches than to dig holes in the ground. But it was hard nonetheless and progress was slow. Nobody thought for a minute that these trenches would be of any use. Why would the Soviets fight in trench warfare with us to take over a few run-down mud shacks? But who knew? Perhaps the Soviets were that stupid.

In any event, by the end of November, the war preparation projects were completed. Our company was so well protected that there were trenches and air-raid holes everywhere. In fact, it turned out that these projects did have lethal powers. That winter, many of the cattle and horses roaming the land in search of dried grass fell into the ditches and died from being trapped.

We hadn't had emergency drills at night for several weeks, because the work building air-raid shelters was exhausting. But the second night after the air-raid shelters were built, emergency whistles woke us up.

This time, we were told, Soviet bombers had been spotted about a few hundred kilometers to the north. Before the commander could issue an order, a messenger came rushing over to report that the aircraft were now only 50 kilometers away. The commander ordered us to run to the air-raid shelters.

We rushed to our shelter. I was leading the pack of our half squad of people. The hole was just big enough to squeeze into. I soon reached the bottom and could feel the hole being filled by the bodies of others. There was too little room and it was pitch black. I was suddenly overcome by a strong sense of fear. What if the shelter collapsed? I knew I would have no chance of surviving.

As we were waiting for the Soviet bombers, my feeling of fright became more and more acute. Finally, I could take it no longer. I shouted I couldn't breathe. By then, everyone was frightened, fearing the hole could collapse. There was a unanimous shout and everyone hurried to squeeze out. Finally, all of us did, emerging like ghosts from graves. I felt enormously relieved. But we had to keep quiet in case the platoon leader saw us and ordered us to go back in again.

The Soviets never came. But there were human fatalities nonetheless. There were accidents in other companies. People were killed digging these shelters. Some of them collapsed, burying people inside.

The next spring, when the ice melted and the grasslands turned green, some friends and I took a walk to the air-raid shelters.

None had held up. We even had a hard time finding the location of the one we'd built. All that remained was a slight concavity where it had collapsed into the ground.

★ ★ ★

It was not until the 1990s, after the disintegration of the Soviet Union, that China and Russia finally settled their border disputes on Zhenbao Island by dividing it between them. It was also in the 1990s that China signed a treaty with Kazakhstan, which was already independent from Russia, to resolve the border dispute in the Terekti region.

Chapter 8

Repairing the Earth

In the 1960s and 1970s, China was still a largely agrarian society. The numbers are staggering when compared with those of the United States. In 1970, about 83 percent of China's total population were farmers or rural residents, compared with 4.6 percent for the United States. Yet the Chinese population was four times that of America's; China's agricultural population was 70 times that of the United States.

The United States and China are of roughly equal size, in terms of total area. But the United States is endowed with much greater agricultural gifts: Cultivated land in the United States represents 17 percent of its total territory whereas in China it is only approximately 13 percent. Therefore, China's cultivated land is only 73 percent of that of the United States, but worked on by 70 times as many farmers, to feed 4 times the population.

As such, China's rural areas were extremely poor and farming was backward and primitive. We worked the earth with shovels, hoes, and sickles, tools that were mostly unchanged from those our ancestors had used 3,000 years ago. Some agricultural jobs, such as seeding (e.g., wheat, corn, vegetables), planting (e.g., rice, potatoes, saplings), and weeding, were done by hand, as ancient people had done probably 50,000 years ago or even earlier. With such ancient tools or no tools at all, the yield was meager even from the most fertile land. It is fair to say that Chinese agriculture in the 1960s and 1970s was barely enough to feed the population even in the best of times.

Whereas US farming had already been largely mechanized for decades, Chinese farming in the 1960s and 1970s was by and large done by manual labor. Farming was hard work anywhere in China, but it was much tougher in infertile areas like the Gobi, where peasants could barely scrape out a subsistence living.

It is estimated that during the Cultural Revolution approximately 16 million educated youth, representing about 10 percent of China's urban population, were sent to the countryside, particularly to remote border areas and poor regions. Whereas much of the rest of the world was undergoing a process of urbanization, China, uniquely, was doing the opposite, forcing millions of young urban dwellers to migrate to poor rural areas. Official newspapers hailed the Cultural Revolution as "unprecedented in history." It truly was, in many ways, against historical trends.

★ ★ ★

Our mission in the Gobi was to farm. I doubt that anyone had seriously considered the feasibility of large-scale farming in the Gobi Desert, but the idea was not entirely crazy. Our farm was located only about 15 kilometers (~9 miles) from Lake Wuliangsu and about 50 kilometers (~30 miles) from the Yellow River. West of the lake lay the Hetao ("River Loop") plain, where the Yellow River takes a sharp bend to the north before looping down and continuing its eastern course to the ocean. This was the river's most fertile region. Periodic flooding from the sediment-rich river and a well-developed network of irrigation canals made the area ideal for farming. It produced an abundance of crops familiar throughout northern China, such as wheat, corn, sorghum, potato, pumpkin, watermelon, and other types of melons.

The Hetao region was already well populated and the land was well cultivated since the Qing dynasty (1636–1912). Our place was outside the Hetao, however, and our land was barren and sandy, which is what the Gobi is known for. Our mission was to cultivate new land, carving farms out of the Gobi. There already were a few pockets of land that had been made arable. Urat Farm, where our company was based, had been one example, a small agricultural enterprise run by the dozen or so old-timers we called "old farm workers." Over time we learned that the "complicated backgrounds" of these old farm workers, about which we'd been warned, referred to their checkered personal histories. Some of them used to be homeless; others had run afoul of the law and served their time. The government sent them here to cultivate land for agriculture in order to feed themselves. Over the years, they picked the best land and built a modestly sized farm. They were producing enough to feed themselves and still have a surplus to sell.

Then we arrived. Our first challenge was water. Farming requires water, and, of course, there was not much of that in the Gobi. But Lake Wuliangsu was nearby. The Yellow River was not far away. It was possible to channel water from either one to our land. Indeed, that was the brilliant idea of our leaders. They reckoned that as long as we could build an irrigation system of canals and ditches, we should be able to turn the arid land into a fertile farm. All it took was our labor, which was plentiful and cheap.

For that purpose, we were made to dig ditches throughout the year, every year, in all kinds of weather conditions, rain or shine, scorching heat or freezing cold. With a vast area to cover, there was no hope we would ever complete our work, so we worked on digging ditches endlessly. According to Liu Baoquan, digging ditches was one of the four most tiring things in the world (the other three were making bricks, harvesting wheat, and having sex).

Regardless of how much water we managed to bring to our land— and we built enough canals and ditches to bring in plenty—we had no hope of producing crops in a meaningful way on much, if not most, of the land, we tried to cultivate. This had to do with the soil conditions.

The land in the Gobi was usually covered by sand and gravel, much of which had to be removed before the soil could be transformed into farmland. But that was just the start. In much of the Gobi, the soil was highly saline and alkaline, so much so that large tracts of land looked like they were covered by dirty snow in the hot summer. The saline-alkaline crust prevented the soil from "breathing," suffocating crops. Most crops, especially wheat and corn, whose tolerance for saline is low, do not grow in such soil. Only some tough thorn bushes grew here, and even those struggled to survive.

We made an effort to treat the soil. We mixed it with sand carried over from wherever we could find it. Supposedly, sand aerates the soil to allow the water to nourish crops more effectively. That sounded good in theory, but in reality it did not really work. To treat a large area of land required much more manpower than a few hundred of us, with our bare hands, could provide.

You might think that irrigation would help improve the soil, flushing out all the salt and alkali. To the contrary, it only made the problem worse. The water we channeled to our land came from either Lake Wuliangsu or from the Yellow River. The lake water itself was somewhat saline, and the water from the Yellow River picked up salt and alkali from the ground it flowed through. Irrigation with such water only made the soil worse as salt and alkali in the water seeped into it. When you ponder what it cost in terms of labor and resources, the project was an enormous drain from the beginning.

In the first year, our crops were a total failure. They would not get better. We worked so hard throughout the year to plow the land, to fertilize, to build canals and ditches, to irrigate, to weed, to spread insecticides, and to harvest under the blazing sun or in the rain, day and night (irrigation was usually done at night). But we produced less, far less, than the seeds we sowed, after a season of backbreaking labor. It would have been better if we had simply consumed the seeds as our food supply. We put so much time and sweat into the most barren parts of the land, and in the end, we failed. The labor of the few hundred of us was no match for the Gobi.

★ ★ ★

At the subheadquarters of our regiment, located between our company and Company No. 9, there was a little shop. It sold some basic goods such as soap, needles, and thread. It also sold canned food. A can of cooked pork cost 2 yuan, 40 percent of my monthly pay of 5 yuan. Unlike most of the boys in our company, I didn't smoke. Nor did I drink. I spent most of my money on buying canned pork. Among my friends, we shared each other's food no matter how hungry we were. Typically, each person only got a single bite out of a can, as there was never enough to go around.

Hunger also drove us to eat everything we could catch. If we caught a stray dog, we ate it. If we caught a stray cat, we ate it. I once joined others in eating an owl that Liu Xiaotong had found dead somewhere near our barracks. A horse died and its carcass lay near the outhouse. Not everyone wanted to eat a dead horse. Some of us including myself cut pieces of meat from the carcass. We ate it for many days. Given the circumstances, it was delicious.

We lived quite far away from the locals. The nearest village was about an hour away by foot. Some boys snuck into nearby villages to steal chickens. If they were caught, they were likely to get beaten up. So they only raided the villages at night. It was rather easy to snatch a chicken from its coop where they slept. Eventually, the locals learned how to deal with the thieves by building a long tube made of mud bricks at the entrance of the chicken coop. The tube was longer than an arm's length so the thieves could not reach the coop.

★ ★ ★

In large parts of northern China, north of the Yangtze River and south of the Great Wall, wheat seeds are planted in early October. They sprout when the weather is still warm and grow for about a month and a half to about 30 centimeters tall (~1 foot) before winter comes. During the winter, they wither away as the land turns brown or, when covered by snow, white. Even though their stems above the ground appear dead in winter, their roots remain alive. The more snowfall the better for them, because snow provides needed water when spring comes. Winter in most parts of northern China is not cold enough to damage the roots of the wheat. Peasants here have a saying: "A good snow heralds a good harvest next year."

When spring returns in late March, wheat plants begin to sprout out of the soil and grow again. I think the reason for winter wheat to be planted the previous year is to allow the roots to take hold deep in the soil before winter, so that in spring the wheat can grow rapidly and ripen in early summer, before the summer rains.

We were farther north. In Inner Mongolia, as in almost all the regions north of the Great Wall, we grew "spring wheat," as opposed to winter wheat. Seeds were sown in springtime, not the previous winter.

Because the winter so far north is extremely cold, it would not only kill the crop above the ground but also the roots when the ground freezes. In the Gobi, the ground is frozen solid in wintertime and to just break the surface is exceedingly difficult.

The sowing season for spring wheat was at the end of March or beginning of April, when the soil had thawed and migrant birds were beginning to return from the south. It was also a time when the roads were muddy and travel was difficult. We called it *fan jiang*, or frost boiling, which causes upswellings of mud from below the surface when the frozen earth thaws. To work in the fields in early spring, we had to pick our way carefully in order not to get stuck in the mud. Too often, vehicles, including horse-drawn carts, sank in the mud and it took the joint efforts of beasts and people to get them out.

Company No. 3 was supposed to help us with their tractors and machines. But we rarely saw them. The political instructor told us many times: "People with free time are prone to trouble." Therefore, he kept us busy with manual labor but left the machines idle.

There was another reason why machines were seldom employed. They broke down all the time. None of us knew if the breakdowns were caused by mechanical problems, because only the operators had the knowledge and skills of a mechanic. We suspected the frequent mechanical problems were just excuses for the machine operators to steal a break, and our company leaders, none of whom knew anything about machines, could be easily fooled.

An exception to the machines' idleness was that tractors were used for sowing. The time window for sowing was short, a week at most. It was impractical to plant hundreds of hectares of land manually, no matter how hard we worked. The seeds were mixed with insecticides before they were planted. Machines could mix and spread insecticides much better than we could by hand. The insecticides were to kill the mole crickets that lived in the soil and would eat the seeds. There were many mole crickets and we could hear them chirp at night. There was a popular expression among us: "Don't stop planting wheat just because mole crickets chirp," which means you should not let little problems or risks prevent you from doing what is necessary. I still follow such wisdom today.

I took part in the wheat planting every spring. A tractor pulled a sowing machine that looked like a long trough with many holes at the bottom. Two of us stood over the trough on a narrow piece of wood board. As the tractor moved, the holes in the trough opened and closed to let out the insecticide-laced seeds. We bumped up and down with the trough, using our hands to spread the seeds over the holes.

As we worked, we were constantly covered in dust and dirt and by plumes of insecticides stirred up by the crawler wheels of the tractor. We called our work "eating dust." When the tractor stopped to refill the seeds in the trough, only the eyes and dirty teeth of my coworkers were visible under the layer of dirt. It was not only the dust we ate, but also a powerful cocktail of dirt, engine exhaust, and insecticides. Cui Xianchao was lucky. He was bespectacled, and behind his glasses he could keep his eyes open when waves of dust blew into his face.

These insecticides were effective poisons. Locals used the seeds mixed and soaked with insecticides to bait and kill waterfowl along the shores of Lake Wuliangsu. The birds dropped dead quickly after eating the seeds. The hunters then took the dead birds to our barracks to sell. It was so rare for us to eat meat, and we were so hungry for it, that these wild delicacies sold well. I had not worried too much about dipping my hands into insecticide, but I knew it was dangerous when swallowed. The temptation of the meat, however, was too strong to resist.

Coincidentally, I was reading an insecticide manual, not so much because I wanted to learn about insecticides but because at that particular time I had run out of books to read. I had learned that the chemical composition of insecticides was highly acidic. Alkali should neutralize the acid, I reasoned; if we soaked the bird in soda water, maybe the poison would be neutralized. I had absolutely no idea if my theory was correct. Nonetheless, that was exactly what we did. We soaked the birds in soda water for a couple of hours before cooking them. They were absolutely delicious. None of us died from eating the birds' poisoned meat, either because my method worked or our bodies were a lot tougher than the birds'.

It was not until many years later that I learned that the most common insecticide we'd used in the Gobi, DDT, had been banned in many other countries. In Inner Mongolia, we used nothing but DDT, not only as an insecticide for crops, but also to spray indoors to kill mosquitoes and flies. I must have had a healthy dose of exposure to DDT over the years. I am positive my body's tolerance level for poison is quite high, but I don't quite believe that what does not kill you makes you stronger.

★ ★ ★

If our farming yielded less than the seeds we used, why did we do it at all? We had no answer for this question. Nor, I think, did our leaders. I guess there was always the hope that next year would be better. But in truth, we did worse each year. Our hard labor was wasted. We described our work as "repairing the Earth" because it was so ambitious, and yet so futile, pointless and backbreaking.

The description came from a song titled "Song of Educated Youth" that was banned by the authorities but secretly circulating among us. It was composed by an educated youth just like ourselves, who came from Nanjing, a major city by the Yangtze River and once China's capital under Nationalist rule. His song struck a chord with us, as it not only described our job in the Gobi but also resonated in our hearts:

> *Ah, … Nanjing*
> *My lovely hometown;*
> *Ah, … Nanjing*
> *When will I be able to go back to you?*
> *In the blue sky*
> *White clouds fly;*
> *On the bank of the beautiful Yangtze*
> *Is Nanjing my lovely ancient city*
> *My hometown;*
> *Ah, the bridge is like a rainbow*
> *Bettering the colorful clouds;*
> *Across the Yangtze*
> *Is the great Zhong Mountain*
> *Where my home is;*
> *Said goodbye to mother,*
> *Farewell home,*
> *Golden student era*
> *Now in the history book of the youth*

Never to return.
Ah, the road of the future so hard
So long.
The steps of life
Deep and shallow in a remote strange land.
Rising with the sun
Returning with the moon
Heavily repairing the Earth
Is the glorious and sacred duty, my destiny.
Ah, ... Our two hands embroider the Earth with red
Red all over the universe.
Looking toward tomorrow
Believe it, it will arrive.
Ah, ... Nanjing.
My lovely hometown
Ah, ... Nanjing
When will we be able to return to you, to you?

There was no better description for our job than "heavily repairing the Earth." All year round we dug in the earth, rain or shine. In the end, we produced hardly anything.

At the time, none of us knew where the song had originated. I later learned that the composer was Ren Yi, who was just 21 years old when he wrote it in May 1969. For this, he was arrested and sentenced to death in May 1970. Fortunately for Ren, the commander-in-chief of the Nanjing Military Region was General Xu Shiyou, who was also the head of the city of Nanjing. Xu was a war hero with a hot temper who repeatedly clashed with the Rebels. The Red Guards could not do anything about Xu because he was one of Mao's favorite generals. When Ren's death sentence landed on the general's desk, he felt sorry that a 22-year-old boy would die for a song and commuted his sentence to 10 years in prison.

★ ★ ★

Digging ditches was hard labor. We would not know how hard until we began to dig below the surface. Under the gravel was a layer of sticky clay. In springtime, when ice crystals were still visible in the earth, the clay was particularly thick, requiring the strength of one's whole body just to push a shovel into the ground. Often, it was impossible to dig out the clay by lifting the shovel. Instead we had to cut the clay like a piece of cake on four sides before lifting a large cube of earth out of the ground. Once the clay was dug out, it often stuck to the shovel and was difficult to shake off. I had to use my full body strength to do so. After a day's work, not only were my arms sore, my back and legs were aching as well.

The blacksmith of our company made our shovels. The blades were hammered out by hand. As such, the surface of the blade was never smooth, no matter how we tried to flatten it. It bore dents and marks from the hammer, and mud and clay would stick to a marked-up, dented blade and make the shovel impossible to use. The only way to make it even and smooth was to use it repeatedly and to grind it with gravel until the steel shone.

My shovel was my pride. I used it so often, and I ground it with a piece of broken brick so much every day, that eventually its surface was almost like shining armor. Such a tool made my work much less frustrating and more productive. When its surface became smooth, it cut like a knife and I could throw the clay out of the ditch. I cared for my shovel so much that Liu Baoquan said I should marry it. It was indeed the most precious possession I had.

The blacksmith shop in our company was located in a tiny brick house. The blacksmith, Master Hu, was of medium height, dark-skinned, with a strong and muscular body. He was a friendly and helpful man and always smiled before he spoke. He was a man of few words, but he was a straight shooter. He talked directly to you, no non-sense. My good friend, Li Rongtian, was Master Hu's only apprentice. Li Rongtian was also of medium build but thin. His skin was pale, just like any city boy, and, without his working apron, he didn't look at all like a blacksmith. Like Old Cui, Li Rongtian was a 66er, three years my senior and more educated than most of us. He and I were among the few who continued to read whatever books we could find, so we were close. I was somewhat envious of him because by not having to work in the fields, he had more time to read.

Li Rongtian believed that wasting time was the biggest sin one could commit against oneself. My whole life since then has been influenced by this wisdom he had shared with me. I still feel a sense of guilt when I find myself with nothing productive to do, such as when on vacation.

I went to the blacksmith shop to help out from time to time. The tools of a blacksmith were quite simple: a little furnace to heat up the iron, a bellows, a heavy iron anvil with a flat surface the size of about two palms, a few pairs of different-sized pliers, a couple of big sledgehammers, and a few small ones. The first step in forging a piece of metal was to heat the iron in the furnace until it was red-hot. To make the fire burn more intensely, the apprentice pushed and pulled the bellows. I sometimes helped handle the bellows. Once the iron was hot, the master took it out of the furnace with a pair of pliers and placed it on the anvil. Then with the pliers in his left hand holding the hot iron, Master Hu would use a small hammer with his right hand to strike the iron where required. His apprentice would then swing a sledgehammer in a full circle before striking where the master had struck. This way, the master basically directed with his small hammer where the sledgehammer should strike. The symphony of hammers striking the hot iron was loud and rapid as the hot iron was formed into the desired shape. If the iron cooled before taking shape, it had to be put into the furnace to be reheated.

I tried to help in the blacksmith shop. It was an extremely hard job. Swinging the sledgehammer required strength and effort, but also precision. Missing the spot where the master had struck would earn his glare at best or a scolding. It was dangerous if you missed the mark too much and you certainly would not want to hit your master by mistake. But unlike carpentry, which I also tried, the job of a blacksmith allowed mistakes; you could always reshape a piece of iron. But if a carpenter cut his wood too short, there was no cure and the wood piece was wasted. Therefore, the rule was "err on the short side for a blacksmith but err on the long side for a carpenter," because it was easy to stretch a piece of iron and to cut a piece of wood shorter, but not the other way around.

Later in life, I always marveled at and appreciated the skills of sculptors of masterpieces, especially stone sculptors, because they cannot make the slightest mistakes. One wrong cut with a chisel, and the whole piece is ruined. That kind of precision is just so hard for a rural blacksmith to imagine. It seems Michelangelo never missed his chisel by a hair in creating the giant statue *David*, which stands 5.17 meters (17 feet) tall. That is hardly in the realm of humanly possibility, and he certainly defied the common wisdom: to err is human. Great sculptors like Michelangelo and Auguste Rodin were truly divine.

★ ★ ★

Spring in the Gobi came quite late. It was not warm until late April or even May. We began to work in the fields in March or earlier, as soon as the ice started to thaw. Despite the cold weather, almost all boys worked naked from the waist up and sometimes, when there were no women around, we worked in our underpants because doing such hard work made us sweat. We worked almost naked was not only to cool down, but also to save clothing; we were rationed only two sets of clothes each year, and they wore out quite easily. It also allowed us to tan gradually as the days grew warmer. The spring sun did not burn as badly as the summer's. By the end of April, we were thoroughly tanned. After that, no matter how much the summer sun of the Gobi beat down on our backs, the skin would only get darker but would not peel off. My skin remained quite dark through the year, until deep into the winter.

One of the hardest parts of being a farmer was cutting wheat at harvest time. Wheat ripened in late June and early July, when the weather was hottest. Once ripe, the wheat needed to be taken in as soon as possible, typically within a couple of weeks, before the summer rains came, as the rain would damage the wheat. The short time window made the work extremely intense and fast-paced.

Harvesting wheat was done entirely by hand. We didn't have any machines for this. I marveled as I read about mechanized harvesters in foreign countries. One such machine probably would do the work of 200 of us.

The tool we had was a sickle. The Chinese sickle is different from the European kind. Chinese sickles look exactly like the ones in the hammer and sickle logo on the flag of the Communist Party. The Chinese sickle has a short handle that can be held by one hand, whereas European sickles are long-handled and held with two hands. The European sickle, a scythe basically, allows the user to work in a standing position. The farmer swings it from right to left to cut down the wheat as he moves forward one step at a time. Using a Chinese sickle, one needs to bend down, wrap one's left arm around a handful of wheat, hold the sickle in the right hand, and, once the blade catches the stems near the roots, sharply pull the sickle in your own direction to cut down the wheat. The farmer moves one step at a time after each cut, but always in a bent or squatting position. This motion was hard on the back and legs, which became sore after the first 100 meters (~100 yards). After a day's work, it became difficult to straighten up and you would ache all over. The scorching summer sun beating down on the head, neck, and back just added to the misery.

We carried buckets of water to the field, but soon drank it all. There was no shade to shelter from the blazing sun. From time to time, some of us passed out from heatstroke as the temperature rose. We had to follow a schedule to avoid the hottest hours during the day. We would get up at about 4 in the morning and work until about 11 a.m. Then we would come back to our barracks to have lunch and rest. We would return to the fields at 3 in the afternoon to work until about 8 p.m., or around the time of sunset.

This was also the time when swarms of mosquitoes would attack most relentlessly. Lake Wuliangsu nearby was a great breeding ground for mosquitoes, and they thrived, attacking cattle and people. They were big and could bite through clothing. Since we did not wear clothes as we worked, we were bitten all over and there was no way to fend them off. With clothes, the heat was suffocating and we sweated profusely. There was no escape from their attacks in the sweltering heat. While we could not feed ourselves by farming, we helped contribute to the food supply for the Gobi insects with our own bodies.

Chapter 9

Battling Frozen Lake

To Mao, politics trumped everything else, including the economy. But not even he could ignore economic realities and the need to feed 800 million people. So in the late 1960s and early 1970s, Mao's exhortation to "grasp the revolution and promote production" appeared with ever-greater frequency in newspapers, indicating that economic conditions were becoming increasingly dire.

But as production resumed in fits and starts nationwide, the need for revolution was never far from Mao's mind. Those who had forgotten to follow the revolutionary line of the Party, or those who engaged in economic activity that was considered to be capitalist, got into trouble. In spite of that, the nation seemed to be taking a breather from political campaigns to go back to work. Unbeknownst to all, another political storm was brewing.

Lushan, or Mount Lu, is one of the most scenic mountains in the country. Located in China's southern Jiangxi Province, it had for centuries been a favorite place for Buddhists to build their temples and for poets to meditate. Pleasant and cool in the summertime, it became a favorite place for Communist leaders to hold major meetings. Mao called one such meeting in 1959 "a meeting for fairies," because staying up in the mountains felt like being a fairy in the mountain's picturesque ambience.

But this place would not be remembered as a fairyland. It was during the 1959 Lushan meeting that Peng Dehuai, the former defense minister, was purged after criticizing Mao.

In late summer 1970, the Party's central committee held a ple-
nary session there. Mao had gone up the mountain in a good mood,
ready to celebrate the victory of the Cultural Revolution. But as the
meeting progressed, he became agitated. Mao smelled a conspiracy,
led by his chosen successor.

By then Liu Shaoqi, the former president, had died in prison. The
position of the president itself had been eliminated. Lin Biao, Mao's
new chosen successor, proposed to restore the position of president.
He proposed that Mao, who held only the position of Party chairman,
also be named the president of the country. Several senior leaders,
including Chen Boda, Mao's longtime secretary and ghostwriter, and
a number of generals close to Lin Biao, were enthusiastic supporters
of the idea since they thought Mao would like such flattery.

Mao thought it was a trap. The real purpose, he believed, was to
make Lin Biao the head of state and to leave Mao sidelined. After
remaining silent for a few days, he attacked the supporters of Lin's
idea for having ulterior motives. Mao was not ready to dump Lin Biao
just yet, presumably because the nation was not ready for another
shock. In the end, Chen Boda was made a scapegoat, accused of
having launched a surprise attack against the Party. Chen was kicked
out of the Politburo, stripped of all his positions, and jailed.

Mao's method was always to discredit his opponents in public
opinions, knocking them down in the minds of the public. A nationwide campaign "to criticize Chen Boda and to rectify the work style
of the Party" was launched. Mao described the supposed attack by
Chen and his coconspirators as akin to "dynamiting Mount Lu into
flatland and stopping the earth from churning."

By then the nation had grown accustomed to Mao's various
political campaigns. This one, while it seemed to come out of left
field, did not really surprise anyone. But almost no one understood
the real purpose or target of the campaign at the time; it would not
become obvious until more than a year later.

Internationally, the Vietnam War grabbed newspaper headlines
every day. Even we, in the isolated Gobi, were aware of the events
from radio reports. The antiwar movement in the United States,
especially on college campuses, was increasingly supported by the
public, according to polls. As the United States and the Soviet Union

fought real wars through their proxies, such as in the Middle East and in Vietnam, the Cold War was in danger of turning hot. The Nixon administration was looking for ways to extract the United States from the Vietnam quagmire and to tilt the balance of power in world affairs in favor of the United States against its Soviet nemesis. No one knew, not even the political players themselves, that all these dynamics would have profound implications for the United States, the Soviet Union, and China in the years to come.

★ ★ ★

It was too cold, almost unbearable. I had forgotten to wear my hat, made of padded cotton with long flaps hanging down to cover my ears, and it felt as if my ears were being frozen off in sharp, cold bites. My body was chilled to the bone. I was marching with the rest of my platoon, loosely scattered across the Gobi wasteland out of any sort of formation. There was no trail, but we were trying to walk in a straight line, as best we could, in the direction of our destination, the nearest shores of Lake Wuliangsu, about 10 kilometers (~6 miles) away.

The wind was so strong that we marched with our bodies bent forward through the swirling dust and sand. I looked up, once, and saw the rest of my platoon covered in sand from head to toe. We were walking fast to keep warm, but not fast enough. It was just too cold. I used my hands to cover my ears, which did not help much, and soon my hands were also frozen stiff. I felt pain so sharp in my nose, ears, and hands that I had to talk myself out of crying.

It was early December 1969, and our platoon had been ordered to the lake to cut reeds. It would be the first of many years I would make this journey. Reeds grow in the lake near the shore, to a height of 2 to 3 meters (~6 to 9 feet). They shrivel and dry when winter comes and the lake freezes, but they still stand tall on the ice. Reeds are made of strong fiber that can be turned into pulp to make paper. Our job was to cut them down, collect them, and transport them to a paper mill near Urat Qianqi tens of miles away.

Out of six platoons in our company, only one was lucky enough to stay behind. The rest, three platoons of boys and two of girls, were ordered to march to the lake for the assignment. I packed my belongings in a bag that would be transported on a truck. I put my cotton jacket, fur hat, and long johns in the bag because I anticipated I would feel hot while hiking. The truck could not take everything. So each of us had wrapped our bedding and a few pieces of clothing into a bundle and tied it with a travel strap so it could be carried like a backpack. We each carried our own washbasin on top of it. The backpack weighed only about 10 or 15 kilograms (~20 or 30 pounds), but walking on such a difficult surface it weighed more with every step.

After loading the truck, the entire company was assembled for an oath-taking meeting. This was just a simple ceremony to pledge to work hard. Then we set off.

It was a cloudy day with a mild wind. Soon the wind picked up as we moved forward like a herd of sheep, picking our way to avoid sand dunes and frozen ditches. At first, I chatted with my friends as we walked; we were curious about what was waiting for us.

Just to get to the lake from the company camp was a test of fortitude. We had grown accustomed to marches by this point, and 10 kilometers (~6 miles) would normally take less than two hours on a good road in fine weather. But the weather had turned, and there was no road and no trail leading to Lake Wuliangsu. Until we could no longer see it through the swirling sand, the barren Gobi stretched around us, with nothing but shifting sand dunes, gravel flows left behind from when the Yellow River spilled over its banks, frozen ditches, and the occasional dried-out thorny shrubs rolling about with the wind.

Without a trail, we had to follow our own sense of direction, guided only by the sun that filtered weakly through the clouds. The land was covered here and there with yellowish-white salt and alkali above loose soil, so with every step we sank a little into the earth. To walk on such terrain at night would be dangerous as one could easily get lost and freeze to death. Even during the day it was tricky.

Most of us boys used old rope to tighten the jacket around our waists to prevent the wind from getting in. I had never thought a rope could be such a critical tool to keep warm. Of course, wrapping an old rope around the waist was not a great fashion statement. Most women didn't use a rope belt and they collectively seemed undaunted by the cold. They usually walked clumsily with their arms folded tightly across their stomachs, each hand deep into the other sleeve, but they seemed to like this way better than wearing ropes. It probably worked as well as a rope around the stomach, but it was also difficult for them to balance without being able to swing their arms when walking with a backpack against a sandy gust. If you have seen how penguins walk, you know what I mean. They tuck their wings so close to the body that they have to sway from one side to another to keep balance while walking. Besides, sometimes we needed our gloved hands to cover our ears, which, if the cold wind was strong, could easily get frostbite, even under the flaps of the hat.

Our bodies leaned dramatically forward into the wind as we walked. Usually when the sandstorms were strong, most of us would wear a white surgical mask to protect our noses from frostbite. It helped, but frost would form around the edges of the mask from our breathing, and you had to wipe it off your eyes to be able to see.

The cold was almost unbearable, especially in my head because I didn't wear my fur hat. After Bawan, Old Cui offered his own hat to me. I refused it several times before accepting it. When we were getting close to Nanchang, wind mixed with sand came from behind, stirring up clouds of sand and dust, so much so that there was hardly any visibility. I looked at the people around me. Everyone was dirty, with dust covering us all. Our hands were frozen stiff.

The coldest part of the body was our feet, because our cotton shoes simply did not insulate them from the cold ground and the wind. The shoes we were given were no match for the Gobi cold, and so the only remedy was to walk as fast as we could.

★ ★ ★

Lake Wuliangsu is China's eighth-largest lake and today covers an area of about 300 square kilometers (~115 square miles). When I was there five decades ago, the lake was about 500 square kilometers (~200 square miles). A lake situated in the middle of a desert is an unusual phenomenon. It was created when the Yellow River changed course about 100 years ago and the diverted water settled on this low land. In fact, the entire region, stretching for thousands of square kilometers, is 5 to 6 meters (~15 to 18 feet) below the water level of the Yellow River, even though our region is about 1,000 meters (~1,000 yards) above sea level. From some locations, on a clear day, we could see the river above the distant horizon, like a shining silver belt zigzagging across the sky; this was because the riverbed was way above the land around it and had to be contained with ever-rising dikes.

Unlike the rest of the barren Gobi, the lake teemed with life. It produced Yellow River carp. It also attracted thousands of waterfowl during the warm months. The birds stayed until autumn, when they migrated to escape the severe winter. They would return in spring to lay eggs in the thick forests of reeds that grew in the lake. The fish and the fowl provided a living for a few villages around the lake as well as a couple of Construction Army Corps companies.

The lake was overgrown with tall reeds that extended from the shore several hundred meters (yards) into the lake. The reeds grew to 3 meters (~3 yards) or more in height. From the shore of the lake, one usually could see only walls of tall reeds, not a body of water. Only from a boat, once you'd emerged from the tall reeds, could one see and appreciate the lake's vastness. In wintertime, the reeds would turn yellow and dry up as the lake froze over, poking up from the ice like thin bamboo trunks. Their roots, under water, remained alive and the reeds would sprout again in springtime.

The ice in winter could be as thick as a meter (~3 feet) or more, frozen solid. Fully loaded trucks and tractors could drive on it, and in parts the lake became the flattest highway imaginable. But vehicles could only drive close to shore; toward the center of the lake, walls of ice thrust dramatically into the air. This is because ice takes up more volume than water. The lake first froze by the shore. As it froze toward the center, the expanding volume pushed the ice in the middle of the lake upward from the surface to form the ice walls. Walls of icebergs cutting through the middle of a shining frozen lake surface were a beautiful sight to behold. Except, when I was there, usually it was too cold for anyone to have the heart or mind to appreciate the scenery.

★ ★ ★

Winter comes early to the Gobi. The reed-cutting season began in the first week of December, when the lake was already completely frozen. Every winter for my years in the desert, when farmers were resting indoors, we were ordered out onto the frozen lake to cut and bundle the dried reeds before transporting them to the paper pulp mill. It was hard labor, and a harsh place to live, when the temperature often dropped to −20° C (−4° F).

The reed-cutting season was about six weeks, during which we lived and slept in shacks or huts we built, either on the ice of the lake or on the shore. By the end of the reed-cutting season, the lake looked like a bald head just after a shave.

Reeds are a tough material, like bamboo. They do not easily rot. The stubble of the cut-down reeds would stay there for a number of years. If the water level of the lake fell from one year to the next, the stubble from previous years would protrude above the surface of the ice. When you pushed the reed-cutting tool across the surface of the lake, its blade would meet the resistance not only of the tall reeds but also of all the stubble of previous years, making it doubly or triply hard to push forward.

★ ★ ★

After maybe a three-hour walk, we finally reached the shore of the lake. To my surprise, the only shelter for us to sleep in was a structure of thin reeds wrapped around a metal frame, built by an advance team directly onto the lake's icy surface. It was big enough to house our entire platoon of 30 people. Once we stopped walking I felt frozen. There would be no respite from the cold inside the tent-like shack. Inside we found there were no beds, only the ice floor covered by stacks of reeds onto which we laid our bedding. It was impossible to light a fire inside because the reeds were combustible, so the temperature inside and out was the same. The women in Platoon No. 6 did try to build a fire, I suppose because they could not take the cold anymore. Their shack caught fire and burned down just as we were about to go to sleep one night. It was fortunate nobody was seriously hurt.

There was no hot water for us to wash ourselves. We had to dig a hole in the ice to fetch water, which was so icy-cold that most people did not bother to wash. The kitchen was situated on shore, a short distance away. Those working in the kitchen used dry reeds as fuel to boil water from the lake in a big cauldron. This was our source of drinking water. The lake water tasted bitter and salty. I found it almost undrinkable.

I soon discovered, though, that the lake ice tasted pure and fresh. I did not know the science behind why ice that formed on the surface of a brackish lake would be free of the alkali and salt of the water below it. But to quench your thirst by sucking on a piece of ice would drive you crazy because it takes too long to melt, and by the time it does, it has left your mouth numb from the freezing cold. Once we began our work on the frozen lake, we would dig, chew, and suck ice every day, because there was no other source of fresh water.

A meal was served before it got dark. It was the usual *wotou*, a type of cone-shaped cornbread, and a soup: hot, salty water with a few pieces of pumpkin and almost nothing else. But the soup was warm at least, which warmed me a little. We were quite demoralized by the bad food and the cold and exhaustion after a hard day of marching and setting up camp. At the evening roll call, Political Instructor Zhang made an announcement to all of us standing in a formation facing him.

"Each of you will be given an overcoat of lamb," he bellowed, and then he paused.

We erupted into cheers. That was great! Just what we now needed. Such a surprise.

"That is impossible!" he continued.

We laughed. He spoke so slowly and with such long pauses, that our hopes were lifted by the first part of his sentence, only to be dashed when he completed the rest of it.

"But, to give you meat for every meal . . ."

Hooray! That would still be wonderful. Our spirits were lifted again.

". . . is also impossible!" he finished his sentence when we quieted down.

We had no idea what he was trying to say. So we stayed silent. He continued:

"We will give each of you two *liang* (3.5 ounces) of lamb meat in your soup from tomorrow on!"

The audience was quiet, waiting for him to complete his long breaths between phrases. After a few awkward seconds, he just turned and walked away. As he walked, he looked very pleased with himself. We were incredulous. Was this speech for real? But we applauded.

That night the 30 of us squashed together in our little shack made of reeds. Below our bed of reeds was the frozen surface of the lake. We could hear the howl of the wind outside the shack. The little wick in a small bottle of kerosene oil burned dimly with a streak of black smoke rising above it. The burning wick would waver and dim from time to time in rhythm with strong gusts of wind outside. I put all my clothing—jacket, pants, and everything else—on top of my quilt to provide some more layers. I was still shivering. My face felt as if it was freezing solid. Each breath blew out a column of mist that would mix with the smoke blown out by Platoon Leader Liu, who was lying next to me. He had swapped his cigarettes for a pipe, but he still smoked incessantly. All we could talk about was the two *liang* of lamb meat in our soup tomorrow. We had not seen meat for a long time, so this promised improvement in our diet went a long way to boost morale.

My frozen feet refused to warm up for a long time even under the cover of the quilt. I felt so cold that I curled up in a ball. Just when I was about to doze off, I felt something jump into my quilt and crawl right under my right shoulder blade. I pressed it with my shoulder and the thing wiggled violently. Then I realized it was a rat that must have been searching for a warm place. I had no idea what rats did on a frozen lake, maybe to eat the tiny seeds found in stalks of reed. I pressed hard on it, trying to kill it with my body weight. I did once kill a nest of rats in my bed by crushing them to death back in the company barracks. But this one got away.

I tossed around and could not sleep for the whole night. Either I felt very cold on my shoulders, or my ears were hurt from the cold. Whichever way I turned, it was uncomfortable. The next morning, I could not open my eyes, as they were frozen shut with a layer of frost over them. I had to gently cover my eyes with my hands to thaw out the frost. Our shoes, which we had left on the ice floor, had all frozen in place. We should have put some reeds under the shoes to prevent them from getting stuck. At night, since nobody would go out of the shack to urinate because of the extreme cold, some people had relieved themselves in a washbasin, the same one we used to fetch food and to wash ourselves. The urine in the basin was already frozen solid. We had to light a fire with the dry reeds under the basin to free the solid piece of yellow ice and throw it out.

It was time for breakfast, but none of us wanted to get out of our beds because outside it was so cold. Platoon Leader Liu got up and brought back a washbasin of warm *mizi* porridge and *wotou*. After eating, we felt warm enough to get out of bed. I quickly put on my clothes and ran out. Even though the sky was clear, it was extremely cold. My nose hurt.

I went out to see an endless forest of tall reeds on the lake. I ran around for a while in an effort to warm up. The ice under our feet was solid and slippery. A few of us took turns using a hoe to break through the ice to fetch water from below. It took a long time. The ice was as solid as marble. Finally, we got through, and we could reach water, but, just as the day before, very few of us wanted to wash our face with this icy cold water. Those who did only did so out of habit.

Going to the toilet here was much more pleasant than the open-air toilet in our company camp, which was far from our sleeping quarters, stinking to hell and so full of frozen feces that one had to stand and squat on top of them to do one's business. Here I could just walk into the reed forest and do my business anywhere without having to worry about stepping onto anything. But it was so cold.

A few of us went to build outhouses, one for men and one for women, on the shore later in the day. The makeshift outhouse had a simple design. We needed to dig a small ditch in a circle, and then we planted reeds in the ditch to form a wall. But the earth was frozen solid. I swung the hoe all the way over my head, but the impact only marked a white spot on the ground. Halfway through our work, the freezing wind began again. Here in the Gobi winter, if there was no wind, it was barely bearable. When the wind blew, the wind chill could be killing. It took us half a day with three breaks in between to finish building the outhouses.

★ ★ ★

Each of us was given a tool to cut reeds. It was a sturdy rectangular frame made of strong wooden bars on three sides and an iron blade at the bottom. The edge of the blade was rather dull, but it served its purpose. The short wooden bar of the rectangle opposite the blade served as a handle. There was another wood bar across the middle of the frame for reinforcement, so it would not wobble. The length of the frame was just about as tall as a person. To use it, one would hold the handle, lean the blade on the surface of the ice against the root of the reeds, and push the frame with all one's might. The edge would cut down the reeds, many of them with each push.

After we collected our tools, we were divided into work teams. Then we set out onto the frozen lake. We would cut down the reeds, collect them from the icy surface, bundle them together, tie the bundle with crushed reeds, which became soft and could bend like rope, and then pile the bundles into stacks for later collection. We piled bundles of reeds very high on ice sledges and then pulled the sledges to the pulp mill some 50 kilometers (~30 miles) away. The minimum quota for each of us was half a metric ton (~1,000 pounds) of reeds a day. Of course, we were encouraged to make a bigger contribution to the Party and the country if we could.

To tie each bundle tight, we would wrap the rope made of broken reeds around the bundle, pull the two ends of the rope in opposite directions with all our strength, using our knees to push the reeds together before securing the rope with a knot. It was a backbreaking job. The crushed-reed ropes were also sharp on the edges and could cut our hands through our gloves.

Soon we learned that this stop-and-go method was too inefficient. We would never be able to meet our quota of a half-a-ton per person per day. We devised a better way to work with each other. For a while, I would do the cutting by pushing the reed cutter as hard as I could, one step at a time, felling the reeds to one side. Xiaotong would collect the reeds, bundle them, and tie them up before stacking up the bundle. When I got tired, we would rotate, so he would do the cutting and I would do the bundling. This division of labor meant that at any given time we needed only one reed cutter. That saved the burden of having to carry two cutters onto the lake every day. It also increased our productivity.

We were fed two meals a day while assigned to cut reeds. The breakfast consisted of *wotou*, salty vegetables, and thin porridge, none of which was appetizing. I had to force myself to swallow five *wotou* every morning in order to get enough energy to last the day. It was so cold inside our shack that the food was cold before I was able to finish. Eating breakfast was so uncomfortable that it took serious effort just to eat and swallow food.

We would go to the lake after breakfast and come back for dinner. No food or water was provided to us during work. There was the ice, of course, which was the only source of fresh water. But without any tools, it would be impossible to break off any to chew. One could die of thirst staring at the millions of gallons of frozen water under one's feet. On the first day of work, we did not know to bring a sharp tool for digging up ice, but we soon learned.

That first day on the ice, Liu Xiaotong and I worked hard. Soon, I was sweating from head to toe. Even my underwear was completely soaked. We did not want to soil our clothes with sweat because washing them would be a serious undertaking. We typically wore the same clothes for weeks at a time. Now that I was hot, I removed my cotton jacket. Soon I was only wearing my undervest. Finally, I removed my undervest too. Bare-chested, I was steaming in the cold air. Now I was working half-naked on a frozen lake in subzero temperatures, pushing the reed cutter with all my strength, one step after another.

By about 2:30 p.m., I felt colder and colder even though the sun was at its warmest. I was running out of fuel because my stomach was empty. Soon, I was almost completely out of energy, and chilled through to my core. I put my clothes back on, one piece after another. But no matter how hard I worked, I felt cold. I began to shiver uncontrollably. We didn't have a watch so we didn't know exactly what time it was. But we could tell it was 4:30 or 5:00 p.m., time to call it a day. An official blow of a whistle signaled the cutoff time. But we had to wait for a long time before that whistle finally came.

When we got back to our shack, we were completely exhausted. I was so hungry that I felt as if my stomach was touching the inside of my back. We were all so looking forward to the dinner today because of the promised two *liang* of lamb meat in our soup.

When the soup was brought back from the kitchen, we saw only a few pieces of diced lamb meat. We asked incredulously, "Where is our two *liang* of meat?" We speculated that the cook must have given all the meat to the company leaders to suck up to them. When we later asked the political instructor what happened to the promised meat, he said he meant meat soup, not chunks of meat. Yes, we should have known better than to believe his promise.

★ ★ ★

The good thing about working in the reeds was that they helped to block out the never-ending wind. It felt quite pleasant with the sun over our heads. When we took a break, we could lie on the stack of reeds we had just piled up and enjoy the warmth of the sun.

But one could easily get lost in the forest of reeds. Once inside it, you could not see anything but reeds all around you. So deep into the lake did the reeds grow that even if you walked in the right direction, toward the shore or toward the center of the lake, you could walk for a long time without emerging to reorient yourself. If you walked in the wrong direction, say parallel to the shore as opposed to perpendicular, then you would never get out. The lake was about 50 kilometers (~30 miles) long and oval in shape, and you could walk in circles forever.

Despite the girls burning down their shack on the ice, we discovered that building a fire on the ice of the lake was not dangerous enough to melt the ice completely. Because heat rose, the ice under the fire would not melt too much. We were usually not permitted to light a fire close to reeds, lest we set the reeds on the entire lake on fire. Most of the boys were smokers and they smoked during breaks, but there was never a fire. I used to think that if we were to get lost, I would start a fire anyhow to send out a distress signal, even at the risk of starting a larger fire. For that purpose, I always carried a box of matches. But it never came to that.

★ ★ ★

In the patches of thicker reeds, the job was getting harder, requiring the full physical strength of a strong boy. I was assigned to work with HaBai, the boy from Hohhot, and Yang Shengchen from Beijing. HaBai and I each carried a cutter. Shengchen was responsible for gathering and bundling the cut-down reeds. If he could not keep up with us, we would stop to help him. We began to work with abandon. Shengchen was capable. He could gather and bundle all the reeds that the two of us cut down. When the whistle blew for break, we had already done 58 bundles. One bundle weighed 15 kilograms (~30 pounds). There were three of us, so we needed to do 100 bundles to meet our quotas. When we finished tying up 100 bundles, I felt starved and exhausted.

For the girls, the walls of reeds with stubbles on the surface of the ice were like brick walls, impossible to push the cutter through. The company leaders decided to mix girls with boys in teams. Two girls joined three of us boys to form a five-person team. Yan Chongjie and I were responsible for cutting down the reeds. Shengchen and two girls were responsible for gathering, bundling, and stacking up the reeds we had cut down. It surprised me that Chen Fengqin, one of the two girls, was almost equally as fast as Shengchen. She rushed this way and that, working hard to gather and bundle reeds without a pause and without even raising her head. She impressed us all.

During the break, the girls gave us a few *mantou*, white-flour steam buns. That was a treat as we rarely had them and even if we did it was for dinner. It seemed they only ate half their ration and saved the rest to share with us. We were touched knowing how precious these were when we didn't have enough to eat every day.

But not everyone worked hard. The other girl in our team, whom I only remember by her nickname, "Half Alive," did not make much of an effort. She had acquired her nickname, in fact, because people thought she looked half dead at work. Of course, people used her nickname behind her back. She just didn't really care to make an effort at work; and cared less about what people thought of her. She went about in her lazy and leisurely ways, contributing little to our collective efforts. She would stand in a corner, expressionless, weaving ropes with reeds slowly and endlessly. That was all she did, while careful not to cut her fingers. We often lost sight of her because we had moved ahead cutting reeds.

Reeds, when cracked as necessary to soften them up to make into ropes, could cut like a blade. Shengchen's hand was so deeply cut that blood was spurting out. I checked the wound and found the skin on his finger was cut through, exposing the fatty tissue. I tried to stop the bleeding but couldn't. It was fortunate he had some bandages with him, so I roughly dressed his wound and let him return to the camp.

We were short-handed without Shengchen. But the other girl, Chen Fengqin, was such a workhorse. I was pushing the cutter and she was right behind me collecting reeds I had cut down. I exerted all my effort in the hope of creating a distance between her and me, so that I could steal a break to catch my breath from time to time. But no matter how hard I worked, I just could not shake her off my tail. I felt frustrated that I couldn't outdo her, but I had to admire her for being so able and so dedicated.

We continued the same routine every day, going onto the lake after breakfast and returning to our shack as dinnertime neared. This was the hardest work I had experienced thus far. Every day, we came back to our shack exhausted. As the days progressed, we cleared an ever-larger swath of reeds, so that we could see the surface of the lake from the shore all the way to the horizon. As we expanded our battlefield, the clearing became wider and wider. We couldn't cut down all the reeds. There were places where the remaining stubbles from past years were so thick that it wouldn't be worth the effort. Now we didn't have to worry about getting lost, but we had to walk farther and farther out on the ice in search of reeds to cut.

What I couldn't get over was the hunger and cold in the afternoon. Some of us would save a *wotou* from breakfast to take with us. But my breakfast ration was never enough for me and there would be nothing left to take. When I occasionally saved a piece, it was already frozen solid by the time I wanted to eat it, and biting was hard on your teeth.

The food was so bad that I found it hard to swallow. Yet I had to eat it to suppress my hunger and maintain energy. I was hungry and yet eating was not an enjoyment. I described this dilemma with the food given to us in an entry in my journal on Friday, December 10, 1971:

The few bowls of mizi last night gave me extreme stomach pain, waking me up in the middle of the night. It hurt so much that it was hard to bear. I massaged my stomach to ease the pain but to no avail. I couldn't go back to sleep because of my stomachache. I had to get up to find some water. Fortunately, there was some water in the pot. I collected a bundle of reeds and boiled the water. I felt warmer after some hot water and the pain eased. I tossed and turned all night without being able to sleep.

Maybe it was psychological, but I still felt my stomach bloated when I got up in the morning. I struggled to keep up during the morning drill. It was again wotou for breakfast. I feared that my stomach wouldn't be able to take wotou today, but I was too embarrassed to ask Dr. Yin for a patient meal. I begged Yan Chongjie to help but he didn't think he would be able to get it for me, as patient meals required a prescription. Fortunately, Wang Juyuan heard of my pain and went to the doctor to ask on my behalf. Before breakfast time, Dr. Yin came and said he had prescribed the patient meal for me. Upon hearing it, my stomach already felt much better. The patient meal was wheat-flour lumps soup and two mantou. After eating the patient meal, I ate another wotou because I was afraid the patient meal would not last and I would feel hungry cutting reeds in the frozen lake. Even though my stomach still wasn't full, I didn't dare to eat any more, for fear of upsetting it again. The squad leader Wang Fuquan asked me to rest in the hut, but I declined. If I didn't go to work, it would be too hard for the rest of our team.

Mantou, made of wheat flour, were much more agreeable to the stomach than *wotou*, made of corn flour. But *mantou* was considered a luxury; we had to eat *wotou*, as well as *mizi*, the coarse fake millet, every day.

By this time we knew to carry a sharp object, such as a knife or a sickle, when going into the lake, to dig out ice when we got thirsty. I found a new use for my sickle one day when I spotted a small dead fish, about the length of my hand, floating under the ice. I gauged that the ice there was probably no more than 30 centimeters (~1 foot) thick because the fish was clearly visible. The sight was so tempting that I immediately set to digging it out. Making a hole in the hard ice with a sickle was no small feat. I dug and dug nonstop. By the middle of it, a small crowd of three or four people had gathered around me. We took turns to dig. I don't know how long it took us, but it was hours. Finally, we broke through the ice and I gingerly reached into the water and grabbed the slippery dead fish. I had to do it carefully in case I inadvertently pushed it away from the hole, wasting all our effort.

Once back on shore, our little group found a spot out of sight of the others. We cooked the fish—by lighting a fire with dry reeds and boiling it in plain water melted from ice in a washbasin—without any flavor added to it, as we did not have anything to add. After it was cooked, each of us shared one small bite of it. Nobody cared to ask how long the fish might have been dead. It was delicious.

As we enjoyed the treat, someone related a story about the good food the imperial court was served long ago. He had heard the story from Hou Baolin, a famous stand-up comedian, who had told it in one of his shows. The story had it that Dowager Empress Cixi fled Beijing after the forces of eight foreign powers invaded in 1900 during the Boxer Rebellion. After a few days of bumpy travel in a horse-drawn stagecoach, food was running out and the empress and the rest of the royal family were starving. The eunuchs found some food from a farmer's home in a poor village. It was a dish of spinach and some watery rice porridge. Empress Cixi was so hungry that she ate it all and thought it was delicious.

The empress asked the eunuch, "What am I eating?"

The eunuch said, pointing to some spinach, which was green with red roots, "Old Buddha, this dish is called green parrot with red beak. And that bowl was a soup of pearl, emerald, and white jade."

The empress was pleased.

When Empress Cixi eventually returned to the imperial palace after the crisis, she asked for the same dishes. But the palace chefs, with all their ingredients and skill, could not reproduce the food to her taste. Hunger made anything appetizing and delicious.

I wrote to my parents about my afternoon bouts of hunger and cold working on the ice. My father sent me a small bag of bitter chocolate. It helped a lot. Just one small piece would keep me from shivering so much. Unfortunately, a small bag did not last long.

Before the Lunar New Year in early February, we had basically cleared the lake of the reeds within our assigned territory. The month-and-a-half long season of cutting reeds was over. We packed up our belongings to return to the company camp. It really felt like going home.

★ ★ ★

During the winter of 1970–1971, we lived through the season in Fanshengedan, a cluster of mud huts with holes in the walls and roofs. It was a surprise that this place even had a name. The mud huts were situated on a mound surrounded by sand dunes whose shape and position would change after a sandstorm. The wind blew often. When it did, sand and dust would come in through the numerous cracks and fill the air in the hut. We did our best to patch up the holes.

Fanshengedan was a 20-minute walk from the shore of the lake. We didn't mind the walk to the work site because it was much better staying on shore than living on the ice. But the huts here could only accommodate our platoon, not the entire company. So for this season, our company was scattered in different locations nearby.

But the greatest improvement from the previous year was that we built a small stove in the hut, out of mud bricks that we made ourselves, with a small chimney going out through the roof. It is an art to building a good mud-brick stove. Bad stoves leak smoke, which can be dangerous. And if a stove burns too efficiently, then most of the heat goes out through the chimney and is wasted. Almost everywhere we camped, we had to build stoves. I became quite skilled at it.

There were of course no beds. We slept on a *kang*, built with mud bricks. Six or seven of us slept on it. The *kang* would be heated by the burning stove, and the warmth would stay for a long while after the fire was extinguished. The *kang* served as our bed as well as a place to sit during the day. We sat on the *kang* cross-legged, chatting with one another, playing poker or chess. I usually occupied a corner to read.

★ ★ ★

In the Gobi, there was little vegetation. Scattered here and there were a few tough short plants growing out of the sand and gravel, making us marvel at the resilience of life. The local people had a few head of cattle and horses, as did our company. These animals grazed on whatever they could find. Cow dung was a valuable resource, and often the only source of fuel for us in the wintertime. Dried cow dung burns well and doesn't smell so bad.

Collecting cow dung was a major undertaking and we would only do it in winter when the manure cakes were completely dry. The dung was scattered all over across the Gobi. We used either a basket or a sack to hold it. It would take hours to fill even half a sack, so the dung was precious. Dried cow dung burned easily. It only took a piece of newspaper to light it. It would burn for maybe 10 or 15 minutes. We would light the stove just before bedtime, to get the hut warm enough to get into bed. We also used it to boil water, either for drinking or for washing, using the all-purpose washbasin.

I cannot tell you what a luxury it was to be able to sit around a burning fire in the deep winter of the Gobi, especially when the wind howled like a loud whistle outside. It was a wonderfully warm feeling while it lasted. But cow dung was scarce and never lasted long. We spent so much time looking for the patties, and we burned them very carefully and sparingly, only when absolutely necessary.

Years later, when I first arrived in the United States, I was amused to hear the expression people use when strongly disagreeing with someone: "bullshit." I chuckled and thought: "That stuff used to be dear to me."

The local people had an ingenious way of catching fish. They used reeds to build an underwater fence in a part of the lake where they knew fish tended to congregate. Without being able to pass through the barrier, the fish would swim along it to a deeper part of the lake. At a certain point, another fence of reeds was erected in parallel with the first fence and the two fences formed a channel in the water. The channel eventually led to a trap encircled by reed fences. The trap, called a fish bag, was built in such a way that fish could go in it but could not back out. This whole thing was like an underwater labyrinth in the lake formed with reeds. It guided fish to swim into the trap. To catch the fish, one only needed to scoop them out of the fish bag with a net. In the summer, you could do this from a boat. But in wintertime, you only needed to stand over the fish bag on the ice.

★ ★ ★

The local people owned the fish bags. We lived so close to so much fish, yet we could not touch it, legally. The local people also knew how hungry we—the Construction Army Corps soldiers—were and how capable we were of stealing food. Locals with bird guns, which were shotguns that blew out "iron sand," or birdshot, would guard some of the bags at night. The shot killed birds, not people. But it could easily scar you or blind you. You didn't want to get shot in the face, or, of course, anywhere else on your body.

But no risk could deter the starved. The bold ones in our squad would go out at night to steal fish. In 1971, we were issued black denim uniforms. These uniforms were great for stealing at night because they perfectly blended in with the darkness. So dressed, some boys would go out to steal fish. Somehow none of our friends were ever caught or hurt, though sometimes they were shot at. I never participated in the adventures, not because I felt it was a wrong thing to do. Then again, I didn't feel it was the right thing to do. But I certainly shared the spoils.

Ding Desheng was now the squad leader. He was a 68er and had finished his first year of senior high school. He was tall with crudely cut hair and a straight back. He never ordered people around. But his leadership by example was hard to follow, because he worked like a horse. Most people had no chance keeping up with him. After work, he would be the first one to go to the lake to fetch water for all of us. He would clean and grind reed cutters not only for himself but also for others. For this, he earned the respect of us all, and also a nickname: Dasheng. It means "great saint" and was the name for the all-powerful and capable Monkey King in the Chinese fairy tale, *Journey to the West*.

Dasheng had his saint-like qualities. But he was too uptight and rigid as a person. He never joined our gossips to complain about the leaders. Although he wouldn't stop those who went out to steal fish, he wouldn't touch what they brought back. For this, we also derided him for being "too revolutionary," a term reserved for someone considered too zealous or naïve, to the point of being oblivious to the harsh and plain reality we lived in. The rest of us had long turned into cynics. It wasn't a badge of honor to be considered "too revolutionary," but at least people had some grudging respect for a true believer and hard worker like Dasheng.

One night, a group of adventurers led by Li Baoquan and Liu Xiaotong came back with some stolen fish. We were all awake, anxiously awaiting their triumphant return. It was past midnight. Baoquan pulled a couple of fish from a sack. What a catch. All of us were very happy. We immediately set to work. Someone fetched water and I scraped the scales off and cleaned the fish. Then we put the fish and water in a washbasin and we set it on the stove.

Fortunately, we had enough cow dung to light a fire in the stove. Soon the water was boiling, and the delicious smell of cooked fish began to permeate our hut. All of us were chatting excitedly while waiting for the fish to be cooked. All except Dasheng, who lay on his part of the *kang* with his head turned away from us, his eyes closed. We knew he couldn't be sleeping amid so much noise, commotion, and the smell of the fish being cooked. But nobody bothered to invite him to join the fun, knowing he didn't approve of what we were doing.

When the fish was finally cooked, we shared it. Everyone was so happy with this great and delicious food in the middle of the night, even though the fish was simply boiled in water. Just then, we heard a sob. Gradually the sob became louder. Then it became uncontrollable. We turned to see that Dasheng was crying. He was so hungry that the feast was tormenting him mentally. Yet he couldn't bring himself to join us. The pains of hunger had brought him to tears. Nobody asked him to join us, but we all knew that nobody among us needed an invitation. It was up to him. In the end Dasheng didn't have a bite of the fish. He was a man with strong principles, a saint.

★ ★ ★

The new black denim uniforms we had been issued for the winter were much more durable than the flimsy green uniforms we used to have, but they were ugly. You can imagine the sight of all the boys and girls in dark black from neck to shoes.

Working with the sharp reeds tore up our clothes quickly because when bundling the reeds, we needed to hold them with our hands, arms, knees, and the whole body. Each of us was issued a pair of white knitted cotton gloves. It was impossible to work without them because the sharp reeds could easily cut through the skin and flesh of our hands. It was also freezing cold, and while the thin cotton wasn't enough to keep warm it was better than nothing. We wore these gloves while pushing our reed cutters, and to stack and bundle the reeds. Usually they didn't last a day or two before holes appeared. Within three to five days, they would become shredded. We usually wore two pairs of gloves if we had them, both to make them last longer and to stay warm for as long as possible.

My mother had been sent to a farm in the northeast. She had a pair of fleece-lined sheepskin gloves made for me, covered in green cloth. I wore them proudly because they were better gloves than anyone else had. The sheepskin was also quite resistant to wear and tear. Even after the green covering totally wore off, the sheepskin would not break. I used them for a number of years, to the envy of my friends. The job on the freezing lake was infinitely more tolerable with this pair of gloves.

★ ★ ★

We repeated this routine of battling the reeds and the elements on the frozen lake every winter, year after year. And each year, I dreaded the reed-cutting season and hoped our platoon would be spared the ordeal, if only for once. We were never so lucky.

Chapter 10

The Longest Night

China's economic policies were modeled after those of the Soviet Union, which was a so-called centrally planned economy—what Western observers derisively called the "command economy"—in contrast with the free market economy of the West. The command economy owed its creation to Joseph Stalin, who institutionalized the state control over industry on a scale hitherto undreamed of.

This was not what Marx or Lenin had envisioned. Karl Marx believed that private ownership of capital goods, or the means of production such as factories and businesses, led to the exploitation of the workers and the concentration of wealth in the hands of the capitalists. But he also believed that socialism was not possible without a society having gone through capitalism first. By his theory, socialism should not happen in agrarian societies such as tsarist Russia or prerevolutionary China, neither of which had gone through the stage of capitalism.

Lenin went further, bringing socialist revolution to Russia and deviating from Marxism by establishing a socialist system in a peasant society. But soon after the 1917 Bolshevik Revolution, Lenin discovered that socialist economic policies did not work; widespread famine ensued. In 1921, he introduced a "New Economic Policy" or "state capitalism," which allowed some private enterprise and private farming.

Stalin, however, expropriated the private ownership of businesses, collectivized farming, and established an economic model of central planning. Stalin's Russia was able to rapidly industrialize because the government controlled so much of the nation's resources.

It was this Stalinist model that China had borrowed in the 1950s. But China was even more of a peasant society in the 1950s than Russia had been in the 1920s, and poorer. Nonetheless, Mao was convinced that socialism was the way to develop the Chinese economy, even if it meant forcing China to modernize faster than many believed possible. Hence programs like mass collectivization and the Great Leap Forward, which even Soviet leaders such as Khrushchev considered insane.

Undaunted by these failures, Mao went further still. The Cultural Revolution removed all the "capitalist tails," or moderate economic policies instituted by Liu Shaoqi and Deng Xiaoping to stabilize the economy, such as allowing peasants to own a tiny plot of land to grow vegetables or raise a pig for their own family use. Now the government at different levels controlled the production of everything, often with no planning or even a good reason, as long as it was in accordance with "revolutionary" principles. For example, when Mao said, "Grain is the key in agriculture," many communes cut down their fruit trees and stopped producing cash crops to make way for producing more grain.

The Construction Army Corps was an extreme form of a "command economy," as the system was literally under military command. There might have been some plans we were following, but if so they were perfunctory; the officers in charge knew practically nothing about planning, nor much about farming. They did not lack for ideas, but most of those ideas were quite stupid.

The Inner Mongolia Construction Army Corps was not alone. By 1971, there were 12 such corps, plus three "agricultural construction divisions," scattered across the country in remote and poor regions, with more than 2.4 million "troops" enlisted. Like ours, they were all organized like giant military units and engaged in production of one kind or another at the whim of officers who were not held accountable for the economic performance of the units under their command.

★ ★ ★

"The curtain of the night fell gradually. Soon, it was completely dark. A bright full moon hung in the sky and shone over the vast land. The work site appeared pale under the moonlight and a mood of misery hung over it. We were still working intensely under the moonlight. I used all my strength to hold up my body, which was about to fall over, as I carried the heavy basket filled with muddy soil running up the bank of the canal. I fell several times but each time I picked myself up and persevered. You should know it was not my physical strength that kept me going. It was only my willpower, which seemed endless."

The above paragraph was in a letter I wrote to my parents on May 12, 1971, two days after finishing the longest stretch of hard labor I had endured in my life.

"The mood of misery wasn't caused by the moonlight," my mother later wrote me, in case I didn't know, "it was in your mind. Cheer up."

That was all she could do to help me.

Like all the deserts in the world, the Gobi is a desert due to lack of rainfall. To grow crops, we needed to bring water by canals and ditches from Lake Wuliangsu or the Yellow River. In the spring of 1971, we were dispatched to dig the Yihe Canal, or the "Righteousness and Harmony Canal." It does rain occasionally in spring and summer, and we were supposed to complete our section of the canal before the rain came. Because of the urgency, we no longer had to walk the 20 kilometers (~12 miles) to the work site: instead we rode in large hauling wagons hooked up to a tractor. But it still took 45 minutes to an hour to get there.

Before dawn on May 9, as usual, we started out in the tractor-hauled wagons for the canal site. There was no wind. It was an unusually fine day.

The terrain along the way was covered with a thick crust of salt and alkali. Even in the burning heat, its whiteness reminded me of a deep winter snowfall. The wagons stirred up a thick dust of salt and sand that the wind whipped at us. Moments into the journey, we felt as if our bodies were made of salt dust, sandy to the last pore.

We huddled together, our eyes and mouths clenched, submerged in the roar of the engine. The salt burned into our skin relentlessly. It was difficult to breathe. We had learned not to speak, lest our teeth scrape and our lungs fill with grit.

We had by now become experienced with the weather. We knew it would be quite hot toward noon, so, despite the morning chill, most of us left our padded jackets behind. By the time we reached the canal, it was already hot. Our spirits were high, and we set to work immediately.

Although Yihe was to be a large canal, where we were working there was no water for miles. Our task was to dig up the damp red clay, put it into baskets, carry the baskets up the 2-meter-high (~6 feet) bank, and unload them at the top. Filled, a basket weighed about 100 kilograms (~200 pounds), twice my weight. The girls loaded the baskets, and two boys carried each end of a shoulder pole with the basket hanging in the middle of the pole by a rope.

We had been told that the project was pressing and important, and we were enthusiastic laborers. Our enthusiasm was boosted by the fact that young people from other companies and even other regiments were sometimes summoned to the site to help us. No one wanted to lose face. There was an implicit challenge to show ourselves to be the most persevering and strong.

Our company leaders came around from time to time to inspect our work. Anyone caught stealing a moment's rest would receive a reprimand.

I was paired off once again with our "saint" squad leader Dasheng. He had to work hard to set an example for everyone else. That meant I had to work as hard as he did as we carried a basket of earth between us with one single pole on our shoulders.

Instead of just walking with the basket, Dasheng and I ran. We would carry it up the bank and back so quickly that the poor girls assigned to fill our basket were breathless. It wasn't easy to run into the strong sandy wind carrying such a heavy load of muddy earth. Dasheng seemed never to tire. Even during breaks, when everyone wanted to lie down, Dasheng would go around trying to cheer us up. I was a hard worker, too. It surprised me to find that I could keep pace with Dasheng, for he was a lot stronger than me.

★ ★ ★

Carrying heavy loads on the shoulder had been a daily chore for me for two years. Even so, the canal work was unusually tough. After carrying more than 50 kilograms (~100 pounds) for 10 hours a day, my right shoulder had become red and swollen. It was painful to the touch when I awoke. It would take an hour or two of carrying again for the pain to subside. After a while, my shoulder would become numb. But my shoulder was in pain for the first few hours every day.

That day, the pain was quite severe. Dasheng had run so fast the day before that I had bruised my shoulder badly keeping pace. Dasheng must have been in as much pain as I, but he did not show it. As usual, we pushed ourselves to run faster than the others.

There were two physical barriers we had to overcome every day. One was pain, early in the morning. The other was fatigue, which came later in the day. When I was exhausted, I felt I couldn't get up again if I had sat down. I just had to keep going, until my second wind set in, as if I was running a marathon.

I asked Dasheng how he was feeling.

"I'm all right," he answered. "I hope lunch will be here soon. Can you hold out?"

As he said this, he stumbled. His fall was such a jolt to my shoulder that I almost fell myself. After we had righted ourselves, I told him I didn't think I could go on.

To my surprise, Dasheng let out a long howl that sounded like a battle call. Then the howl turned into a work song of the kind that I'd heard from laborers hauling heavy loads. His voice was loud and rhythmic. There were rapid words, then a chorus of "Hei Yu Lo."

The sound was startling. Everyone turned to look. Oblivious, he sang on.

I suddenly realized how music came into being and appreciated its primal power. The cry not only synchronized our legs, it also cheered us up. Dasheng became a song leader. After his words, the entire company echoed with him, Hei Yu Lo, Hei Yu Lo, Hei Yu Lo ...!

We quickened our steps.

Lunch arrived on a horse-drawn cart. It was *wotou*, salted vegetables, and *mizi* porridge. Each of us was permitted three pieces of *wotou*. I devoured mine in minutes, and there was no more. I gulped down the porridge to fill my stomach.

It was important to take in as much liquid as my stomach could hold when it was available, for there was no water in the area. Even in the small village a half-hour's walk away, the well didn't provide enough water for its own villagers. Although we brought as much with us as we could, the water buckets were drained quickly under the hot sun.

The lunch break was too short and the sun was very hot. In this vast openness, there was no place to hide. The only protection I had was a worn straw hat.

The afternoon seemed long. Dasheng became silent. But we had found our rhythm, so that even without the work song we moved along briskly.

By midafternoon, my throat was parched. The water was long gone. A trek to the village was out of the question since it would take much longer than a break allowed. Around the bank of the canal, some distance from where we were working, there was a secluded area surrounded by mounds of earth where the boys would go to relieve themselves. Since there were hundreds of people working at the site, it wasn't easy to find a place to answer the call of nature.

Dasheng had noticed that near the mounds of earth there were puddles of water from the last rain. He suggested that we go there during the next break.

Indeed, we found that there were a few puddles in the shadows where the sun could not reach. But they were filled with wigglers, baby mosquitoes. Otherwise, the water did not look too bad, although of course we were not sure if there was urine mixed in.

I was so thirsty that I didn't care. I knelt, closed my eyes, and drank to quench my thirst. Dasheng did the same. We must have swallowed hundreds of mosquito larvae. Then we went back to the work site, joking that we'd discovered a unique high-protein drink. Although we both knew the danger of that type of water, such risks had become secondary to the need to stay hydrated. We really had no other choice.

We resumed carrying earth up the bank. The bank grew higher, becoming more difficult to climb. Every step meant more effort. Our sweat and the salty dirt in the air made our skin burn. Our shirts grew stiff with salt and dried sweat. The girls who shoveled earth into our baskets had been bending so low for so long that they had to struggle to straighten themselves.

By five o'clock, my stomach was empty and I felt weak. Without food, I felt chilly even under the hot sun. There was a break and I sat down without feeling any better. I wondered how I could work the hours until dinner being so terribly hungry.

A few of us were sitting or lying in a kind of circle. Everyone was hungry, but we were happy that there was a break. We were talking about whatever came to mind.

Cui Xianchao started to talk about the famous dishes served at well-known Beijing restaurants and state banquets. He spoke as if he had eaten them hundreds of times, and, because he was older than we were and spoke with conviction, we believed him. The more we thought about food, especially good food, the hungrier we became, and the more we wanted to talk about it. I thought then that if I ever got back to Beijing, I would spend an entire day eating.

Old Cui asked us in a mysterious tone: "Do you know what type of food is the best and most expensive?"

"Bird's nest! Shark's fin! Sea cucumber!" everyone cried. In fact, I didn't think any of us had even seen, much less tasted, any of these delicacies, although we had all heard of them.

"No. The best and most expensive food is bear fetus. It's very nutritious and good for the brain." We were shocked. We had heard of bear paws, of course. But bear fetus? How could you get one?

"Well," Cui said, smiling, "That is precisely why it is so expensive. Did you know that Marshal Chen Yi once had a dish of stewed bear fetus that cost 3,000 yuan?"

In retrospect, I have no doubt he just made this up to entertain us, but he achieved his intended effect; none of us knew any better.

Since we had never heard of this dish, the thought of eating it didn't make us salivate. But 3,000 yuan for a dish? We were making about five yuan a month. So it would take us 50 years to earn enough to buy a dish of bear fetus.

"Well," Li Baoquan said, breaking the silence. "I don't want a dish of bear fetus. But I would call him grandpa whoever brings me a dish of stewed pig's feet."

"I want a roast chicken," another shouted.

"I will be quite content if someone can share with me a piece of *wotou*. Anyone saved anything from lunch?" Zhou Wanling looked quite desperate.

"How would you reciprocate such a favor?" Cui asked.

"I would call him grand-uncle." Zhou smiled, sighing.

"All right, then," Cui said with alacrity. "Everyone is a witness. If I get you some *wotou*, you will call me grand-uncle."

"I certainly will," replied Zhou.

We were all laughing. We knew that Cui had eaten his ration of *wotou*, and we seriously doubted he could produce any more. We were curious to see what trick Cui could pull out of his hat. It would be quite a loss of face if he could not deliver on his promise.

To our great amusement, Cui stood up, turned toward the women, and began to walk over. When we realized that he was not just pretending, we were shocked. He was going to ask the women for a piece of *wotou*!

At that time and place, people of the opposite sex barely even looked at each other, let alone talked to one other. Any such contact with the opposite sex was regarded as decadent or bourgeois. Love was indeed a very dangerous word. It was unthinkable that anyone would walk toward the girls and talk with them in broad daylight for everyone to see. We couldn't believe he could be so thick-skinned.

We knew that some girls could not finish their ration of three pieces of *wotou*. We didn't dare ask them for their leftovers, and they usually would not offer to share them either. But Cui could do things and get away with them because, I suppose, of his age, as he was considered a big brother to most of us.

In no time, Cui came back with a piece of *wotou*. We all marveled at his courage and accomplishment. The women were all watching us and listening. Zhou was intensely embarrassed: Now he had to call Cui "grand-uncle"—in front of the women.

"I'm not hungry anymore," he pleaded.

"No! No! Call him grand-uncle!" we all shouted and laughed.

Cui had mercy. "All right," he said. "Take the *wotou*. But I will keep your promise in reserve. You can fulfill it when we are out of earshot."

Zhou nodded with relief as we doubled over in laughter. He devoured the *wotou* in seconds. All of us were swallowing hard, too, salivating in sympathy.

When work resumed, my head was dizzy and my legs felt as if they were filled with lead. I fell several times as we climbed the bank of the canal, but I managed to get to my feet again each time without losing the shoulder pole. Dasheng wasn't faring much better. The sun was already low on the horizon. There was half an hour left in the workday and we were both eager for it to end.

Dasheng said he was going to relieve himself and asked if I would go along. As soon as we were out of sight, he took a half piece of *wotou* from his pocket. I couldn't believe my eyes. This man, well known in the company for his voracious appetite, had saved such a large portion from his meager ration for this moment of need.

He offered the piece to me, and I was nearly moved to tears with gratitude. The sight of it was so tempting. I couldn't accept, knowing that he was probably hungrier than I. But he insisted. Finally, I agreed to split it with him and we finished it quickly.

Although physically the *wotou* aroused an even stronger feeling of hunger, psychologically I knew that now I should be doing better since I had just replenished my body with some nutrients. We could continue. I was grateful to Dasheng.

Usually a whistle signaled the end of the working day around six o'clock. But time passed very slowly and we didn't hear the whistle. By seven o'clock, the whistle had still not sounded. I was puzzled and so was Dasheng, but we were all good soldiers, and no one questioned the delay.

Soon, the sun disappeared from the horizon, painting the evening sky pinkish red. It was a beautiful sight, but it was hard to appreciate the beauty of nature when we had to fight for every step with the little strength we had left. Soon the curtain of night fell and there was a chill in the air.

May 9, 1971, was April 15 by the Chinese lunar calendar, a lunar register that is designed so that every fifteenth of the month there is a full moon. There was not a cloud in the sky and the entire work site was brightly lit by the chilly glow of a full and bright moon.

We continued our work, but our pace slowed down considerably. Our hunger again became relentless. I fell more often now. We were still running most of the time, especially on the way back from the bank with an empty basket. But I more and more appreciated the time it took for the girls to fill the basket. I was secretly hoping that they would be so tired that they would fill up the basket slowly. I could see layers of white salt stains on the back of their clothes, these poor teenage girls who had grown up in big cities, now working like mules.

Stars rose one after another. At first, their light was faint against the bright shine of the moon. But more and more of them appeared. Soon the sky was covered with shining and twinkling stars. There was a light wind. We were so hungry.

At around eight o'clock, the whistle finally blew. To our shock, this wasn't a signal to go home. Some food had arrived, and this time there was no rationing. Everyone could eat as much *wotou* and porridge as his stomach could take. From this we knew that we would be there for quite a bit longer. But for how long, no one bothered to tell us. We had already been working for 14 hours.

With filled stomachs, we went back to work. My movements had become mechanical. I didn't feel anything anymore. I couldn't feel tired and I was no longer hungry.

At about 10 p.m., there was a loud whistle. Thank heaven and earth the workday was over. We threw down our shoulder poles with relief. Finally, it was time to call it a day. Or so we thought.

But we were quite mistaken. It was not the end of the day. To our amazement, another horse-drawn cart arrived, this one with another meal, one we rarely ate—white rice and boiled spinach. Out here, if we saw some white rice on the Chinese New Year we considered ourselves lucky. Spinach was even more of a treat. The sight of such wonderful food drove us crazy. Again, we were told we could eat as much as we wanted.

I'd just stuffed myself on *wotou*, wolfing down as much as I was able. Now I wasn't even hungry. I couldn't remember the last time I had seen this delicious food, and I might not see it again for many months.

I did something I had never done. I went to a quiet place and stuck a finger down my throat. This induced violent vomiting.

The discomfort was intense. But with an empty stomach, I ate a hearty meal of spinach and white rice, though the pleasure was psychological, since I wasn't feeling hungry when this meal arrived.

This unusual abundant supply of food did not bode well for us. Nobody told us when we might expect to break. The unusual food sent a message that we might have to spend the whole night working. But that would be physically impossible. Surely our leaders wouldn't try something like that.

Then an order came. The platoon leader came around to say that we had to finish the canal to meet the deadline. We wouldn't be allowed to leave until it was completed. At this, some people simply disappeared into the darkness or deserted. Most people stayed, however. But even Dasheng was nearing his limit. The wind of the Gobi penetrated my bones. Our shoes were filled with sweat. As we walked, they made a *pu-chi, pu-chi, pu-chi* noise. We counted the steps, one two, one two, one two.

Around midnight, we had a break. The temperature had dropped below freezing. Few of us had brought cotton-padded coats. We didn't feel so bad while working, but now the cold air chilled us to the bone.

Someone had a brilliant idea. He suggested that we pile up onto each other to keep warm.

No sooner had he spoken than we all heaped up on each other. Those who were unfortunate enough to be at the bottom shouted for mercy, but soon we could barely hear them. There were moans and laughter. Reluctantly, we got up. We didn't want to kill anyone.

Someone started to sing. Others joined in. It was the workers' anthem, "The Internationale."

How ironic that in a place supposedly ruled by the working class, we felt like the oppressed for whom the Belgian composer Pierre De Geyter had written the song. We sang it not to celebrate the international cause, but to resonate with the feelings of a slave.

The singing grew louder. When it ended, there was complete silence. We could only hear the howl of the wind. Then Xiaotong's voice rose in a sad song from an old movie about a slave looking forward to the return of the Red Army. Few people knew the tune, so we just listened.

Throughout the night, the North wind blows;
The North wind blows across the Mountain of Ke.
The slaves of Mount Ke
Sleep with hunger, cold and snow.
Blood and tears
Form red crystals and pearls,
Iron chains on necks chilled to the bone.
The slaves look forward,
Look forward to a short winter night.

. . .

Brothers, brothers,
When can you bring us good news?

The song aroused so much emotion that some wept. My eyes were also glossy from emotion. As in the song, we felt so much like slaves, and we too wanted the night to be over soon, but the night was so long.

Back at work again, I struggled with the heavy load. My steps became heavier and heavier. My head grew blank and dizzy. I sneezed constantly, wishing I had some warm clothes. But I had given my jacket to someone else, and he had gone off to sleep somewhere. Time was crawling like a lazy snail.

Finally, a trace of light appeared on the horizon. One after another, the stars faded away. Soon the Morning Star disappeared to give the sky over to the rising sun.

We were still working. My head was buzzing like a beehive. My whole body was numb, but my limbs kept moving.

Before we knew it, the sun beat down on us again. The heat of early summer was again torturing us. Most of the boys who had snuck away earlier in the darkness had returned. We were all too exhausted to speak. One kilogram felt like 10; each step was a hard struggle.

Finally, the canal was completed, and we stopped. We looked at our accomplishment with awe. It was hard to believe that a crowd of hungry and cold teenagers had moved so much earth.

We had worked for 31 hours straight.

I could not climb into the wagon and had to be pulled on. I collapsed to the floor. As people stumbled on top of me, I did not feel a thing. All sensation had left me.

When we got back, I did not even have the strength to wash off the dirt and sweat but fell immediately into bed and into a deep stupor.

* * *

About a week after that, we heard that the course of the canal had been miscalculated. The section we had built was too high for water to flow through. That part would have to be abandoned and a different course built.

The futility of our labor, pain, and suffering in building the Yihe Canal was but one example of many such experiences of ours. We were resigned to it. But these experiences turned us into cynics, disillusioned with the whole purpose of us being there and later with the system.

But was it the fault of our commanders, or the system we found ourselves in? At that time, I could only think about the absurdity of the system of our Construction Army Corps. It would be years later when I realized the entire economic system of China at the time made no economic sense. No wonder that we and the nation were trapped in dire poverty even though the people were no less hardworking and industrious than in any other country.

Chapter 11

Unforgettable Movie Night

Jiang Qing was pretty, charming, and rebellious in her youth. In 1935, she left her native province of Shandong at the age of 21 and became a film actress in Shanghai, the only place where films were made in China. She starred in a number of movies and acquired some fame in entertainment circles, although she was generally considered a second-rate actress. Many years later, as the wife of Mao Zedong, she would consider herself to be the sole authority on arts and culture in China.

In 1937, Shanghai fell to Japanese invaders. Jiang Qing left the city the next year and fled to Yan'an, the headquarters of the Communist forces. She married Mao at the end of 1938, when she was 24 and he was 45. It was Mao's third marriage. The union was controversial within the Party's leadership because of rumors of her checkered past, including previous relationships and marriages. It was said that the central committee approved the marriage with the condition that she not be allowed to participate in the politics of the Party.

After the founding of the People's Republic, Jiang Qing kept a low profile. She was made the head of the films section in the Party's propaganda department, her rank equivalent to a bureau chief in a government agency. But by the time of the Cultural Revolution, her star had risen. She was made the deputy head of the powerful Leading Group for the Cultural Revolution, arguably the highest decision-making body during that period. She was hailed in official media as the standard-bearer of the revolution in cultural affairs, in large part because of her involvement in the creation of the so-called Model Plays.

Mao had thought that old traditions and culture still dominated the arts in the New China. This, he felt, should not be allowed to continue. One objective of the Cultural Revolution was to replace the old cultural institutions with revolutionary new ones. Operas and plays should sing the praises of revolutionaries and common folk instead of the emperors, generals, and beauties of long-dead dynasties that were common in traditional performances.

Beginning around 1966, Jiang Qing had helped create what became known as the "Eight Model Plays," a series of modern Chinese operas with revolutionary themes. These plays were initially supposed to be models for creative artists to emulate and follow, and as such they shared the stage with traditional plays. But the storms of the Cultural Revolution cleansed all forms of entertainment of their feudal or capitalist residue. Nearly all forms of performance art—every film, every play, and every opera—were deemed "poisonous weeds" and were rooted out or banned, except for the Eight Model Plays. Radio stations played them, and nothing but them, incessantly, every day. For a country with more than 800 million people and 4,000 years of recorded history, cultural life became very simple: eight revolutionary model plays.

★ ★ ★

After a day's hard work, we usually found some way to entertain ourselves. No matter how tired, some found the energy to play volleyball or basketball. Others would sit on the *kang* playing poker or chess. Then there were the talented people like Liu Xiaotong, who had taught himself the basics of many musical instruments. He could play harmonica, accordion, violin, and the two-stringed *erhu*. Wang Dacheng, Cui Xianchao, and Yan Chongjie could also play the *erhu*. When they played together as a quartet, people would gather around and listen.

Radios were little help in relieving the monotony of our lives. All stations broadcast only the sound tracks of the six Peking operas and two ballets known as the "Eight Model Plays." Everything else was regarded a poisonous weed and was banned. We had heard these revolutionary performances so many times that almost everyone knew them by heart. In fact, although I was somewhat tone deaf as a singer and was frequently off-key, even I could sing the part of every character and perform them in full.

Cui liked to sing. So whenever Xiaotong played the *erhu*, we would urge him to sing with the music for us. He had a reasonably good voice and it was very loud—a crucial requirement for Peking opera. We all enjoyed his performances, especially the way he stretched his vocal cords, and when his singing was out of tune. We found it hilarious in those moments to see how serious he was, his face contorted with effort.

The most exciting but extremely rare event of our lives was going to see a movie. The regiment had a movie projection team that made the rounds from barracks to barracks. It was equipped with an eight-millimeter projector and a diesel power generator. In remote places like ours, more than a whole day's walk from headquarters, we would be extremely lucky if a movie was brought to a place near our barracks. Of course, it was almost always a film showing one of the eight revolutionary model performances.

One day in early summer we heard that the Tenth Company would show a movie that night. Incredibly, the movie was not one of the eight productions, but rather, *Lenin in October,* an old Russian film depicting Lenin and his comrades during the October Revolution of 1917. It had been dubbed into Chinese and released in China long before the Cultural Revolution. Somehow, this movie had been "liberated" as a revolutionary piece of art because now the leadership said that Lenin had been betrayed by the Soviet revisionist regime.

The Tenth Company was about two hours away by foot and there was no direct road. But nobody gave any thought to the distance. After all, we often walked that long each way to work. Two hours were nothing for such a reward.

The summer night fell late, so it was still light out when we finished our dinner around six and set out. Our whole company of several hundred marched en masse. We figured that if we went south, we should run into the Tenth Company. Since the movie would not start until it was completely dark, we had plenty of time.

We usually marched in a formation, but since this was free time, the whole crowd just moved along without any order at all. The boys led the way. We maintained a respectable distance from the girls, as usual.

There was a spirit of happiness in the air. Among the young men, there was chattering and laughter. The young women were much quieter, but we could hear them chatter and giggle as they walked a little distance behind us.

We were traversing the land crisscrossed with ditches. We had to tread very carefully because this was the irrigation season and water was flowing from the ditches everywhere. It would be very uncomfortable if we got our shoes wet.

Occasionally we would run into a trail that followed the direction we were headed, and we would speed up. But soon it would curve, and we had to get off the trail to head in what we believed to be the right direction. Nobody was exactly sure where the Tenth Company was, but since we were walking together, we relied on each other to find the direction and just walked south. At this time of the year, the wind blew from the south. We could not be too wrong if we walked against the wind.

We walked and talked for almost an hour and a half. The compound of the Tenth Company was still not in sight. In fact, other than the vastness of the land, we could see nothing. Soon dusk fell and it became more difficult to find our way, as everything looked the same in every direction.

"Do we know where we are headed?" someone shouted.

Nobody answered. It did seem curious that we hadn't run into the Tenth Company yet. We grew anxious. The starting time for movies was invariably nightfall. That meant that we had half an hour or less. We might miss the first part. We quickened our steps.

All of a sudden, I stepped into water above my shoes. The grass under my feet was quite tall so it was difficult to see. I swallowed my cry to avoid calling attention to what had just happened. There were at least 20 boys in front of me. They must all have stepped into the water. Yet none had let out a sound either. This was because no one wanted to become a laughingstock by being the only person who was wet—and if he had to be wet, he didn't want to spare the rest of us. So the first boy just kept silent and must have been chuckling to himself by now, knowing that everyone else behind him had also stepped into water, like lemmings. We all marched across the water silently, everyone secretly laughing. A few dozen of us passed through this swampy area without disclosing our mutual fate.

We were, however, eagerly waiting to hear what would happen to the young women behind us. Sure enough, we heard a loud shriek. One of them had stepped into the water and screamed. All the boys burst out laughing. We had pulled a trick on the girls. It was interesting that none of us had betrayed the secret, yet the first of them had let it out. I guess we were full of mischief at the time and looking for ways to entertain ourselves.

After the first cry, the women stopped in their tracks. We kept walking but turned our heads to watch. We could see them only vaguely, as it was already getting dark quickly. Behind us, they were obviously discussing what to do. But we knew they could not do anything but follow us; the road back would be equally long and treacherous. So, just before we could no longer see them, we heard some splashing sounds. As we expected, they were crossing the swampy area and running to try to catch up. They continued to follow us, at a respectable but closer distance. It was now totally dark.

We walked and walked. Finally, we heard a dog barking. We were all excited to be close to our final destination, or so we thought. But other than barking, there were no other sounds. If this had been the Tenth Company, we all felt we should have heard the sound of a movie.

To our disappointment, we had come only to a small village with a few houses. We sent two people to ask for directions. They soon came back with the news that we had made a mistake: We had been walking southeast instead of southwest. Now we had to turn west.

According to the villagers, the best way to reach the Tenth Company was to walk on the bank of a large irrigation ditch winding its way to the Tenth Company's vegetable fields. If we followed the ditch, we would not get lost again.

It was a dark night, and the bank was treacherous. Although it was wide enough to allow two people to walk side by side, the surface was by no means smooth, and there were puddles of water everywhere.

We picked our way forward, trying to avoid stepping into the water or slipping off the sides.

There were numerous occasions on which one needed to work and walk at night in the Gobi: irrigating the fields, herding the cattle and horses, and even going from the barracks to the outhouse. It was important to learn how to walk at night, especially now that it was summer, a time when ditches were filled with water. It didn't take much for the entire landscape to turn into pockets of mud. At that time of year, it was difficult to drive a tractor or a truck even during the day because it could sink into the mud, and so would a horse-drawn wagon.

I was an experienced night-walker by then, and I knew the basic rules. You should always look far ahead, not down at your feet. Otherwise, you could not walk fast, and it was easy to get lost. You shouldn't use a flashlight because then you could only concentrate on a short distance and you would lose your sense of direction. But it was good to carry one just in case. While several of us owned flashlights, we couldn't afford to buy batteries. We carefully conserved our batteries by using the flashlights as little as possible.

It was important to be able to differentiate between different types of terrain. We created a saying that served as a guide for night walking: "The shining is water, the dark is mud, and the white is solid ground." Water reflects light best, even very faint light from stars behind thick clouds, so it appears somewhat shiny. Mud does not reflect light at all, so it seems dark. The road looks white, as it is neither as reflective as water nor as absorbent as mud. Human eyes, I found, can easily be trained to see in the dark.

But there must be no artificial light at all. Even a small light will make it difficult to distinguish water, mud, and solid ground. Whenever there were a few electric bulbs in the distance, I found it difficult to recognize the road under my feet.

Now we walked briskly, picking our way around puddles of water and mud. I was silently calculating how much of the movie had been shown and how much was still left. I knew that everyone was thinking about the same thing. Having gone so far, nobody wanted to go back without seeing at least part of the movie. We just hoped that we could get there before it ended.

By then we had walked about three hours. It had been dark for about an hour. That meant that the movie was already half over if it had started when darkness fell. There was still no sound or light ahead.

Old Cui was walking beside me. He had poor vision, which became worse at night. Even with his glasses on, he could not differentiate between water, mud, and solid ground. I had very good vision. So the two of us walking together made a good pair. As usual, he was telling me stories.

He was talking about Mr. Ulanhu, the deposed party secretary of Inner Mongolia. Every year in Inner Mongolia to this day there is a big festival called Nadam, at which Mongolians gather to compete in various traditional games and sports, such as archery, wrestling, and horse racing. Horse racing is popular in Inner Mongolia, and at Nadam there are several types of races. In one of them, horses are only allowed to walk, but not to gallop. If the horse gallops, the rider is immediately disqualified. The trick is to let the horse walk at maximum speed without breaking into a gallop. Mr. Ulanhu always participated in the horse-walking event, presumably because he would have no chance to win if competing with the younger folks in such rather wild and dangerous games as "grabbing a lamb."

I didn't know until later in life that English-style riding is much more refined; the rider's position controls the horse's gait—how it moves its legs while walking, trotting, cantering, or galloping. British-style riders also synchronize their body rhythms to rise and fall with the leg movements of the horse. Once out of rhythm, riders have to "change diagonal" to get back in sync with the horse. We weren't that sophisticated, and there was no practical point in being so, either. I suppose what we called "walk" would include what English-style riders call "walk and trot," and what we called "running" would in English style be considered either cantering or galloping.

In the Gobi, we rode in the Western style similar to cowboys in the United States, and there wasn't so much attention to the form and style of riding, probably because our horses were much more suited for real work as beasts of burden than for show or other purposes. Indeed, the Mongolian saddles are much closer in style to Western saddles, as are some other details about how to saddle up and ride a horse.

Years later, I was astonished to discover that in stables in the United States and in Britain, horses aren't fed at night. In the Gobi, it would be considered a gross negligence and animal cruelty if the caretaker of a horse did not get up many times a night to add hay to the trough to feed the horses. We even had a saying: "A horse can't maintain its weight without eating hay at night." I think we had to feed the horses at night not only because they work during the day with little time for eating, but also because our feed was low in protein, whereas in the riding stables in Europe and America, the horses eat much more grain and plant protein than what we consumed as farm laborers ourselves. Some of our people even stole grain-based feed from the stables to exchange with local villagers for tofu to avoid starving ourselves. It is no exaggeration to say we were literally competing with other animals for food.

But, getting back to the story, Cui Xianchao told me that many horses for competition at Nadam were trained as walking horses. They did not know how to gallop, but they could walk very briskly. Unlike galloping horses, which would tire out after a rather short distance, a walking horse could walk the whole day. Therefore, as a means of transportation, good walking horses were more valuable than running ones.

Mr. Ulanhu was a good rider. He had been a cavalry leader in the Red Army and was one of the most senior ethnic Mongolians in the Communist Party. Even though he was already old, he had always won the walking horse race every year. Now, of course, he could no longer participate because he had been deposed.

"You know how he beat the young riders?" Old Cui asked. Then he told me that every other rider was instructed by the organizers of the game not to outperform Mr. Ulanhu. But he would have been angry if he had realized this, or if he had felt he won too easily. So the race had to be close: All the young riders would whip their horses relentlessly, while at the same time holding the reins tight so that their horses would not pass Ulanhu's. It always appeared that he had won a tough and fair race. And as he was being congratulated for being the best rider of the grasslands, he was the only one who did not know that he had been allowed to win.

We both laughed, and so did the people within earshot.

"It would be great," I said, "if we had a horse. Then for sure we would be there in time to see the movie."

"I'm afraid," Cui said, "that it will be over by the time we get there."

"I would be happy if I could see even half an hour of the movie," someone said with a sigh.

We did not have much hope. After more than three hours of walking we were tired, and the Tenth Company was still not in sight. Our purpose now seemed simply to reach the Tenth Company, regardless of whether we could see the movie.

All of a sudden, someone shouted: "Be quiet and listen!"

We stopped and strained our ears. We heard the faint sound of a loudspeaker coming from a distance. As we walked toward it, it became clearer. It was the movie.

We excitedly quickened our steps. We were almost there. We could still see no lights, but if they were all watching the movie, and if we could not see the screen, then we would not be able to see any light at all. If we followed the sound, we would find our way.

About 15 minutes later, we marched into the compound of the Tenth Company. Just as we walked in, a big crowd of happy people walked out. The movie was over.

We stood in the center of the field where the movie had been shown, not knowing what to do. We were tired, hungry, and thirsty. But that was not important. The only important thing was that we had missed the movie. We could sense the excitement in the crowd that came out of the compound. The movie must have been great.

We decided to send representatives to the leaders to see if they would run the movie again for us. We knew that the chances were slim, but we did not want to leave without having tried. Three of us, including Cui and myself, went in to talk with the company leaders. We told them how many hours we had walked to see the movie. We would have to travel at least two hours back, even if we did not get lost. We would be very grateful if they could do us this great favor.

Finally, the leaders of the Tenth Company took pity on us. The Tenth Company was located closer to the center of things, near the regiment headquarters and the town of Urat Qianqi. They knew that we were much more culturally starved than they. Moved by our determination, or perhaps afraid that we would refuse to leave without seeing the movie, and thus that any delay would mean an even later bedtime for them, they agreed.

When we made our announcement, the group cheered. I felt happy not only about the prospect of seeing the movie but also because I had helped in the negotiations.

We sat down on the ground in front of a raised white canvas that served as the movie screen. We all had good views. I found a brick to sit on, so I even had a seat. Gobi summers were dreadful less because of the heat than because of the mosquitoes. They were less of a problem when you were walking, but once you sat down, they swarmed all over you. If you clapped your hands at random, you would kill quite a few. I now had to move my hands constantly around my head and slap myself on the legs and arms.

The movie was indeed old, and the picture was no longer clear. The film must have been shown thousands of times. But the quality didn't really bother me, and I was soon absorbed in the plot. It was about how the Bolsheviks, led by Vladimir Lenin, had won the 1917 October Revolution.

One unusual scene showed some people meeting to plot political intrigues on the balcony of a theater. On stage was the ballet *Swan Lake*. A group of small swans, young women, were dancing to the beautiful music. These women were scantily clad, with their figures fully shown. I had never seen the body of a woman so exposed. It embarrassed and excited me at the same time, I must admit. And I was certain that the others around me were feeling the same way. The morality of our time was such that it was deemed risque if any woman so much as rolled up her sleeves or pants when working, or if she wore anything that showed the curves of her body. In fact, all the young women dressed in the same oversized baggy uniforms. Anything that might suggest their gender was regarded as nonrevolutionary and bourgeois.

Cui told me afterward that young people in Beijing would go to this movie just for this 30-second "pornographic part" from *Swan Lake*. For days afterward, Baoquan said that he would surrender to the Soviets if they should invade. "Russian girls are beautiful," he marveled.

The conclusion was quite touching. There was a shortage of food in Russia right after the October Revolution. Lenin's former bodyguard, whose name was Vasily, I think, was sent to supervise the transportation of grain to what was then St. Petersburg to feed the workers. He completed his task and was reporting to Lenin when he collapsed onto the floor. The doctor found that he had fainted because he was weak from starvation. I had great sympathy for this man. Like him, we were handling grain daily; like him, we were hungry and teetering at the edge of starvation most of the time ourselves.

At the end of the movie, Vasily was saying good-bye to his wife. She secretly put a piece of bread into his pocket. He hugged her, and secretly took the bread out of his pocket and put it back onto the table, whispering, "There will be grain. There will be bread."

From that day on, whenever there was a shortage of food or we were hungry, someone would say, "There will be grain. There will be bread."

It was past midnight when the movie was over. We thanked the projectionist and set out for home. The way back was much easier, and we did not get lost. We talked about the movie on our return journey the whole time. When we got into bed, there were only three or four hours left to sleep before another workday began.

The long night was certainly worth it. Who knew when we would experience such a rare cinematic treat again?

Chapter 12

Barefoot Doctor

n 1950, the year after the founding of the People's Republic of China, the average life expectancy in China was 41.6 years. In 1960, during the Great Famine, it dropped to 31.6 years. Creating a health care system for a poor, sprawling country with more than half a billion people was a daunting task for China's new rulers. The country suffered from a severe lack of medicine and a shortage of medical professionals. Medicine was almost absent in the rural areas, except for the scant coverage provided by traditional medicine men. The government thus attempted to improve access to health care by creating a new public health system designed to give priority to prevention over treatment.

In the 1950s and 1960s, the Rural Cooperative Medical Scheme (RCMS) established a three-tier system for rural health care access. The RCMS functioned on a prepayment plan that drew funds from individual contributions, a village collective welfare fund, and subsidies from the government.

The first tier consisted of village doctors, who were trained in basic hygiene and medicine, including Western and traditional Chinese medicine. Not every village had a doctor, but where they did exist, they provided the most basic form of health care. For any illnesses a village doctor could not treat, patients were sent to township health centers, the second tier of the RCMS, which consisted of small outpatient clinics staffed by government medical professionals.

The third tier of the RCMS, the county or provincial hospitals, handled the most serious cases.

The rural areas were "lacking in doctors and short of medicine," as a popular saying had it. Mao strongly pushed to bring medicine to the countryside by providing basic health care training to peasants and medicine men, thus promoting what became known as the "barefoot doctor" system. The name was derived from the need for these doctors to work in the paddy fields barefoot during planting season in the southern part of China. When the educated youth were sent down to the countryside during the Cultural Revolution, a number of them were given basic training to become barefoot doctors.

By 1976 an estimated 1.5 million barefoot doctors served China's rural areas, covering approximately 85 percent of the total population. Thanks largely to economic reforms and the de-collectivization of rural farms in the 1980s, however, the funding and organizational rationale of the RCMS collapsed; by 1984 barefoot doctors served just 9.6 percent of China's population. Soon, the name "barefoot doctor" had become passé and replaced with "rural doctor." Barefoot doctors became history, at least in name.

Today, China's health care system consists of hospitals, including primarily public hospitals and a growing number of private medical institutions, and insurance programs. About 95 percent of the population has at least basic health insurance coverage. China is scheduled to provide affordable basic health care to all residents by 2020.

★ ★ ★

I was sitting on a little folding stool in front of our room reading. It was June 3, 1971. The windy season was over, and the sun felt comfortably warm. Suddenly, I heard someone shouting my name.

It was Little Xie, the messenger from company headquarters. He had been in our squad when he first arrived from Yuyao, a town in Zhejiang Province in the south. He was tall and handsome but introverted; he rarely spoke. Political Instructor Zhang had taken a liking to him and given him the job of messenger. Little Xie didn't have to go to the fields anymore. Because he was now so close to the leaders, many people tried to curry favor with him. He took advantage of his enhanced status and went from one platoon to another, inviting himself to meals whenever someone returned from home leave with machine-made noodles or canned meat.

But Little Xie didn't forget his lowly squad mates. He was a frequent visitor, sharing gossip about what was going on at headquarters. Now I greeted him warmly and asked what was new.

He looked at me mysteriously, smiling. "Instructor Zhang wants to see you," he informed me.

"What for?" The political instructor had never summoned me before. I thought perhaps I might have done something wrong.

He wouldn't satisfy my curiosity, or perhaps he didn't know. "You'll find out soon enough. He says it's urgent."

The company office was right behind our platoon. I stopped reading and hid my book under my pillow before going to the room the political instructor shared with the commander as both office and bedroom.

"Report!" I announced myself loudly outside the door.

"Come in." Instructor Zhang was sitting on his bed, facing the door. Apparently, he was expecting me.

He didn't invite me to sit down, and my heart beat nervously as I raked my brain for what offenses I might have committed unintentionally or by accident.

Finally, he spoke. "Little Shan," he began. I was startled to hear such an intimate greeting, the first ever from the instructor. Usually, he called me by my full name. "Do you like medicine?" he asked. I was even more puzzled and did not know how to respond. I thought perhaps he was questioning my courage.

"I don't really like medicine, but I am willing to take it when I'm sick. 'Good medicine is bitter but beneficial to your health.'" I quoted the Chinese proverb and tried to smile.

"Do you know anything about it?" he asked. I didn't have the foggiest idea what he was driving at, so it was useless to try to avoid trouble. I answered him directly.

"I have read some chapters from the *Manual for Barefoot Doctors*. I was in poor health when I was small and had all kinds of illnesses. I took a lot of different drugs."

"Very good," the instructor said. I still could not figure out where he was going with the conversation. Was it perhaps my knowing something about medicine or my poor health when I was small?

Now his face grew more solemn. He cleared his throat, and I knew he was going to tell me why I was there.

"The Company Branch Committee of the Communist Party has decided to make you a medic or barefoot doctor. This has been determined after lengthy discussion, based on the recommendation by Dr. Yu. You leave tomorrow morning for the regiment hospital in Batou for training for three months." He paused, staring as if he had made an announcement on behalf of God. "Do you have any objections?"

Objections? I was almost dizzy with joy. I tried to conceal my excitement and replied carefully, reciting a line familiar to everyone from war movies. "No. I obey the decision of the Party."

"Good. In any case, the matter has been decided." The instructor fell silent, seemingly waiting for me to speak. But I didn't want to express my happiness for fear that I would show "petty bourgeois sentiment" or hints of disliking hard labor in the fields. If I had known better, I would have said a few words of gratitude, but I took his words literally. I didn't think personal thanks would be appropriate for a decision made by the Party, of which he was the physical embodiment.

Apparently disappointed by my silence, Instructor Zhang said something about living up to the trust placed in me by the Party and the leadership. Then he said, "I will expect you to give me acupuncture for my arthritis when you come back." He lifted the corner of his mouth for the first time and dismissed me.

I was so happy that I wanted to shout and somersault. But there were people everywhere, so I hurried to find my friends to tell them the big news.

Cui Xianchao said that this was the first good decision that the company leadership had ever made. Huang Shurong teasingly asked me not to forget him when I became a man of importance. Li Rongtian was more thoughtful: he told me I should thank Dr. Yu for the nomination.

But someone said that Dr. Yu had gone to regiment headquarters. There was a rumor that he might be transferred permanently. That made sense. That was why they needed a new medic.

Dr. Yu liked people who read books. He must have seen the barefoot doctors' manual on my bed. I could not get over the fact that although I had never exchanged more than a few words with him, he had chosen me.

The next morning, I packed my clothes and quilt. Most of my good friends took the day off from the fields to see me off. It was exciting for everyone that one of us had been chosen to become a doctor.

As it turned out, the delivery truck that I was supposed to get a ride with would not arrive until after 5 o'clock, and we had to go to the Third Company to catch it.

So off we went. I felt happy surrounded by so many friends, who were carrying my belongings and cheering me on. We had to pass through the compound on our way, and the people who had just returned from a day of hard work were hanging about waiting for the dinner whistle. I felt as if we made a parade.

When we arrived at the Third Company, the driver was off having dinner. Despite my urgings, my friends refused to go back to eat. When we finally got under way, I waved goodbye to the crowd. The driver marveled at what a friendly place my company seemed to be.

It was well after dark when we arrived in Batou. Through the headlights, I could see rows of houses just like the barracks in our company. Someone helped me with my belongings, guided me to my room, and then disappeared. I was given a room all by myself, apparently vacated when a squad was dispatched to work somewhere else. It wasn't until after I was in bed that I realized I hadn't had dinner. I went to sleep on an empty stomach.

At breakfast, I saw that there was much stricter rationing here, presumably because people here weren't engaged in any types of hard labor. I was only given one piece of *wotou*, one bowl of corn-flour porridge, and some salty vegetables. Usually, I could eat four or five pieces of *wotou*, but there was no more. Well, I thought, now that I didn't have to work in the fields, one piece was probably enough to last the morning.

I would be trained in basic medicine and taught how to treat common illnesses. The training sessions were held in a large warehouse. Most of the 20-odd students were medical workers from the regiment hospital. The rest were, like myself, from different companies. Most of them had considerable medical experience already and were here to improve their skills. I was one of the very few who had never been exposed to medicine, other than taking it.

The instructors were from the regiment hospital. Unlike barefoot doctors, who received only the most rudimentary training, these were real doctors who had had formal medical education in military medical schools.

In the first days, an instructor went over the anatomy and all the systems of a human body with the aid of a large picture. The last part of his lecture was on the reproductive system. He went through this rather perfunctorily. The vast majority of our patients, the Army Corps soldiers, would be teenagers too young to worry about reproduction. Besides, the leadership of the Nineteenth Regiment had issued an order that soldiers were "forbidden to develop a love or marital relationship" for at least three years. If we dealt with local peasants, the instructor said, it would be our duty to reduce their rate of reproduction by educating them in population control and by dispensing birth control devices.

After the "Western analysis of anatomy" class, another instructor talked about how Chinese medicine viewed the body. Instead of talking about different "systems," Chinese medicine was based on the study of the five *zang* and six *fu*. To me, Chinese medical theory seemed much more complicated and philosophical than Western medicine. The doctor used terms similar to those in Western medicine, but they had different meanings. For example, one of the five *zang* of the human body was the heart. But the symptoms of "heart problems" in Chinese medicine included insomnia, mental disturbances, nosebleeds, and premature ejaculation. The concept of high blood pressure did not exist.

The anatomy classes were followed by study sessions on Chairman Mao's works. The instructor told us that if we were armed with the theory behind Mao Zedong Thought, we would better serve our patients.

To dispel any doubt about the connection between Chairman Mao's teachings and medicine, he related a story about "capturing the principal contradiction."

Mao had written a long essay, "On Contradiction," in which he espoused the concept that contradictions existed everywhere and in every problem or issue; to solve a problem, the key was to find the principal contradiction. "Once the principal contradiction is captured, everything else will be resolved as if being cut through by a sharp knife."

The instructor said, on a hot summer day in a big city, a pedestrian suffered a heart failure and collapsed. A doctor happened to walk by, and he went over to find the man unconscious. He felt for a pulse but there was none. The situation called for immediate action. He started to apply pressure to the man's chest but was unable to restart the heart. The only hope was direct hand massage to the heart. But that would require open-heart surgery.

Well, the instructor continued, the doctor happened to have an old pocketknife. On the spot, in front of the crowd, he used it to cut open the man's chest. Then he applied direct massage. When the ambulance arrived, the heart was beating. In the hospital, the man was given large doses of antibiotics, for the pocketknife operation would almost surely lead to a bad infection.

"Assuming you were a trained surgeon with years of experience, would you have dared to open the chest of a patient with a pocketknife amid a crowd on the street?" the instructor asked.

We all looked at one another. Everyone knew that open-heart surgery was a major operation. It was hard to believe that someone had done it with a pocketknife on a street. Of course, none of us had ever seen that type of surgery. But even for those few who had some idea, the scene was hard to imagine. We all shook our heads in disbelief.

"Why not?" the instructor pressed us.

Someone raised his hand hesitantly. He said that first, it would be impossible to tell if a direct massage would revive the person; second, how could he stop the bleeding without any help; and third, there would be a good chance that the infection would kill the patient anyway. The risk of failure was too great.

I nodded my head in agreement.

"Risk!" the instructor exclaimed. "A revolutionary isn't afraid of risks, because he is not concerned about himself. For a revolutionary doctor, the task is to treat the patient, regardless of the chance of losing the patient or humiliating himself before others. As for the technical problems, Chairman Mao guides us to the answer in his teachings on capturing the principal contradiction." The instructor paused, creating an effect of suspense. Seeing that we were all listening, he continued, "There were many contradictions in this situation. If he didn't open the chest with his pocketknife, the patient would surely die. If he did, there would be bleeding and infection. But if you compare death with bleeding and infection, which was the biggest problem?"

Obviously, it was death.

"The doctor, following the teachings of Chairman Mao, decided that death was the principal contradiction and other issues were secondary. Once the principal contradiction was resolved, other problems would in turn become principal contradictions to be dealt with. So he opened the chest. Once the man was brought back to life, the medical workers could tackle the problems of bleeding and infection. So you see," he concluded triumphantly, "Chairman Mao's teachings are sharper than a surgeon's scalpel."

I had to scratch my head at this feat of logic. I had been unaware that Chairman Mao's teachings had such universal applications.

Dr. Yu taught the sessions on diagnostic techniques. I was very grateful to him, so I was extremely attentive. Dr. Yu was a rather serious person who seldom smiled. He would suddenly call out a name and ask the victim to interpret what he had discussed. Because of these surprise attacks, most people were a little afraid of him.

One day the subject was peritonitis, the infection of the peritoneal tissue that covers the inner stomach. Dr. Yu was describing some causes and symptoms. Toward the end of the lecture, he said that gastric puncture caused by an ulcer could also lead to peritonitis. Then he turned from the blackboard and asked:

"Could somebody tell me why gastric puncture can lead to peritonitis?" To my horror, he was looking at me.

I could feel the blood drain from my face. I was the only one who had never had any medical experience. *Oh, please, Dr. Yu, I have no idea why gastric puncture can lead to peritonitis*, I thought.

I heard my name. I searched Dr. Yu's face for mercy, but there was only inquisitive gravity.

I stood, with a sense of despair. But suddenly a thought came to me. I heard my voice tremble, "A gastric puncture would cause gastric juice to leak out. Peritonitis could be caused by the irritation of the peritoneum by the gastric juice."

I did not know if I had made any sense. But Dr. Yu smiled broadly and announced emphatically, "Absolutely correct."

I grew dizzy from nervousness and relief. I was so happy that I hadn't let him down—everyone knew that Dr. Yu had selected me for the course.

During the break, a young woman named Liu Ying came over and asked me how many years I had studied medicine. She could hardly believe I had never studied before.

"No wonder. I could see you were very nervous just now. You were trembling and your face was as pale as a piece of white paper. But how did you know the answer, then?" she asked.

When I told her it was intuition and logic, she shook her head in disbelief. I asked her how long she had been a barefoot doctor.

"Two years. But I haven't studied medicine either."

It was my turn to disbelieve. How could she practice medicine for two years without having studied it?

"Simple. At first, I just did what the military doctors asked me to do. After I had some experience, I could treat some minor problems. 'Learn from practice,' you know," she said, quoting a line from Mao.

It was little wonder that there were so many "medical accidents" in the regiment and division hospitals. I had heard, for example, how a woman once had an operation on her stomach. After two weeks, her wound still had not healed, and more and more pus kept coming out. When she went back, the doctors found through an X-ray that they had left a pair of surgical scissors in her stomach. So she had another operation to retrieve the scissors. This time, they left a roll of gauze in her stomach. She had to be operated on for the third time. Li Baoquan once told me the best thing the doctors could do would be to install a zipper. That way they could open her stomach whenever they wanted.

We studied both Western and Chinese diagnostic techniques. While Western medicine relied heavily on instruments and lab tests, a doctor of Chinese medicine had to know how to *bamai*, to feel the pulse. The index, middle, and ring fingers were used to sense many things about the pulse, but it was very difficult for an inexperienced doctor to discern the very subtle differences. The doctor instructed us to feel each other's pulses to practice.

This "practicing on each other" method of learning soon became a little scary. We had to give each other injections. I was not afraid to play doctor, but I was most reluctant to be practiced upon. The instructor recited Chairman Mao: "There must be sacrifice when there is a revolution." This little sacrifice, we were told, was nothing in the service of learning useful skills for the revolution. We should feel happy. But whenever I was practiced upon, I cringed, closed my eyes, and "prayed" the words to myself over and over: "There must be sacrifices."

To this day, I wonder how doctors learn all their techniques without being tortured or torturing others. I had saline injected into my buttocks numerous times, acupuncture all over my body, and blood drawn repeatedly from both arms. These were all unpleasant experiences. I, in turn, inflicted the same pleasure of learning upon my fellow medical students. There was only one exercise in which I absolutely refused to participate: intravenous transfusion. I couldn't bear the thought of having my blood vessels loaded with saline. Fortunately, when I said that I would certainly pass out, the instructor spared me.

Acupuncture was a little better. Each of us practiced on ourselves. Everyone was given a small box containing different-sized needles. We were supposed to implant these on the correct points on our own bodies. I found this difficult to do. I was able to push the needle into my skin, but no matter how determined I was and how hard I pushed, I just couldn't feel what the instructor told me I should. He said I was too tense. But how could I not be tense, pushing a needle into myself?

My first attempt to apply what I had learned of diagnostic techniques was on myself. I began to suffer from insomnia. I would be awakened by the slightest sound, such as the wind blowing past a window. At first I thought I was studying too hard without sufficient exercise, so I started to run long distances in the morning and stopped reading half an hour before bedtime. But I still could not sleep.

After consulting several books, I realized my insomnia was probably caused by malnutrition. Once I began my medical studies, I became a "person detached from production" for rationing purposes, meaning my rations were only two-thirds or less of what they had been when I belonged to the category of "person in an agricultural company."

I had never felt that the ration for an agricultural worker was enough. The "detached from production" ration left me hungry almost all the time. Besides, our daily diet had consisted only of corn flour, sorghum, and pumpkins ever since I had first arrived, with no meat and few vegetables. That was certainly not enough nutrition for a 17-year-old.

Although I thought I had accurately diagnosed my problem, there was nothing I could do about it. If there was not enough food, there was not enough food. I wrote a long letter to my father and asked him to send me a package of food by mail, especially wheat flour, canned food, and chocolate.

The training course had been scheduled to run three months, but apparently the regiment leadership had decided that the training of a barefoot doctor did not require so much time. The instructors had to squeeze all the classes into five weeks. Just when I thought that I was getting a slight taste for the medical profession, the training was over.

Dr. Yu arranged for me to go out on a fishing boat on the last day of my stay, since Batou was located right next to Lake Wuliangsu. It was a dinghy with a sail, manned by two boys from the Eighth Company. Their job was not to catch fish, but to ship cargo to another company.

I had never been out in a boat on the lake, although we already had spent two winters cutting reeds on its frozen surface. This was summertime and there were numerous waterfowl. I expected a fun trip.

We set out early. One boy used a pole to propel the boat, while the other held the rudder. We moved slowly through thick forests of reeds. There were throngs of mosquitoes everywhere. Fortunately, we had raincoats that we used to cover our heads and arms. I was told it would be a bad idea to swim near the reeds, for the mosquitoes could kill you.

When we cleared the reeds and moved out onto the lake, the mosquitoes disappeared. There was a vastness of calm water dotted with fishing boats. The boys raised our sail and the dinghy really started to move. I felt I had stepped into a fairy tale.

We passed a fish bag, and the boys netted out some large carp. This would be our lunch. Each one weighed 5 or 6 *jin* (~5 or 6 pounds). I thought that two of them would be sufficient for the three of us, but the boys smiled and said that the way they prepared the fish, the three of us would need five.

I wanted to help cook, but they told me just to watch. To my astonishment, they cut off the heads and threw the bodies back into the water. Having been hungry so often and for so long, I could hardly bear to see such senseless waste.

The boys said the most delicious part of a carp was its head. They had to throw the bodies away because there was no way to keep them fresh. But whenever they could get hold of some cooking oil they could make dried shredded fish, which was easy to store. Once we got back, they would give me some to bring back to my "poor brothers."

The fish heads were indeed delicious. But there was not much meat on them. The boys said I must have starved to death in my previous life, because I just could not eat enough. I told them I couldn't remember the last time I had fish. And I had never had fish so fresh.

★ ★ ★

The training class at Batou provided but the briefest introduction to medicine. I realized there was a great deal more to learn, but "learning from practice" was the only way. Fortunately, there was an advantage to practicing medicine on a farm: There was no specialization to speak of, so I got a taste of everything. If someone was sick, I had to find out what was wrong, prescribe medication, fill the prescription, sometimes administer the medicine through infusion or injection and, occasionally, if the illness was serious, nurse the patient.

Including myself, the Fifth Company now had a rather large medical force. A Dr. Yin had recently been transferred in to replace Dr. Yu. Because Dr. Yin had been accepted into a military medical school shortly before the Cultural Revolution, he was nominally a medical school graduate, although he had not received much real medical education before his school was shut down. He was in his late twenties, tall and with a flat face. He stuttered, especially when he spoke to women.

There were two other medics. One was Wang Xinquan, a boy from Tianjin. He was taller than most boys, but his mannerism was almost feminine. He spoke softly. When he walked, his hips swayed more than a woman's.

There was also a young woman four or five years older than me named Gao Xiaorong; she was short and somewhat overweight. To be sure, most of the young women in our company looked chubby whereas most boys looked emaciated, probably, I gathered from some readings, because all we ate were carbohydrates, which were more easily turned into sugar and fat in young women than in young men.

Dr. Yin usually stayed in the company clinic. So did Gao Xiaorong. Wang Xinquan would go to the fields with the platoons occasionally. I was the only one who went to the farm field with my platoon every day. I was truly a barefoot doctor who was not "detached from production," although in the Gobi, unlike in the rice paddy fields in the south, nobody took off their shoes when working. I enjoyed this, because I didn't want my "poor brothers" to think that I was now different from them.

I reported my return to the political instructor as soon as I got back from Batou. He seemed pleased to see me and asked me not to forget that this opportunity to practice medicine had been given to me by the Party. I should work hard to live up to the expectations of the Party. He did not need to mention that he represented the Party. In fact, he was the Party.

"I need acupuncture for my arthritis. Gao Xiaorong is no good. When you think you are good enough, come treat me," he said before I was dismissed.

I knew that my acupuncture skills were limited. In the hands of a good acupuncturist, a patient should not feel it when the needle goes in, and he should feel only numbness and a sense of swelling after the needle has reached the right depth. I could not achieve this effect on myself. Perhaps, as my instructor had said, this was because I could not relax.

Li Baoquan volunteered to be my guinea pig. He said gallantly, in Tianjin ruffian tradition, that he was not afraid of "stabbing both sides of his ribs with a sharp knife for the sake of his friend." He was true to his word. Every day after dinner he would lie on the *kang* allowing me to plant needles all over him. When I hurt him he would curse me for being clumsy and stupid. But I was happy to see that I was making progress with my skills every day.

Soon I had settled back to the daily routines of farm life. In the morning, I would go out with the platoon to work in the fields, carrying a first-aid bag. Every evening after dinner, while the others relaxed, I went to the company clinic. I fell in love with medicine. My work was more tiring now, but I really enjoyed being able to help those who were sick.

The clinic was where I spent all my spare time. When there were no visitors, I would write down the Latin names of all the drugs we had. Dr. Yin said it was not necessary, and besides, without knowing anything about Latin and without knowing how to pronounce the long words, it would be difficult to remember so many. But I was not discouraged. I enjoyed being able to memorize them.

I remembered my promise to the political instructor to treat his arthritis. I was flattered by his insistence and I appreciated fact that he took me, a freshman in the profession, so seriously, when he could have gone to the other two barefoot doctors. After much practice on Li Baoquan, I was ready to give it a try.

I went to consult with Dr. Yin to get a better idea of the instructor's case. Dr. Yin was strictly a doctor of Western medicine. As far as I knew, there was no cure for arthritis in Western medicine. Aspirin could help relieve the symptoms, but it would not provide a cure. Acupuncture did not promise a cure either, but it might alleviate the problem without the irritating side effect of an upset stomach from aspirin.

Dr. Yin seemed uninterested in my inquiries about the instructor's medical history. While listening to me, he kept his eyes fixed on the cover of a medical manual. Without raising his head, he said, stuttering, "The in . . . instructor is in excellent health. He won't be ki . . . killed by your acupuncture. So, just do whatever you want, he'll be fine."

I was a little annoyed. I would not have called somebody with arthritis in excellent health. Dr. Yin did not seem serious about the matter. Could it be that he was scornful of acupuncture? After some hesitation, I said, "Dr. Yin, you know I am a neophyte at this. I really need your help. It would give me a better idea of the best way to treat him if you would tell me his medical history."

There were no such things as medical records in our camp. The company clinic was supposed to provide only basic medical help for daily ailments. Nobody ever thought it necessary to keep a record. I would not be able to find out anything about the political instructor without Dr. Yin's help.

He moved his stare away from the medical book and smiled his typical embarrassed smile. "I cer . . . certainly would like to help you in any way I can," he said. "But you know that there is little I can do to help him. I have given him aspirin re . . . regularly. But I . . . I think he throws away more than he takes. He said he was for . . . getful. It must be that his problem does not bother him much. The instructor is a man of much . . . much . . . much thunder but few raindrops. So don't be too serious about it."

I did not like what I heard. I thought that as medical professionals we should care deeply about someone's medical problem. Obviously, there was nothing I could gain from Dr. Yin.

I took a rubber knee hammer and went to the political instructor's bedroom. I found him and Company Commander Zhang playing poker with two young women. I felt uneasy about disturbing them and stood there with a silly smile on my face.

The political instructor raised his head and beckoned me closer. I reported that I had come to check on his knees. I said I was ready to treat him, but I could come back when he was free.

"Good, good," he said, "Why don't you sit down and have a game of poker with us? Are you good at Advantage?"

How dare I? What would people say if they knew I had played poker with young women in the political instructor's room? Besides, I was not a poker player.

So I politely refused, saying that perhaps I should come back another time. I could see that the political instructor was not too pleased, but he turned to the others and said, "I knew that Little Shan would be a good barefoot doctor. See, he is now ready to treat this stubborn problem of mine. I would like to go to the fields every day with all the soldiers. But this damned arthritis troubles me all the time."

"Political Instructor, at your advanced age, you should take more rest. Don't risk your health with us young kids," a young woman by the name of Wang Lianxi chimed in. She was with the cooking squad and was rumored to be a big *mapijing*, or ass-kisser.

I took a hard look at this woman. How could she be so shamelessly flattering? The political instructor was no more than 40, and she was talking about his advanced age. Then I caught the company commander resting his hand against her thigh. Noticing my glance, she brushed him away.

I was disgusted to see the commander's contented smile in the midst of the women. I thought it would be best if I left.

The next day, I came back and examined the instructor's knees. I was puzzled by what I found. Everything seemed to be all right. His reflexes were excellent. But he said that his knees were very painful and that he had had this condition for many years. He also told me that he regularly took the aspirin prescribed for him by Dr. Yin. But he was reluctant to submit to a blood test. "Why don't you just give me acupuncture from time to time?" he suggested.

I did give him acupuncture that day, but I did not feel that I really knew what I was doing since I did not understand what his problem was. I told Dr. Yin about my puzzlement, and he simply said that acupuncture should be good for the instructor.

The next day, Instructor Zhang came to our platoon and told me in front of everyone how much better he felt after the acupuncture. When he left, Li Baoquan said that the political instructor should thank him because he had acted as my acupuncture guinea pig.

Soon after, we received an order from the regiment that everyone should be tested to find out their blood type as part of our preparations for war, in case there was a need for a blood transfusion. For two days we were busy drawing blood samples. I made sure to take a little extra from the instructor because I wanted to see how bad his arthritis was.

I tested his blood twice. Both times, the result turned out negative. The test for arthritis was the simplest of all tests, and there was no way I could have made a mistake. That turtle egg (a term of endearment similar to "son of a bitch") did not have arthritis at all. He was just inventing a reason not to go to the fields. That pot-bellied lazy pig. Hypocrite. He was even worse than the company commander, who did not pretend to need an excuse not to work. I felt stupid for having spent so much time thinking about how to treat him.

I went to tell Dr. Yin what I had found. He said indifferently that he had told me the instructor was in excellent health. No wonder he was not interested. He had known this all along.

I told some friends the story about the political instructor. Everybody agreed that the instructor was the biggest turtle egg under heaven. But all of them advised me to keep quiet about it.

"The Monkey King could not somersault out of the Buddha's palm," Li Baoquan said. "Instructor Zhang could make your life miserable if you offend him. If he wants you to treat him again, just plant your needles on all the wrong points and let that turtle egg have a good time." Fortunately, the instructor did not ask me for acupuncture again. I thought that either Dr. Yin had told him what I had found or he thought he had already achieved his purpose by letting everyone know that I had treated his arthritis. For weeks, I thought all the time about what I should say if he came back. I could not stop thinking about what a turtle egg he was.

* * *

The clinic was always busy between work and curfew times, especially after dinner. Some complaints varied with season and weather, but most remained constant throughout the year. The most frequent problems included stomachache, dysentery, back pain, arthritis, frostbite, heatstroke, heartburn, head colds, and minor gynecological problems such as cramps.

It was simple enough to treat most of these common issues, but it was difficult to eliminate the causes. Stomachache and dysentery were caused by bad food and unclean water—all our water was contaminated by dirt as well as human and animal waste. The kitchen usually boiled its water first, but when we were working in the fields we often had no choice but to drink from ditches. In summer, stomach problems were routine.

We sometimes tried to use traditional Chinese medicine to prevent diseases. We put alum into the water to make the mud sink to the bottom. In summer, I would collect the stems of eggplants, dry them in the sun, and store them for use in winter. The liquid from boiled eggplant stems was effective for frostbite. But most diseases were caused by poor living conditions and hard labor, which could not be prevented.

Occasionally, there were more severe cases of illness. The first really sick patient I treated was Cui Xianchao. He came down with a high fever and was vomiting constantly. At first, I thought it was just a common cold and gave him some aspirin and other drugs to relieve his symptoms. Overnight, his case worsened. He coughed so hard that he could not sleep—and neither could the people who shared his room.

Soon Cui became severely dehydrated, and Dr. Yin ordered that he be given an intravenous transfusion of normal saline and penicillin injections. I also gave him injections of metamizole sodium, known as analgene, to relieve his fever and pain. Because he needed full-time attention, I was excused from going to the fields. I nursed him as he lay there panting. I read him books out loud and, when he was up to it, we would discuss the contents.

No sooner had Cui Xianchao recovered than Liu Xiaotong became sick. He had such a severe toothache that he could not eat or sleep. His left cheek was so swollen that his face was distorted. His gums bled. But there was nothing we could do other than give him antibiotics. He urgently needed to see a dentist.

The nearest one was with the division hospital in Urat Qianqi. With Dr. Yin's help, I secured the permission of the political instructor to take him there. But the truck that brought our food from Urat Qianqi every two weeks would not arrive for a week, and the company leaders did not think that an illness as insignificant as a toothache was worth dispatching a special truck. So poor Xiaotong had to wait.

While we were waiting, Xiaotong was absolutely miserable. He moaned constantly, both hands over his swollen face. To relieve his pain and give him a few hours of sleep, I gave him injections of dolantin, the strongest analgesic we had. But after a few days, I had to stop because I was afraid he might become addicted.

It seemed there had to be something else I could do to relieve the pain, and I consulted some traditional Chinese medicine books. In one of them, I found a remedy for toothache in the form of the poisonous yellow liquid a toad squirts from its warts when threatened. Since the liquid was poisonous, the book warned, it had to be used sparingly and carefully.

Xiaotong, desperate, was quite willing to try the "toad treatment." So I went out and captured a large grotesque-looking toad and put him in a washbasin. I gently touched his back with a cotton swab. I could see he was unhappy: his belly started to grow. I applied a little more pressure, palpating the warts. Suddenly, yellowish liquid squirted out. The force of it was such that some of the goo landed on my hand. I immediately swabbed up the rest. Xiaotong, standing by, opened his mouth and allowed me to spread the "medicine" along his gums.

After a bit, he announced that his gums were numb. The medicine worked. Encouraged, I collected more yellow ooze in the same way.

Unfortunately, the toad became uncooperative after a while. There was no way that I could preserve this "toad product," and Xiaotong's numbness lasted only a short while. After several days of this unorthodox treatment, Xiaotong and I gave up, concluding that Western medicine was more convenient, and did not taste nearly as bad.

One day, Dr. Yin asked me to give an intramuscular injection to a young woman of the Fifth Platoon. She had been in bed for several days. Dr. Yin could not find anything wrong with her and concluded that she was suffering from hysteria. But when the pain attacked, she rolled around, sometimes falling onto the floor if no one caught her. Several people had to hold her down for the injection of pain reliever.

This went on for several days, and I became uneasy about the therapy. I suspected that her pain was probably more psychological than physical, and that the injections were probably more effective on her mental state than anything else. I decided to try something different.

I took a syringe filled with saline and a little harmless vitamin B12 and went to her dormitory. The liquid vitamin B12 was an unusual pink. I told her we had just got hold of some imported medicine that was exactly right for her. I asked her to steel herself, because this special medicine would be painful when injected. She grew tense and made an excuse to avoid the treatment. But I insisted, telling her this would take care of her condition. The placebo effect worked. This was the last we heard of her pain. She was cured once and for all.

As Construction Army Corps soldiers, we were privileged to receive free medical care. We barefoot doctors were poorly trained, but at least we could provide basic care and administer some medications. If the problem was beyond our skill, we could send the patient to a hospital. But for the local peasants, medicine was a luxury. They had to pay if they came to our clinics, for they were not part of the same administrative system. Many of them had never been to a doctor in their entire lives.

One day, when Dr. Yin happened to be away, I was on duty when a local peasant mother in her thirties came in with a three-year-old boy in her arms. The little boy's face was red, his lips were blistered, and his eyes were tightly closed. He was hot to the touch and had a high fever.

The woman was crying. I could tell at a glance that the boy was at risk of dying. His mother said he had been having convulsions.

Normally we would send a seriously ill patient to the division hospital in Urat Qianqi. But I was afraid that the child would not survive a bumpy journey in a tractor or truck, even if we could find such a vehicle. I decided I had to treat him myself.

As I examined the boy, I was filled with fear, knowing he could die at any moment, literally in my hands. But I did not have time to be afraid. I listened to his lungs and could hear the moist rale and shallow respiration through the stethoscope. His pulse was weak and rapid. I concluded that he was suffering from lobar pneumonia.

The most urgent thing was to bring down the fever and stop the convulsions. I also had to apply antibiotics to stop the respiratory infection. I sent someone to fetch Gao Xiaorong, my fellow barefoot doctor, and set to work.

The clinic had only two little rooms, one of which served as a pharmacy and the other as a treatment room. There was nowhere I could ask the mother to go, so I let her stay in the room. Between sobs, she told me she had not come earlier because she had no money to pay for a doctor.

Gao Xiaorong came rushing in. She had become a barefoot doctor two years earlier than I and was more experienced. She agreed with my diagnosis and plan, and we set to work.

A test of the boy's leucocyte count, a type of infection-fighting white blood cell, confirmed my diagnosis. We gave him an injection of analgene to bring down the fever. Gao gave him a skin test to determine if he was allergic to penicillin and streptomycin. We were both holding our breath because if he were, we would be out of options. But he was negative, and we gave him a large injection of a combination of both antibiotics. Then we put him on intravenous transfusions of both normal saline and glucose. Throughout this process, the boy did not utter a single cry. I became more and more scared. What if our treatment failed? We had no backup plan. He could die if this did not work.

Now we had to wait for results. The mother had been sad when she first came in, but now she looked frightened. I allowed her to come and sit by her child, but seeing all the tubes, she dared not touch him. I felt pretty desperate, too. All I could think was, "Please don't die."

Gao Xiaorong and I took turns bathing the boy's body with alcohol-soaked cotton to help bring down the temperature. While I was not doing anything, I held his hand as if to inject energy from my body into his.

To our delight, the boy's temperature started to subside shortly before dinner and the convulsions stopped. The mother stopped sobbing. By bedtime, his breathing and pulse had become less rapid and slowly normalized. We gave him more antibiotics. At nightfall, the mother was calm enough to go back to her village to report the news to her family.

I stayed with the boy throughout the night and added to the transfusion bottle several times. Shortly after dawn, Gao came and told me to get some sleep. I was so tired that I fell asleep despite the noise of the day. It was midmorning when I woke up again.

I could hear people talking before I reached clinic door. I rushed inside to find the boy awake, his big head leaning weakly against the pillow. His mother was showing him a homemade toy. I knew he was out of danger.

The fever came back that afternoon, but only briefly. The antibiotics proved to be effective on this child who had never been exposed to any medication before.

It turned out that his father was a horse-cart driver who was away on some business. I could imagine how devastating it would have been if the boy had died in his absence. I felt grateful that the child had lived, although I was not sure to whom I should be grateful.

The mother wanted to bring the boy home, fearing a longer stay would be too expensive. But I could not let this boy go yet. After consulting with Gao, we told the mother the treatment would be free. I told her to bring the boy back whenever he got sick and there would be no charge. Nobody would know if we had used the medicine on an Army Corps soldier or on somebody else.

The boy was shy and would not talk to anyone but his mother. But he had a rapid recovery and by the third day did not want to stay in bed. When he went home a few days later, he was a healthy little boy, if a bit weak.

★ ★ ★

At that time, the newspapers were reporting miraculous "newly emerging things" as a result of applying "invincible Mao Zedong Thought." In medicine in particular, there were many such stories. A People's Liberation Army medical unit used acupuncture to cure the mute and the deaf, for example. The newspapers said that the first words these formerly mute people spoke were, "Long live Chairman Mao." There were reports of discoveries of new acupuncture points to cure all types of diseases. Even the official *Manual for Barefoot Doctors* had a special section on "new acupuncture therapies."

Naturally, I read about these developments with keen interest, although I remained skeptical. For curing the mute and the deaf, for example, the newspapers reported that the doctors applied acupuncture needles to points behind the neck, which traditional practice specifically warned against as extremely dangerous. But there were other new therapies that seemed less dangerous. One of them was "rooster blood therapy," which became popular among people who had chronic diseases. The therapy involved drawing blood from a rooster and injecting it into humans. One of our neighbors in Beijing had bought a large rooster for that purpose. But the neighbors complained about his crowing, so the old lady had to make a muzzle for the poor cock.

Although I was skeptical of such discoveries, I was curious, too. One day Gao Xiaorong told me that Zhang Fengmei, the company bookkeeper and a good friend of hers, had learned of a new therapy that she wanted to try.

Zhang Fengmei was a reasonably good-looking woman from Tianjin. She had a mild case of acne that embarrassed her greatly. Others would not have admitted that this bothered them, because concern about appearance was regarded as bourgeois. But she was close with Gao and had asked her to find a cure. Gao had mentioned it to me, but all I could find in books was a recommendation to eat less fat and more fruits and vegetables. Of course, in the Gobi there was hardly any fat in our diet and we almost never saw fruit.

The new treatment that Zhang Fengmei had read about was "self-blood therapy." It involved having about five cc's of blood drawn from one's own veins and immediately injecting it into one's posterior. I had no idea what the scientific basis for this was, but Zhang was quite determined to try it. Gao knew that I liked to try new things and asked me to help.

Gao and Zhang were very careful to keep the operation a secret. I appreciated their trust and the fact that they had involved me in this conspiracy, and I was eager to find out if this was indeed a miracle cure, since many others in the company also had acne. When we were ready, Gao explained the procedure to Zhang and told her not to be bashful because she would have to pull her pants down as soon as we drew the blood from her arm.

I was nervous and excited. I also felt funny about the "logic" behind this. I just could not figure out what the difference was between having the blood in one's veins and in one's posterior muscles. Would it stimulate some kind of immune reaction? Anyhow, there was no harm trying, or so I thought.

Zhang was very cooperative and the procedure was completed in about three minutes. In the days following, we repeated the same treatment several times. For the next few weeks, I would stare at Zhang's face whenever I saw her to see if her problem was cured. To my disappointment, there did not seem to be any difference. Discouraged, Zhang gave up. But I have had my eyes open for a cure for acne ever since, and I still haven't found a truly effective therapy in spite of many claims.

Some people who had been diagnosed as chronically sick had received permission to return to their home cities. Such permission had to be issued by the division hospital, where there were trained doctors and testing facilities. But there were many ways to fool a doctor. For example, one could go home if one had tuberculosis, and people devised a way to fool the X-ray machine: They put tincture of iodine on a piece of adhesive plaster and put it on their backs; iodine absorbs X-rays and leaves a shadow resembling tuberculosis. It was only after this method became common knowledge that a stop was put to it. All X-rays had to be taken from several angles to make sure the "TB" had not been taped on.

The most dramatic success in obtaining a permanent return home due to illness permit was achieved by a boy named Wang Kang.

One day, one of his roommates asked Dr. Yin to come check Wang Kang's leg, which had stopped moving completely. Dr. Yin checked the involuntary responses and found everything normal. But Wang said that he no longer felt that his leg existed. Dr. Yin thought it might be another case of hysteria and decided to try the same trick I had used with the girl from the Fifth Platoon. But still the boy's leg would not move. After two weeks of this, there was clear muscular atrophy: his leg had visibly shrunk. Puzzled and concerned, Dr. Yin sent him to the division hospital.

The doctors there could not find anything wrong either, but they hospitalized Wang for further observation. The next day the doctors found that his bed had been moved from next to the door to a more comfortable place by the wall. Wang claimed he did not know how the bed had moved. He said that he had woken up to find it in its new position. The doctors had no evidence to prove anything else. And there was no question that his left leg was much smaller than his right one now.

Wang stayed in the division hospital for a whole month, where he limped around on a pair of crutches. His case had all the doctors puzzled. Finally, they concluded that he had better seek help in his hometown, Tianjin, and issued him permanent home leave. He came back to the company to collect his belongings.

On the day of his departure, many of us went out to see him off. He was comfortably seated in the driver's cabin of the truck. There were handshakes and farewell exchanges. Finally, when the truck pulled off, Wang threw his crutches out the window. "Enough of this!" he shouted. Only then did we realize that he had been feigning it all along. You have to admire him for his discipline and the extraordinary suffering he had to go through to pull this off.

I had not been sleeping well since coming back from the medical training course. I was suffering from neurasthenia, I believed, and my major symptom was insomnia. Despite my exhaustion, I continued to go to work without taking time off. I wanted to contribute enough to be worth the few *wotou* I ate every day. Moreover, I wanted to be with the people of the platoon, so nobody would think that I was any different now that I was a barefoot doctor.

I sought a remedy for my problem. I read in some medical books that neurasthenia generally occurred after tension caused by higher nervous system activity when mental activity reached a state of exhaustion. There was no question that I had been studying hard, and I had always liked to read. But I strongly believed that the real cause of the problem was malnutrition.

The package of food my father had sent me was long exhausted. I began to spend all my monthly wages, five yuan, on food. When the shelves in the small shop were empty, I would go with friends like Cui Xianchao and Liu Xiaotong to a village quite far away to buy a chicken or two. When we pooled our wages, we could get a couple of chickens at a time. We always shared everything among whoever came into the room when the chicken was being cooked. So one person could only have a few bites of chicken meat once in a long while. But our meager monthly pay was only enough to buy one chicken apiece and there was not much I could do to improve my nutrition intake.

Then I learned that vitamin B complex was supposed to nourish the nervous system and to improve my sleep. For some reason, our clinic was stocked with injectable vials of vitamin B complex. I started to give myself an injection of vitamin B complex every day. It was an awkward exercise, putting a needle into my own behind. It was painful to begin with, and it was even worse when I was pushing the liquid into the muscle. But the practice of doing self-injection at my medical training now proved useful. I don't know if this had an actual or psychological effect, but I began to sleep better after several shots.

I stole a rooster once, but not for the meat. Since I didn't sleep well, I woke up at the slightest noise. For a long while, a rooster's crowing awakened me before the sun rose. It was so annoying and painful. I decided to act. One night, I caught the rooster in his coop while he was asleep and I twisted off his head with my bare hands. I had to walk a long way to dump the body in a ditch. I knew there was no other way to silence him, so I had to murder him, as he literally was driving me to the edge of sanity.

I doubt that a farmer laborer has sleep problems, as the day's hard work tires him out and drains his energy, inducing him to sleep. But a combination of hard labor, not enough to eat, and intensive reading whenever possible would fray your nerves, no matter how physically exhausted you are.

I eventually recovered from my frequent insomnia, once I was able to get enough nutrition in my diet years later. But to this day, I don't sleep well, a reminder of my days in the Gobi.

★ ★ ★

One of the tasks of being a medic was to administer vaccines to protect against epidemics. The first one I helped with nearly got the entire company killed.

It was a vaccine against the bubonic plague—in sparsely populated Inner Mongolia, there were field rats. Plague was endemic in this area of China during my time in the Gobi. The last time the Fifth Company had been vaccinated had been shortly before we arrived about two years earlier. There was thus the need to vaccinate those of us who came after.

Dr. Yin was away from the camp so all three of us medics were involved. The vaccine came in powder form. Wang Xinquan, Gao Xiaorong, and I diluted it with normal saline according to the instructions given to us by the regiment hospital. It took an entire day to vaccinate the whole company. Li Baoquan had avoided it the last time, and I was jeering at him for being so chicken-hearted as to be afraid of a small shot in the arm. But he replied that if everyone became immune to the plague, there would be no way for him to get the terrible disease either.

I would not listen to this nonsense. Since I was closer to Baoquan than anyone else, I got Yan Chongjie and two others to help me hold him down. We vaccinated him by force, as if he were a pig. Baoquan was strange. He didn't mind being used as a guinea pig for me to practice acupuncture, but he would not submit to a shot that was supposed to be good for him.

The next day was a day off because of the expected side effects from the vaccination.

There were side effects—but they were entirely unexpected. Overnight the arm in which I took the shot became red and swollen. I thought it was normal. But by afternoon I felt all the symptoms of a bad case of influenza. Everyone else was faring the same. We were all in bed. Few of us wanted to eat that evening.

The second day was awful. My whole body alternately burned and felt very cold. I knew I was running a fever. I had never expected a vaccine would have such severe effects. Could I be allergic?

I was not alone, though. No one who had been vaccinated could get up. I checked all our temperatures to discover we all had fevers. Baoquan was complaining that I had brought him suffering. I had a splitting headache and could hardly keep my eyes open. I felt so weak that it took great effort just to go to the outhouse and back.

Chapter 1   Man-Made Famine

With paternal grandpa Shan Xingsan and brother Shan Weizhong in 1957.

With mother, Wang Wenli, and brother in 1959.

With mother and brother in Beijing's Beihai Park on May 1, 1962.

Chapter 2 School Cut Short

Family portrait, c. 1962. Left to right, front row: Brother, maternal grandma Song Pei'e, the author. Back row: Aunt Wang Wenfang (mother's younger sister), mother, father Shan Yi, and sister Shan Weimin.

With brother and sister, c. 1965.

Chapter 4　Turmoil Under Heaven

In October 1966, at a well said to be dug by Mao Zedong at Sha Zhou Ba, Ruijin, Jiangxi Province, capital of the "Chinese Soviet Republic" from 1933 to 1934. Left to right, front row: Wang Yuanbo, the author, Qin Zhiqiang; back row: Wu Junjie, Huang Zhengfu, Zheng Lian, He Yuzhou.

At Huang Yang Jie, Jing Gang Mountain, Jingxi Province, in October 1966. Jiang Gang was the first Red Army base Mao established in 1927. The monument commemorates the victory of the Red Army over the Nationalist troops. The inscription on the monument is by Zhu De, Commander in Chief of the Red Army: "The Memorial of Victory in the Battle of Defense at Huang Yang Jie." From left to right, Wang Yuanbo (with cane), unknown, the author, and Wu Junjie.

Chapter 5   Exiled to the Gobi

The author, in Urat Qianqi, shortly after arrival in the Gobi in 1969.

The author, horsing around without a saddle in the Gobi.

Chapter 9 Battling Frozen Lake

With Li Baoquan (right) in front of self-built makeshift reed-and-mud hut in Xiao Ming Sha by Lake Wuliangsu during reed–cutting season (December 1970 to February 1971).

Eating ice dug out of the frozen lake to quench thirst during reed cutting.

Author, cutting reeds on the frozen lake in deep winter.

Liu Xiaotong, bundling up cut-down reeds and piling them up on the frozen lake.

Chapter 12   Barefoot Doctor

With Liu Xiaotong (right).

With Li Baoquan (right), company barracks in the background.

Chapter 15   Pigs Don't Fly

With airman and pig squad captain Yi Kong (right).

The author chasing a bull.

Chapter 17   Desert Dreams of College

At farewell to Zhang Yingfan, who was selected to go to college in September 1971. From left to right, front row: Wang Chunlian, Cui Xianchao, Yan Chongjie, Li Baoquan; back row: the author, Li Rongtian, Zhang Yingfan, Wang Dacheng, Liu Xiaotong.

Gobi friends on home leave in Beijing, 1974. Left to right, front row: Cui Xianchao, Yang Yulong, Li Changsheng, Wang Dacheng; back row: Ding Desheng ("Dasheng" or "Great Saint"), Yang Shengchen, Liu Xiaotong, Li Rongtian, Qin Zhiqiang, Huang Shurong, the author, Li Zhuangzhong, Wang Zutong.

Chapter 18   Last Convulsions of the Revolution

Tiananmen Square on April 4 1976. The author took the pictures of the mass protest against the radicals led by Mao's wife, Jiang Qing, in the name of mourning Premier Zhou Enlai, who died on January 8 of the same year. The crackdown on the next day marked the event as "April 5th Movement" of 1976 in Chinese history.

Chapter 19   Roads to Rome

With Bin Shi at the Great Wall, summer 1978.

With Bin in 1979. We were married in 1980.

Chapter 20   Old Gold Mountain
Chapter 21   The People's Republic of Berkeley

The author (far left) chatting with Dianne Feinstein, then mayor of San Francisco, in 1980.

The family finally together in San Francisco in summer 1985.

Our family with the Cassous at Berkeley, 1987. From left to right, front row: son Bo, wife Bin, April Cassou; back row: Philip Cassou, the author.

Chapter 22   Ivy League Professor

In my office at the Wharton School of the University of Pennsylvania, 1990.

Lecturing a Wharton class for senior executives, 1990.

Berlin, March 17, 1990. The author (hand up in a victory sign) and Wharton colleague Isik Inselbag.

Berlin, March 17, 1990. Wharton colleague Skip Rosoff sarcastically gesturing to compare a Mercedes (left) and the shoddy boxy car (right) made in East Germany.

With wife Bin, son Bo, and daughter LeeAnn on her first birthday in October 1992.

Wharton kids: Bo and LeeAnn in 1993.

Family in Grand Teton Park in 1995.

Epilogue

The Gobi in 2005. To protect the sparse vegetation, only camels, considered to be endangered, are still allowed to graze the land.

With Zhang Zhiqiu (Er Gou), right, at Fanshengedan by Lake Wuliangsu, with the crumbling barracks used during reed-cutting seasons in the background, on July 10, 2005.

I knew something was wrong. I staggered to my feet and went around the camp. I checked several rooms and other platoons and found the same situation everywhere. As I was going around, I felt as if I were walking on a cloud. The veins in my forehead were pounding so loudly and rapidly that I thought my head would explode.

I finally found my way to the clinic. Gao Xiaorong was on duty. She did not take the vaccine because she had done it before. I told her I was afraid that the high fever was damaging my brain and asked her to give me an injection. After some discussion, we decided to give pain and fever relief medicine to anyone who needed it.

It occurred to me to check the vaccine. No vaccine should have had such a powerful effect. I looked at the label of the vaccine bottle and at the instruction sheet that came from the regiment hospital. What I saw made me tremble with fear. The instructions from the regiment said that each bottle should be diluted to use for two adults. The tiny print instructions on the label said that each bottle should be used for *20* adults. Each of us had been given 10 times the normal dose. We were exhibiting the exact symptoms of bubonic plague. I had no idea if we would survive our self-inflicted epidemic.

I showed my discovery to Gao Xiaorong and staggered back to my platoon with a medical kit. I knew that there was nothing I could do but wait and hope that the effects of the vaccine would pass. But I gave medicine to everyone just to relieve the fever and pain a bit. I trembled as I did my job. Then I went back to my room, climbed onto the *kang*, and collapsed.

Gao Xiaorong made an emergency call to the regiment hospital. The company leadership alerted headquarters that there had been a "medical accident." A rescue team headed by Dr. Yu arrived the same day.

They stayed until everyone was fully recovered a few days later. It was fortunate that there was no permanent damage to anyone. Later, I heard that we were not alone. The doctor who wrote the instructions for us sent them to several companies. If he had missed by another decimal point, he would have wiped out maybe hundreds of us with one stroke of his pen.

★ ★ ★

It gave me great pleasure to serve as a barefoot doctor, although it meant much more work for me. I liked interacting with people and I enjoyed bringing them back to health. I was learning a great deal. But in spite of my hard work, I knew the political instructor and the company commander had begun to dislike me more and more. The instructor's attitude toward me changed drastically after I found out that he did not really have arthritis. Soon, I offended Commander Zhang as well.

The commander often came to the clinic for cough pills. One day Gao Xiaorong told me the commander didn't have a coughing problem; he wanted those cough pills because they were sugarcoated. He would put the tablet in his mouth, suck the sugar off, and spit out the rest.

I didn't like what I had heard. Didn't he know that medicines were expensive and that local peasants didn't have easy access to them? How could he waste cough pills like that?

Then one day he came in when I was on duty and asked me for some pills. I told him that he had to get a prescription from Dr. Yin before I could give them to him. His face grew redder than usual, and he said coldly and menacingly, "Why do we need you if you can't even give us some medicine?" Then he stalked out.

I feared then that my days as a barefoot doctor were numbered. A few weeks later, I was unceremoniously booted out of the clinic: I was told I would not need to come to the clinic anymore. There was never any announcement. A new full-time medic was appointed to take my place. And I resumed my full-time duties in the fields with the comrades of my squad. My medical career was over.

Chapter 13

Brickmaking the Ancient Way

Who could have imagined that hopping onto the wrong bus could trigger a chain of events that would change the world?

In the spring of 1971, Glenn Cowan, a 19-year-old American Ping-Pong player, was participating in the World Table Tennis Championships in Nagoya, Japan. After practice one day, Cowan mistakenly got on the wrong shuttle bus. Instead of seeing his American teammates, he was surprised to find himself surrounded by the Chinese national team.

While most of the Chinese players avoided talking to this gangly American with shoulder-length hair, Zhuang Zedong, China's best Ping-Pong player, stepped forward to greet him and shake his hand. They chatted through an interpreter, and before Cowan got off the bus, Zhuang gave the American a gift: a silk-screened picture of China's Huangshan Mountains. The next day Cowan returned the favor with a gift of his own: a T-shirt he'd found in a Nagoya market, emblazoned with a peace symbol and the Beatles' lyric "Let It Be." "Photographers caught the incident on film, and the unexpected goodwill between the US and Chinese teams soon became the talk of the tournament," as one account put it.

For more than 20 years, there had been no diplomatic relations between China and the United States. Encouraged by this friendly encounter, the American team suggested to the Chinese team that they make a visit to China after the tournament. This was not a decision that a Ping-Pong team could make, and the matter went all the way to the Chinese foreign ministry. After deliberating, the ministry recommended to Premier Zhou Enlai that he not extend an invitation. On April 4, 1971, Zhou passed the ministry's recommendation to Mao with his own comment that the time did not seem to be ripe to reach out to the Americans. Mao circled his agreement with his pencil on April 6. And that would have been the end of it—except that the chairman was still thinking about it.

At about 11 o'clock that night, Mao had already taken his sleeping pills and was resting his head on the table in a state of drowsiness. Wu Xujun, Mao's head nurse, was eating her dinner next to him. Suddenly, Mao, without raising his head, muttered to her to call the foreign ministry and tell them to "invite the American team to visit China."

Wu was surprised; this contradicted Mao's standing instructions. Mao had once told her that whatever he said after taking his sleeping pills did not count. She looked at the chairman, who was sitting on his bed, with his head buried in his arms on the dining table. The nurse did not move or respond.

After a while, Mao raised his head and struggled to open his eyes. "Xiao Wu, you are still here eating. Why aren't you doing what I've asked you to do?"

Wu said in a loud voice, "Chairman, what did you say to me just now? I was busy eating and I didn't hear it clearly. Would you repeat?"

Mao repeated his instruction. Wu was still unsure and said, "You already circled the document from the foreign ministry during the day to say no invitation. How come now you say to invite? You already took sleeping pills. Do your words count?"

Mao waved his hand firmly and said, "They count. Hurry or it will be too late."

Just as the US team was preparing to leave Nagoya, they received the invitation to visit China. After checking with the US embassy, the team accepted.

President Richard Nixon had written as early as 1967, "We simply cannot afford to leave China forever outside the family of nations." But as he later noted wryly in his memoirs, "I had never expected that the China initiative would come to fruition in the form of a Ping-Pong team."

In July 1971, Nixon sent his national security advisor, Dr. Henry Kissinger, on a secret mission to Beijing where he met with Premier Zhou Enlai. On July 15, the US president shocked the world by announcing on live television that he would visit China the following year. The weeklong visit took place from February 21 to 28, 1972. Nixon hailed it as "the week that changed the world."

★ ★ ★

Just as winters came early to the Gobi, spring came late. While Beijing would be warm by May Day, the temperature here still fell below freezing at night. On windless days, the cool temperature felt quite comfortable, especially for working outside at some strenuous task. And when the weather was cool, flies and mosquitoes did not bother us.

I welcomed spring with mixed feelings. I was always happy when the dreadfully severe winter passed because it meant there would be some green enlivening the otherwise dull landscape of the Gobi. But I hated the inevitable spring sandstorms. Spring also meant that we would again have to return to the fields, and the endless, relentless tasks of plowing and seeding the ground, digging ditches, building ridges, and tending irrigation canals. We repeated this same cycle year after year.

In the spring of 1972, a rumor went around that one of the platoons would be assigned to serve as masons, building houses for the company. I heard that our platoon had a good chance to be picked, because Platoon Leader Liu had lobbied hard for us, arguing that Third Platoon had always done agricultural work, and it was time for a change. When we asked, Liu just smiled and said that we should wait and see.

It was true. Our platoon became the designated "barracks construction platoon" and we would learn to be masons. We were all happy and excited, without really knowing what we were in for. At least it was a welcome change from farming. We soon learned we were to build a storage house and a row house for the kitchen squad, made from bricks. We had no bricks and were therefore also responsible for making them—300,000 bricks for various projects, according to the company leadership. At the time, bricks were a luxury. At four cents per brick, 300,000 bricks would be worth about 12,000 yuan, or equal to the total annual pay of 200 of us.

Squad Eight set to repairing and restoring an old kiln, long abandoned and in disrepair, while our squad prepared the brick-making ground, a large patch of ground near the kiln. This was where raw bricks, after we had shaped them in a mold, would be placed to bake in the sun before firing. We carried soil in two baskets on a shoulder pole. We layered this fine-grained, good-quality soil on top of the ground, and used large brooms to smooth it. Then we carried buckets of water to wet its surface. The ground had to be smooth and flat, so we then pulled a heavy stone roller back and forth across it. We repeated the layering and smoothing of the earth until we built a solid flat surface that was some 300 square meters (~3,300 square feet) in size, about one and a half the size of a tennis court. We started work on the brick field on March 23, 1972, and construction took almost two months. We had to stop from time to time when the weather changed and the temperature plunged below the freezing point because we could not work on frozen ground.

Our kiln was four or five meters (~13 to 16 feet) tall and from a distance it looked like a small volcano. Its firing chamber was made of bricks, as an arched tunnel led from the entrance to the mouth of the kiln where coal was to be fed. The brick inner shell of the kiln would be covered with clay for insulation from inside and by layers of earth from outside, with an opening on top to give it the look of a small volcanic hill. I liked to climb on top of it, a vantage point from which one could see quite far.

About 40 meters (~130 feet) away from the kiln there was a small shack where the former kiln masters had lived. Squad No. 8 moved into it. Their job was to keep rebuilding the kiln during the day and to safeguard the brick ground at night.

We began making bricks in mid-May. I was teamed up with HaBai, the Mongolian boy, and Yan Chongjie. Yan was shorter than both HaBai and me, but he was muscular and strong. HaBai often cracked jokes. Yan was a man of few words. I was happy to be in a strong team, and thought that, with our strength, we should probably be able to beat any other team at brick making.

The problem was, none of us had any real brick-making experience, let alone skill, and nobody was there to teach us. We all thought it was a simple matter of using a mold to turn clay into the shape of a brick. How hard could it be? Well, it was not so simple, as we soon found out. We had to waste many batches of raw bricks before we learned how to do it right.

The process involved several stages. First, we needed to prepare the clay. This was probably the most crucial part because it would directly affect the quality of bricks. It was very much like making dough, only on a much larger scale. The trick was in mixing just the right proportion of sand, clay, and water so the brick would hold together and not crack when fired.

To get clay, we dug it out of the Gobi floor and then mixed it with sand. Then we poured water fetched from a nearby ditch onto the mound of sandy clay to thoroughly moisten it. As one of us poured on water, another person used a shovel to turn the pile rapidly to make sure that the water, sand, and clay were thoroughly mixed. This process demanded hours of hard labor.

The wet clay needed to sit overnight so the water would seep through evenly, leaving it smooth and free of any chunks of unmoistened clay that might cause imperfections. The next morning, the clay had to be stirred and mixed again until smooth and soft. The more it felt like flour dough, the better quality the bricks would be.

For the second stage, we formed bricks with a mold. This was like making cupcakes, but, again, on a much larger scale. Each mold made two bricks. The mold looked like two rectangular wood boxes joined together and positioned side by side. After dusting the mold with a light layer of sand to make sure the clay would not stick, we'd each put our mold flat on the ground. We would squat down, grab a piece of clay with both hands, lift the clay up to almost eye level while standing up halfway, and then throw the clay into the mold with all our might. It was crucial to use as much strength as possible. If the force was not strong enough, the clay could not fill every corner of the mold with one throw. Filling it in would affect the quality of the brick, as the brick would not look like one piece.

In one continuous motion after throwing down with the clay, we'd use our right hand to sweep across the opening of the mold to remove the excess. Then with a piece of wood resembling a large ruler, we would swipe across the opening again, to make the surface as smooth as possible.

Next, we'd carry our mold some 20 meters (~65 feet) away to where the newly made bricks were left to dry and very swiftly turn over and empty the mold. If the brick was not perfect, it was destroyed right away.

The newly molded brick would be left for about a day until it was half-dried. Then we would touch it up with a flat wooden board by ever so slightly tapping the edges to make them sharp. Finally, when the bricks had completely dried in the sun, we would stack them up and clear the ground for the next batch.

Unfired bricks could also be used in construction, but houses built with them would not last very long. Our bricks would be baked in the kiln nearby. The kiln could fire some 40,000 bricks at a time. Although there were about 30 people in our platoon, we had about 20 hands on a regular day because many did not come to work for one reason or another. If we averaged about 200 bricks per person a day, 10 days' labor would be required to make enough bricks to fill the kiln, a process we would have to repeat between seven and eight times to make the quota of 300,000 bricks that the leadership had set for us.

★ ★ ★

Preparing clay was a very dirty job. We were covered with mud from head to toe by the end of the day. As we worked, we were soaked in sweat. Since it would be troublesome, if not impossible, to wash our clothes every day we usually wore only a pair of underpants. At the end of the day, we would go to the ditch, fetch some water with a bucket, and pour the water over our heads to clean off the mud. When the weather was warm we jumped into a nearby pond. This waterhole, however, was used not only for washing ourselves, but also for drinking water. Cattle drank and bathed in it, too. The water became so dirty we were concerned we would get sick from drinking it; so later we used a horse-drawn cart to carry a large metal container of water drawn from the well at the company camp some distance away for drinking water.

We soon learned that making bricks with a mold was much more tiring physically than preparing the clay. It was taxing on one's back to repeat the motion of bending down, throwing clay into the mold, straightening up, lifting the mold, running the distance with it, and bending down again to dump it. It was a painful repetition of bending and straightening with a heavy load.

Our initial efforts did not yield as many bricks as we had hoped. The mound of clay we prepared was gone quickly. When we tallied up the bricks the three of us made, we found that there were about 600, only about 200 bricks per person. Yet everyone was so tired we did not feel like walking the distance back to the company barracks. To make matters worse, we learned that Dasheng's team made about 300 bricks per person. We had to work harder or smarter to improve our productivity. I found it hard to imagine how we could work any harder, as we had certainly given it our best effort.

Exhausted, we dragged our feet back to our barracks. I was so tired that night that I, unusually, did not feel like reading anything. I spent the evening lying in bed listening to Baoquan talking about his life as a little hooligan in Tianjin and some other nonsense. His team only made about 100 bricks per person, but Baoquan could not care less about their productivity. He said he would not risk his precious health to be a hero worker.

"You prove yourself to be a book idiot for driving yourself so hard making bricks. Take it easy, like me," he advised. "Let HaBai and Chongjie do the work. How can you match strong guys like them? Steal a break whenever you can. Nobody is going to give you even one more *mantou* to eat for working so hard."

I fell asleep even before the lights-out bugle blew, as Baoquan and Zhou Wanling were still bragging about the adventurous trips they took last fall stealing melons from peasants' fields.

I woke up in the middle of the night and my whole body ached so terribly that for a long while it was difficult to fall back asleep. My back was the worst part: It was in pain constantly. Other parts did not feel much better either. My arms and legs were also very sore. I lay in my bed wondering if there was any way we could alleviate our hard work and make more bricks.

The next day we had to start the process from the very beginning. Step one: preparing clay. I learned that both HaBai and Yan Chongjie were in pain, too. HaBai was complaining that he was dead tired. Yan said that he was exhausted also. We all felt quite discouraged that we were behind some others in the number of bricks we made. We felt it was a loss of face. We also felt challenged because ours was a strong team and we should be doing better. Somehow, we had to catch up and make more bricks.

HaBai was not known as a hard worker in the platoon, although he had the build for it. Yan was more of a sporadic type. When he was in a good mood, he could work like a horse and few could match his strength. If he was feeling down, he did not care to work at all. I liked HaBai but was never close with him. Yan was one of my closest friends. Even though the two of them might skip a day or two or steal a break when we worked on our own, they both worked hard when we were together as a team. None of us would be willing to let the others down. Counting muscles—and by that I meant HaBai's and Yan's muscles, as mine were rather pathetic in comparison—we were a strong team. Although I myself was not muscular, I was known for my endurance and capacity for hard work. I hated to be left behind by anyone. There was an implicit competition among us to see which team produced the most. Whichever team I joined for whatever job, we had always had that competitive urge to beat other teams. I think that competitive urge is innate: We were not paid a penny more for producing more, but we surely felt good to have done better than other teams.

I found it hard to understand how other teams could be so productive, as we certainly exerted our very best efforts. There had to be a better way to do it.

We went around to see how others were doing their jobs. As expected, some people were just taking it easy, not caring how many bricks they made. But the few groups with strong hands, like the one led by Dasheng and Platoon Leader Liu, were working hard. Liu had had some experience making bricks in his home village before he joined the army. Dasheng's group was doing even better. We could see that they were using a different method entirely. They divided up the job among themselves so that each person was specializing in one function, either throwing the clay or transporting the mold.

After a little discussion and consultation among ourselves, we decided to divide our responsibilities so that each person could specialize in one function of the process. This was really teamwork. Each one had to do his part of the work quickly, otherwise he would hold up the entire "production line."

For my part, I had to run with the fully loaded mold, empty the molded brick onto the ground, and then run back with the empty mold. Two wet bricks were heavy, probably weighing five to six kilograms (~11 to 13 pounds). Running with them was so hard that soon I was exhausted and my heart beat rapidly. My legs became weak and I began to feel nauseated. But I continued, trying to keep up with the other two. Soon, the feeling of nausea was gone. And our work became synchronized. Every so often, we would rotate roles to give our bodies a break.

Now we were making more bricks. Soon, we were counting about 300 bricks per person each day. The work was still tiring, but much more productive. As we gained experience, our output increased. In a week or so, the combined output by the three of us stabilized at around 1,000 bricks a day.

Soon, every team adopted the method. Nonetheless, it was backbreaking labor and, as the days passed, everyone became more and more exhausted. Even though we had become more productive, we found it increasingly difficult to keep the output at 1,000 bricks a day for our three-person team.

One day Political Instructor Zhang came to "inspect" our work. Baoquan greeted him, calling him "General" as usual. Zhang beamed, protruding his belly even further and smiling from ear to ear. The humorous thing about the political instructor was that he could never tell if anyone was mocking him. He always felt good about himself. He was rather pleased with our work, and announced that, in a week or so, we would start to fire the kiln. The company would invite an experienced kiln master from somewhere to guide the work. Therefore, he exhorted us to work even harder to make sure that there were enough bricks by the time the kiln master arrived.

It was easy for him to say, we thought grimly. I did not think that we could work any harder than we were, after having honed our technique. HaBai sneered that the political instructor certainly would not hurt his back by chattering while standing up. Baoquan, though, knew exactly how to deal with the political instructor. "You can't be serious with him," said Baoquan. He challenged the political instructor to join his team to make a few bricks. In a good mood, Zhang agreed.

Baoquan suggested that Zhang throw clay into the mold as the job did not require running back and forth, which would be hard for the overweight instructor. We were all amused to see him splashing mud all over himself, clumsily filling the mold. By the end of the day, he looked like a general wearing a Peking opera mask. To hide his embarrassment, he declared that he was too old to compete with us youngsters. That was the first and last time we saw him making bricks. But at least he knew now that making bricks was a hard job.

When the stacks of raw bricks we made were dried out, we found, to our dismay, that the quality of our bricks was not uniform. Some batches were perfect and others less so. In one batch, every single brick cracked after it dried. Apparently, the sand content in that batch was too low.

It pained us to throw away the thousand or so bricks that we knew contained so much of our sweat and effort. We learned a lesson and had to be careful mixing clay with enough sand so that this type of waste would not happen again. But the next day, we made a major mistake to the other extreme. The prepared clay contained so much sand that the bricks would not stay together in one piece. The whole batch was wasted. It was not until about two weeks later that we finally mastered the perfect balance of sand and clay.

Once we had enough dried bricks, we began to transport some back to the barracks where some houses would be built with unbaked bricks. Our team loaded bricks into a cart drawn by an old cow that plodded along slowly. But when we were about to be passed by a horse-drawn cart, surprisingly the cow began to run fast to keep up. Even the cow had a competitive spirit. We doubled over with laughter sitting on the pile of bricks on the cart, as we passed the boys in the cart drawn by the horse.

One day some time later, I captured a horse grazing alone near our brick-making ground. Usually a horse grazed with its herd. If you saw a lone horse, its owner was usually somewhere nearby. But this one was grazing all by himself, with no one in sight. Nobody knew where he came from. Maybe he was from Outer Mongolia and traveled here in a sandstorm. In any case, we harnessed him on our cart. He was much faster than our cow and we were all delighted with him because we won every race with other carts. But one day he somehow got startled as we were racing and the cart overturned, throwing all of us, along with our bricks, to the ground. Fortunately, no one was hurt. But our horse began to limp after we put him back into harness. He must have hurt his leg. We could not let an injured horse work so we let him go.

The spring weather of the Gobi frequently changed. More often than not, it was windy. When the wind blew, it stirred up a lot of dirt and sand. It was particularly difficult to make bricks against a strong sandstorm. At the end of the day, there would be mud all over our bodies and sand in our mouths and ears. I hated the inconveniences caused by windy days and sandstorms.

★ ★ ★

For the most part, while we were at this work, I had not been reading. It was impossible. I felt so exhausted that I did not have the strength to hold a book or to concentrate. I would simply collapse into my bed after washing the mud off my body from head to toe, getting up only to eat dinner. I was amazed to find that both HaBai and Chongjie were in much better shape. Although they were as tired as I was when we first started, they seemed to have become used to this hard labor. Yan would take out his *erhu* after dinner to play a tune from a Peking opera, and HaBai sometimes would howl out a piece of opera when Cui Xianchao was around. Baoquan was the same, fond of talking about life at home in Tianjin and the strange things happening there. I felt great enjoyment simply reclining on my quilt and pillow, watching and listening to them. But I was reluctant to go outside even when the weather was good because my back and legs ached so much that even going to the outhouse required an effort. Every night, I went to sleep earlier than them, but I still did not feel rested enough in the morning. I wasn't sure how long I could last.

We had not had a break for several weeks. I felt that each day, my fatigue increased. We all longed for a rest. Even one day off would be so good. Now I had to struggle to get out of bed every morning and after a short noontime nap. In the first few days, I was too tired to even eat dinner. But as we settled into a routine, our rations became more and more inadequate for my appetite. Platoon Leader Liu complained to the political instructor that our platoon deserved a larger ration because of our hard labor. Surprisingly, Instructor Zhang agreed, allowing us one more *wotou* with dinner. Baoquan took the credit, saying that the experience of being a laborer for a day must have convinced the "General" that we indeed deserved a little more. But there was still not enough to eat.

I had a reputation as a good worker that I did not want to ruin. Besides, I was thinking that I had to be worthy of the food that we were provided. Baoquan said I was being naïve. He argued that if we worked hard, we were simply contributing to the welfare of those who never had to work, such as the political instructor and the fat-cat officers in the regiment headquarters. I could not argue with him. I knew that I was doing my job, which I considered to be my responsibility. But by that time, HaBai and Chongjie had started to take turns being on "sick leave."

★ ★ ★

I was thinking of ways to mechanize the process of making bricks. The techniques we were using seemed ancient. In fact, they were. Many years later, on a trip to Italy, I noticed that bricks found in the ancient Roman city of Pompeii (which had been buried by volcanic ash and pumice in the eruption of Mount Vesuvius in 79 AD) had been made using much the same technique. There had to be a more modern way of doing it. I had seen dough-making machines in the noodle shop at the grocery shop near our home in Beijing. The principle of mixing clay to make bricks should be similar, except the machine and the power required had to be much larger for the large quantities of clay and sand.

I went to consult with Li Rongtian.

Li was clever with his hands and had inventive ideas. When it came to mechanical things and machines, he knew better than anyone. I believed that he would have little difficulty designing a brick-making machine if he set his mind to it.

Li went with me to the brick-making ground. After thinking about the problem for a while, Li agreed with me: Making bricks was just like making noodles or steamed buns. He, too, had seen the noodle-shop machines, which basically consisted of a large mixing bowl in which dough was created from flour and water. Then the dough would be pushed out of the container through a chute with a spiral shaft. The dough came out, shaped like a thick noodle, which a revolving steel wire would then cut into pieces. The same technology could be used to build a brick-making machine, Li said. But a brickmaking machine would require a container made with thick cast iron. Furthermore, a diesel engine was necessary to power the machine.

I was encouraged by his words and the thought that we would save our backs and legs and not have to work like slaves every day. Moreover, we would be able to produce more. Our bricks would be superior to those made the old-fashioned way. I urged Li to give some careful thought to it and try to draw a blueprint or a design for such a machine. Li agreed.

I told both HaBai and Yan Chongjie about my conversation with Li Rongtian. They were as excited as I was. But they were skeptical about how our project would be greeted by the company leaders. We needed the leadership's backing for the purchase of some components. Although it was our consensus that the company leadership could probably not care less about how hard we had to work, I thought they would be interested in the productivity increase a machine like this would produce. After all, the political instructor and the company commander were eager to fulfill their production targets, which would make them look good to higher authorities.

Li Rongtian doubted we would secure the leadership's support. To my disappointment, Li seemed to have second thoughts overnight, and when I visited him after dinner the next day he was no longer enthusiastic about the project.

He had, however, drawn some designs on a piece of paper. He said the odds were low that leadership would buy into it, because they did not like anyone with ideas that disrupted the status quo. And, of course, there were challenges. For example: What if it turned out not to be technically feasible? Where would we get the materials? Would the regimental leadership allocate iron, steel, and a diesel engine to Company

No. 5, which was, after all, an agricultural company? Li argued that neither the political instructor nor the company commander would be willing to take the risk, no matter what encouraging words they might say about it. Perhaps, he said, it was best for both of us just to accept the facts and resume our primitive backbreaking work.

I could not steer him away from his skepticism. In fact, I agreed with his analysis about the willingness of the company leadership to get involved. But I argued that if we could demonstrate the technical feasibility of such a project, the leadership might go for it out of self-interest: If this idea worked, they would win praise from regiment headquarters. I just could not give up the appealing prospect of being liberated from the unbearable hardship of making bricks by hand. My own sanity and survival, in some sense, depended on it. Besides, what did we have to lose?

Li Rongtian held his ground, saying only that he would consider it. I went back to my room crestfallen. After much thought, I decided that I should have a discussion with the political instructor to find out how he would react to such an idea. If I could persuade him to let us try, Li Rongtian would have no reason not to help.

It was difficult to tell what Instructor Zhang really thought. He tried to appear seriously interested in what I had to report. My dilemma was that I could not tell him just then that this project would require the company to commit some resources. That would turn him off immediately. But I did not want to give him the idea it was easy, either.

The political instructor did not say anything for a few minutes, as if deep in thought mulling over my proposal. Then he spoke and said he saw no reason to oppose the project. Had I ever seen a machine of this type, he asked me? And how much would it cost?

I told him that it was going to cost him something. We could not build a machine without component parts. I told him we would need a diesel engine, at least. All other parts had to be cast-iron. It was not going to be a small project. I told him that once the machine was built, it would ensure that we met our production target of 300,000 bricks in two months. In fact, I continued, the machine would be able to produce that quantity in one month. I had heard that a company of the Fourteenth Regiment, near Urat Qianqi, had a machine of this type. I told him that with his permission, I would go there with Li Rongtian to investigate.

The political instructor said that he would think a bit more and talk with Li Rongtian himself. He then promised to advise us of his decision.

That evening, I went to bed hopeful of a favorable outcome. Just as I was about to fall asleep, I heard the howling sound of a sudden sandstorm. It whipped the window violently, making sandpapery scratching sounds as it blew past the panes. Sand and dirt came through cracks in the door and windows, and the room was quickly filled with dust. I found it hard to breathe and covered my mouth with the corner of my quilt. I was glad that I was in bed early so I didn't have to go to the outhouse in the storm.

I hadn't been asleep long before I was startled awake from my dreams by a sound like someone rapidly beating a drum. It came from the roof. I realized it was heavy rain. I pulled the quilt a little tighter around myself. But my thoughts flew to the dried bricks stacked up in the brick field. What would happen to them? I dreaded the thought. I was hoping that the rainstorm would quickly pass. But it lashed the roof and the windows through the night. Knowing that worrying about the bricks in the fields was futile, I resigned myself to sleep.

The next morning, the rain seemed reluctant to leave. The sky was overcast with thick clouds, but a patch of clear blue on the horizon announced the rain's retreat. The air, washed clean by the storm, was fresh, mixed with the sweet taste of wild grass. But our bricks . . . I thought. How much of our labor was washed away?

It would be some time before breakfast, so I went to the brick-making ground to see for myself. The road, soaked with the rain, was drenched and muddy, and so was I by the time I reached my destination. Just as I expected, the rainstorm had wreaked havoc on our handiwork. The bricks that we had left to dry were completely destroyed, reduced to no more than little mounds of shapeless clay. The bricks that were already stacked up fared a little better, but the first couple of layers on the surface were largely gone. I felt chilled to the bone, and a sense of futility overtook me as I gazed out on the quiet field. So much of our sweat and hard labor was gone, and so easily. The damage was not distributed evenly. Some fields, like ours, suffered more than others. Those closer to the shack had pieces of sheets and rags covering the brick stacks. Apparently, the people of the eighth squad fought hard against the storm to protect the bricks, but their efforts were clearly no match to nature.

I walked to the small shack where the eighth squad was staying. Most of them were still in bed. I could tell what an awful night they had had: Every corner of the hut was piled high with dirty, soaking-wet clothes and shoes plastered with thick mud.

Those who were up told me how they braved the rainstorm to try to cover the stacks of bricks with their own sheets. They knew they were fighting a hopeless battle. There were too few people trying to cover too many stacks of bricks. Once they exhausted all their sheets, they used their own quilts. No wonder some of them were sharing one quilt.

When I came back from the brick-making ground, it was time for breakfast. I reported to everyone what I had seen on the brick field. Those whose work suffered slight damage took some pleasure in others' misfortune. Those who heard of severe damage in their field looked quite miserable. But the gloomy mood soon lifted when the platoon leader came to tell us that we did not have to go to the brick fields today. It would not make sense, as the ground was soaked with water. It would take a few days to dry up. We would have political study sessions instead. This was welcome news, as everyone was longing for a break.

The rainstorm made me even more determined to investigate the possibility of building some kind of brick-making machine that would alleviate our hard work. I went to Li Rongtian's place to talk with him about my conversation with the political instructor. Li was now quite negative about the whole thing and suggested that I was creating trouble for both of us. I could not persuade him to see the merit of my proposal with my words alone. I felt that he could not appreciate how badly we needed some alternative means to ease our hard labor. With this in mind, I invited him to come with me again to see our work at the brick field.

Li was noticeably touched when he saw the miserable remains of the bricks lying battered by the rainstorm. When we came back, he went to the political instructor himself.

That evening the power generator broke down, which happened with some regularity. The time was spent in darkness, but, as luck would have it, the rainstorm also brought us a surprising delicacy:

We had some frog meat. Xiaotong had captured several strings of frogs from near Lake Wuliangsu. It had been a long time since we had had any kind of protein, and the frog meat tasted delicious.

★ ★ ★

The next morning, Li Rongtian came in before I got up. He had already talked with the political instructor, who had agreed to our proposal to investigate the technical feasibility of a brick-making machine. We decided to travel to Urat Qianqi to visit the "making-bricks-with-machines" company of the Fourteenth Regiment.

The only mode of travel readily available was a tractor-hauled wagon. I dreaded the ride. It was so uncomfortable that, if we took it, by the time we reached Urat Qianqi, all our bones would be shaken loose traversing the bumpy road. Li and I decided to go to Xishaliang, a big village where we could catch a bus. Though it meant several hours of walking, it would be preferable to the tractor-hauled wagon.

The journey was not bad. We were chatting as we walked and were in no hurry. We spotted a few people in the distance by the roadside. As we came closer, I noticed that they were surrounding a cow that was lying on the ground. The cow had a bad wound on its hind leg. It was bleeding, and the peasants did not know what to do to stanch the wound. I took a quick look and decided that it must have been the work of Construction Army Corps soldiers, probably inflicted by a sharp piece of metal. Perhaps this cow had strayed into the Construction Army Corps compound. The local peasants would not do such a thing to a cow.

I offered to help, and Li Rongtian explained to the peasants that I was a barefoot doctor. I asked someone to collect some dried grass, and when we had a stack of it, I burned it to ashes. The ashes I applied directly to the wound, in layers. At first, the cow's blood was still oozing out. But the bleeding soon stopped. Newly burned grass ash is the best folk remedy to stanch bleeding and reduce the chance of infection. Since it is created by fire, the ash is germ-free.

The whole process took about 40 minutes. By the time we were done, the peasants were pleased and grateful. They wanted to get the cow up and walk her back to the village. I suggested that they wait for another hour or so until the wound dried up a bit. They thanked us profusely. Just then, a tractor-hauled wagon passed by. It was their village's tractor. They were kind enough to stop the vehicle and helped us onto it. Both Li Rongtian and I were amused by its serendipitous appearance: We had taken this road to avoid a tractor-hauler. Yet we eventually ended up on one. Since we spent a lot of time caring for the cow, we were glad to accept a ride.

After a short but bumpy ride, we reached Sudunlun, where the Fourteenth Regiment was situated. The roads were lined with trees, a rarity in the Gobi. The Fourteenth seemed to be doing much better than we. We saw an auditorium where they would have performances by regiment soldiers. People even seemed better dressed, although they wore the same standard uniforms of the Construction Army Corps as we did. Rongtian and I felt like a pair of country bumpkins riding into town.

We asked around and found our way to the brick company. As chance would have it, we hitched a short ride on yet another tractor-hauler, this one loaded with coal.

The brick-making machine was being repaired when we arrived. This gave us a chance to study it and talk with the people, who were friendly and open with their knowledge. We drew some blueprints of the machine and the brick makers described how it functioned and answered all our questions. The object itself was heavy, with large bulky components. As we had expected, the mechanism itself was quite simple. We had not been far off in thinking that it would look like a noodle-maker. We were surprised to learn it was powered by the engine of a tractor, a perfect solution that had somehow never occurred to us.

This machine could produce 20,000 to 30,000 bricks per day. Looking at the raw bricks stacked high around the machine, we saw immediately they were of high quality. Compared to our bricks fashioned by hand using the ancient method, these were uniform and much more solid, thanks to the heavy and consistent pressure on the machine-extruded mixed clay.

Then we learned the machine's cost. It would be about 3,000 yuan, an astronomical figure for us, and that was not counting the cost of the tractor as the power source. Getting hold of a tractor would be a challenge. Our company did not have one, and, in our regiment, they were all kept at the Eleventh Company, which was in charge of agricultural machinery; we would have to borrow a tractor from them. I wondered if our company leadership would be capable of even considering the required investment, although, of course, it was well worth it.

Meanwhile, I was impressed with the officers of this company. They were warm, modest, and candid with us, without the familiar air of pretentious importance we had become used to with our own leaders. I noted with interest that all the soldiers of the company lived in brick houses, but as leaders of a "brick-making company," the officers lived in low mud shacks. Rongtian and I had a long conversation with their political instructor, who impressed me as sincere and caring. I could not help but feel respect for the man. It was little wonder that the people we talked to here were happier than we were. Their standard of living was noticeably better. I told Rongtian that I wished we had leaders like this in our regiment. It was a shame that leaders of this type were so rare.

Then we said goodbye to the political instructor and the others who had helped us out.

Once alone, we walked around to see more. We visited the Fourteenth Regiment's shop and were pleasantly surprised to see cookies, milk, and red bean–flavored popsicles there. These were things we had not seen for what seemed like an eternity. We learned that all these goodies were made by the people of the Fourteenth themselves. We bought some, and they tasted excellent by Gobi standards. We concluded that good leadership really made a big difference.

On our way home, we were lucky to see a horse-drawn wagon driven by a man in his sixties. We offered him a popsicle to give us a ride. The wagon swayed slowly forward, but we were content with not having to walk a long distance. We got off at Xishaliang and ate our last cookies in a deserted, crumbled hut. All the way home we could not stop talking about what we'd seen that day. We both were impressed by the machine and the spirit of the Fourteenth Regiment but discouraged by the cost of our dream machine.

At dinner back in our barracks, everyone wanted to hear what we had seen at the Fourteenth Regiment. A bleak mood prevailed when they heard the price tag, and HaBai summed up the collective feeling by calling our political instructor "a bowl of fake millet." "He may give

you all the nice words in the dictionary, but he won't do anything if he
has to lift a finger," HaBai observed.

★ ★ ★

I kept thinking about how we could present our findings to the political instructor. There was a movie showing at a nearby company that
night, but I was distracted and came home before the feature. In the
dim light of a kerosene lamp, I jotted down a few thoughts to prepare to negotiate with the political instructor. I felt like I was preparing
for an examination that would determine our future, even though the
chance of success was slim.

Cui Xianchao came back before the movie was over, too. He tried
to soothe my anxiety over the machine. He said I should not worry
about something that I did not have any control over. "You've done
your best," he said. "Man proposes and God disposes. Have a good
night's sleep. If the political instructor doesn't want to do it, just pretend
that you never had the idea."

I read an article in the *Reference News* before I went to sleep. It was
called "Agricultural Revolution in the United States" and described in
some detail the technological level of American agriculture. Relative
to our experience as farmers, it might as well have been science fiction. I was wondering why capitalists controlled such advanced tech-
nologies, and why it was so difficult for us to mechanize our work.
Perhaps it was because we had too many people. If there were not
so many people, the leadership might think harder about using some
machines.

I went to sleep, not knowing what tomorrow would bring.

In the end, we didn't get the machine.

★ ★ ★

It was back to hard labor. We continued to make bricks, while the
eighth squad was busy rebuilding the kiln. In two months, we had
enough sunbaked bricks ready. The kiln was ready to be loaded and
fired. The company invited a kiln master to direct us. Some of us were
designated as kiln operators, including myself. We worked in shifts of
three or four hours each after the fire was started.

The kiln needed to be loaded first, with about 40,000 unbaked bricks. The goal was to position them inside the kiln for optimal heat flow. Each brick had to be placed with minimal or no contact on its two flat surfaces with another brick. The bricks were stacked on top of each other on their sides. Rows of bricks were staggered horizontally and vertically. If bricks were placed too close to each other, some might not be thoroughly fired and baked. If they were too far apart, 40,000 bricks could not fit into the kiln. It had to be perfect. With the help of the kiln master, we got the hang of it quickly.

The kiln was loaded from the bottom first, accessed through the stoking tunnel, which we would later use to feed coal into the kiln. As the stacks of bricks rose, that entrance was soon blocked. Then people had to carry the bricks to the top of the kiln by climbing a slope of packed earth we had built. Through the opening on top, we would hand the bricks a few at a time to someone inside the kiln, who would in turn pass the bricks down a line of people until they reached the operator who would place them in the right places.

The company dispatched a women's platoon to help us. The surface of a brick was rough, like sandpaper. We used our bare hands to handle the bricks. Most of us did not have work gloves. It would not have mattered anyway because a new pair would have worn out in less than an hour handling these bricks. Unlike working with a shovel, our hands did not form calluses handling bricks. Instead, our skin would simply abrade off. I noticed that even before the loading of the kiln was completed, the lines and wrinkles of our palms and the pads of our fingers were worn clean away. If we had to make a fingerprint, it would have been a smooth surface with no lines.

When the stacks of bricks rose to the top of the kiln, the bricks in the last layer were placed close to each other to form an inner seal. We would put earth over the top layer of bricks to fully seal the kiln, leaving only a few small holes, some of which served as chimneys and others allowed us to observe the conditions within the kiln once it was going. After the kiln was sealed, it was ready to be fired. We used coal to fuel the kiln. Inner Mongolia was a coal-rich province, although we rarely had enough coal in the wintertime. The coal mines were far away from where we were, so coal had to be shipped in. We used a handcart to bring coal next to the mouth of the kiln inside the entry tunnel. Then we used pieces of wood to start the fire, to which we added coal.

The tunnel was part of the airflow system. Air flowed through the tunnel into the kiln, and the heated air inside exited by flowing up and out through the chimney. To make a good batch, once the fire started, it could not stop until the bricks were fully baked. Half-baked bricks were useless. Therefore, we had to take turns feeding coal into the fire continuously for days around the clock.

Feeding the fire was a tough and dirty job. The fire had to be strong enough to bake all the bricks in the kiln to a red-hot color like molten iron. Inside the tunnel it was hellishly hot. The fire, right in front of our faces, belched choking black smoke, which filled the tunnel. From time to time we had to lean into the inferno, using an iron bar to loosen the burning coal and remove the ash slabs to allow the fire to burn better.

I learned to keep my body low, bending beneath the smoke that floated up. The closer to the ground I stayed, the less smoke I inhaled. From time to time, though, I had to get out of the tunnel to gulp for fresh air. We worked like this for hours at a time each shift. Our bodies were covered with coal dust and smoke. Each work shift was hell. The conditions in the tunnel varied with the weather. When the sky was clear and there was wind, the fire burned well and there was little smoke in the tunnel because the barometric pressure was high and airflow was good. But when it was overcast and still, when the barometric pressure was low, it became almost unbearable; the fire could not burn well and the tunnel would be filled with suffocating smoke. It was the worst if it rained, when I felt as if the tunnel itself became a chimney with the hot, dirty, choking smoke flowing right into my face, nostrils, and lungs. If you think smoking is bad, try inhaling coal smoke and you will consider tobacco smoke a form of clean air.

The night shift was particularly tough, as I had to fight drowsiness as well as heat and smoke. There was a wooden bench next to the fire's mouth, where we could sit during the intervals between feeding coal. Sometimes, when I got too tired, I would lie on it for a few minutes. Fortunately, two people worked each shift, so we could take turns running out of the tunnel to gasp for air. When the night sky was clear, I looked up to see it filled with stars. They shone brightly because all around us was complete darkness. There was no artificial light in the

Gobi at night. Usually a person with an exhausted body was oblivious to beauty, as I knew from experience. But it was on nights like this I felt that I saw breathtaking wonders few others had the privilege of seeing, like the burning inferno under my feet and the stars above my head.

A few days after firing the kiln, I went up to the top of kiln to look down into it through the observation holes. It was a beautiful sight, because the bricks were radiating bright red, like cubes of molten iron stacked into intricate patterns.

The kiln master came back from time to time to check the color of the bricks in the inferno. He told us to stop the fire when he determined the bricks had been baked. We had to wait for a few days for the kiln to cool down before the bricks could be removed and we could learn how well we had done. Completely exhausted after four or five days of firing the kiln, now we could finally take a break. It felt like I had just escaped from hell.

We were amazed our first kiln of bricks was successful. The bricks came out the way they were supposed to. We unloaded the kiln while the bricks were still warm, but no longer hot. Again, two platoons of people joined in the work of taking the bricks out of the kiln. The bricks were loaded onto carts of all types, drawn by horses, donkeys, and cattle. We also used wheelbarrows to move the bricks back to our barracks.

In about two months, we fired the kiln four times and made about 120,000 bricks, not counting breakage. That was enough for our needs for the year, probably with some to spare and ship to other companies.

Now that we had bricks, we began building houses. There was no need for a design or blueprint, as the houses there were identical and simple. Each row had three doors. Inside each door, there were two rooms, one inside and one outside, connected by an opening without a door. All the houses in this part of China were situated in such a way that their doors and windows faced south, away from the winter winds from the north. Each of the south-facing rooms had a window as well.

A women's platoon was assigned to help us. Their job was to help carry bricks and other supplies. Our job was to lay the bricks and build.

The first step was to mark out the shape of a house on the ground where walls would be. Then we dug into the earth to turn the marks into rather deep ditches. We laid the foundation by putting layers of stone or bricks in the bottom of the ditch. Once the wall rose above the ground, we put either baked or unbaked bricks on the wall, layer after layer. Our own dorms were made of unbaked bricks, but the company office and kitchen were made of baked red bricks.

We used some tools to ensure quality. A level spindle was a must to make sure that the foundation was built on a precisely level ground. We also used the spindle to make sure that each layer of bricks on the wall was exactly level. We also used a plumb line, a string with a small weight attached at the end, that would ensure it dropped in a perfect vertical.

After the walls on all sides reached a certain height, those on two ends continued to go up in a triangular shape, converging to a point at the top. A large wood beam would be placed on the top of the walls facing each other to support the roof. We had to wait for weeks for the wood to arrive, as it had to be shipped in. We also needed wood to make doors and windows. Huang Yuliang, a boy from Zhejiang Province in the south, was the company's carpenter. I think his father was a carpenter, too; he was quite skilled. I tried to learn to be a carpenter myself, but I never could do it well. Meanwhile, we spread and covered the walls inside the house with mud to cover all the cracks and holes and make them smooth. Before it was too cold, we completed our task of building new housing for our company.

I then worked as an electrician, wiring each of the rooms of the new house. What I learned about building radios in elementary school turned out to be more than enough to handle the job, which did not require much more than connecting some electric wires to a bare bulb. I liked being a mason and an electrician. It was gratifying to see some tangible results of our labor in the houses we had built, much better than wasting it all in the fields where crops did not grow.

Chapter 14

Petition to Mao

Li Qinglin was an elementary school teacher in suburban Putian, in Fujian Province. On May 6, 1973, the postman delivered a letter to him, in a large envelope on which was printed in red the name of the sender: "The Office of the Central Committee of the Communist Party."

Li's heart missed a beat. He knew immediately that this was a response to a letter he had written to Chairman Mao the previous December. When he opened it, he could not believe his eyes. Mao himself had written the letter.

Mao's letter read: "Comrade Li Qinglin, 300 yuan is sent to help you put food on the table. Similar things are too many in the country. Please allow [us] to solve them in a coordinated way."

The letter was dated April 25, 1973. On May 10, Li received 300 yuan from Mao.

It was of course extraordinary for an elementary school teacher in a small town to receive a personal letter from Mao. Li had written to complain about the plight he and his family were in. His son had been forced to volunteer to become a farmer in a poor province. The place was so destitute that his son could hardly make a living and had to ask his father for help. Li and his wife were already living hand-to-mouth, and had nothing to spare. In addition, his younger son was about to finish junior high and was faced with the same prospect as his brother. In desperation, Li decided to write a letter to Mao. He had never expected Mao to personally write him back.

Mao's letter was soon published in newspapers and touched off a wave of official examination of the problems associated with the "going up to the mountain and down to the countryside" movement. These problems included everything from unnecessary hardships to negligence to the abuse of the young students at the hands of government officials. Looking back, many among the educated youth are still grateful that Li Qinglin had sent his letter; their lives were somewhat improved after the publication of Mao's response.

Li himself became an instant star. He was made a member of the People's Congress. But since he was inexperienced in politics, he became something of a pawn of the radicals in the top leadership; they spurred him to heap accusations against their political opponents for the problems his letter had exposed.

Li's luck did not last. Soon after Mao's death and the arrest of the Gang of Four, the most powerful faction of the Communist Party during the latter part of the Cultural Revolution, Li himself was jailed. In 1978, he was sentenced to life imprisonment for "counterrevolutionary crimes" and was sent to a labor camp to serve his sentence. He was paroled in 1994, after 17 years. He lived off government welfare and the money occasionally sent to him by anonymous former educated youth, who remembered the impact of his letter. He died destitute in 2004 at age 73. His children erected a tombstone on which is inscribed the full text of Mao's letter to him.

★ ★ ★

"Oh, that is more than any patience can endure! God, Who sittest on the brazen heavens enthroned, and smilest with bloody lips, looking down upon agony and death, is it not enough? Is it not enough, without this mockery of praise and blessing? Body of Christ, Thou that wast broken for the salvation of men; blood of Christ, Thou that wast shed for the remission of sins; is it not enough?"

Those were the words that went through the mind of Padre Montanelli, a character in the novel *The Gadfly* by Ethel Voynich, after having lost his son. At the time, I was so mesmerized by the book that

I could not put it down, and I read through it in one go, overnight. The book had long been translated into Chinese and was banned, like almost all other books. But I somehow came to be in temporary possession of a copy. Even though the story was set in the 1840s in Italy, I felt the hardship and pain experienced by its main character, Arthur Burton—whose alias was The Gadfly—and his mental struggle; it somewhat resembled the anguish we were experiencing. Burton renounced his religion, having become completely disillusioned with it, but he could not let go of his love for the padre, who turned out to be his biological father. He tried in vain to persuade the padre to abandon God to be with him. But the padre clung to his faith, in effect sacrificing his son. Now the padre was tormented by his loss: was his sacrifice not enough?

Before he and Arthur parted company for eternity, Padre Montanelli prayed to God for a divine intervention, only to be mocked by Arthur in his stuttering voice:

"C-c-call him louder; perchance he s-s-sleepeth."

The story touched me deeply and I found myself identifying, even to this day, with The Gadfly's cynicism about authorities of any kind. Were our sacrifices not enough? What would be our salvation? Who would answer our call?

After having been told so many lies and so much nonsense by those above us, most of us had lost all confidence in authorities. We did not believe in anything anymore. If I learned anything in the Gobi, it is to be always skeptical of authorities of any kind, especially the self-proclaimed ones. But at that time many of us still believed in Mao and Premier Zhou. We thought they must have been blindsided by what was going on in the system. If only they could hear us, they would have intervened. If only they had known the truth . . .

The truth was ugly.

The Army Construction Corps did not help in any way to develop or transform the impoverished countryside for the better. In fact, we only made things much worse. By my calculation, we were consuming three or four times the amount of food we produced every year. Yet we were made to continue to toil on the land throughout the year and to waste all the resources we put into it. We were stuck, in a hopeless situation, led by officers who did not want to be there. They did not care about how much we produced. Their only job seemed to be to drive us to work hard—for the purpose of keeping us occupied. Yet the harder we worked, the more resources we wasted. It made no sense. But nobody, to my knowledge, was questioning this whole enterprise.

There was no morale to speak of. Everyone hated the place and wanted to leave, if only it were possible. Life could not be worse. After a day of hard, fruitless work, the only entertainment was to lie in bed, chatting about the cities we came from, about food, and about girls. Love was taboo, so boys could only talk.

Without the freedom to go home or to get out of this place for anything better, it felt our lives were not so different from those who were sent into exile in Siberia as described in Russian novels.

Yet we were told we should feel fortunate because "three-quarters of the world population still lived under oppression and exploitation." We should be happy with our lives knowing that people in the capitalist societies led a miserable life. None of us believed that anymore.

My views of this were tempered by listening to broadcasts of programs of the Voice of America and the BBC we picked up on shortwave radio, and from reading whatever I could find, including *Reference News*, an official newspaper, which our company regularly received, although always a few weeks out of date. *Reference News* was a collection of clippings from the foreign press, including the Associated Press, Agence France-Presse, and Reuters. For some reason, the *Christian Science Monitor*, a US publication, was frequently referred to, so the name, which in Chinese sounded odd to me, stuck in my head. From this newspaper, I felt somewhat up to date with goings-on in the world. A fool would know our own living standard was barely at subsistence level and could hardly be worse. Yes, there were a lot of people living in poverty in the world in what Mao called Third World or developing countries. But the living standard in the developed countries, all of which were capitalist societies, was without a doubt better—although at the time, I could not comprehend how much better. Of course, they had a long history of industrialization and China was only building itself from a low base. But we were certainly not contributing to it and, if anything, we were doing our share of dragging it down. Looking around, it seemed that the entire Construction Army Corps was a gigantic waste of labor and resources.

We were meant to learn from the poor peasants to help transform our world outlook. How was that working? In truth, the peasants hated and feared us, for good reason. We competed with them for water and land, and we outnumbered them by far. The Army Corps sealed off a large swath of Lake Wuliangsu from the locals who had lived off its bounty for many years before our arrival. If a local were caught "stealing" fish and reeds from what was now "state property," he would face stiff fines. There had been no need for the locals to venture far from where their villages were to catch plenty of fish in the lake before our arrival. But the Construction Army Corps so overfished that the lake was producing fewer and fewer fish for a much larger population. No wonder: we lived so close to the lake, and yet it was extremely rare for us to have fish to eat.

Whenever a fight broke out between Army Corps soldiers and the local peasants, it was almost always the locals who got beaten up. So many among us had nothing to lose because our lives seemed so meaningless anyhow, that some of us did not think twice about resorting to violence.

The Construction Army Corps gained a bad reputation as a bunch of unruly guys prone to violence; I heard stories that some peasant mothers frightened their kids to bed with "The Army Corps soldiers have come!" The kids would stop crying and hide in their beds right away. I didn't know if the stories were true, but it was certainly reflective of how the locals viewed us, like a bunch of bandits.

There was savagery on both sides. When a lone Army Corps soldier, well known for his fights with the locals, was caught by a group of peasants, they cut off one of his ears. The Army Corps soldiers retaliated by catching a peasant and slicing off both of his.

Once, I heard, a local peasant was caught by some of our soldiers near the regiment headquarters. He was locked up in a small hut guarded by two Army Corps soldiers. Bored with their job, the two of them decided to have some fun by playing tricks to tease the poor peasant. They stood near the window of the hut within earshot of their prisoner.

One said to the other: "It is so troublesome to keep watching this bad guy. I want to finish him off."

The other said: "Great idea. I still have a bullet in my rifle."

Then they opened the door and marched inside with their rifles. The peasant stared nervously at the muzzles of their guns. One of them stepped forward and declared, mimicking the heroes in revolutionary model plays:

"You are a counterrevolutionary. On behalf of the Party and the people, I hereby sentence you to immediate execution!"

Then he aimed and pulled the trigger. Upon the sound of explosion, the poor peasant collapsed to the floor. But it was a dummy bullet. It was just a cruel joke.

The two mischief-makers laughed their heads off. And the poor peasant could only grit his teeth.

How could we expect to build a good relationship with the peasants? How could we possibly learn anything from them? The whole idea seemed like a joke, and a very cruel one at that.

Since we lived not much better than animals, some of us started to act like them. Many people became hot tempered, and gang fights were a common occurrence. Much blood was shed as we fought among ourselves. Some bullies were held in awe and fear, while the weak were bullied.

I was considered a nerd and lightweight, but even I got into physical fights a couple of times when I was attacked for no reason; I still bear a scar on my head, which had to be stitched up after being smashed by a heavy ceramic bowl full of hot noodles thrown with full force at my face. (Yes, although you should have seen how the other guy looked.) At another time, I narrowly escaped with my life when a friend and I were chased by a group of ruffians from Company No. 10 wielding shovels just because we had exchanged a few words with a young woman, which, I guessed, might have provoked the jealousy of some boy there. They stopped us right outside their barracks as we were leaving. A tough-looking guy came right to me without a word and swung his fist at my head. Only quick reflexes allowed me to fend it off with my left arm and, with my right fist, I punched him hard in the stomach before yelling to my friend, "Run!" I took off like a rabbit. My friend did not react as fast and he received a few blows before he could get away. There was no better strategy than running as we were so outnumbered and outgunned. I had never run so fast in my life. We were spared the worst. I had to calm down and hold back my friends at our own company who had picked up shovels and other weapons of destruction ready to seek revenge when they heard of our narrow escape. Based on my personal experiences, I can understand how gang violence can easily escalate.

I was convinced that the top leadership of the country did not know what was going on in these remote areas, where the local officials routinely abused their powers and ruined the lives of young people. I could not believe that the wise leader Chairman Mao would allow this situation to continue if he knew what was going on. Premier Zhou Enlai would certainly put a stop to this waste of lives if he knew.

I had an idea. How about writing a letter to Chairman Mao and Premier Zhou and reporting what was going on in Inner Mongolia? Surely they would intervene. They might change the leadership of the Army Corps. Perhaps the whole thing would change.

I shared my idea with Li Rongtian and Hua Zhenhao. Hua was not a member of our inner circle, but he was a friend of Li and myself. Both of them were more senior than me by schooling. Whereas I only finished elementary school, Li had finished junior high school, and Hua had completed one year of senior high school. Both were considered among the few more-educated people in our company. Both liked to read and think as well. Hua was a somewhat private person and did not socialize much. It seemed that he only cared to talk with those whom he considered intellectual equals. I trusted them. I knew that they, too, were concerned with larger issues, like the future of the farm, the future of the Construction Army Corps, and ultimately the future of the country.

They saw eye to eye with me. Together we started to draft a letter.

We wanted to keep it short, knowing the leaders would be too busy to read a long letter. We would simply report the serious problems we had seen. We debated whether the letter should be anonymous or bear our signatures. We decided to sign our names. If, upon reading the letters, Chairman Mao or Premier Zhou wanted to investigate what was going on within the Army Corps, it would help if they knew how to find us. We were, of course, concerned about reprisals, if the letters got into the wrong hands. But we figured nothing could be much worse than the status quo. On the other hand, why should we fear reprisals when we were doing the country a service? We made up our minds.

We worked hard on the letter. Night after night, we would discuss and debate every point, revising it again and again. Finally, the letter was complete, and I copied it onto clean paper carefully.

The theme of the letter was simple: We were concerned about the country and would like to draw your attention to a grave matter. The letter combined calm analysis with a passionate plea: This situation at Construction Army Corps should not be allowed to continue. In the letter, we reported that the Construction Army Corps was nothing but evil. In fact, we "credited" the Construction Army Corps with "three evils." First, we said, the Army Corps was an evil to the young people. There was no education of any kind. We were not learning anything. Moreover, we were not producing anything. We mentioned the meager crop yield. It was a total waste: of productive assets, of valuable resources, and of our youth.

Second, we argued, the Army Corps was an evil to society. Look at the harm we had brought to the area around us. We did not have enough to eat, so some of us would go out to steal from the peasants, everything from chickens and dogs to pigs and cattle, anything that was edible. We would fight with peasants for irrigation water, for land, and for the right to fish and cut reeds in the lake. The peasants hated us so much they said that we were worse than the Nationalist troops, or even bandits.

Third, the Army Corps was an evil to the state. We did not produce anything and could never generate enough to cover our expenses and costs. Every year, if proper accounting had been taken, it would show we operated at a big loss. This had been going on for four years since we had arrived. Without any drastic measures, this situation was expected to continue indefinitely, at great cost to the government.

Therefore, we pleaded, "Please, *ninlaorenjia*"—or "you old man," referring to Mao with an expression of great respect, as age is associated with wisdom in Chinese tradition—"please do something about it. We soldiers of the Construction Army Corps need help. Please help us and please save us. Please save the peasants and other people around us. Please save the state from the harm of the Army Corps."

We turned the letter into two, one to Mao, and one to Zhou with similar content. We signed and sealed the letters in silence, as we were keenly aware of the risks we were taking. But we were not quite sure how to get such a letter to the great leader himself or to the premier. We knew enough not to mail the letters directly from our barracks. We were certain they would be intercepted and would never find their way out. The letters could clearly be read as an indictment against the leadership of the Army Corps, and that would bring all kinds of reprisals against us. We decided it would be best to send the letters to some people in Beijing and ask them to mail the letters out from there.

I thought of asking my parents. I did not think that my father would do it, but my mother might. She had just returned to Beijing after spending the past three or four years in two separate labor camps. (These camps were referred to as May 7th Cadre Schools, so named because of a letter written on that date in 1966 by Mao, who suggested cadres should also be sent to the countryside to do manual labor to reeducate themselves.) I was hesitant to ask her to take the risk. I knew she would worry about my safety. Who else could help? Liu Xiaotong's father came to mind. He once openly complained to me, railing against the entire Army Corps system. I thought he might be willing to help.

In the end, we decided to send one copy of the letters to Xiaotong's father and another one to my mother, asking them to post the letters from Beijing. We would send the letters from the regiment's sub-headquarters, where there was a mail collection box.

The next day, I took out a horse from the company stable when nobody was paying attention, as none of us had the privilege of using one. Without saddling him, I jumped on his back and spurred him to a gallop for the short ride. I was excited about what this letter would bring, and I wanted to catch the last postman of the day.

Near sub-headquarters, the horse and I barreled around a tight corner at the walled courtyard of the medical clinic, still at a gallop. Just as we rounded the corner, I saw an electric pole dead ahead. It was too late. It seemed inevitable that the horse would crash into the pole. I reined him in hard.

Startled, the horse swerved and reared up on his hindlegs. I was not prepared for this move. The horse reared to his full height, front legs flailing, and I was thrown to the ground. When the horse returned to earth, one hoof glanced past my face. I turned to avoid it, too late. The hoof's blow hit my right eyebrow as if someone punched me. There was no pain.

My right hand reflexively went up to my eyebrow and came away bloodied. Then a lot of blood came, covering my hand and streaming down my face. I could not gauge how badly I was hurt, and I still did not feel the pain.

I retrieved the package of letters now thrown on the ground and calmed down the horse. Horses are sensitive animals, and I felt grateful to this one, even though I was hurt; he must have withdrawn his hoof as soon as he felt my face beneath it, or otherwise my skull would have been crushed. I needed to seek medical attention quickly, and I was right outside the walled yard of the medical clinic. I could not ride anymore, but before I let the horse go, I climbed onto its back, stood up on his back with my hands on the wall, scrambled over the wall, and jumped into the garden of the clinic. This would save time, instead of walking around the walls to go into the clinic through its front door. I still wanted to mail the package.

A few nurses were in the courtyard, tending Chinese medicinal herbs growing in its garden. They must have been shocked to see someone jumping down from the wall with a bloodied face. I quickly assured them that I only wanted some medical help.

The doctor who saw me said that the wound needed stitches. I refused. The last time a barefoot doctor had stitched me up after my head was badly cut in a fight, it left a scar on my left temple. No, I said. Just patch me up. I could not trust the medical skills of those quack doctors who were as poorly trained as I was.

They did as I asked, and the wound eventually healed with hardly a trace, or I might have had trouble finding a wife.

Emerging from the clinic with my head heavily bandaged and my right eye covered, I remembered my mission. Feeling like a zombie, I walked to subheadquarters, and into the mailbox I dropped the package on which so many of our hopes rested.

As luck would have it, I ran into Old Duan, the deputy commander of our company, as I was heading back to camp on foot. He was on horseback. Old Duan was the last person I wanted to see at that moment. He stopped and asked me what happened. I dared not tell him that I was thrown off a horse because he would know that I had stolen one. "Nothing," I replied, as nonchalantly as I could, "I bumped into something by accident," which of course was the honest truth.

The deputy commander must have been amused to see me like that, because he laughed and rode away. I knew he did not buy my story, and he must have thought that I had been in a fight.

I dragged myself back to the barracks. Despite my injury, I felt relieved and happy that I had sent the letters out.

It was October 8, 1973.

Much later, when I went back to Beijing for a visit with my family, I learned Xiaotong's father did not send the letters out, fearing they would bring us trouble. He sat me down and had a long conversation with me about being careful in our actions. Although I understood and listened respectfully, I was determined that the top leadership should know about what was going on in the Gobi.

It was my mother who posted our letters. First, however, she did something quite characteristic of her. She carefully copied them out, every character, in her own calligraphy. She was a professional secretary, and she thought my handwriting was not neat enough for such an important letter to state leaders. After making sure everything was proper, she sent them out by regular mail.

It would be some time before we heard of the letters again. They did bring me trouble. They brought trouble to all of us. But we would only find out later.

Chapter 15

Pigs Don't Fly

At about 6 o'clock in the morning on November 9, 1949, just five weeks after Mao declared the founding of the People's Republic of China, a Convair CV-240 passenger airplane took off from Hong Kong's Kai Tak Airport. Within about 20 minutes, 11 more aircraft—3 Curtiss C-46s and 8 Douglas C-47s—followed it into the sky, one after another, in the first rays of the morning sun. The flight plans submitted to the control tower showed destinations that included Taipei, Haikou, and Guilin, all Nationalist-controlled cities that had yet to be captured by the advancing Communist forces.

The 12 aircraft belonged to two Nationalist-controlled airlines, the China National Aviation Corporation (CNAC) and Central Air Transport Corporation (CATC). In the lead plane sat two important passengers, Liu Jingyi, CEO of CNAC, and Chen Zhuolin, CEO of CATC.

Once airborne, all 12 aircraft made a big circle, altering the direction of their flight toward the north, in the direction of Communist-held China.

Led by the two CEOs, the aircraft crews were either defecting (as the Nationalist government called it) or leading an uprising (as it was hailed by Beijing). They and their aircraft were headed to join the new Communist government in Beijing. They had to fly in and out of the clouds, staying far out of range of the Nationalist air force, to avoid

249

being shot down. The crew of one aircraft was so nervous that one of its pilots mistook a bird for a fighter plane sent to chase it.

After eight hours of flight, the CV-240 touched down at a military airport in the western suburbs of Beijing. The other 11 aircraft flew to Tianjin, a city adjacent to Beijing, and landed safely. The defectors sent out an open telegram to announce their decision to sever ties with the Nationalists and to serve the new government. They were all given a hero's welcome. Zhou Enlai, the newly appointed premier, hosted a banquet in their honor.

Soon after this incident, more than 4,000 Hong Kong employees of the two Nationalist airlines announced their decision to switch their allegiance to the new Beijing government as well and left the British colony to return to the mainland.

These defecting crewmembers and employees, as well as the aircraft they flew, became the foundation and backbone for the first airline of the New China.

The incident is known in Chinese history as "the uprising of the two airlines."

★ ★ ★

"Thank you. Thank you," a gray-haired man said gently as I poured the leftover soup of boiled pumpkins into one of his two buckets. Then he lifted them up with a pole slung across his shoulders and walked with his load slightly swinging back and forth to the next squad. He was collecting leftovers for his pigs, as his job was tending pigs in the Pig Squad.

His name was Yi Kong. He was one of us and yet he was much older, older than our parents.

Among the teenagers and young people of our company was a group of older adults from the Civil Aviation Administration of China, the CAAC. They had been "sent down" to reform their ideological outlook. Once they had been airplane pilots, technicians, and administrators; the youngest was in his thirties and the oldest, Yi Kong, was nearing the retirement age of 60. Some of them had been affiliated with the old Nationalist regime before the revolution. Others had been sent down because they belonged to a discredited faction of Rebels within the CAAC.

Everyone knew and respected Yi Kong. He usually wore an old leather flight jacket, an unusual and precious item if ever there was one. He always had a smile. He was tall and handsome with a wrinkled face. Despite his age, his back was as straight as a military officer's.

He worked hard at his job. To collect food scraps, he placed empty gasoline barrels in front of each platoon's barracks. When the barrels were filled with leftovers from many meals, typically the tasteless boiled pumpkins we were so tired of, he would go around to collect them with two buckets on a shoulder pole and carry the scraps back to the pigpens.

Almost every day we would see him, either carrying the buckets or herding the pigs. He carried a small stick to guide them, looking for a place for them to graze. Since there was not much food for people, there was never enough for pigs. They usually had to eat grass or whatever little vegetation they could find. They were so skinny that they looked more like wolves than pigs, and their stomachs hung to the ground because they had been fed with so much liquid.

Because Yi Kong was kind to everyone and because of his age, we all called him Old Yi to show our respect. Even the company leaders, who usually treated all their subordinates condescendingly, used this honorific to greet him.

Old Yi did not socialize much, even with the others from the CAAC. At meals, he would come to the dining area with a tin bowl to collect his portion, and then take it back to his room near the pigpens and eat alone.

I heard many stories about the man. He had a "complicated" background. He had served in the Nationalist air force. After the Anti-Japanese war, he became a pilot working for the national airline under the Nationalists. He earned fame as one of only few Chinese airline captains in Old China—almost all the rest were Americans. The other one later became the captain of Premier Zhou Enlai's special plane.

In 1949, the Nationalist government fled the mainland, and all its civilian aircraft were flown to Hong Kong. Old Yi was disgusted with the corrupt Nationalist regime and saw hope in the Communists. He and some others decided to defect. With this group of pilots and the aircraft they had brought back, the new government built its first airline, the predecessor of the CAAC.

I got to know Old Yi when I was a barefoot doctor. He came to the clinic, complaining of runny nose and a fever. It turned out that he was allergic to pollen, and his allergies were so bad that he had developed bronchitis. I was able to give him some relief from his allergies. I liked him immensely, and it made me feel good to help him.

One day, Old Yi said that some of his pigs were sick. They ate little and seemed listless. Since there were no veterinarians in the Gobi he thought that I might be able to help. So I went with him to check on the pigs.

Several of my "patients" were confined to one pen, lying in a corner. It did not take me long to note that all the sick pigs were coughing. It was the first time I had seen animals cough, and they did so in very much the same way humans did. Their symptoms pointed to an upper respiratory tract infection, which was surprising to me considering how pigs sniffed the muddy or dusty ground with their snouts all the time without ever getting sick. There would be zero chance for a human not to catch bronchitis or pneumonia by doing the same. It befuddled me how they got sick in the first place, but nature works in mysterious ways, and bovine influenza occurs from time to time.

As with humans, my first professional move was to take their temperature. The only way to do this with a pig was to insert the thermometer into its rectum. It became immediately obvious that the first patient did not like this. The pig became agitated and broke away from the pen, thermometer and all. My friend Huang Shurong, who was now a kind of assistant pig-keeper, was about to chase the animal and subdue it. But Old Yi stopped him, saying it would be even more troublesome if the thermometer broke inside the pig. We decided to let it go, knowing that it would come out sooner or later.

Although I had never treated animals, I thought there should not be much difference between a pig and a person, as we are both rather advanced mammals. It was too bad that they could not complain or allow their temperature to be taken. Otherwise, the only difference was that pigs were a little heavier, warranting a proportionally larger dose of whatever I would give a human, or so I thought.

But since we only had a fixed allocation of antibiotics, there would not be enough to treat the pigs. Besides, antibiotics would be ineffective in case it was a viral infection. I decided to try Chinese folk medicine.

In Chinese medicine, one type of treatment for common diseases is *guasha*; *gua* means scratching and scraping, and *sha* means a rash or redness. The patient lies on the bed, facedown. The doctor holds a coin, dips it in water, and scratches the patient's back, one stroke after another, dipping the coin in the water after each stroke to make sure that the coin does not cut the skin. After a while, the back becomes very red. According to the theory of Chinese medicine, some types of disease, such as coughing, are the result of an imbalance between cold and hot or yin and yang; *guasha* gets the hot "fire" out of the body and restores the balance. In medieval times, European doctors performed bloodletting, draining the blood of their patients, which was probably the same idea.

It was difficult to imagine how I could treat the pigs with *guasha*. I consulted a veterinary book and found there was a related technique that involved letting out some blood by cutting the pig's ears. I decided to give it a try.

It was fortunate that Huang Shurong was with the pig squad now. He was the only one with enough strength to tie down a pig. According to the description in the book, I carefully made triangular cuts on the ears of each of the patients, who did not know what was good for them and screamed loudly.

It worked. A few pigs started to eat almost the next day and recovered quickly. For those that did not totally recover I did use antibiotics, as I suspected a bacterial infection. Huang got hold of some genuine veterinary syringes. They were made of steel and functioned like an impact drill. I would walk near a pig and push the needle in when it was not paying attention. Before it had time to respond, the injection was over. I wished it were so easy with humans.

Pigs were much more responsive to antibiotics than humans. Within a few days, all the patients were happy and noisy again. After this episode, the three of us, Old Yi, Huang, and myself, became self-taught veterinarians. Whenever there was a problem with the pigs, we would discuss the symptoms, consult some books, and figure out what to do.

★ ★ ★

The pigpens were located at the back of the compound right behind the kitchen. Several pens were built around four sides of an open yard, where the pigs would walk around and feed. Each pen was half-covered by a roof, under which the animals would sleep. Pigs may appear to be dirty animals as they bathe in mud, and they do excrete plenty. In fact, the pigs always kept their sleeping quarters under the roof clean, and even in raining or snowy days, they would get up at night to walk out of the roofed area to the farthest corner of their pen in the open air to do their business. They would go out if not confined. In this regard, they are not different from dogs.

Adjacent to the pens was a small room that functioned as a kitchen for the animals. Old Yi and Huang would dump collected leftovers into a big pot—vegetable roots, pumpkin skins, and old cabbage leaves, mostly—and then boil them. As far as I could see, the pigs loved this food, or more accurately, whatever they were fed.

The room that Old Yi and Huang shared was right beside the pigs' kitchen. It was a small room with a *kang*, similar to mine. Although five or six of us lived together in my squad, there were only the two of them here. Two wooden luggage cases under the window served as seats, and another served as a table. Compared to my living quarters, theirs were much more comfortable and spacious.

There were only a few rooms in the entire company that were adequately heated, because coal was scarce. The head office where the company commander and the political instructor lived was one. Another was the clinic. Because they had to cook for the pigs, the pig squad also had plenty of coal. In the deep winter, when it was extremely cold outside, it felt cozily comfortable to sit on Old Yi's *kang* and talk. To this day, I have fond memories of Old Yi's face reflecting the dancing fire and of the pigs making comforting noises on a heap of straw on the earthen floor.

Although they could do nothing about the lack of food, the pig squad did good work. When a pig had a litter in winter, Old Yi and Huang would make a "bed" for them inside their own room so that they would be warmer.

Old Yi was the best-paid man I knew at the time. As a reward for bringing aircraft back from Hong Kong, he and his coconspirators were given a salary paid in cash but pegged to a certain number of sacks of rice. Fixing salaries in terms of sacks of rice became common during the hyperinflation that marked the last days of the old regime. Although Old Yi had to take a big pay cut when the Cultural Revolution started, he was still paid 300 yuan a month, compared with the 5 yuan I was paid.

We used to joke that Old Yi's pigs were probably the most valuable pigs in the entire country, if not the world. The pig squad contributed three or four pigs to the company each year. Old Yi's share was not more than two. Each pig was worth no more than 125 yuan. So Old Yi's contribution to society was about 250 yuan. Yet his annual salary was about 3,600 yuan.

What a huge waste of talent that such a highly paid aviation expert was made to raise pigs whose value was a fraction of his reduced pay. But such waste of talent or worse was on a national scale.

Old Yi sent half his salary to his wife, who lived in Hohhot, and spent the rest. He was generous with us. There was not much to buy where we lived—the shelves of the small shop some distance away were usually empty. Sugar was sometimes available but most of us could not afford it. Whenever Old Yi bought sugar, he shared it with us. He would fill his tin box with sugar and put it on the windowsill. At mealtimes, people would come around to help themselves. He would, from time to time, also put out a bottle of hot pepper that was also popular.

Huang was quite protective of Old Yi and said he should not waste money this way. There was no way for Old Yi to improve the living conditions of so many of us, so Huang figured, why waste the money on the wolves? A few spoonfuls of sugar would not make a difference for anyone. But I knew that everyone appreciated Old Yi's generosity. Old Yi suffered from hemorrhoids, which were made worse by the coarse food and hard work. While most of us used newspaper, Old Yi had a roll of real toilet paper. Although it was rough, it was far softer than newsprint. That was the only thing he would not share.

Aside from the hemorrhoids, Old Yi was legendary for his robustness. Even in his late fifties he still had perfect eyesight. He told me that when he was still one of the best-known pilots in the CAAC system, a newspaper reporter came to interview him about the secrets of his health. She expected him to talk about exercise. To her disappointment, Old Yi said that his secret was not to exercise much.

That was Old Yi. He worked long hours at a slow pace. Other-wise, he would sit in his room, reading or resting with his eyes closed. I asked him why he thought there was no need for exercise. He said the human body was like a machine. If left idle, it would rust. But if you overworked it, it would wear and tear and break down. The best way to maintain it was to use it in moderation. A man would fall ill for lack of movement. But he would not live long if he overworked himself. Since a man's work was already demanding, there was no need for additional exercise. I remember laughing hard about this. I did not know if he was pulling the reporter's leg because Old Yi was not known to tell jokes. I was sure what hard laborers like ourselves required most was more rest, not more exercise; but an office worker or a pilot would probably rust without exercise.

★ ★ ★

Since I was one of the few close friends of both Old Yi and Huang, I liked to go to their pig-food kitchen to chat and read books. Their place was relatively secluded, so I could read away from the public eye, and it was quiet so I could concentrate without being disturbed.

Old Yi was by far the best-educated person in the whole company, yet raising pigs required little of his knowledge or rich experience. In retrospect, his education had probably brought him more trouble than benefit. People from the CAAC told me that the Rebels accused Old Yi of being a "reactionary technical authority." Because of this, he was sent to the Gobi to "reform himself."

Probably to avoid trouble, Old Yi did not possess any books, to my knowledge, except an obligatory copy of *The Selected Works of Mao Zedong*. But he took an interest in whatever I was reading and was happy to answer my questions if there were things in the book I did not quite understand.

I subscribed to a popular-science magazine, *Aviation*, one of the few magazines still allowed at the time. At the same time, I was reading basic textbooks on physics, including aerodynamics. I remember feeling so happy after having understood how a pair of wings could carry a large aircraft into the sky, given the required speed. Old Yi would read every page of that magazine. I asked him why he was interested, as those articles must have been like kindergarten stuff to him.

Old Yi smiled and answered simply: *kai juan you yi*, "Merely to open a book is beneficial." He did not have anything else to read.

The officially published four volumes of *The Selected Works of Mao Zedong* contained Mao's writings only up to September 1949, a few days before he proclaimed the founding of the new People's Republic. The thinking behind his policies after 1949, as reflected in his speeches in internal meetings, was thus largely unknown to the general public.

I owned a few "rare" books. Among them was a set of volumes containing some speeches of Mao that had only been internally published for senior officials. But when the Red Guard ransacked homes and libraries during the chaos, these speeches attracted attention. One of my "rare" books contained Mao's speeches and writings written since 1949.

I had never thought of Mao as anything other than a wise leader. But when I read what he said during the 1950s and 1960s, I grew skeptical. He sounded unbelievably naïve, even to a 16-year-old like myself. For example, during the late 1950s, the "rapid growth" of the Great Leap Forward was followed by three years of the Great Famine. But leaders at various levels reported astronomical output to show the effectiveness of the policies. Annual industrial and agricultural output was said to have increased 10, 20, and sometimes more than 100 times. The figures were so ridiculous that even though I had been out of school only for a few years by then, it was obvious to me that they could not possibly have been true. But somehow Mao seemed to accept them as facts and take them as proof of the success of his policies.

Mao also seemed to think China would soon achieve the ultimate state of communism, and with it the abundance of social and material well-being that Marx had envisioned. He was concerned about what to do with all the extra food and goods that the Chinese people would not be able to consume.

Although I believed China was a strong country in the world, and that the oppressed people in capitalist countries were starving, I had begun to question how strong China really was. Looking around me, we did not have enough to eat. It did not take an expert to realize that we were not productive. If China was on the verge of communism even then, I wondered, why were we so poor? I did not dare think that

Mao might have been delusional, but I felt sure he was overly optimistic about the economy under his policies.

I let Old Yi borrow these works of Mao. From then on, whenever I went to the pigpens, Old Yi was deep in his reading. He was usually careful not to let other people see that he was immersed in something. But he did not have to hide now that he was reading Chairman Mao. Occasionally he would lay down the volume and chat with me about the contents.

My doubts about Mao were forbidden thoughts. But we were quite secluded, and there were only pigs to hear us. By then, I had enough trust in him that I did not hesitate to share my thoughts.

Old Yi's judgment on Mao was reserved. In fact, he was reluctant to speak of Mao. I could understand this, because to criticize the great leader was too dangerous. But I kept asking questions about socialism and capitalism, about China's past, present, and future, and her position in the world—all subjects that came up repeatedly in Mao's works.

I knew that Old Yi had been abroad and, as an expert on aviation, his students and trainees included dignitaries from the Third World countries. However, despite my curiosity, it was difficult to get Old Yi to talk about his past. He would always smile and say, "Read and study. You will learn more than I have."

He also refused repeatedly to teach me English, saying that he had learned a nonstandard dialect. In fact, he was protecting both of us from getting into trouble. I gradually realized that he was being careful not to put himself in a position where he could be accused of influencing my thinking. The risk was less if we discussed facts and concrete experience. I found he was less reluctant to answer questions if I made them specific.

After Old Yi finished reading the volumes by Mao, I asked him his thoughts on Mao's obvious optimism about China marching into the communist stage of economic development. Old Yi said he did not know what level of economic development communism was supposed to reach, and what "material abundance" in a communist society meant; China was still poorer than many capitalist countries in the world.

I was surprised. *China was poorer than many capitalist countries?* I was brought up believing that China was a prosperous socialist country and that the people of the world looked up to Beijing as the center of world revolution. I knew that we were poor in the countryside, and there must have been other poor places in China as well. But I had thought that the oppressed people all over the world were much poorer.

I asked Old Yi how he could be so sure. It was true that he knew little about other countries and their standard of living now, he admitted. But he had been to the United States in the 1940s as an officer under the Allied Forces command and had seen what that country looked like then. He said that if what I had just heard was shocking, he had more shocking news to tell me: The United States in the 1940s was much richer than China today.

I found it impossible to reconcile this with what I had been brought up to believe. But there was no question in my mind that Old Yi was telling me the truth. I was grateful that he would share such a secret with me.

He gave me an example to help me understand. He said that in the 1940s, US shipyards were turning out more than 15 ships every week as part of the war effort against the fascists. Even if fully mobilized today, Old Yi said, China could not produce that number of ships in a whole year.

Through repeated questioning, I learned more from Old Yi about the foreign lands he had been to. It turned out that he had served on a US battleship and traveled all over the world. This was probably the "darkest part" of his personal history, as far as the authorities were concerned, as he had worked with "American imperialists." But he said that the United States had been a friend to China in the war against the Japanese.

I became very curious about the United States, our second-greatest enemy after the Soviet Union. My impression of the country softened after Old Yi told me that Americans were among the friendliest people in the world. I thought that Chairman Mao was right: You should always distinguish between a government and the people of a country.

I asked old Yi about the poverty of the oppressed working people in capitalist society. It was true, Old Yi said, that there was a large gap between rich and poor in the United States. But it was also true even then, that the poor had a higher standard of living than an average citizen of China today.

Subversive words. But Old Yi had to know about rich and poor. He was the highest-paid person I had ever met. If he said China was poor, how could I not believe him?

The sudden realization that I had been misled all my life left me feeling disappointed and delighted at the same time. There might be other things I never knew. Meanwhile, I felt fortunate that I could learn so much truth about the world from Old Yi. I was so ignorant. But I realized that the only way out of my ignorance was to continue to study and learn. For this, the conversations with Old Yi were very valuable. I found it ironic that I was supposed to be re-educated by the peasants in the countryside, yet I learned a great deal more from a "reactionary technical authority" with a counterrevolutionary background.

★ ★ ★

The pigs were generally allowed to roam free, but they had to be summoned to eat. So twice a day, Old Yi could be seen chasing his pigs with a stick while making a beckoning sound of "Lou Lou Lou."

I think it was Huang Shurong who had the bright idea of using a whistle to call the pigs at feeding time. Once the pigs learned the sound, they would rush to the trough when they heard it. But this was confusing for the people. While the pigs could distinguish the sound of Old Yi's whistle, we confused it with the whistle that announced our own meals. So every time we heard a whistle, we would look to see if the pigs were rushing toward the pens.

I liked to watch Old Yi feed the animals. Pigs were impatient. As he poured the feed into the trough, he would fondly reprimand them with the words "Naughty, naughty."

He was fond of his subjects, as we jokingly referred to his pigs, and had given each one a name. The one he was most fond of was a female named Cao Cao, after the politician-general of the Three Kingdoms period (AD 220–280). Perhaps because she was Old Yi's favorite and was fed a bit more and better than the others, or perhaps because she was an enterprising forager, Cao Cao looked like a real pig, with a plump, round body. She would come whenever Old Yi called her name. But unlike other pigs, Cao Cao never ran to eat. She was always composed, just like the politician-general who was her namesake.

Cao Cao was a free spirit, and sometimes she would miss a meal, occasionally wandering off and returning late in the evening. Old Yi somehow found out that she was visiting a breeding stud that lived in another company of Construction Army Corps, about one hour's walk away, a very long distance for a pig. We had no idea how she found her love. Old Yi joked that Cao Cao was violating the rules, since any contact between boys and girls was frowned upon. But Cao Cao didn't seem to care, nor did Old Yi obstruct her romance. The next thing we knew, she was pregnant.

Old Yi was happy that Cao Cao was expecting. He took even better care of her as her belly grew larger. In winter she gave birth to a fine litter. I went to Old Yi's room after work to find her lying on the floor by the fire with a group of pink piglets sucking at her teats. As she lay stretched out, she made low sounds of contentment.

Old Yi told me that he and Huang had had a long night. They had to play midwife to Cao Cao because of her difficult labor. They had to reach inside and pull each piglet out by hand, and a pile of their blood-stained clothes lay on the floor.

Soon Cao Cao was up and about, a group of small piglets chasing after her and stumbling upon one another. It must have been comforting for Old Yi to see Cao Cao have children. He would herd the Cao Cao family into a special area and feed them special meals.

In February, the Chinese New Year approached. Everyone looked forward to a good meal. The thought of eating meat tantalized us, and to our joy the leaders announced the slaughter of a pig. Since there were a few candidates, we never imagined that Cao Cao would be in jeopardy. But the commander decided that she would provide the most meat.

Old Yi, Huang, and all the young women in the company wanted to save Cao Cao, as she had become quite famous. As head of the squad, Huang went to argue with the leaders. He said that Cao Cao should be kept for breeding. Besides, he pointed out, a sow's meat would not taste good. But his objections were overruled. The leaders couldn't care less about future generations of pigs. The fact was that regiment rules said that no company could slaughter more than one pig, and Cao Cao was the fattest. The leaders always did what they wanted. Who would listen to someone arguing on behalf of a pig?

I went to the pig squad on the day of the slaughter. Usually, it was the duty of Huang and Old Yi to tie up the pig, and someone from the kitchen would do the butchering. But Huang said he could not find Cao Cao. After everyone was enlisted in a long search, she was found roaming around somewhere. But Huang would not help catch her. There was no help from Old Yi, either, for Huang had dispatched him to the village shop to buy supplies. The butchers had to chase Cao Cao all over the compound and her screams were so loud that she could be heard everywhere.

Old Yi came back after it was all over. If he had any feelings about the loss of Cao Cao, he did not show them, not even to me. When we spoke of Cao Cao some time later, he only quoted a proverb of which Mao was fond: "A man should be afraid of being well known; a pig should be afraid of being fat."

★　★　★

It seemed to me that Old Yi never had a temper. He was always calm and kind, smiling to everyone, old and young, boys and girls alike. Nothing seemed to upset him. In contrast, I had such a strong sense of love and hatred that I did not even want to speak to the people I did not like, such as the leaders of the company. I offended them, which was probably why I eventually lost my job as a medic.

I told Old Yi how I called Instructor Zhang a real pig when he flatly refused to allow me a home visit when my father was ill in Beijing.

Old Yi told me he worried about this quality of mine. He said that I should try to learn to be tolerant, and to think before I did anything so that I would not regret it.

I could not understand why he showed such respect to the company leaders. Everyone else despised them. They knew almost nothing about agriculture or anything else. The only thing they were experts on was how to make people miserable. They always asked the kitchen for special meals. And they never worked in the fields.

In Old Yi's view, the leaders were not bad people by nature. They did not like it in the Gobi any more than any of us did. If they were harsh or unpleasant to us, it was because they were angry about being here in the first place. He said I should try to understand them.

Besides, he pointed out, the leaders could make my life wretched and I would not be able to do anything about it. If they did not want you to have a home visit in three years, then you would not see your parents for three years. Sometimes, Old Yi advised me, it was worth it to swallow your pride. "You don't lose a piece of your flesh when you call him Commander," he reasoned.

Old Yi told me that he was a carbon copy of me when he was young—passionate and emotional. He used to always speak his mind. But this attitude had led to a lot of suffering. He had now learned never to get emotional about anything.

In his youth, Old Yi had been one of the first students at the new Air Force Academy of Guangxi under the Nationalist regime. It must have been in the 1940s or even earlier. He had been a good student. But as graduation neared, a dispute erupted between the students and the authorities, and the students decided to boycott the final examination.

In a military academy, anyone who disobeyed orders could get into serious trouble. But the students remembered the old saying, "Punishment cannot be meted out on all." They decided that if there were an investigation to find the ringleader, everyone would stand up. The authorities could not punish everyone.

Sure enough, everyone was summoned to an academy-wide meeting. The chief instructor demanded that the ringleader stand up. As planned, Old Yi sprang to his feet, expecting everyone else to follow suit. But he suddenly felt lonely. Everyone else had remained in his seat. Only one other person in the entire room had stood up with him.

The other person turned out to be a nephew of Bai Chongxi, the provincial military commander and governor. Obviously, he had nothing to fear. But Old Yi was not allowed to graduate with his class. Although he graduated a year later without losing his rank, he learned a bitter lesson.

Since then, he said, he had had many similar experiences. Someday I, too, would become seasoned and hardened. But he did not want me to risk smashing my head against a wall to learn a lesson.

Since he was always so careful about everything, I wondered once if he had ever done something that he regretted. He answered that he regretted to have passed the chance to join the Communist Party.

A colleague of his from the CAAC told me that once Old Yi flew an aircraft back in a dense fog with fuel running out. Everyone thought that the aircraft would be lost, because with the primitive equipment aboard there was no way for him to land safely. Accidents were not uncommon in those days. He could try to crash-land in the peasants' fields outside the airport, but people would probably be killed and the aircraft destroyed.

Miraculously, after approaching the runway several times, he managed to land the aircraft safely. He was given a big award for saving the plane. Because of this, his Party secretary had tried to recruit him.

He did not hold anything against the Party, Old Yi told me, but he did not want to join. He told the Party secretary that he could serve the interests of the Party very well as an outsider. As a Party member, one had to attend Party meetings and obey the Party discipline. Old Yi did not want be bound by these strictures. Despite being assured of a "Party ticket," he passed.

During the Cultural Revolution, this decision came back to haunt him. Old Yi became the target of class struggle. His children suffered because of their father's "black" family background. There was little Old Yi could have done about his past—he had, after all, flown for the Nationalists—but they would have fared much better had he not declined to be a Party member. Yes, he concluded, he would not regret his choice if it were just him. But he had inadvertently caused his children misery.

The day after he told me about the regret of his life, Old Yi said he had had a nightmare. He dreamed he was being dragged onto the stage of a class struggle session. As he bent low to hear the charges, a Rebel cited the crimes he had committed against the Party. He was reminded that he came from a landlord family, that he had been a Nationalist Party member, and that he had flown bombers to bomb the "liberated areas" controlled by the Communists. For all they knew, he was a Nationalist spy who had pretended to be a member of the uprising against the old regime.

Old Yi related his dream calmly, but I could tell that he was disturbed. He had never mentioned his family background or his membership in the Nationalist Party to me. He said as a military officer it had not been unusual to become a member—indeed, it was mandatory. He had defected to the Communists because he was disillusioned with the old regime.

Many years later, I learned that Old Yi had been physically beaten by the Rebels who had accused him of plotting to defect to a foreign country. Of course, no evidence was offered, nor was he given a chance to defend himself. His accusers tore apart everything in his house but found nothing; they beat him to force a confession.

Given his experiences at the hands of the Rebels, I think that Old Yi must have been happy in his exile with us. Life was hard, but no one bothered him here. He was glad to have friends like myself, even though, as a teenager, I could not appreciate how difficult it must have been to be separated from his wife and children. He was respected by everyone here, including the company leaders, because of the dignified yet modest manner in which he conducted himself, and for the diligence with which he was doing his job as a pig herder.

One of my most cherished memories of Old Yi is from the summer of 1971, when the company was engaged in the hard work of digging the Dongba Canal. One day, it was scorching hot and the drinking water we brought with us was quickly consumed. We sent someone back to the barracks to fetch some water. Two hours passed and he had not returned. We were so thirsty that some people had collapsed. Then somebody standing on the bank called out, "Water is coming!"

I saw a tall, lean figure with a shoulder pole moving slowly in our direction. The boy we had dispatched, Yang Shengchen, was much shorter. As the figure got closer, I recognized Old Yi. He had carried two full buckets of water weighing over 50 kilograms (~100 pounds) for 10 kilometers (~6 miles) under the burning sun.

We all rushed to greet him. He stopped, put down the buckets, and wiped his forehead. He was soaked in sweat and his face was mottled pale and red. We all asked what had happened to that damned Shengchen. Old Yi reported that he had suffered a heatstroke. Since there were no other men around, Old Yi had taken it upon himself to bring us water.

Before we started to drink, someone suggested that we wet a towel and let Old Yi wipe his face. Against his objections to the waste, we stood and watched him wipe his face. I can still remember his expression of content as we gulped down the precious water. He was like a father to all of us.

★ ★ ★

In the spring of 1973, Old Yi left the farm for Hohhot. It was a time of "implementing new policies." His old work unit had been taken over by the military, and those for whom there was no evidence of crimes were allowed to return to work. They were needed to run the airline. All the employees of the CAAC were issued air force uniforms and prepared to report for duty.

I was happy and sad at the same time—happy that Old Yi was finally able to leave this terrible place and that he could rejoin his family after so long, but sad because I would miss his company and his teachings so much.

Old Yi comforted me, saying that the road ahead was still long. All happy things eventually came to an end, as did all sad ones. "There is no banquet that doesn't end in the world," he said. But our friendship would endure, because it had been forged in a time of hardship.

Many of us turned out to say goodbye to Old Yi and his group. They left for the train station in an open truck. Old Yi looked very different in his air force uniform, like an old general, with white hair peeking from under his cap. He was smiling and waving. The truck started to move. A cloud of dust engulfed it, and it was soon out of sight.

A few months later, a friend of Old Yi's came back to settle some business. He said that on the trip home their hard-seat section of the train was so crowded that the two of them had to share one seat. Since he was the younger man, he had insisted that Old Yi sit. Then he had an idea: He went to the head conductor and claimed that he was a guard to Old Yi, who was his commanding officer. At that time, Chinese military uniforms did not bear any insignia to indicate rank, and Old Yi, with his straight back, white hair, and uniform, looked like a high-ranking officer indeed. The conductor hurriedly ushered them into a first-class compartment, where they rode in comfort all the way. Old Yi never found out why they were treated so nicely.

Sometime later, I received a parcel in the mail. It contained a book titled *The English Duden: A Pictorial Dictionary*. I opened it to find pages and pages of illustrations, each identified and described in English. The book was inscribed to me: "*Comrade Weijian to kindly keep. Gifted by Yi Kong on November 18, 1973 in Hohhot.*"

Soon he retired and went back to his hometown, Guilin, in Guangxi Province, to live on a street named Long Yin ("Hidden Dragon" Road). I lost touch with him after that.

Chapter 16

Half the Sky

A Korean friend and his wife once invited my wife, Bin, and me to have dinner at their home in the United States, where he was studying. His wife was a great cook, and all of us enjoyed the food as well as the lively conversation during dinner about various subjects. My friend would get up from the table from time to time to help her serve the food and clear away the dishes.

More than 10 years later, we visited with them at their home in Seoul, South Korea. It was palatial in comparison with where they had lived in the United States. In addition to my friend's salary as a professor, they both came from wealthy families, and lived quite comfortably. But this time around, Suzy would not sit at the table to eat with us. She was busy cooking, serving the dishes, and pouring drinks. My wife and I repeatedly asked her to sit down to eat, but she declined. Her husband made no effort to invite her to the table.

Puzzled, I asked him why. Don't forget, he told me, that we're in Korea now. It was traditional in Korea for women to not sit at the table with men and guests. My wife and I protested, especially because we were so close with the couple and used to eat together in the United States. "Don't be so old-fashioned," we politely chided our host. He only smiled and reminded us that Korean traditions had come from Confucianism. "We had learned it from your ancient ancestors," he said.

That Confucianism still reigned so supreme in modern Korea surprised me, especially considering the fact that our friend had been educated in the United States—and had a PhD, no less. But what he said was true. I remembered my visit to my mother's home village decades earlier, and how my own grandmother, aunt, and sister would not eat until the men had finished their meals. This tradition was in keeping with Confucius' teachings, which espoused the need for everyone to obey social and domestic hierarchies and their own positions in them. Confucianism required the respect and deference of the young to the old, of women to men, of men to their superiors, and ultimately of all to the emperor. Of all the schools of thought that proliferated in ancient times, Confucianism had prevailed in China because it suited the emperors the best. It legitimized the existing social and political hierarchy, put everyone into his or her own place, and promoted social harmony. Emperors since the Han dynasty in 206 BC had loved the sage and his ideas, as did the rulers of Korea, Japan, and other neighboring countries.

The Communist Revolution was supposed to change all that, as the revolution itself was aimed at overthrowing the existing social and political order. Unsurprisingly, the Communist Party had promoted gender equality throughout its history. While men still dominated its leadership, there were many women revolutionaries enlisted in the Communist cause, some of whom had taken part in the epic Long March of the Red Army and had risen to prominence. Gender equality was enshrined in the first constitution of the People's Republic, adopted in 1954. Mao had famously said, "Women hold up half the sky," although he might not have been the first one to use those words.

In spite of the official promotion of gender equality, old traditions die hard. Confucianism remains deeply rooted in China, including the social bias against women, as it does in many other countries influenced by the Confucian culture.

★ ★ ★

I was sitting outside our barracks reading one lazy Sunday afternoon when a military jeep of the kind usually reserved for high-ranking officers sped noisily into the compound and came to a screeching halt.

Our camp did not have anything faster than a horse or more modern than a beat-up bicycle. We did not see many vehicles, let alone a military jeep. Everyone rushed outside to find out who was paying us a visit.

To our amazement, three uniformed policemen, pistols in their holsters, got out of the jeep. They strode purposefully toward the second platoon's barracks. I hadn't seen a policeman since I left Beijing, and I followed the crowd after them. They marched inside one of the dormitories and came out pushing Zhang Zhiqiu, nicknamed Er Gou (Second Dog), ahead of them. Holding his arms tightly, they escorted him to the commander's office, one officer on each side and the third following close behind.

Old Duan, the deputy commander, let the policemen and Er Gou inside, but stopped the crowd from following them. He would not answer our questions. But a story quickly spread among us: Er Gou had raped his girlfriend.

It had been rumored that Er Gou and Cui Hua (not her real name) had been "friends" for some time. As "talking love" or dating was forbidden, any rumor of this type was usually just that: a rumor. Anyone who wanted to "progress"—which meant anything from joining the Party to going back to the city—would never allow himself or herself be the focus of such gossip. But Er Gou, a boy from Beijing, never seemed to care. He did not seem to have any desire to join the Communist Youth League. He occasionally got into fights.

I do not know where Er Gou got his nickname. Chinese parents sometimes would give their children the most humble or worthless-sounding nicknames for their safety in life so that evil spirits or ghosts would not bother carrying them off. "Gou Sheng," a dog's leftovers, so worthless that even a dog would not eat it, was another popular boy's nickname.

Although Er Gou was known to be a good worker, he was no favorite with the leaders. He could never be bothered to flatter our higher-ups. Instead, he went about doing what he liked, including finding himself a girlfriend.

Cui Hua was with the Sixth Platoon. She had a reputation as a flirt. This was probably because she always had a ready smile. In those days, any girl who smiled easily at boys was regarded as a flirt. I had just thought she was friendly. Now it seemed that there really was something going on.

The whole story eventually came out. It turned out that Er Gou and Cui Hua had been dating secretly for a time. Then, perhaps out of fear they would get caught, Cui Hua decided to break up. She told Er Gou that they should concentrate their energies on building socialism instead. Er Gou was hotheaded and felt humiliated at being dumped. After drinking some liquor, he had stormed to the Sixth Platoon barracks and shouted for Cui Hua to come out. Scared, she refused, and her roommates told Er Gou through the window that she was not in. This further enraged Er Gou. He kicked open the flimsy barracks door, found Cui Hua, and dragged her out of the room into the darkness.

As the other girls and the company commander were out searching for them, Cui Hua came back. When questioned, she told the commander that Er Gou had dragged her to the half-finished row house and raped her.

Commander Zhang did not do anything that night to Er Gou and told Cui Hua to keep quiet. But he called regiment headquarters. The next morning the officers arrived in their jeep and arrested Er Gou.

All afternoon, the police were busy. They photographed a pair of women's underwear, presumably Cui Hua's, which were pinned to the sunny outside wall of the Sixth Platoon barracks. They also spent time "collecting evidence" at the half-finished housing project. Shortly before dinner, the police brought Er Gou out of the office and pushed him into the jeep, handcuffed. The jeep drove away in a cloud of dust.

Although there was no official announcement of the incident, Commander Zhang happily leaked the story wherever he went. He could hardly conceal his excitement whenever he spoke of it. He described the incident in such detail that it seemed as if he had been an eyewitness. Nevertheless, he sternly warned us that Er Gou's trouble was the result of "not earnestly studying Chairman Mao." From time to time, he would scornfully refer to Cui Hua as "that bitch." He would not say what was going to happen to Er Gou, only that he was not going to get off easily.

Most of us had rarely had any real contact with the opposite sex. The male and female platoons were always segregated, and there were never visits or opportunities to mingle. Although some street-smart boys like Li Baoquan liked to talk about sex, nobody believed they had any grounding in experience. That was why this incident of reported rape was so shocking to all of us.

Someone came back from regiment headquarters a few days later to report that Er Gou had denied the charges. He insisted there had been no rape. He said he had taken Cui Hua to the half-built housing project, where he had "lain on top of her for a moment" and let her go. Soon, the boys began referring to Er Gou as one who had committed the crime of *pa-yi-hui-er* ("lying on top for a moment").

A month later, Instructor Zhang called a meeting to announce Er Gou's sentencing for his crimes. The instructor introduced an officer from division headquarters. He was tall and heavily built. He stepped forward and, without wasting time, shouted: "Bring the counter-revolutionary criminal!"

Two policemen pushed Er Gou out from around the corner. We were surprised because nobody knew that he had been brought back to the company. Er Gou, his hands cuffed behind his back, staggered forward with his head bowed low and his back hunched. His head had been shaved and his face was haggard. He had lost weight, and his clothes were in rags. It was obvious that he had been roughed up. A sudden fear ran through us, for he looked so miserably different from his familiar self. There was a hushed silence. After a moment, he raised his head and searched the crowd. I sensed that he was looking for Cui Hua, but she was nowhere to be seen.

Although I had not known Er Gou well, I found it difficult to reconcile him with my image of a counterrevolutionary criminal and rapist. Like everyone else, I was anxious to hear what the police were going to do to him.

The officer announced the offenses. There was nothing we had not already heard: Er Gou had committed the crime of rape. The officer went on to read the rest of the document, which explained what had caused him to fall: He had become a counterrevolutionary criminal because he had not paid attention to studying the works of Chairman Mao and had neglected to reform his ideology. However, the officer said, Er Gou had a good attitude and had confessed his crimes. According to the policy of "leniency for confessing, penalty for resisting," he would receive a light sentence of four years' imprisonment and hard labor. After this announcement, the officer sternly warned us against failure to remold our ideology, which, he said, would lead us to where Er Gou was today.

The meeting ended. The policemen led Er Gou to his room to collect his few belongings. A small crowd followed. We could see that he was weeping. Later, I heard from his former roommates that Er Gou murmured to them he regretted what he had done, but still maintained his innocence.

I think many in the company had some doubts whether Er Gou was guilty as charged. It was obvious he had been roughed up during interrogation, as we could tell from his appearance on that sentencing day. It would not have surprised many of us if he had confessed under duress. Soon after the incident, Cui Hua was transferred out of the company.

There were several "educational" meetings after Er Gou was sentenced. Commander Zhang and Instructor Zhang took turns giving us lectures about the vice of love. They said that we should throw our whole hearts into the construction of the countryside and into the task of reforming ourselves to have a proletarian world outlook. Anyone caught "talking love" would be dealt with severely. They said we should concentrate our love on the Party and Chairman Mao.

I did not think that it was necessary for the commander and the political instructor to be so concerned about our world outlook on love and sex. Anyone who ever wanted to get out of this place would not be involved in a romantic relationship. Only those who were considered "old"—in their late twenties—could have an open relationship with someone of the opposite sex. In general, if anyone were thought to be involved in a romantic relationship, he or she would be automatically excluded from consideration for factory work, college, or Communist Youth League membership, anything that might have meant a chance to get out of the Gobi. Although such opportunities arose rarely, the hope, no matter how dim, was a strong enough incentive for us to stay away from romances. It was not enough to stay clean—one had to stay above suspicion. If people even thought that you were involved with someone, you were doomed to stay in the Gobi.

This situation made it very difficult for anyone who truly wanted to pursue a romance with someone else. Because such relationships had such harsh consequences, those who dared sin had to do so in absolute secrecy. Rumors would fly if a girl and a boy so much as exchanged a few words or even smiles. Any expression of interest could get one in trouble if the other party reported it to the company leadership. This happened a few times. A boy would write a love letter to a girl. If to his misfortune she was very "revolutionary" in her thoughts and wouldn't consider devoting herself to anyone but the Party, or if she were just not that interested in him, she would give the letter to the company commander. The commander would then read the letter to the entire company at the next roll-call meeting. The boy was not just humiliated but, worse than that, he lost all hope of ever making progress. It would have been unthinkable in those days for a woman to take the initiative in writing such a letter. A similar humiliation could get her killed.

But there were exceptions to the rule forbidding talk about love. Army veterans who were old enough and senior enough could pursue relationships openly, without having to worry about gossip. It was open knowledge that Platoon Leader Liu had a girlfriend—the leader of the Sixth Platoon. They were both in their early twenties, but it felt to us like they were of a different generation.

The best these veterans could reasonably expect out of life was to be able to return to their home villages, as most of them came from rural areas, whereas we city kids had different prospects. Only the educated youth from the cities stood a chance, however remote, of going to college or working at a factory. The veterans did not have to worry about sacrificing their future for a romantic relationship. In fact, their greatest wish was to marry a city girl and settle down. A man with a position, such as a platoon leader, would have little trouble finding a girlfriend.

But there were those veterans who found it difficult to land a girlfriend among the educated youth. One of them was Old Hou. In spite of his status as a veteran, Hou was only a common soldier in the second platoon. He was not a Party member either. Hou was short, stocky, and rather unattractive. To his distress, he found it difficult to elicit respect, not to mention affection, from the educated youth. He was so concerned about his romantic future that he went to the political instructor to ask for help in solving his problem. The instructor told Old Hou to spend more time studying the works of Chairman Mao.

Hou liked a girl by the name of Shi Xiuling. I have to say that Old Hou had very good taste. Xiuling, who became a barefoot doctor after

I did, was tall, slender, and pretty, with large eyes. Hou decided to write a letter to express his affection for her and delivered it in person one day at the barracks' communal well. Instead of being flattered, she was frightened and soon turned the letter over to the company commander. Since Hou was a veteran, Commander Zhang did not read the letter openly at the company meeting to shame him. But he took great pleasure in telling everyone about it, taking care to make fun of Old Hou for his misspelled words. When Xiuling learned that many in the company knew that she was being pursued by Old Hou, she developed such hysteria that she had to be sent to the division hospital.

Although spurned, Old Hou would not give up his pursuit. He wrote another letter to Xiuling, telling her that he was only 25 years old despite the fact that he looked 30. To dispel any doubts, he said that he would swear to Chairman Mao that he was indeed 25. Moreover, he demanded to know why the girl did not love him.

According to Commander Zhang, who amused himself telling us the story, Old Hou quoted Mao in the letter as saying that "there is no love without a reason and there is no hatred without a reason in the world." A true proletarian, he said, should love another member of the proletarian class. "I am a proletarian, why don't you love me?" he demanded. "If you do not love me, you do not love the proletariat."

The logic in his reasoning was compelling, but it did not work.

The furor over the letters continued, and Xiuling's hysteria returned. She had to be sent to the division hospital again. The political instructor had to issue an explicit order forbidding Old Hou to communicate with her in any way. As a consequence of this episode, Old Hou earned the nickname of "true proletarian."

Because the male and female platoons were kept apart, there was only one place where people of the opposite sex could possibly meet openly, and that was the company office, where Commander Zhang and Instructor Zhang wielded their power. They alone decided who would be allowed to join the Communist Youth League or the Party, two of the surest ways to progress. The power these two held over us was immense. It was they who decided who got what job. They could send some people to factories or colleges and block others. Power was attractive, and as its center, the company office drew many people every day. People found all kinds of excuses to visit.

Commander Zhang was overweight and clumsy and grew uglier when he smiled. His voice was rough like a donkey's. He was so lazy and so slow that the boys nicknamed him "Old Idiot." The women called him, slightly more respectfully, "Idiot Commander." He always treated boys harshly but was pleasant to the girls.

One day, Li Baoquan rushed in and excitedly announced that there was "exceptionally good news," a term that usually referred to the publication of a "highest edict" from Mao. Sometimes that would mean a drastic change of course in either domestic or foreign policy. The last time there had been an issuance of a "highest edict" had been a year earlier in 1972, when it was announced that US president Richard Nixon would visit China.

So what was the "especially great good news" this time? I asked Baoquan. He grinned from ear to ear. "Old Idiot has been detained at regiment headquarters."

Old Idiot had been detained because he was found to have committed "mistakes of lifestyle," a euphemism for sexual misconduct. The old turtle egg had been caught at last. Baoquan put on an air of authority and reported what he had learned.

A boy and a girl from our company were caught in a tryst one night in a corner of the threshing ground. Old Idiot was coming back from a hunting trip on horseback. He had the privilege of carrying a rifle, which he used to hunt rabbits and foxes to "improve the quality of his life," as he said. He spotted the boy and girl and was furious that they had dared to violate the order against romantic relationships. He chastised them and ordered the boy to go back to his barracks to write a self-criticism and wait for his punishment.

Both the boy and the girl were frightened, knowing that this discovery would seal their fate, depriving them of any chance for a better future. The boy left. Then Commander Zhang turned to the girl. He said that he would keep the episode to himself . . . if only . . .

From that night on, the commander summoned the girl to "exchange views" with him from time to time. No one suspected anything since it was normal for the company leaders to give lessons in correct ideology to any one of us at any time. The commander took the girl to the threshing ground, to the fields, or wherever he could find privacy.

The boy, frightened, stopped seeing the girl. He was surprised that nothing ever happened to him, as if his transgression had been forgotten. He was even grateful that the commander was willing to overlook his wrong deeds. But then the girl got pregnant. As the relationship between the boy and the girl hadn't progressed that far, there was no doubt that the commander was the father. The girl sought out her old boyfriend, and she told him what had happened.

If it had been someone else among the boys, he might have avenged the girl's shame by resorting to violence against the commander. But this boy was a wimp, sniffed Baoquan. All he did was to encourage the girl to report him to higher authorities. The girl was reluctant, because of the shame it would bring. After much hesitation, she made a trip to regiment headquarters to lodge a report. But the move backfired. Commander Zhang said the girl was slandering him, and claimed that the boy was the father, not he.

The regiment authorities launched an investigation into the family background of this girl and her boyfriend to see if she had any motives for slandering an officer. The girl was from a family of poor workers and more or less above reproach. But the boy's father had been a petty businessman before the revolution. The boy was therefore suspected of trying to launch an act of class vengeance.

Just at that point, the regiment headquarters received a letter from the Beijing Military Regional Command, the official supervisory organ of the Inner Mongolian Construction Army Corps, a much higher authority in the military hierarchy. The letter was regarding another young woman of our company, whom I will call Zhang Liling. She had recently deserted, fleeing back to her home in the city.

Her father was a decorated People's Liberation Army (PLA) commander who had participated in the battle to capture an important seaside city during the civil war. During the Cultural Revolution, the Rebels labeled him as a black member of society because he was from a landlord family. Accordingly, Liling had been categorized as a child of class enemies, but she was also considered a child who can be re-educated.

Among those of us in the Gobi, the "children who can be re-educated" generally wanted to prove themselves worthy of the Party's trust by working very hard and behaving carefully. Despite a weak constitution, this girl had been a hard worker, and had been an "active element" in the eyes of the leadership, always going to study sessions and generally currying favor with the leaders. She had tried to prove that she was loyal to Chairman Mao and the Party.

A few months earlier, Liling's platoon had been dispatched to a place quite far from our barracks. After they had been there a few days, Commander Zhang arrived and ordered her to go fetch an "important document" back at the company camp. When she went back the girl found in the commander's drawer an unimportant document and a love letter addressed to her from the commander. Among other things, he told the girl that as a re-educable person, she should get close to the Party. In the eyes of Commander Zhang, he was the Party. He promised to take care of her.

Liling was indignant. The incident shattered her idealistic image of the Party. She had grown up in a military compound, and never expected such behavior from an officer of the PLA. She had genuinely believed that she could atone for her father's sins by working hard, for the Party taught that redemption was possible.

As Liling was returning to her platoon on horseback, she encountered the commander lying in wait. It was already dark. When he tried to stop her, she spurred her horse forward in an attempt to run him over or to get away from him. But the horse was startled and threw her into a ditch. Old Idiot attacked her. Liling, still in the ditch from her fall, tried to fend him off with her whip. At just this moment, a horse wrangler passed by, and Old Idiot fled. The horse wrangler did not see Old Idiot and did not know what was going on but helped Liling catch her horse so she could ride back to her platoon safely.

Liling wrote to her parents about the commander's attack. They were so worried that they told her to get away. This was risky. Many deserters were caught and brought back. A deserter was often condemned to the hardest of all jobs, without any hope for a better future. But Liling got away and took a train back to Beijing without incident. In fact, at the time I had been surprised that there was not much discussion of her desertion by the commander in the company meetings afterward. Now I knew why.

By coincidence, Liling's father had been exonerated and had assumed his senior position in the military just before she arrived home.

He immediately sent a letter to the Beijing Military Regional Command, enclosing the commander's love letter to his daughter.

This did Old Idiot in.

He was urgently summoned to the regiment headquarters. He never returned. The timing couldn't have been worse for Old Idiot. In addition to his offenses and the letter from the Beijing Military Region, a document signed by Premier Zhou Enlai was at this time being circulated to all the country's Construction Army Corps. The document dealt with a case involving a regiment commander of the Northeast Construction Army Corps who had sexually exploited hundreds of young women under his command. The premier ordered a thorough investigation of all similar cases. Old Idiot immediately became a prime target for our leaders, who could now report the effectiveness of their work in carrying out Zhou Enlai's order.

At the time, my friends and I did not realize that Old Idiot was not an isolated case. It turned out that he was just one of thousands of officers around the country who were preying on young women. The number of revelations that poured out was shocking. Within a few months, several commanders and political instructors in our division were arrested for their "lifestyle problems." The political instructor of Eighth Company was arrested for having slept with practically every young woman under his command. One of the young women who had earned her way to college in his bed turned him in after she got back to Beijing. In many cases, it emerged, the young women had gotten something in return: Youth League or Party memberships, the opportunity to go to college, or work at a factory in the city. But who could blame them? After all, these were innocent young women whose fate was entirely in the hands of their commanding officers. And some of those officers were out of control.

According to official documents, in the Yunnan Construction Corps, a battalion commander raped more than 20 young women. A political instructor, Zhang Guoliang, raped dozens of educated youth. In Heilongjiang, the regiment commanders and chief of staff raped 50. In Inner Mongolia, where we were, there were reports that 209 officers raped 299 women. Arrests of officers in the Construction Corps were made in Inner Mongolia, Xinjiang, Guangzhou, and Yunnan.

We were ecstatic when Old Idiot was taken in and hoped he would receive a harsh sentence. But when his case was decided months later, all he got was dismissal from military service. He went back to his home village. We were all disappointed and were not quite sure if it was a punishment at all.

It was good to get rid of those bad eggs. But who knew how many others were never caught? After all, their power enabled these officers to do what they did. Those who remained still had absolute control over our fate and future.

Chapter 17

Desert Dreams
of College

Liu Bang was the founding emperor of the Han dynasty, one of China's most significant periods. The Han dynasty lasted 426 years, from 206 BC to AD 220, and is widely viewed as one of the pinnacles of ancient Chinese culture.

Liu Bang himself, however, made for an unlikely patriarch. A former rebel leader from a peasant family, he despised intellectuals, especially the followers of the great sage Confucius. He was known to urinate into the hats of Confucian scholars to show his contempt. One day during one of his military campaigns, he was sitting on his bed in his tent having his feet washed by two young women of his court. When it was reported to him that an old scholarly looking man was outside waiting to see him, he flew into a rage and said, "Tell him I am busy with the big affairs of the country and have no time for Confucian scholars."

When Li Yiji, the visitor, heard this reply, he put his hand on his sword, angrily stared at the reporting guard, and yelled, "Go back to tell him, I am a drunkard from Gaoyang, not an intellectual!"

Upon hearing this, Liu Bang immediately stood up in his bare feet and asked Li to be invited in. From that point on, Li became Liu Bang's trusted advisor. Once Liu ascended to the throne, one of his first official acts was to pay homage at the temple of Confucius in the sage's hometown, setting a precedent for dynasties of Chinese emperors to follow for the next 2,000 years.

Formal education and learning had a long and revered history in China. The Chinese word for university is *da xue* (*da* means big and *xue* means studies), which originated from *tai xue*, meaning imperial college. Imperial schools, intended solely for the purpose of training government officials, dated back 3,000 years. The system was formalized about 2,000 years ago by Liu Bang's descendants in the Han dynasty and had continued with little change throughout the centuries.

The first modern national university in China was the Imperial University of Peking, founded in 1898 as a successor to and replacement for the imperial college. The name was later changed to Peking University. Mao Zedong was a librarian there at one time. Equal in fame and stature with Peking University today is Tsinghua University, which was founded in 1911, the last year of the Qing dynasty, thanks in part to an initiative by the United States.

The United States was one of the eight foreign powers that had crushed the Boxer Rebellion in 1900. The Qing government was required to pay indemnities. In 1909, President Theodore Roosevelt obtained congressional approval to return the overpaid part of these funds on the condition that it would be used to secure scholarships for Chinese students to study in the United States. Tsinghua College was established in 1911 to serve as a preparatory school for these students. The YMCA in the United States recruited faculty members for sciences, and the college's graduates transferred directly to US schools as juniors upon graduation.

Like the first emperor of the Han dynasty, Mao also held intellectuals in contempt, even though he was an astonishingly well-read man. He detested the formal education system that he thought indoctrinated young souls with old ideas against the revolution. Yet eventually and grudgingly he conceded that the country still needed formal education. "Universities are still needed," he admitted. "Here I mainly refer to those teaching science and engineering. But the terms need to be shortened and education needs to be revolutionized."

★ ★ ★

The room was dark, illuminated only by a flickering burning wick dipped in a small bottle of kerosene, and it was quiet, except for the faint and breaking voice coming out of a radio. Three of us huddled together on a *kang*, listening intently and trying to catch the words drifting out of the radio mixed with the noise of static. We were listening to the Chinese program of the Voice of America (VOA).

Suddenly, there was a loud voice: "Aha! I have caught you listening to the enemy station!"

We all turned around and froze. Instructor Zhang stood by the door. We had been so absorbed in the broadcast that none of us noticed him quietly sneaking into our room. Listening to American imperialist propaganda was a serious offense. We were in deep trouble.

I could see the sly smile on his face even in the dim light. He was clearly very pleased with himself for having caught us red-handed.

Someone immediately turned off the radio. But it was too late. Then there were a few seconds of dead silence, as nobody knew what to say or do.

Finally, I broke the silence. "So what?" I said. "If you put us in jail, the food there will be better than here and we wouldn't have to work so hard."

None of us had ever been in jail or knew what it was like. But that was the only thing I could think of to bluff him.

He seemed to be surprised by my words. He thought for a few seconds and then said in a nasty tone, "That's true. I can't let you little kits of a rabbit get off easy."

"Little kits of a rabbit" was what he fondly called us, a term similar to "turtle egg" or the equally "endearing" English expression "son of a bitch."

Then he walked over and sat down on the *kang*. Leaning forward, he asked in a low voice, almost whispering, "What were you listening to?"

Incredibly, he seemed to be suggesting he wanted to join our little conspiracy. I supposed he could not suppress his curiosity.

We were in fact still trying to sort out the meaning of a major piece of news heard from "enemy stations." In spite of its almost total ban on foreign publications, China never banned shortwave radios. That was probably because the country was so large that a vast majority of the rural population would not have been able to receive news and propaganda from Beijing without them. I had a shortwave radio my mother had given to me, whose reception was good enough to allow me to listen to foreign stations including VOA, the BBC, and Radio Moscow, all of which had frequencies that broadcast in Chinese. Of these, VOA was the most interesting, because of the variety of its programs. Radio Moscow was the most boring, as its propaganda was no more entertaining than Radio Beijing.

It was the first week of October 1971. I had heard various foreign broadcasts over the past few days speculating about something big happening in the Chinese capital, although nobody seemed to be able to confirm what it actually was. All anyone knew was that Beijing had canceled the annual military parade in Tiananmen Square on National Day, October 1. This had never happened since the founding of the PRC in 1949. But there was no official explanation given, prompting a frenzy of speculation among foreign observers about what had happened behind the scenes.

Radio Moscow reported that the cancellation had something to do with Marshal Lin Biao, Mao's designated successor and second in command in the Chinese leadership. But it offered no more than rumors or hearsay.

Those among my closest friends who cared about matters like this had become more and more anxious to find out what was going on in Beijing. Foreign radio stations were the only source of such sensitive information. Now that we were caught and cornered by the political instructor, we had to tell him what we had heard.

"Really?" He was very intrigued and told us to turn on the radio. We immediately obliged, eager to draw him into our crime. Now that Instructor Zhang was compromised, we were able to relax and turn our attention to the radio. But we did not hear any new information that night.

It was not until early November that we learned the true story. On an unusually sunny day for November, our platoon joined the rest of our company in an assembly to hear an important proclamation from the central command. We all sat on the ground in formation, making a kind of outdoor auditorium facing the sidewall of a row of mudbrick houses, which shone brightly in the winter sun. Soon Xuan, the political commissar of the regiment, strolled to the front to read an official document. We knew we could expect some surprising news. The last time he was here, a few months earlier, he had announced that Henry Kissinger, a representative of China's mortal enemy, the American imperialists, had secretly visited Zhou Enlai and that Mao himself had invited President Richard Nixon to visit Beijing. What could it possibly be now?

Through rumors and our foreign radio stations, some of us already had an inkling that something major had happened in Beijing, and that it could possibly be related to Mao's successor, Lin Biao. Still, the news shocked all of us.

Lin Biao had plotted to assassinate Chairman Mao, Commissar Xuan declared. But the attempt had failed because the great leader, who was ever wise and farsighted, had foiled his plot. Consequently, on the night of September 13, 1971, Lin had scrambled onto a French-made Trident aircraft together with his wife and son to flee the country, in an attempt to defect to the Soviet Union. His plane had run out of fuel shortly after crossing the Mongolian border and crashed in the desert near the town of Undurkhaan, a few hundred kilometers north of where we were.

It was an astonishing turn of events. More than just about anyone else in the leadership, Lin Biao was the one who had carried the banner of the Cultural Revolution for Mao. He had created and promoted the Little Red Book of Mao's quotations and he had waved it in his hand wherever he had gone, setting an example for the rest of the country. Now he had wanted to kill Mao?

★ ★ ★

Mao was devastated by the defection of Lin Biao and fell gravely ill for a period of time. With Lin out of the way and Mao utterly drained of his vigor by the event, Zhou, the premier, began to bring some order back to the country. Some purged officials were brought back to power and some prominent scholars had their names cleared.

In late 1971, official newspapers printed another one of Mao's highest edicts: "Universities are still needed. . . . Students should be selected from among workers and peasants who have had practical experiences."

In fact, he had made those remarks in 1968. But as Zhou moved to undo some of the Cultural Revolution's excesses, the central authorities chose this moment to publicize it.

I had always wanted to go to college. But in the Gobi, this increasingly felt like a pipe dream. It was going to take a miracle for me to get out of the place. To comfort myself, I would tell myself to keep reading. If I did not have a chance to go to school, I could still educate myself, and that kept up my motivation to learn. But how nice it would be if I did get the chance.

With the publication of Mao's remarks, many colleges reopened. Professors, who had been targets of persecution and sent to the countryside, were now being summoned back to teach.

It had been six years since China's entire system of higher education had been shut down. Most of us had spent the last few years laboring in the countryside. People of college age, like me—18 or 19 years old—had never attended middle school. But there was no need for academic qualification. There would be no exams. Instead, a "revolutionary" process of student selection was devised. Students would be chosen from the ranks of those having had at least two years of work experience among peasants, workers, and soldiers, through a system of "recommendation by the masses," meaning election by one's peers. They also had to meet political criteria, like good work performance and a working-class family background.

This, I realized, could be the miracle I had been hoping for. I was certain that I met the basic qualifications: I was a hard worker and was perceived as such. I had never been in a relationship with a girl or done anything else that would keep me out of contention. People were fair-minded, I thought. A good worker deserved to be considered.

And as our tenure in the Gobi had lengthened, good workers had become harder and harder to come by. Most people had long ago stopped working in the fields on a regular basis. Out of 150 boys, probably no more than 20 or so still cared to go to work every day. I was one of them. I was by no means physically strong, but I proved I could tough it out.

The catch was that I was not on good terms with the company leaders.

In September 1972, the leadership selected three people to go to college. One of them was a friend of ours, Wang Yingfan. He was to go to the Beijing Institute of Foreign Languages to study Polish. Counter to the stated rules of the selection process, the decision was made in secret, without any input at all from the masses, who were officially supposed to recommend candidates. All of us were excited, nonetheless, that he had been given the opportunity to go.

We celebrated. This was a big event in our lives and we were letting off steam. We talked and talked, about the past, the present, and the future, for it seemed as if a future were suddenly possible.

We were delirious with excitement. At one point, referring to our friend's study of a foreign language, I remarked, "Perhaps someday all of us will meet up in Paris or London."

Someone else chimed in, "Or maybe New York."

We all laughed at this joke, which also embodied so many hopes and dreams that had been repressed for so long. None of us really thought this might come true. We said it lightly, carried away by our joy of the moment.

Someone reported the conversation to the company leaders. The next thing I knew, I was the target of a public criticism against my bourgeois outlook on life, because of what I had said about Paris and London.

Despite its absurdity, the charge was a serious blow to my college chances. According to my critics, my remarks revealed that I aspired to a "capitalist lifestyle." My accusers suggested the reason I was always reading was that I wanted to become somebody someday, which, by definition in the dictionary of the working class, was bad. A number of different squads and platoons, including, surprisingly, women's platoons, put up posters that criticized me. I supposed it was easy for them to write such denunciations in accordance with the wishes of the leaders, since they did not know me personally.

I felt hurt, and also concerned about my future. But I held up, despite my anguish at being singled out as a target of attack by so many. I hated the snitch who had informed on me, and I could not understand how people could sink so low as to please the leaders by stepping on other people's heads.

But the criticism also made me think about how others saw me. Why were so many people joining in with accusations? They did not know me, or my friends, at all, and I realized that our tight circle could be perceived as elitist and exclusive to those on the outside. We spent our free time reading books, and we passed around everything we could get our hands on, from Chinese histories to Russian novels. Most people spent their leisure time playing poker and chess. I thought myself to be above such useless pursuits or wastes of time. And maybe that was my problem: people did not like people who were too different.

The criticism against my bourgeois outlook on life was a wake-up call for me and taught me a painful lesson. I began to wonder how I could win more people over as friends. With the women's platoons, it would be difficult and risky to even try, given that contact between the sexes was frowned upon. But I could improve my relationship with the boys. If I achieved that, the company leaders would not be able to isolate me.

★ ★ ★

As the criticism against me subsided, I started my own public relations campaign.

I thought hard about how to become more popular and decided I had to spend more time socializing. I wanted everyone to see me not just as a nerd but as one of them.

Time spent socializing meant time taken away from my studies. That was a big sacrifice because I already felt I had too little time to read. Most people on the farm did not go to the fields to work, but I worked every day. Since farm labor, no matter what kind, was never light, I would be exhausted after work. After dinner I had only a few hours to myself before bed. Yes, time was precious to me.

And yet I regarded the sacrifice as necessary. I decided to use one hour every day, no more and no less, to improve my social relationships; I called this my "socialization hour." I would simply wander into a room, sit down, chat with a few of the guys, and tell a story or two. When the time seemed right, I would say goodbye and go to another room. I went from one room to another in rotation. This way, I made sure that I got to as many people as possible.

But that was still not enough. How could I stand out? How could I impress the women's platoons so they would not regard me as the nerdy one and remember me when the election time for college came? Women, as Mao put it, held up half the sky, so I needed their support when the occasion called for it.

I hit upon an idea.

Sports were popular on our farm. There were matches between platoons in volleyball and basketball almost every day after dinner, weather permitting. When there was a match, almost everyone, boys and girls alike, came out to watch, though the sexes did not mingle. Good athletes were popular and everyone knew them.

It would be much easier if I'd been a basketball or volleyball star. But I had no experience in either sport and had little chance of learning now. In fact, no team would allow me to play with them, as I would probably cause them to lose the game.

Then I thought of something different.

I had noticed that while there was a volleyball match almost every day, there wasn't anyone who seemed to know the precise rules of the game, and there was never an official referee when teams from different platoons played each other. That, I had realized, was my chance.

I wrote a letter to my father in Beijing, asking him to send me a book explaining the official rules of volleyball for international competitions. When it arrived, I spent many nights studying and memorizing it, until I was well versed not only in the rules of the game but also in the hand signals used by professional referees. Volleyball was one of the most popular sports in camp. Many boys participated. And while none of the girls played because it was considered unfitting, they always watched and giggled on the sidelines.

One day, as a game was just about to start, the teams asked for a scorekeeper. I immediately volunteered. The players just laughed at me. Because I had never played, they doubted my scorekeeping abilities. "Let me give it a try," I pleaded. "Maybe I can do it." Without an alternative, they agreed, and the game started.

I strictly applied all the rules of the game in refereeing. My decisions were precisely executed, complete with hand signals that really surprised and pleased the crowd. I was immediately accepted as the official referee for platoon-level volleyball matches. From then on, I was invited to be the judge whenever a serious game was played. I received much attention. And, to my satisfaction, I was becoming popular.

I would have been more popular if I also picked up basketball refereeing. But that much running around would have exhausted me, especially after a day of work. I decided to stick with volleyball. I was more noticeable (and it was less tiring) to sit in my referee's chair, high above the net. I loved it when some player fouled with a light step out of bounds during a serve. Then I would blow the whistle and give him a penalty. He often would protest, but I would overrule him. The eyes of the crowd were on me as I delivered my decision. Then the onlookers would back me up with testimonies of what they saw. My authority was accepted and respected. It felt great.

I could feel people becoming friendlier toward me. I was also respected for being a hard worker; although most people did not work, they respected those who did. It took strong will and determination to stand the cold, the heat, and the hardship to go to the fields every day, and people knew that. With my newfound popularity, I felt sure I had an advantage over other contenders for a chance to go to college next year. Ironically, thanks to the campaign against my bourgeois outlook on life, most people now knew that I loved to read and study and could infer that I was probably better qualified for college than others.

When the time finally came for the annual college selection process, in early summer of 1974, there was a big surprise.

In the previous year, I had led a small protest movement over the college candidate selection process. The official line was that candidates had to be "recommended by the masses around them," through an election, but, in truth, the company leaders made the decision. We demanded a change and lobbied for a true election. The protest had fallen on deaf ears.

We were resigned to the idea that 1974 would be a repeat of the previous year. Still, everyone was curious to see who would be the lucky ones chosen. It was like announcing a lottery number, although not everyone had an equal probability of winning.

On August 15, 1974, at a company meeting, Instructor Zhang announced that an ad hoc committee would be formed to lead and supervise the selection of candidates for college this year. He then read four names. The committee would consist of the head of the logistics unit; the head of Platoon No. 6; the political instructor himself; and me.

I was sure that everyone was as surprised as I was. Who was I? It was well known that the company leaders didn't like me. And nobody had forgotten about the criticism against my bourgeois ideas. Moreover, I was not a member of the Communist Youth League, and anyone worth anything in the eyes of the leadership was a member. I was the last person anyone expected to be a member of a committee of any sort. And this one might be the most powerful body ever formed in our company, because it could promote some people to heaven, which was what going to college felt like.

Quickly, a few friends and I huddled to analyze why the leaders had decided to include me on this committee. We decided they did it to dispel potential accusations of favoritism; since I was a known trouble-maker, my presence would bear witness to the idea that it would be a fair selection process. I was the window dressing they needed to make the process look fair and aboveboard.

Every squad had a heated discussion about whom to select. Candidates were nominated and ballots were collected. The discussions were recorded in minutes and organized as the "views from the masses." All the ballots and opinions were sent to the company office. The four-member committee then tallied the ballots.

The results were announced at the next company meeting. The commentaries that came with the ballots were also read out.

Cui Dehui received more votes than anyone else. He was known as a hard worker, a person we all thought would someday work himself to death. He was also a member of the Party. There were only two or three Party members among us. He was well liked, and he was also a favorite of the leaders. His chances were the best.

To my surprise, I came in second, with just slightly fewer votes than Cui Dehui. I had never thought that I would receive so much support. My public relations campaign must have worked. In retrospect, Instructor Zhang had made a big mistake. By including me in the committee, he gave me visibility and legitimized me in the eyes of the people.

Our company was given a quota of nine places for colleges. Out of this, I ranked second. And I was present at the committee meetings for the final selection. Nobody, including the political instructor, could veto my chances in my presence. Therefore, my candidacy sailed through without major issues. I was elated. My luck might finally have turned.

But of course, it's never over until it's over. I was only "recommended" by the company to the regiment headquarters, which would in turn decide whom to submit to the division headquarters and its Party committee. It would be foolish to celebrate now. Anything might happen. I had learned through cruel experience that one should never be happy before a decision was made official.

Although my heart was no longer in it, I began to work extra hard. I understood that everyone was watching me. Showing signs of joy would be taken as evidence that I had not truly embraced my mission in the countryside and was just waiting to get out of here. That would provide the leaders with an excuse to terminate my candidacy. Every day, when I went to the fields with others, I would bow my head low and put on a serious face, as if I didn't care about what awaited me. Nobody could tell that I greeted every day with nervous excitement, anxiously awaiting the announcement I felt would change my life. I worked longer and longer hours to prove my good intentions.

I waited, and waited, and waited. For several weeks, there was no news. I had no idea where that recommendation had gone. Would the regiment Party committee back me up? Usually they would go along with a company's recommendations, since slots were already reserved for the regiment leadership's own favorites and there was no need to grab slots from the companies. But my case was unusual. Among all the candidates recommended by the 11 companies in the entire regiment, I was the only person who was not a Youth League member. Would they automatically strike my name?

I felt my life was at a critical juncture. Yet I had no control whatsoever over my own destiny. I anguished over the thought of eventually being rejected. I felt helpless and the anxiety was killing me.

Several weeks later, Instructor Zhang called a meeting. The regimental authorities had approved the following comrades to go to college, he announced. One name after another was read. The total came to nine. My name was not among them.

I felt as if a bucket of ice water had been dumped on my head and a dagger stabbed into my chest. My stomach churned and I felt like passing out. My heart was filled with anguish. I knew that everyone was watching me, including the political instructor, who sent stealthy glances my way. He must have been feeling intense pleasure at my disappointment. It would delight him even more if I let my emotions show. I fought with my own feelings to keep my composure, forcing out a bright smile as if to say, "I am so happy that I can stay with you guys forever." On our way back to our barracks, I congratulated those who were selected and chatted with friends, trying to look cool.

That night, I walked out of our barracks deep into the openness. It was dark. There was no moon, not even a star in the sky. I walked and walked. Tears streamed down my face, and I choked. I felt lost. When I was safely out of earshot, I started to cry aloud. Then I began to yell. I was yelling into the darkness. No one could hear me. I was tearing my lungs out, shouting and yelling myself hoarse in frustration and sadness.

I came back very late that night, but I felt better. Life had to go on; there was always a future. I vowed that I would not let myself down. I would pull together and continue to try. I dreaded the thought of getting stuck in this godforsaken place. I had already been through so much, but I would not lose myself in despair. To give up was to commit a sin against myself, I reminded myself time and time again. And I would never give up.

★ ★ ★

Soon, I learned why I was taken off the list for college. The letters that my friends and I had written to Chairman Mao and Premier Zhou had somehow made their way to the recipients' offices. We heard of the response from Mao's office from some people working at the regiment headquarters. The three of us never saw the response ourselves, and we never knew whether Mao read the letter himself. But as a result, his office had sent a directive to the Army Corps requesting that the issues brought up in our letter be addressed in an "appropriate way." It further instructed that these youngsters had good intentions and their complaints should be heeded.

The leadership of the Army Corps was not amused that some of their charges had complained about them to the chairman himself. It was fortunate for them that the chairman's office merely asked them to address the issues brought up in the letter. It could have been worse. They could have lost their jobs.

The regiment leaders were angry. But they could not say anything. They knew they were not permitted to openly punish those who had written to the chairman. But reprisals could take subtle forms, and they were patient.

It was about this time that my candidacy for college came up for approval by the regiment Party committee. I was rejected in a unanimous decision. The official reason given was my age: I was too young (at the age of 21) to go to college, they said, and they replaced me with an older person.

There was one consolation. My good friend Huang Shurong received the approval to major in steelmaking at a Beijing college. He was four years my senior, and by the following year he would have been too old to be considered. It was fortunate he was selected. Still, my dreams of going to college had been dashed. It took a while to recover from the pain.

The summer of 1975 came. The college recruitment season began again. The company leadership decided to follow the same format for candidate selection as last year. This time, I was not included in the selection committee. The political instructor did not want to take any chances.

A friend of mine, Zhang Yingjian, nicknamed Old Number Nine because he had recently transferred from Company No. 9, was included on the committee. Yingjian was the deputy leader of our platoon and a hard worker. He was chosen because he was regarded as unbiased, having just come from outside the company. To me, it was a stroke of luck that he had been selected, because he kept me informed of the committee's deliberations.

As before, all the platoons and squads in the company nominated and voted for their candidates. The voting took place on August 10, 1975, and the results were announced the next day. Old Number Nine won the most votes. I came in second again, trailing him by a narrow margin. I received 118 ballots, 25 more than the previous year. Regardless of whether I got to go to university, I was congratulating myself for having not given up since last year's disappointment, and for having persevered to get this far. I had seen others give up and stop working after a failure. They quickly lost public sympathy and attention. I think because I kept it up, people supported me and elected me again.

The selection committee had a meeting. The committee had grown since last year to include all the platoon leaders and some key officers of the company. The committee had another round of voting on the candidates nominated by the platoons on August 14, 1975. Nine members voted for me, and two against. Instructor Zhang counted the votes. Somehow, he dropped one of the votes in my favor so I had a tally of eight. Old Number Nine noticed and told me. He didn't raise an objection for fear of offending the instructor and risking his own chances to go to college. I couldn't blame him.

Mao had said that the decision-making process within the Party was that of "democracy and centralization." The political instructor announced that the democratic process was over, and now he would "centralize" to make a final decision. He and the commander decided to remove my name from consideration even though so many voted for me.

This year, to prevent arbitrariness and abuse by the company leaders in the selection process, the higher authorities required that the file of each candidate include comments by "the masses." The political instructor asked the squads to evaluate each chosen candidate and submit comments. After the comments were collected, a meeting was held. A representative from each squad read the commentaries aloud before the assembled group.

People had good things to say about some candidates, including Old Number Nine, but not others, especially those who received few ballots. When it came to Xu Anqi, a young woman who had received only a fraction of my vote count, the reviews were especially harsh. One commentary said she was seen bringing expensive cigarettes to the company leaders' homes, suggesting that she was trying to bribe the leaders. One after another, commentary from different squads was read out.

It was supposed to be an honor to be nominated. Candidates expected to receive compliments. Instead, Xu was humiliated in public. She began to sob and quickly broke down in tears. She stood up in front of everyone and left the meeting, crying. The one who really lost face was the political instructor. But he kept his composure.

Although nothing was said about me at the meeting because I was no longer on the list, Old Number Nine told me later that many people went to Instructor Zhang afterward to complain about my exclusion. I will be forever grateful to these people for speaking on my behalf.

Perhaps because they were embarrassed by this show of support for me, the company leaders decided to make a gesture.

I was reading a book in my room one day when I was told the political instructor wanted to see me. I went there wondering what to expect. I had no idea what he had in mind. Instructor Zhang had a surprise for me. The leadership had changed its mind, he declared. I was to be an officially nominated candidate. I was careful not to show any emotion, but I was delighted to have made a small step once again toward my dream.

I learned later that this was not so much a change of heart as it was a trick on the part of company leadership to please their subordinates. They had nominated two more candidates than allowed by the quota, a total of 11 candidates for 9 slots. Therefore, I was merely an alternate candidate, and the second of two alternates at that. I would be considered only if the higher authorities disqualified two people. My chances were remote at best. But maybe, just maybe, I might get lucky this time.

Once again, the list of candidates was submitted to the regiment headquarters. I dreaded the prospect of being rejected again. There was indeed, I later learned, some debate at the regiment committee meeting about me. Three young people on the committee, all of whom were educated youth, strongly supported me in the deliberations. I never met these people in person. But apparently, they liked what we had written in our letter to Mao and thought well of me. Largely because of their support, my name received approval, although I remained the last of two alternate candidates.

I was summoned to Batou, to regiment headquarters, along with the other college candidates, to have a physical checkup. This was a crucial step. Colleges were very picky at the time. Even the slightest health problem could lead to disqualification. I thought this was unfair. Anyone who could bear the hardships of labor in the Gobi was physically fit enough to sit in a classroom. But the rules were the rules.

I knew I was in good health, but I was nervous. What if they discovered something I did not know about? A suspicious blot on an X-ray, or an abnormal blood test result? Any unexpected health issue would cost me my future.

It turned out I was in such good health that the examining doctor couldn't even find a cavity in my teeth. But because I was nervous, my blood pressure was elevated, at 130 over 90. I had the nurse take it several times, hoping it would return to a normal rate. But my blood pressure kept going higher and higher, I suppose because I was getting more and more anxious. The nurse also thought she detected a heart murmur.

This of course made me even more anxious. I had come this far. Now I was being told I could not go to college to read books because I was deemed not physically capable, even though my health never prevented me from working like a mule all these years? I knew there was nothing wrong with me. The blood pressure was due to nerves. The heart murmur was pure nonsense. I had listened to my heart many times while training as a barefoot doctor. There was nothing abnormal about it.

I went to Dr. Yu. Without even bothering to put a stethoscope to my chest, he pronounced that I had a perfectly normal heart. On the medical checkup form under blood pressure he wrote "120/80"—perfectly normal.

And that was it. I received a squeaky-clean bill of health; my medical file showed not the slightest abnormality. I was pleased. Dr. Yu was such a good man.

★ ★ ★

Wang Decai, my platoon mate, was not so lucky. He was nominated for a spot at a vocational school, a notch below university or college. But his X-ray revealed a tiny shadow on his lungs, presumably calcified tissue from a long-ago case of tuberculosis, from which he had fully recovered without ever knowing it. The poor guy was disqualified and now had to go back to do hard labor.

While I felt awful for Decai, his removal meant I moved a step closer to being a full candidate. Still, when the final list was submitted to division headquarters, I remained only an alternate. And as far as I could tell, that was as close as I was going to get. After all these years of work, this seemed teasingly cruel.

Shortly afterward, news came that a young woman from my company, Xiao Geng, was removed from consideration. The reason? She was two centimeters too short of the height requirement for college. Height obviously had nothing to do with her fitness to study, but again, the rules were the rules. Luck was with me, and I finally moved up to be a full candidate. I didn't feel too sorry for Xiao Geng, as she had received the least number of votes among all the candidates. I did feel that it was unfair to her or anyone to be rejected on the basis of height.

I was at long last one of the nine lucky names to be considered for college. But I still needed final approval from division headquarters, and my chances were far from assured. I fretted daily; rumors came from division headquarters suggesting I had been taken off the list, only to be contradicted by later reports that I was still on.

My diaries from this time reflect my anguish:

September 8, 1975, Monday, heavily overcast, rained last night:

"The hope for college is very dim. . . . I fret either sitting or lying down. [The leaders of] the regiment hate my guts, which is what I have expected. Earlier the college recruitment office already nominated me as a candidate, but the members of the committee got my name off the main list and pushed it to the alternate list. The list was submitted to the division headquarters. At this moment, no one was dropped from the main list. There is no hope for me. I have done all I can and now I have to wait for the disposal of my fate. I feel restless and anxious."

September 10, 1975, Friday, cloudy to clear:

"There was rain last night. Bad news came, suggesting I was taken off the list again. Later, it was verified to be false. Depressing. Received word today, there is hope again. But there is no final word to calm me down.

"The harvest of *mizi* will begin tomorrow. I ground my sickle waiting for the harvest to begin. I am tormented to death by the wait."

★ ★ ★

Just as I was losing hope, I was called to division headquarters. They wanted me to take a test for college.

It turned out a recruiter from a college in Beijing had bumped into two people from our company in the town of Urat Qianqi. Naturally, they talked about the college selection process. In the conversation, the two from our company brought up my name as someone known to be a bookworm who also worked hard doing physical labor. The recruiter was impressed.

I didn't know what the test would entail. The examination system had long been abolished, and college acceptances were now done on the basis of recommendations.

Li Guozhong, an administrator at the Beijing Institute of Foreign Trade, had come to our division headquarters to recruit one student to major in the study of a foreign language. Since the vast majority of candidates had not received any education beyond elementary school, he wanted to make sure the student he picked could at least read and write Chinese and could be trained to speak a foreign language

I met with Li in a small room in the division headquarters building, but as the interview began I did not know the school he represented. It was my first and only visit to division headquarters during all my years in the Gobi. I was nervous when I walked in, not knowing what to expect. He took out a copy of the *People's Daily*, pointed to a paragraph and asked me to read it aloud. I did, in my standard Beijing Mandarin, imitating as best I could the voice of the broadcaster from Radio Beijing.

After I finished, he nodded: "Very good."

I thought, "a cakewalk," and relaxed.

Then he asked me to write a composition. I did it in his presence and tried my best to impress him. I wrote a five-page essay in which I talked about how the hardship of life in the country's border area had toughened me and changed my world outlook, as I was transformed from a student to a peasant, how I appreciated the necessity of changing the backwardness of the border area, and of changing my own thinking as well. I also talked about the need to acquire more knowledge, and I provided an example of how we used trigonometry to measure agricultural land without having to do it entirely by hand. I then said if given the chance, I would study hard to better serve the people.

Much of my writing sounded like an editorial from the *People's Daily*, peppered with my own experiences to prove the correctness of the Party line and Chairman Mao. I doubted he could find any fault with it.

He slowly read through it as I sat there watching him. I was not nervous because I was confident in my own writing. When he raised his head, I could see he was pleased.

Then he asked what subject I wished to study. I told him that I had been thinking of studying Chinese literature at the University of Inner Mongolia. He asked me why I had picked that university. I said because I knew that it would be the last one on anyone's list, so I would have a better chance to get in. I explained to him that unlike many others, my purpose in going to college was not simply to go back to a big city. I truly wanted to study. That was why I would be happy to be accepted by any college.

That was when he told me he was here to recruit a foreign language student for the Beijing Institute of Foreign Trade. "If you were chosen," he asked, "which language would you like to study?" I answered without hesitation, "French." I could see a hint of puzzlement cross his face before he asked, "Why French?"

"Because I've been studying English for a number of years on my own and I've picked up a good vocabulary," I said. "I think it will be interesting to study another foreign language." This was true. I had read some books and textbooks in English, and secretly listened to the learning programs on the VOA shortwave band. I had studied an English dictionary, and the *English Duden* from Old Yi.

Li Guozhong smiled, seemingly happy with my answer. "No," he said. "You are going to study English. English is spoken by more people in the world than any other foreign language," he explained. "You will have much more use for it than for French."

I would be happy to study anything, of course. So I emphatically nodded my head in agreement.

With that, the test was over and I was dismissed. But I still didn't know what would happen next. I knew I had passed the test, but the final approval had to come from the division headquarters.

★ ★ ★

A couple of weeks passed without further news. I felt every day was an eternity and my despair mounted. I prepared myself for the worst; I had to assume it was going to be like last year when the final verdict came. I was likely destined to spend the rest of my life here, I kept telling myself, and I had to accept my fate. I tried hard to put the whole thing out of my mind, however impossible it was.

On Sunday, September 14, 1975, I borrowed a horse to go to regiment sub-headquarters to visit my friend Wang Dacheng. He was now a member of a team specializing in waterworks that designed canals and irrigation systems. I found him in his dorm. I sat down to chat with him.

Dacheng's dorm was next door to the telephone switchboard that served the regiment sub-headquarters. Each company had a hand-powered telephone in its office. To make a call, one would crank the handle a few times and then pick up the cradle to connect with the switchboard. The operator there would connect the call to the intended party, usually the regiment headquarters. If a call came from the headquarters, the switchboard operator would patch the call through. Typically, only the company leaders had reason to use the telephone.

Dacheng knew the two young women operators. I had a nodding acquaintance with them as well. As he and I were talking, there was a knock on the door and one of the operators poked her head in. She said they had heard my name mentioned on the phone. I immediately jumped up and rushed to the switchboard room. The other young woman was still listening with her headset and motioned for me to be quiet.

After she finally disconnected the phone, she raised her head and said, "It was a call from the regiment headquarters to your company. The person read a list of people approved to go to college. You are on that list."

I was overwhelmed by the news, elated beyond words. My time had finally come. I profusely thanked the two young women. I was especially grateful because the information they had given me was classified, as everything transmitted by that line was; they had leaked important military secrets, which was against all the rules. I hurriedly said goodbye to Dacheng, ran out, untied my horse, jumped onto it, and galloped away at full speed back to my company. After a few seconds, though, I slowed down. I was overjoyed, but I had the presence of mind to tell myself that it would be tragic if I should die or get seriously hurt falling off my horse at this moment. Now life suddenly had become precious.

The first person I met back in the company barracks was Little Xie, the company messenger. When he saw me, he shouted to me that he was just about to go to my dorm to fetch me. Of course, I already knew why, and I followed him to the company office. After I shouted "Report!" the political instructor raised his eyes from a piece of paper in his hand. He looked at me with a serious face as if studying me. For a few seconds, he didn't say anything. I played as dumb as I could, for fear I would betray a hint of what I already knew. Finally he said, "Based on the recommendation of the masses, the company leadership, and the regiment leadership, the division headquarters has given approval for you to go to college." It was the Beijing Institute of Foreign Trade, he said. I was required to return to the capital city.

I had to make an effort to conceal my joy and to keep a straight face. I was so afraid that the leaders would change their minds, that all this would come to nothing. I said something like, "I will never forget Company No. 5 and all my comrades here and I will study hard to live up to the expectations of the leaders and my fellow soldiers." He appeared to be happy with my attitude and dismissed me.

I didn't begin to run until I was safely out of his sight, as I suspected he was watching me through the window of his office. Once I was sure I was not watched, I dashed back to my room.

My heart was already flying to Beijing. I was in a great hurry to leave. There was a tractor-pulled wagon going to Urat Qianqi that afternoon. I decided to take it and leave the company immediately. There was no time to pack. I only took my shoulder bag with a few things and my money. I said goodbye to as many friends as I could. I told Li Baoquan he could have all my belongings, including my new washbasin.

I still could not believe this was really happening, and I still worried that the leaders could change their minds at any moment. I wanted to get out of there as soon as I could. It would be difficult for them to force me back to the Gobi if I had already reported for duty at the college in Beijing.

After a long bumpy ride that seemed to take forever, the tractor-trailer dropped me off at the barracks of another regiment not far away from the town of Urat Qianqi, where the train station was. I needed to buy a ticket for the last train departing that night, and I was hoping tickets were still available. Time was running out and I needed to get to the station as soon as I could. It would take too long to walk. I saw a bicycle standing outside a row of barracks. I didn't know anyone in that company I could ask to borrow the bike. But I noticed it was not locked. I decided to take a chance.

I grabbed the bicycle, jumped onto it, and began to pedal as hard as I could. Just as I rode out the entrance, I heard shouting behind me. I turned to see a crowd of people chasing me, some with shovels in their hands. I was so frightened. I knew if I were caught they would surely beat me up. I got a huge rush of adrenaline and pedaled with every ounce of my strength as I pulled further and further away from the crowd. It was fortunate the bicycle chain did not break even though I was pedaling like crazy. Eventually they gave up chasing me. I was lucky to have escaped with my life. Was it worth it? I didn't know. I was so possessed by the desire to get out of there as soon as possible that I was not even thinking clearly.

Fortunately, tickets were still available, and the last train would not leave for a couple of hours. I bought my ticket and biked back to the barracks where I had just stolen the bike. I was no longer in a hurry, but I felt tired because all my strength had been drained by the narrow escape from disaster just a short while ago.

The people in the barracks were surprised to see me. When I explained why I had had to borrow the bike in such a hasty fashion, they immediately forgave me and warmed up to me. They offered me some hot water and congratulated me on being able to go back to Beijing. One of them said that I was crazy. If they had caught me, they would have beaten me to death, as they thought I was a common thief. A bicycle was, of course, the most valuable personal possession at the time.

I felt much more relaxed when I finally boarded the train that night. I felt safe and my excitement had also subsided. I began to think about my parents and how pleasantly surprised they would be to see me and to learn my good news. I felt bad about leaving all my belongings behind. I suddenly remembered my shovel. I deeply regretted that I hadn't thought of taking it with me. It had been my pride. I had used it almost every day and had taken great care to clean and grind it so its blade shone like armor. I would have kept it as a souvenir, a reminder of my life in the desert.

Now I was sitting all by myself on the train, I began to sorely miss my friends who were left behind. When would they get out? And how many of them would be given the opportunity for a new and better life?

Chapter 18

Last Convulsions
of the Revolution

The Chinese premier, Zhou Enlai, a moderating force under
Mao's leadership, was diagnosed with bladder cancer in 1972.
By the middle of 1974, his cancer had spread. He continued to
work from his sickbed but as his condition worsened, the burden of
running the state was largely passed to Deng Xiaoping in 1975.

Born in 1904, Deng was 6 years younger than Zhou and 11 years
younger than Mao. As a student in France, he joined the Communist
Party two years after its founding. Back in China, he became a senior
member of the Party's leadership in the 1930s and joined Mao's Long
March. In the winter of 1948 he served as the chief commander of
the Communist force that annihilated a superior Nationalist army of
about 500,000 troops in the Battle of Huaihai, a victory that helped
clear the way for the Communist takeover in 1949. He became secretary general of the Party in the 1950s and a member of the core leadership. In the 1960s, he helped Liu Shaoqi run the country, including
managing its economic affairs, after Mao stepped back following the
Great Leap Forward. But he was purged from his positions in 1966 at
the start of the Cultural Revolution and was sent to Jiangxi Province
to do manual labor.

Deng was short of stature—he stood 1.52 meters (less than 5 feet) tall—but strong of will. He suffered a number of setbacks in his long career within the Party, including his exile during the Cultural Revolution, but he was a political survivor. Mao once described him as "a ball of cotton with needles buried in it," meaning that he was aggressively sharp behind his soft appearance. He was one of the most thoughtful and capable of China's top leaders, pragmatic and strongly principled. For this reason, both Mao and Zhou liked him, although Mao complained often that Deng did not listen to him. His pragmatism was reflected in a well-known quotation of his regarding economic policies: "It matters not if the cat is black or white, as long as it catches the mice." That, however, was precisely the issue Mao had with him. To Mao, the whole point was that the color mattered a great deal.

In deteriorating health, Zhou Enlai convinced Mao to bring Deng back to work. In January 1975, at the age of 70, Deng was made vice chairman of the Party, chief of staff of the military, and vice premier, effectively giving him the power to run the country.

In the United States, Richard Nixon resigned as president in August 1974 rather than face impeachment proceedings in the wake of the Watergate scandal. Before his resignation, Nixon had appointed Gerald Ford to be vice president, to replace Spiro Agnew, who had resigned in 1973 for legal troubles of his own. Gerald Ford was sworn in on August 9 following Nixon's resignation and became the only US president never to have run in an election for national office.

★ ★ ★

I arrived back home in Beijing in late September 1975, six years after I had left for the Gobi. It had been an eventful six years for the five members of our family.

My mother, who had been sent to a farm in the northeast for some years, had been allowed to return to her job in Beijing by the time I returned. My father had been away in the African country of Somalia since 1972.

My sister, Weimin, had returned to Beijing a year earlier, after having spent five years in northeast China working on a farm. She was studying computer science at Beijing Industrial University.

My younger brother, Weizhong, was in one sense the luckiest of my siblings, as he was not sent to the countryside. But he was unlucky in other respects.

After graduating from elementary school, my brother was accepted into a vocational school to study chemistry, which he attended between 1974 and 1976. In the first six months, his class was sent to the countryside. There, he lost half of one finger in a wheat threshing machine. Later, working in a chemical factory, he was overcome by a poisonous gas leak. (Known as Zyklon B, the same gas used in the Nazis' gas chambers, it was used as a softener for plastics.) Fortunately, he was rescued in time. He later went to Beijing University to study biology after the formal examination system was restored in 1977.

My father, meanwhile, from around 1966, had been under investigation at his job in the customs administration. During the frenzy of the Cultural Revolution, his work unit could not authenticate his Party membership. Faking membership was a crime, since that was how Nationalist spies were known to infiltrate the Party.

He never told me what the investigation involved, but I knew he had to endlessly recount his personal history in every detail. Proving the authenticity of his Party membership was next to impossible, because there were no membership cards when the Communist Party was outlawed under the Nationalist government. It just required two members to sponsor a new member and bear witness to his membership.

Unfortunately, one of his two sponsors was long dead. The other one was living in Shandong. But during the Cultural Revolution, many of the members whom he had brought into the Party were denounced as counterrevolutionaries. He was so scared of being implicated in a case like this that he simply denied knowing or having introduced my father into the Party. With one of his sponsors being dead, and another refusing to stand up for him, my father was in jeopardy.

Fortunately, according to my mother, the members of the Rebel group in the customs administration were not young students, but responsible adults. They could not find any other stains in my father's history, as he came from a suitably poor family, and there was nothing else connecting him to anything suspicious. The Rebels went to Shandong repeatedly to visit with my father's introductory sponsor, now an elderly man, assuring him that my father had no problems other than not being able to prove his Party membership. Finally, the old man relented and admitted that he had indeed introduced my father into the Party, which freed my father from serious trouble—after living for almost six years under a dark cloud of suspicion.

My parents shielded my father's plight from all of us children. I was oblivious of his troubles; otherwise it would have put great psychological stress on me. A "bad" family background could severely limit one's future, and children from families with a problem background did not have much of a chance in life. I would never have been allowed to go to college if my father had still been under investigation.

In 1972, during my third year in the Gobi, at the time I was making bricks, my mother finally wrote to tell me what my father had been through. She only did so because she could also tell me the news that he had joined a Chinese delegation to the United Nations Trade and Development Conference in Santiago, Chile, as an expert on customs affairs. China had only been readmitted to the United Nations the previous year, and this was the first time that delegates from the PRC joined a UN conference. The fact that my father had been named to the delegation meant that his problems were cleared.

By the time I returned to Beijing in September of 1975, my father had been posted to Mogadishu, Somalia, as a commercial attaché at the Chinese embassy. He would return home the following year. In the meantime, my sister, my younger brother, and I were all back in Beijing, and I was able to spend every weekend with my family in my parents' home.

★ ★ ★

I registered at the Beijing Institute of Foreign Trade, or BIFT (today known as the University of International Business and Economics), located in the northern suburbs of Beijing, on the grounds of what used to be the Beijing Film Studio. Because there had not been any movies made for nearly 10 years, the studio had been abandoned and was now taken over by BIFT.

BIFT was about a 40-minute bus ride from my parents' home, although you could cover the distance on a bicycle in about the same time. Between the bus terminus and the campus was open farmland, where peasants grew vegetables to feed the city. A dirt footpath led through the rows of vegetables to the campus gates.

Inside the wrought-iron gate of the campus, the footpath became a paved road. There was a messenger's office on the left, just inside the gate, with one single telephone for the use of all the students. Past the messenger's office was the cafeteria and a row of flat houses, among them a boiler room and public shower. On the right-hand side, there was a four-story classroom building. At the far end of the road was a three-story dormitory.

The institute had been founded in 1951 but, like almost all colleges, was shut down during the Cultural Revolution. It had reopened and moved to the current location a year or two earlier. Many of the old film studio facilities were not suitable for teaching. To the right of my dormitory were two odd-looking buildings. One was called Big Film Studio, a huge, windowless hangar with high ceilings and a small door, just like a movie studio on a back lot in Hollywood. It was now used occasionally to show movies or hold big meetings. The other was referred to as the Glass Building. The south and east sides of the building were made of clear glass, with no solid walls. I was told actors and actresses had come here to sunbathe without having to worry about getting too tanned because the glass would filter away ultraviolet rays.

A five-story building behind the cafeteria was used as a women's dormitory, and there was a soccer field with a running track where we exercised. The school was still constructing some new buildings for teaching, but I estimated that the campus would not be completed until after we graduated. Still, I thought, the conditions for studying were good. There was plenty of space. Surrounded by expansive amounts of farmland, it was also quite secluded.

The living conditions felt like paradise after the Gobi. The food was infinitely better that the rations I had subsisted on in the desert. I did not have to worry about where the next meal would come from, or if there would be enough to eat. The common showers were in an old building with maybe two dozen showerheads. The shower room only opened two days a week, once for men and once for women. But the water was hot, and compared to the Gobi this was a luxury. On summer days when the shower room was not open, my classmates and I would sometimes sneak in and take cold-water showers to cool off from Beijing's muggy heat.

★ ★ ★

I was relieved once I had formally registered as a student. In China, everyone had an official dossier that accompanied them wherever they went, but which they were never allowed to see. Only the authorities were privy to its contents. The dossier provided all the details of an individual's personal background. If your previous employer had written some damning assessment in the dossier, it might doom your career forever, often without you ever knowing why. When a person moved from one work unit to another, it would not be considered official until the dossier had been transferred. The fact that I was allowed to register meant that my dossier had arrived at the institute without problems.

I would never know what my bosses in the Gobi had said about me in the dossier. I was thankful that no matter how much some of them disliked me, they had allowed me to leave—apparently without writing down anything seriously damaging against me. On the other hand, I reflected, there was really nothing bad they could say because, after all, I had worked hard and I was elected by my coworkers to go to college.

But I just could not get over the fact I was no longer in the Gobi. Every day, I was excited about being at the institute. I still feared that I might be called back to the Gobi. I had a recurring nightmare in which I was told that letting me go to college had all been a mistake, and I was ordered to go back to the Gobi. This nightmare haunted me for many years. I was always happy to wake up, to realize it was just a bad dream.

The institute was divided into four departments. The First Department taught English and was the largest. The Second Department, or the "small languages department," taught a number of languages, including French, Russian, Polish, Japanese, and Arabic. The Third Department specialized in foreign trade, and the Fourth Department taught subjects related to customs administration.

I was enrolled in the First Department to study English. Our class of students was divided up and assigned to 10 classrooms of about 20 students each. Mine was the Second Classroom. Classrooms in Chinese universities were set up like homerooms in US elementary schools. Instead of carrying our books to different lecture halls, as university students would in the States, students would stay in the same room, at the same desk, and teachers of different subjects would come in and give lectures. Of the students in my classroom, there were 13 men and

7 women. Only two were natives of Beijing, myself and another boy, named Chen Min. One girl came from Shanghai. The rest of my class-mates were from rural areas across China.

I believe the recruiters at BIFT had made an effort to recruit stu-dents as young as possible because they believed that the younger a person was, the easier it was for the person to learn a foreign language. The admissions policy required that students be selected from among the appropriate political classes: peasants, workers, or soldiers. A city youngster like myself would have had to work for a few years in the countryside, in factories, or in the military to qualify for acceptance. But someone from a peasant family was already qualified by birth. Therefore, much younger students could be recruited from rural areas.

I was just turning 22 when I started classes at BIFT in 1975. I had always been one of the youngest among my peers because I got into elementary school before I was seven years old. I was also among the youngest among my peers in the Gobi. But here at BIFT, I found myself one of the oldest in my class. Some of my classmates were still teenagers. I also felt older, having been through a lot more than most of my class-mates, many of whom had never left their home village before coming to Beijing for college.

None of us had much formal education. But at least I had finished elementary school. Most of my classmates had not gotten that far before the schools were closed, and therefore lacked even a basic education. For many, their exposure to the world outside their villages was quite limited as well. Some of my classmates had never seen a train before coming to the institute. No matter how young you were, it was hard to learn words like *embassy*, *airport*, *zoo*, and *restaurant* if you didn't know what they meant even in Chinese.

Since schools had been shut down for almost 10 years, there were not many qualified teachers around either. Wang Keli, the head teacher of my English class, and a few others had taught before the Cultural Revolution. Teacher Wang was in his fifties, tall, always smiling and easygoing. We all respected and trusted him. These older teachers were generally of much better quality, as they had received formal instruc-tion. But many other teachers were about my age. They had just grad-uated as worker-peasant-soldier students themselves. One of them, a woman named Li Yan, was a 69er like myself, who also served in the

Inner Mongolia Construction Army Corps. But she had managed to get out a few years before I did, and had recently graduated from the First Language Institute, China's top school for foreign-language studies. It made my heart sink a bit. I felt as if I were already a few years behind where I should be in life.

I had studied English on my own for a number of years in the Gobi. The Voice of America had a daily radio program called *English 900*; one could learn English grammar rules and vocabulary by memorizing the 900 simple sentences it broadcast in a series of lessons. There was also an educational program on the BBC, but I found that the British spoke so fast that it was difficult for me to follow them. Though I had listened to VOA quite diligently, I had never spoken English with anyone. So when a teacher asked me if I spoke any English, no sooner had I opened my mouth to say *Hello, how are you* than he shut me up, aghast. You need to forget whatever pronunciation you came up with on your own, he told me.

Another handicap of mine was that I was not familiar with the alphabet. I had accumulated a modest English vocabulary by memorizing words when I was in the Gobi. But I never really bothered to learn the alphabet. If nobody was teaching you and if nobody spelled a word for you, what was the point? I had to start from the beginning.

Fortunately, all my classmates were starting from same place. While it was unrealistic to expect that everyone would be able to jump from elementary school to college, it became quickly apparent to me that the college education we were supposed to be receiving was not really college-level. Once I'd learned the alphabet, the classes quickly became too basic for me. I began to read the textbooks for second- and third-year classes, and books of other types. I spent a lot of time listening to tapes of English conversation. The teachers told us that the teaching philosophy at BIFT was "listening comprehension and speaking first, reading and writing second." I found that priority suited me just fine. I had no trouble studying to read and write on my own, but I could not learn to understand spoken English, or how to speak it, without practice.

Our classroom was on the second floor. My desk was in the last row by the window, which looked out to the south. I could see trees, buildings, and factory chimneys in the distance. On a clear day, I could even see the new wing of the Beijing Hotel about 10 kilometers (~6 miles) away. Built the year before and standing 20 stories high, it was the tallest and most modern building in the city at that time. There were elevators, I knew, although I had never stepped into one in my life, to take you to the higher floors. Rumor had it that when Mao's wife visited the hotel, her elevator car had to be gently pulled up by hand because otherwise the speed would make her dizzy. The rumor was likely untrue, as I cannot imagine how one can pull up an elevator manually, but it shows how little we knew at the time.

I chose a desk in the corner in the last row not only because of the view but also because I could secretly read extracurricular books under my desk. My desk was usually piled high with textbooks, with the one on top always open. The teacher did not know I was reading something else in my lap when the instruction got boring, which happened more often than not.

All the men in my class lived in the same dorm room, which had seven double bunk beds. I had a top bunk. The best thing was the electric light. When we had electricity in our barracks in the Gobi, it was usually shut off at 9 p.m., our curfew time. But at the institute, all the classrooms were brightly lit with fluorescent light tubes. The dormitory was usually too crowded and dimly lit to read, so we often studied in our classroom until curfew.

I got to go home every weekend. My mother was overjoyed to have me back in Beijing and in college.

★ ★ ★

It was great to be back in Beijing. I had only been home twice for home leave since leaving for the Gobi. On my first trip, in February 1972, my visit coincided with President Richard Nixon's historic arrival in China. On a gray and hazy day with overcast skies and badly polluted air, I saw Nixon's motorcade speed down Chang'an Boulevard in front of Tiananmen Square. There were no crowds on the street to cheer the US president, probably because the Chinese leadership wanted the first-ever visit by an American head of state to be low-key. The country needed time to come around to the idea of a relationship with a nation long seen as China's imperialist archenemy.

By the time I returned from the Gobi there was a US Liaison Office in Beijing, run by a genial former oil executive named George H. W. Bush, who was known for bicycling around the city with his wife, Barbara. Bush, who had previously served as chairman of the Republican National Committee and as the US ambassador to the United Nations, was the second diplomat to be appointed chief of the US Liaison Office in China, serving from September 28, 1974, until December 5, 1975. For all practical purposes, it was an embassy, but it was not called one. A formal diplomatic relationship between the two countries was not established until 1979.

Coming back to the city from the Gobi, I felt that everything had shrunk in size. I was used to the vast open spaces of the desert. In contrast, everything in Beijing looked small and the streets felt narrow. Another big difference was the color of the sky. In the Gobi, the sky was always blue and bright. Beijing's sky was almost always gray, especially on a windless and cloudy day. Many Chinese publications described pollution in foreign countries. But having seen what blue sky looked like, I was already quite conscious that Beijing's air was badly polluted, especially in wintertime when there was so much coal being burned.

There was a shortage of nearly everything in Beijing, even though the capital was still faring much better than the rest of the country. Rationing had been a fact of life in Beijing since I was a child. But now it covered more items, all the way down to furniture for newlyweds. For goods not subject to rationing, store shelves were frequently empty. Shirts and blouses made of polyester, for example, were not rationed like cotton products were. But they were in such short supply that whenever a store had some to sell, people waiting to buy them would form a long line. Most Beijing residents carried a *wangdou*, or net bag, wherever they went. It could be easily folded into a fist or carried in one's pocket; although it was almost weightless it was very durable. If you happened to pass a store that had in stock something you needed, you would wait in line to buy it and use the net bag to take it home. In fact, people lined up to buy things even without knowing what was being sold. Because everything was in short supply, whatever other people needed had to be something you needed as well.

In April 1974, on my second home visit from the Gobi, a few friends and I were wandering around Wangfujing, the best-known shopping street in Beijing. Someone in our group suggested that we play a prank. We found a broken window in a building on the street and a few of us formed a line under the window, as if waiting to buy something. Soon, more people began to queue behind us and the line grew longer. Initially some people asked us what was going to be sold there. We simply shrugged. People in the queue all wanted to know what would be sold but nobody had a clue. That did not prevent the line from growing longer and longer, and the longer it got the more people were attracted to join. Then, one by one, we slipped away from the queue. Looking at the long line of people standing below a broken window, we laughed our heads off. We were the bad boys from the Gobi then.

★ ★ ★

China in the mid-1970s was caught between two feuding factions in the leadership, both loyal to Mao. One, represented by Zhou Enlai, wanted to end the chaos, restore social order, and improve the economy. This was the old guard, the remnants of the pre–Cultural Revolution government. The other force, represented by Mao's wife and her followers, continued to push for class struggle and to attack any policies or ideas that they perceived would breed capitalism. These were the radicals. Mao was the balancer. He needed the old guard to keep the country and the economy going. He also needed the radicals to carry out his continuous revolution. It was a tug of war between the old guard and the radicals, and which faction prevailed at any moment depended on Mao's whim.

I had returned to Beijing at a critical moment in China's history. Earlier in the year, Mao brought back to power Deng Xiaoping. Deng, a member of the core leadership, had been purged in 1966. He had been accused of being the second-biggest capitalist roader in the country, after Liu Shaoqi. Liu had been officially expelled from the Party but Deng was only stripped of all his positions and exiled to Jiangxi Province, where he worked in a factory as a lathe operator. (He was said to have operated lathe machines in his youth as a work-study student in France.) Mao had allowed Deng to keep his Party membership. So he was down but not completely out.

In January 1975, Deng's time came again. Zhou Enlai, standard-bearer of the old guard, was stricken by bladder cancer and hospitalized.

Mao needed someone else capable of running the country. After Deng promised to Mao never to reverse the verdict on the merits of the Cultural Revolution or challenge the accusations that had been made against him, he was made a member of the Politburo, vice chairman of the Party, first vice premier, vice chairman of the Party's Military Commission (of which Mao himself was the chairman), and chief of staff of the armed forces. Despite all these titles Deng was still nominally under Zhou. But with the premier hospitalized, Deng took over Zhou's entire portfolio of responsibility and was more or less running the show, with the blessing of Mao himself.

Deng immediately took action to reverse some of the extreme leftist policies. "All-around rectification," he said, was required to put China's productivity back on track. He rehabilitated many deposed senior officials and appointed capable and experienced ones to positions of power. He wanted factory workers to go back to work, peasants to go back to the farm, professors to go back to teaching, scientists to go back to their research, and students to go back to their studies, instead of spending their time waging an endless revolution. He also wanted trains and buses to run on time. And his measures were producing some noticeable results.

We could feel the changes. At BIFT, most of our time was allocated to academics, as opposed to the words of Mao. There were still some political study sessions but they were typically reserved for the afternoons or for an hour on Saturdays. I hated those sessions, as they bored me to tears and I considered them a total waste of time. I had been through enough and knew better than to take this kind of nonsense seriously. But I was not able to skip these study sessions. It was just not worth the risk to invite that kind of attention to myself. Fortunately, it was just an hour or two a week. Sometimes I would sit in the back of the room and read a history book while others stood up and gave speeches.

* * *

At BIFT, there was not much to do other than reading, studying, and some afternoon exercises. The campus was like a self-contained village. It was quite far away from the nearest store of any kind. There were no restaurants other than the cafeteria, which was closed after meal hours.

There was no television or entertainment other than an occasional movie in the Big Film Studio, typically a foreign film meant to help us study languages. Even the bus stop was on the far side of a vegetable field. Without distractions of any kind, almost all of us immersed ourselves in studying from dawn to dusk. After dinner, students were seen studying everywhere on campus, talking to themselves or with each other loudly in some foreign language. Some students would stay in the classroom, using headphones to listen either to an English-language tape played on a recorder or, by changing a channel, to VOA or the BBC.

There was no food served other than at mealtimes. There were no drinks other than hot water. Some students brought their own tea and poured water over the leaves. I say this because years later when I got to the United States, I noticed that students snacked frequently and had all kinds of drinks (although I found a glass of hot water difficult to come by). Our life was completely spartan, but I did not know it. To me, this place was so blissful, with enough to eat at every meal, central heating in deep winter, and a shower every week. I didn't have to worry about being caught reading in my spare time. Indeed, we were expected to read and study as much as we liked, and I could do so in comfortable, well-lit rooms. I did not know what more to want.

During my first month at BIFT, our deputy Party secretary stood up and outlined the curriculum for the next few years. Overall, he said, we would have a total of 158 weeks at school. Aside from school breaks, 115 weeks would be spent on campus and 33 weeks would be spent "learning from the workers"—traveling to the countryside or factories to work alongside the proletariat—as well as on "open-door schooling," which basically meant internships and language practice. Compared to what I had heard about other schools, this meant BIFT students would actually get to spend a significant amount of time on their studies. It might be taken for granted anywhere else in the world that students were supposed to study. But this was quite unusual for China at the time, where for the previous 10 years it had been taboo to let study of a professional subject take priority over waging revolution. This renewed emphasis on learning was consistent with Deng's new policies.

This newfound liberalism would not last. At Tsinghua University, one of the country's top universities, a dispute was brewing between the deputy Party secretary, Liu Bing, and two of Mao's henchmen, Chi Qun and Xie Jingyi. Chi, an army officer, and Xie, Mao's former secretary, had been sent to oversee the university. But they clashed with Liu and others, prompting Liu to write letters to Mao complaining about their behavior. The letters were entrusted to Deng Xiaoping to pass along.

Mao interpreted the letters as being critical not just of Chi and Xie, but of his Cultural Revolution. In a strong public rebuke, Mao wrote, "The target of their letter is me."

What was not made public until a few months later was the rest of what he had said: "I am in Beijing. Why wasn't the letter sent me directly? Rather it was delivered through [Deng] Xiaoping. Xiaoping is biased in favor of Liu Bing." The problem at Tsinghua, Mao declared, was not an isolated incident but "a reflection of the current struggle between the two lines"—meaning, between the revolutionaries represented by the radicals and the bourgeois reactionaries represented by the old guard, including Deng.

These words of Mao's in November 1975 marked the beginning of yet again another downfall for Deng. A new leftist campaign to fight against "the rightist wind of reversing correct verdicts" began. The phrase "reversing correct verdicts" meant challenging the correctness and conclusions of the Cultural Revolution; it was something Deng had promised never to do. Now Mao said of him: "'Never to reverse,' it can't be counted on."

Initially, this leftist campaign involved lengthy articles in the *People's Daily* critical of "the rightist wind" and political study sessions that would challenge anything considered to represent such a shift in ideology. The articles did not name any names. But reading between the lines, all who followed politics knew that the campaign was aimed at Deng himself.

Now the political study sessions took on a more and more combative and ominous tone. The education policy of China since I first entered elementary school had been to train students to be "both red and expert": to be ideologically and politically correct as well as academically proficient. Now the Party secretary of our department kept reminding us of the importance of being "red." Meetings were organized to criticize Deng's new policies, which were interpreted as focusing too much on being "expert." Deng's name was never mentioned, although everyone knew who had initiated and pushed for those policies.

I had no idea where this new political campaign against the rightist wind was headed or what would come of it. By and large, it had not affected the routine my classmates and I had settled into: going to classes in the morning, a nap after lunch, some study time and exercise before dinner, and then studying after dinner until bedtime. If people were excited and involved in the Cultural Revolution when it first began, by now most were numb to the endless political campaigns, and they participated in obligatory political sessions only perfunctorily.

★ ★ ★

On the morning of January 9, 1976, I got up to hear the radio playing funeral music. Soon the announcement came that Premier Zhou Enlai had died on January 8. Zhou had been a fixture in China's politics, economy, foreign policy, almost everything, throughout my life. He had managed to keep the country together and to prevent it from descending into total chaos under exceedingly difficult circumstances. He was known to work extremely hard and to care about the welfare of common folks. Without him, who knew where the radicals would take the country?

Zhou's death brought grief to a nation already becoming more and more disillusioned with what the radicals represented. The radicals banned any public mourning of Zhou. This outraged the people and in defiance, hundreds of thousands of people walked to Tiananmen Square in the January cold to mourn Zhou. I went there that day to find numerous wreaths in tribute to Zhou piled high at the base of the Monument to the People's Heroes, a 10-story obelisk in the middle of the square bearing an inscription in Mao's calligraphy on its front and another one in Zhou Enlai's handwriting in the back.

After Zhou's death, everyone who followed politics sensed that Deng was about to be removed from power once again. The leftist campaign in the media gathered momentum against the moderate and pragmatic policies both Zhou and Deng represented. The radicals had underestimated Zhou's popularity and influence. Popular discontent was rising, made worse by the veiled attacks on Zhou by the official media.

The pent-up anger was waiting for an opportunity to erupt.

★ ★ ★

April 5, 1976, was Qingming Day, or tomb-sweeping day, a day in Chinese tradition to pay respect to dead relatives. Numerous people before and on that day brought flower wreaths to Tiananmen Square to pay tribute to Zhou. The authorities, now consisting largely of the radicals because Deng was already sidelined, ordered the wreaths to be removed and burned every night. This only prompted more people to come to the square.

On Sunday, April 4, I went to the square to see what was going on. Never before had so many people congregated there in defiance of official orders. I told my classmates this was history in the making. I took with me a small secondhand camera, a Shanghai 58-II. By the time I arrived the square was already packed with people. More were pouring in from all directions, individually and in processions. At the head of each procession, marchers carried large wreaths. The most striking was a procession of workers from the Beijing Factory of Heavy Machinery, who marched behind a heavy truck, carrying on a crane a gigantic wreath made of steel. The wreath must have been at least four meters (~13 ft) across. The night before, the authorities had cleared and burned all the wreaths in the square. Everyone understood the message of the iron wreath: "Try to burn this one!"

The high base of the monument was once again buried beneath piles of wreaths and flowers. White paper flowers left by the visitors covered the ground like newly fallen snow. Pieces of white paper written with essays and poems hung everywhere, on lampposts, on trees, and on fences. Some of the poems were beautifully written, poignant and daring. One such poem read:

I want to cry but noisy devils are yelling
I am sad but wolves are laughing
Pouring wine to commemorate the hero
Raising my brow as I draw out the saber.

Everyone knew the "devils" and "wolves" in the poem referred to Mao's wife Jiang Qing and the other radicals in the top leadership. Another poem read:

There is a bridge on the Huangpu River
The river bridge is rotten and wobbly

Asking Premier Zhou
To demolish it or to burn it down?

Huangpu River is the main river that runs through the city of Shanghai, where radicals in the top leadership were from. The name of Mao's wife, Jiang, is the same character as "river." One of her followers was Zhang Chunqiao, and "qiao," the last character of his name, is the character for "bridge." Therefore, it was clear to anyone that the rotten and wobbly "river bridge" referred to Jiang Qing, Zhang Chunqiao, and the radical gang from Shanghai.

Other poems and essays attacked Jiang and other radical leaders more directly. Few targeted Mao himself, although a couple of bold ones did allude to him by referring to the cruel rule of Shi Huangdi of Qin, the first emperor of unified China, who reigned during the short-lived Qin dynasty (221–206 BCE). The insinuation was lost on no one.

It was later estimated that at the peak there were two million people in the square. People were packed together, shoulder to shoulder, a boiling sea of blue and green. As I worked my way through the crowd to read this essay and that poem along the fences and on the trees, I saw people continuing to pour in from all sides, carrying large wreaths of flowers. The singing of "The Internationale" could be heard everywhere, over and over again. But in spite of the large crowd, people were orderly. Here and there, a man would stand on the base of a lamppost to give a speech, reading from a script and attracting a group of people around him. The crowd was so dense, I was not able to move close to hear clearly what was being said. But it was obvious the speakers were all angry and they raised their fists defiantly in the air as they spoke.

As I mingled with the crowd walking from one part of the square to another, I felt swept up by the atmosphere. Many of the words in the speeches, banners, and poems broke taboos as they attacked the powerful radicals. But the crowd was emboldened by its own size and there seemed to be confidence that the will of the people would somehow prevail. I also felt a tinge of excitement and hope. I didn't see how the will of so many could be defied.

On the night of April 4, 1976, the authorities ordered that all the wreaths be cleared out of the square, which was washed clean in the early hours of the morning of April 5.

★ ★ ★

On Qingming Day, April 5, I arrived in the square in the afternoon with my classmate Chen Min. The crowds were much smaller than on the previous day, but there were still hundreds of thousands of people in the vast square. There were far fewer wreaths at the base of the monument. There was a small crowd, a few dozen people perhaps, in the southeast corner of the square near a redbrick building, which as I later learned housed the command center of the military's Beijing garrison. Earlier in the day a small mob of angry people attacked the building and set it on fire. They also overturned and burned a few police cars parked outside it.

As darkness gradually descended on the square, the crowd began to thin out. Suddenly, at about 6:30 p.m., the loudspeakers affixed on the tall lampposts in the square began to blare. It was the voice of Wu De, the mayor of Beijing. He said that there were bad people in the square who were engaged in counterrevolutionary activities of destruction and making trouble. He urged the revolutionary masses not to be fooled by these bad elements and to immediately leave the square. His speech was repeatedly blared from the loudspeakers. I didn't see any bad people, and we certainly didn't consider ourselves to be bad people.

At about 10:30 that night, Chen Min and I decided to leave to catch the last bus for campus. Just then, I noticed multitudes of workers in tight formation marching into the square. They wore the same work clothes as everyone else but they all carried clubs in their hands. I thought they were there to protest. "Look," I said to Chen Min. "The workers are rising up. The leadership can't stop this thing now." I was quite excited as we left the square.

I later learned that I had been quite mistaken. These marchers were a workers' militia. They were there to clear out the protesters at the order of the authorities. The commander of the Beijing military garrison had personally decided to delay the deployment of forces until late at night, when there were fewer people in the square, or we would have been caught up in it. The militiamen surrounded the square from all sides and, at about 11 p.m., moved in toward the monument at its center. They arrested a few hundred people; many were beaten up. The protests were suppressed.

★ ★ ★

On the evening of April 7, the central radio station broadcast two decisions made by the Party's central committee. The first declared the April 5th Movement, as it became known, to be a "counterrevolutionary incident." The second declared that Deng Xiaoping had been the "black hand" behind the event. Those who went to the square knew that the mass protest was spontaneous. But for months the official media had been attacking Deng without naming him, only referring to "the capitalist roader who does not repent till his death." Now the gloves were off. Deng, the central radio announced, had been stripped of all his positions within and outside the Party. Once again, however, he was curiously allowed to keep his Party membership. For some reason, Mao always had a soft spot in his heart for Deng, treating him differently from almost all those purged from power in the history of the Party.

Back at school, as in every work unit in Beijing, there was a hunt for those who had participated in the April 5th Movement. It was well known I had gone to the square, because I made a point of urging others to go as well. But other than observing what was happening, as millions of others did, I did not take part in any activities that were considered counterrevolutionary, such as distributing leaflets, posting articles and poems, or burning down the police command center. And of course, I wasn't alone.

Still, someone must have told on me. The Party secretary of the English department, Lu Zuwen, called me into his office. He came right to the point: "Did you go to Tiananmen Square?" he asked.

"Yes," I replied, defiantly, "I went there several times and I don't see anything wrong with it. As you know, millions of people went there. I don't think they were all counterrevolutionaries."

"Did you take notes of the essays and poems posted there?" he asked. One was supposed to surrender such notes if one had them. I remembered the photographs I had taken at the square, which I had developed and kept at my parents' house. Those photographs could get me in a lot of trouble.

"I didn't take any notes," I replied, "but I memorized the ones I read." I was thinking, "You can confiscate notes people took. But how do you purge them from my memory?" Then I proceeded to recite for him some of the poems.

Mr. Lu stopped me with a gesture of his hand. Then he stared right into my eyes and he said, "Can you keep quiet and not tell people about what you have memorized?"

At that point I realized he was not trying to get me into trouble. To the contrary, he was trying to protect me. I looked at him, feeling ashamed of myself for having judged him and for being so foolishly defiant. I was quite sure he and I thought alike, but as the Party secretary of the department, he had to go through the motions of carrying out his duties. He was taking a risk himself by not only letting me off the hook, but also by warning me not to be foolish. I felt so grateful and so much respect for him. I thanked him before taking my leave.

Such was the public sentiment at the time. Popular discontent went beyond anger at Jiang Qing or weariness of an unceasing revolution. It represented a final disillusionment with Mao himself. Since the Communist Party came to power in 1949, Mao had enjoyed the status of a savior. Despite his disastrous policies, his stature among the people had not diminished; in fact, it was only enhanced and mythologized to dizzying heights. By the start of the Cultural Revolution, he was worshipped like a god. His words were deemed the ultimate truth. Anyone who disagreed with him or whoever he did not like were immediately perceived as bad actors—in a word, evil. Few questioned his leadership or his infallibility.

But now people were increasingly skeptical. The revolutionary zeal was long gone. Those of us who had experienced the hardships knew that real life was much more ugly and harsh than the utopia promoted by official propaganda. The nonstop political campaigns had become tiring and seemed pointless. Revolution did not fill empty stomachs.

Deng's efforts to rectify the excesses and disorder in all walks of life were welcomed by the populace. Under his stewardship, industrial and agricultural production was up, trains began to run on time, scientists and scholars were back to do research, and the military had been streamlined—all in about one year's time. But much remained to be done and even Deng lamented the problems were "piled up to become too heavy to be restored to normal." But now he was fired again. Where was China headed? Nobody knew, and the public mood was pessimistic and gloomy.

★ ★ ★

The summer of 1976 in Beijing was particularly hot. I found it difficult to sleep. I often had to get up in the middle of the night to go to the washroom with a basin and pour cold water over my head to cool down.

Shortly before 4 a.m. on July 28, 1976, I was awakened by a powerful jolt that almost threw me out of my bed. The shaking continued, accompanied by loud noises, as I was trying to come to my senses. Just then Chen Min, whose bed was below mine, yelled, "Earthquake!" Immediately we all bolted out the door of our dorm, down the stairs, and out of the building into the open air. I could not remember how I jumped off my bunk bed to get out of the building so quickly.

All of us were in our underwear and bare-chested, as it had been so hot when we went to bed. There were a few more powerful jolts, and then the quake stopped. For a long while, we milled around in front of our dorm, a lot of people without much clothing on. Nobody dared go back into the building to fetch clothing in case more aftershocks came.

Soon the day broke. I was in a hurry to go home to find out if everyone in my family was all right. Fortunately, some buses were running. There were thousands of people in the streets, as few dared to venture back into their homes. I arrived home to find everyone outside. Thankfully, no one was hurt. By then, however, reports of casualties started to come in. Falling tiles had killed one faculty member of our institute as he tried to escape from his home. Fearing aftershocks, since we could not go back inside our homes, we built shelters outside. It was summertime, warm enough for people to spend the night outdoors. But there was not enough room in the open space by our home for everyone, so our family set up a tent a couple blocks away, on the wide pavement of Chang'an Boulevard, along with numerous other families. Temporary shelters of all colors, shapes, and materials covered the pavements on both sides of the boulevard. People only went back to their homes to cook their meals. The streets of Beijing became a giant refugee camp, as people were constantly on alert for another quake.

It took a few days for the news to trickle in of what had exactly happened. The epicenter of the earthquake was in Tangshan, a city of more than a million people about 200 kilometers (~125 miles) to the east of Beijing. The quake measured 7.8 degrees on the Richter scale and was rather shallow, just 12 kilometers (~7.5 miles) beneath the surface of the earth. It immediately flattened the entire city, cut off all power, and plunged the area into complete darkness—a total blackout. Because the quake also knocked out all lines of communication and severely damaged the roads, the authorities in Beijing didn't know what had happened until several hours later, when someone drove the four hours from Tangshan to Beijing to report the disaster. It was another six hours before military rescue teams could reach the city. The earthquake claimed the lives of about 250,000 people and seriously injured more than 150,000, including the father and two sisters of my future wife, whom I had not yet met.

The entire city of Beijing came to a halt, because it was not safe to go back into the buildings. All schools were closed, and most workplaces shut down as well. For months, people camped outside, too scared to go back to their homes. Thankfully, there was no shortage of either food or water.

★ ★ ★

In September 1976, classes for a new semester resumed, and I went back to campus. We moved into the former girls' dormitory next to the soccer field, which was now divided in half to house both male and female students. In this building we slept seven people to a room, in four sets of bunk beds, which was an improvement from our old dorm. The building was made of rather thin concrete slabs, so thin in fact that when people ran in the hallway, the footsteps could be heard throughout the floor.

One night shortly after we moved in, someone on my floor ran to the bathroom. Hearing the rumbling noise of his footsteps, one of my bunkmates awoke and yelled, "Earthquake!" All of us jumped out of our beds and bolted out, which triggered a chain reaction. Within a few minutes the entire building was emptied and a crowd of people, men and women, stood outside in their underwear wondering what had happened. It was early September and getting a little chilly outside. Eventually, people went back to their rooms, still feeling jittery. But from that night on, running in the hallway was prohibited.

★ ★ ★

On the afternoon of September 9, 1976, I was studying in the classroom when Chen Min pulled me out into the hallway. He had a secret to tell me. He leaned close to my ear and whispered, "The chairman has passed away."

This was shocking news. In the photographs of him in the newspapers, Mao had appeared frail and senile. But his health, as that of all state leaders, was kept a secret, and the official media always did their best to present him as healthy. I didn't know where Chen Min heard the news, but he would not have told me unless he had been absolutely certain it was reliable. We calmly went back to our own desks to wait for the news to become official. Soon there was a notice that we should tune in to the radio for a major announcement at 4 p.m. The broadcasting system in our classroom was switched away from headphones to the loudspeaker. We were all waiting at our desks.

At 4 p.m. sharp, came the sound of funeral music. All in the room immediately knew Mao had died. Even before the announcer came on, the entire classroom burst into tears. I was crying, too, affected by the others. But I had long harbored the forbidden thought that China's misery would not be over as long as he lived. I felt a tinge of excitement and hope: China was now in uncharted territory. How would the future be different?

★ ★ ★

Back in April, after Deng had been blamed for the Tiananmen Square protests and removed from power, Mao had named Hua Guofeng as the new premier. Hua came from Mao's home province of Hunan. He joined the Communist forces during the Anti-Japanese war, much later than the first generation of Communist leaders such as Mao, Zhou, and Deng. Hua was 55 years old now, and Deng Xiaoping was 72. Mao had probably selected Hua because he thought his mediocre abilities and achievements would be no threat to anyone, as well as for his loyalty.

He was a compromise between the old guard and the radicals; neither group would be able to live under a prominent figure from the other faction. Because of his meteoric rise, he was a relatively unknown factor to the populace.

Hua would surprise everyone.

After Mao's death the most pressing matter for Hua was how to deal with the already defined Gang of Four, which is how the clique of radicals associated with Mao's wife Jiang Qing would come to be known: The group included Jiang, Zhang Chunqiao, Yao Wenyuan, and Wang Hongwen. Mao himself had given them this name. At one time or another he had suggested that they should try to work with others in the leadership, and not just to isolate themselves as a "gang of four." It wasn't a term anyone outside the inner circles of the top leadership had heard before, but it would stick. Zhang and Yao were both writers from Shanghai, and they had been among the most ardent and fervent promoters of Mao's ideas. Wang was a worker from Shanghai who had led a Rebel faction at the start of the Cultural Revolution; Mao made him a member of the Politburo and vice chairman of the Party in 1973. As such, he was considered Mao's heir apparent at one time. But Wang, as the Chinese saying goes, was like a piece of tofu held by a string—he could not be lifted up—and eventually Mao gave up the idea of making him his successor. Nonetheless, he remained in his position in the central leadership.

As one of his first orders of business Hua visited Marshal Ye Jianying, one of the old guard sidelined but not kicked out by Mao. Ye had effective control of the military. The two of them enlisted Wang Dongxing, the director of the office of the central committee, or Mao's chief of staff. Wang controlled the PLA's No. 8341 garrison, whose mission was to protect the state leadership.

On October 6, 1976, less than one month after Mao's death, Hua and his allies made their move. Early that morning, Jiang Qing and other members of the Gang of Four were arrested. The coup d'état was a complete success. They put up no resistance. The event became referred to as "smashing the Gang of Four" in the annals of the official Chinese history. The victors of the power struggle labeled them the Gang of Four to suggest Mao was against them. The truth was that Jiang Qing and her supporters were in power only thanks to Mao's support. When Mao died, their fate was sealed.

The next day, Hua Guofeng was named by the Politburo as Chairman of the Communist Party, Chairman of the Party's Military Commission (equivalent to the position of commander in chief of the armed forces), and Premier. No other person before or since had held all these top positions at once, not even Mao.

News of the Gang of Four's arrest trickled down the hierarchy over the following two weeks. But word of mouth spread fast, especially in Beijing, where so many high-ranking officials resided and had access to secrets from the top. Those in the know whispered it to others, always while reminding the listener to keep it a secret. No one did, of course. The arrests came on a Wednesday. I heard about them by Friday. The following day, as Chen Min and I were leaving campus for the weekend, we came across our head English teacher, Wang Keli. He was walking his bicycle along the path through the vegetable field toward the campus as we were walking in the opposite direction. We stopped to chat with him. When we told him that Jiang Qing and her followers had been arrested, he could hardly believe it.

"It's true," we assured him. Teacher Wang was so excited that I saw tears well up in his eyes.

"I feel things haven't been right these years," he said, before walking away happy.

When the news was officially announced, about a week later, Beijing broke into celebration. People poured into the streets to celebrate. Every drop of liquor in the city was sold out in a day. October was also crab season. People bought them in sets of four, one female and three males, each symbolizing a member of the Gang of Four, to smash them to pieces and pick out their meat. Crabs were soon sold out, too. People celebrated with banquets, eating crabs and drinking *baijiu*, a strong Chinese liquor, all over the town and all over the country.

In spite of his courage and decisiveness, Hua Guofeng clung to the legacy of Mao and insisted the country continue to follow whatever Mao had said and decided. It would take another two years for Deng Xiaoping to return to power and for Hua Guofeng to fade into the background of Chinese politics. But it was Hua who removed the radicals from power and cleared the way for Deng's return. Soon real change would begin.

Chapter 19

Roads to Rome

In July 1977, Deng Xiaoping was once again brought back into the Party's leadership, under China's new leader, Hua Guofeng. Initially Deng's agenda included only the military, foreign affairs, and education. He moved swiftly and restored the college entrance examination system, which had been suspended since 1966.

There were more than 10 million applications for the college entrance exams that year, and 5.7 million people eventually took part. Of those, only 272,297 students were accepted, a rate of less than 5 percent. The new students ranged in age from 13 to 37, which reflected the gap in schooling created by the 10-year Cultural Revolution.

The Construction Army Corps system was dismantled. The "educated youth" who had been sent down to the countryside gradually returned to the cities, including my friends from the Gobi. But it was hard for them to find a decent job; their lack of formal education left them severely underqualified. Many of my friends struggled to find their footing once they returned.

With the leadership's most radical elements purged following Mao's death, changes could be felt throughout the country, but slowly, because Hua Guofeng favored a policy that adhered to whatever Mao had said and done. His legitimacy and power came from Mao, who had designated him as his successor; it was not surprising he remained loyal to Mao and whatever Mao represented. The rest of the new leadership, particularly a faction of pre–Cultural Revolution senior leaders led by Deng Xiaoping, held opposing views. They did not renounce Mao, but they were willing to publicly question his policies. All their experiences and suffering during Mao's political campaigns had taught them that the only test of the truth was not what Mao had said but what worked or did not work in practice. The reality was that many of Mao's policies had been complete failures, disastrous and ruinous for the nation as well as for its people.

In December 1978, after what amounted to a well-publicized debate over Mao's legacy, Deng became the de facto leader of the country. Hua Guofeng, who had resisted changes to Mao's policies, was gradually sidelined, although he is remembered for changing the course of history as the leader of the coup d'état against Mao's wife and her gang of radicals. Deng was free to move ahead with a new policy focused on reform and openness. He knew that to develop, China had to depart from the Soviet-style centrally planned economy and move in the direction of a market-based economy. It also had to abandon its isolationist stance and form better relations with the West.

Jimmy Carter won the election to become president of the United States in 1976. On New Year's Day 1979, China and the United States formally established diplomatic relations. At the end of January 1979, Deng Xiaoping paid an official visit to the United States at the invitation of President Carter, the first Chinese leader to do so since the founding of the PRC in 1949. His visit also provided the Chinese public, for the first time, with an opportunity to get glimpses of the United States, as television cameras followed Deng everywhere while he was there.

Shortly after Deng's return from the States, China launched a border war against Vietnam, purportedly to punish it for its invasion of Cambodia and for its incursions into what China considered its own territory. The war captured the public's attention until it was concluded about one month later. The United States had untangled itself from the Vietnam War in 1975. China and the United States, former enemies, were now becoming friends. China and North Vietnam, former allies, now turned their guns on each other. It is really true that in international relations, there are no permanent friends or permanent enemies, only permanent interests.

★ ★ ★

Part of Deng's education reform was to resume the examination system and to reward academic performance. Before winter break of 1977, we were given final exams, for the first time. The school authorities decided to post all the grades and, more boldly, to reassign classes based on the grades from the finals. Two "fast-pace" classes were formed to include the best students from the 10 classrooms. I was put into one of them. From the next semester on, I would have new classmates. The objective of the new system was to "produce talents faster."

I was assigned to Classroom No. Four, and I was elected the class representative. The new students selected through the nationwide college entrance examination in the last two months of 1977 had begun their matriculation in late February 1978 as well. But we had little interaction with the students outside our own cohort.

The fast pace did make a difference. My new classmates were the best and brightest in their former classrooms. They were competitive, motivated, and always hungry for more from the teachers. We began to study English literature as well as business writing in English. My favorite authors were Mark Twain, for his great sense of humor; Ernest Hemingway, for his simple and short sentences, which were great for a foreign student of English; and Jack London, for the human struggles in his stories and his characters, some of whom I identified with. I also enjoyed the French author Guy de Maupassant, whose short stories, translated into English, were full of surprises, irony, and satire. I loved his short stories so much I translated some from English into Chinese.

By now, I was making good progress with my spoken English, which I practiced with my classmates and with the foreign teachers who came to China for a semester or two. Beyond listening comprehension and speaking, we also spent much time studying English grammar. The basics were not difficult to learn because the typical sentence structure in English is similar to Chinese, with the subject preceding the verb and the verb before the object. The difficult parts of the English language were the tenses, the moods, such as the subjunctive mood, and especially the articles. It did not seem that there were fixed rules on how to use an article. The teachers told us that as we read more and more English writing we would develop a feel for using that part of speech.

I decided that the best way to learn to speak fluently was to memorize English texts by listening to language tapes repeatedly, and by reciting them back loudly and often. I began to memorize and recite every passage, short story, or essay in our textbook from the beginning of the semester. Once I had committed the different expressions to memory, they came to me easily when I spoke the language. Every day, I would find a block of time to walk around campus, reciting all the passages in our textbook from the beginning to wherever it was we had got at that point. By the end of the semester, I could recite the entire textbook from beginning to end. In order to teach myself the subjunctive mood, for example, I memorized such passages as: "Whatever happened to her then may have determined whatever happened to her afterwards, and whatever happened to her afterwards may have driven her to suicide, a chain of events," from the English play *An Inspector Calls*.

I wasn't the only one doing this. Walking around the campus after dinnertime, I frequently passed classmates who were loudly reading or talking to themselves in English, French, German, Polish, Japanese, or Arabic, oblivious to their surroundings and others around them. There was one student in a senior class, by the name of Tang. He not only talked to himself all the time, he would come up to anyone to chat non-stop in English, regardless of whether or not his audience was interested. One of his classmates was so annoyed by him that he yelled, "I will slap your face if you don't stop talking to me."

The institute now had a reading room stocked with foreign newspapers and magazines. There were issues of the *Times* of London, *Reader's Digest*, and the British *Daily Mirror*, whose naked "page 3" girls I found too scandalous to look at, yet too tantalizing to resist.

The English publications were typically outdated, but I didn't care. I was not there to keep up with the news, which I got by listening to VOA and the BBC every day. I was there to learn the language and foreign culture.

Reader's Digest was one of my favorites. It ran a condensed version of the novel *A Town Like Alice*, which I found mesmerizing. I particularly loved the regular feature *Laughter: The Best Medicine*. I remember a favorite joke of mine from that feature: "Men marry women hoping they will never change; women marry men hoping they will change. Both are disappointed."

For the first time since before the Cultural Revolution, bookstores began to sell Chinese translations of foreign books. I bought two plays by Shakespeare translated into Chinese. I found them difficult, even in Chinese.

★ ★ ★

On January 10, 1979, our class graduated, three years and three months to the day after we matriculated on October 10, 1975. In keeping with the system at that time, everyone was assigned a job. None of us had a choice. Those assigned a job in Beijing were considered lucky, both for the living conditions and because Beijing was where the action was. It was the capital, and news traveled here first.

I stayed at BIFT and joined the English Department. Along with a few classmates who were also chosen, I would receive further training, for at least another year, in a faculty training program while serving as a faculty member.

I was given a salary of 49 yuan per month, a bit less than $32 at the official exchange rate, and just about $16 at the black market rate. Still, it was a big step up from the 15 yuan per month student stipend I was receiving previously.

Although I did not realize it at the time, Deng's nine-day visit to the United States at the invitation of Jimmy Carter in 1979 would have an immense effect on my life. It not only paved the way for China to open its door to visiting foreigners, but also allowed Chinese to go abroad to study.

Deng, himself a work-study student in France in the 1920s, had already had the idea of sending Chinese students and scholars abroad to study before he left for the United States. In Washington, Jimmy Carter broached the subject of Chinese emigration with Deng. Under a piece of legislation known as the Jackson-Vanik Amendment to the Trade Act of 1974, the United States was not allowed to grant most-favored-nation trading status (which was important for facilitating China's trade with the US) to any country that restricted emigration. This law was primarily aimed at Soviet-bloc countries, which had restricted travel for Jewish refugees and other religious minorities, but it affected China, a closed country, as well. It was a significant obstacle for increased trade between the two countries. According to Zbigniew Brzezinski, President Carter's National Security Advisor, after Carter brought up the subject, Deng leaned forward and said, "Fine. We'll let them go. Are you prepared to accept 10 million?" Everyone laughed, as President Carter later recalled, although somewhat uneasily. It was said that Carter quickly dropped the subject.

The Americans thought Deng was joking. It would turn out that he was quite serious. His visit heralded China's opening, including allowing overseas studies and emigration, an opening that started with a trickle but became a torrent. Soon so many were knocking on US doors that the limiting factor became the difficulty of getting a US visa.

We continued our studies with more advanced materials. Every week, we took classes in reading, writing, listening comprehension, and speaking, and every week there were tests and exams, which pressured us to study ever harder.

★ ★ ★

In late January 1977, while I was on winter break from school, I met a girl in the office of a mutual friend by chance. I had walked in to deliver a package from my mother to this friend only to find her chatting animatedly with another girl in a navy blue uniform. She was introduced to me as Shi Bin, a native of Beijing but now on a school break from a university in Harbin, in China's far northeast. Bin was pretty, with big eyes and dark hair, and tall at 1.74 meters (~5 feet 8 inches). It turned out that she played professional basketball for the women's team of the navy. I was impressed by her personality—open, unreserved, confident, straightforward, and no-nonsense. I thought, "What a happy girl," very different from many of the girls I had met who looked to have suffered too much in life and wore their miseries on their faces.

I would learn later that Bin had suffered more than most in the most unimaginable way. Just the previous year, while away at school, the massive earthquake struck her home city, Tangshan, and her father and two younger sisters were killed when the family home collapsed; her mother was severely injured.

But none of the pain of that tremendous loss was visible on her sunlit face.

Bin and I left the office of our friend together. She was headed in the same direction as my home so I offered to walk with her.

"Okay. But do you know the way?" she asked.

"Of course," I replied. I was confident in my sense of direction. Even in the Gobi, surrounded by miles of emptiness, I had little trouble finding my way.

"Don't worry," I added nonchalantly, "all roads lead to Rome." Beijing's roads were generally laid out in a grid running north-south or east-west, and this pattern persisted even in the small and narrow lanes, or *hutong*, in residential neighborhoods. So, as long as we walked in the right direction, I was sure we would get to our destination.

As we walked we chatted with each other. I must have been too enamored and lost in conversation to notice where we were headed. We promptly came to a dead-end in a *hutong*.

"I thought you said all roads lead to Rome?" she prodded me, looking amused.

"Most of these *hutong* go straight through." I tried to hide my embarrassment, but in vain. "I suppose this is one of the rare exceptions."

Bin had a good laugh as we found our way back out. Her laughter relaxed me. Unconsciously, my use of the phrase "all roads lead to Rome" foreshadowed the inevitability of our relationship.

★ ★ ★

An opportunity came. In April 1979, I noticed an advertisement for a position at the United Nations in the newspaper. At that time, advertising in newspapers was almost unheard of in China, so the UN ad was particularly prominent, and it immediately caught my attention. It said that the UN would be recruiting simultaneous interpreters from China for the first time. The recruits would be put through a yearlong intensive training program established at the First Foreign Language Institute in Beijing. After the training program, the recruits would be posted to United Nations headquarters in New York City.

A group of us young faculty members from BIFT applied even though none of us had any great hope of being selected. The program was to test and interview candidates from three major cities in China— Beijing, Shanghai, and Guangzhou—and would accept only 25 people in total. Who would want to miss a golden opportunity to go to the

United States and to work at the UN? We were sure China's best and brightest would come out, and the competition would be too difficult for us to have any chances.

Still, I thought there was no harm trying, and it would be a good exercise anyhow. In late April, I sat for the UN exam and did well enough to advance to the next round. I was relaxed when I took that second round of exams, as I had no expectation to be selected from among so many. Although the tests were rigorous and the subjects quite wide-ranging, I did not feel they were particularly hard. I was quite pleased, and somewhat surprised, when I received notice that I had made it into the third round. This thing suddenly looked quite real. If I did get selected, it would change my life. I had never expected to work abroad, and for the United Nations, no less. Now my hopes were up.

The third round was not so much a test as a face-to-face interview with the UN recruiters, representatives from China's Ministry of Foreign Affairs, and professors from Beijing First Language Institute. It was held at the Beijing International Club, a building next to Beijing's diplomatic district. The finalists waited in line to be ushered into the interview room. When it was almost my turn, I suddenly became nervous as hell. I was fully conscious that this would be the chance of a lifetime, for so much was at stake. Afraid to say something wrong, I seized up.

I walked into a big room to see more than a dozen examiners sitting in a semicircle. Some of them were foreigners and others were Chinese. The examiners looked friendly, but that did not ease my extreme nervousness. I was seated in a chair in the center facing the interviewers. Then they took turns asking me questions. I answered them mechanically. I was so nervous that I literally didn't know what I was talking about.

The only question I still remember was: "What do you think about the Cultural Revolution?" By that time the Communist Party itself had concluded that the Cultural Revolution was "10 years of catastrophe" and it was no longer taboo to be openly critical of it. I wanted to say that by the end of the period, the economy was on the verge of being completely destroyed. In my nervousness, instead of using the passive tense—being destroyed—I said "on the verge of destroying." I immediately realized my grammatical mistake but I still couldn't bring the correct expression to mind. My heart sank. I thought I had blown the opportunity. I was quite disappointed with myself and regretted that I missed this opportunity so close at hand because I was not calm enough. I could not get over this nagging feeling of regret for a few days. But eventually I decided to put the whole matter out of my mind. It was July and the summer break began. I shifted my focus to find something interesting to do.

★ ★ ★

Toward the end of August, I returned to the BIFT campus to begin the autumn semester of faculty training. As I passed through the wrought-iron gate, someone working in the messenger's office stepped out and stopped me. "Hey," he said, "you had a letter from the First Foreign Language Institute."

"Where's the letter?" I asked. I knew it had to be about the UN program. I was surprised to hear from them again. "It sat here for some time and eventually we handed it over to the personnel department," the man replied.

I hurried to the personnel department, but nobody could find it. Apparently, the letter was lost. I got on my bike and rode to the First Foreign Language Institute to find out what they wanted.

There, I met with Professor Zhang Zailiang, one of the instructors in charge of the UN program. He said there was good news and bad news. I did indeed do poorly during the interview, and I placed 33rd on the test, and did not make the cutoff to join the class of 25 students who would take the UN translator program that year. But I had done well enough to earn a spot in the second training program, which would begin in the winter of the following year.

Since I had completely given up hope and put the UN thing out of my mind, I was quite delighted by this news. Now it was just a matter of time until I could attend this program, which would prepare me to work as an interpreter at the UN headquarters in New York City.

I went to see Bin to share the news with her. As the weather was hot, we decided to go out to buy a watermelon to celebrate. As we were trying to pick a ripe melon from a stand on the street, I heard someone yelling, "Stop, thief!" A man dashed past, pursued by a group. Without thinking, I dropped the melon and joined the chase. But the thief ran like a rabbit and eventually got away.

When she finally caught up with me, Bin looked worried and said in a reproachful voice, "What were you doing?"

"Catching a thief," I replied, matter-of-factly.

"What did he do? Steal a watermelon?" she asked.

I really had no idea what the offense was. He must have been guilty of something, as he was running away.

"That wasn't worth it and so dangerous," she said. "What if he had a knife? What if he turned around and stabbed you in your eye?"

"Then I would still be a one-eyed UN interpreter," I teased her. From that day on, from time to time Bin would call me a one-eyed UN interpreter.

★ ★ ★

On Saturday, October 27, 1979, Bin and I went on our own to register to be married. There was a marriage license office in a village near the institute. I rode my bicycle with Bin seated behind me on the small baggage rack. The dirt road through the vegetable field was quite bumpy, and I pedaled slowly to make sure that I would not fall and drop my bride into the mud. The village was called Taiyanggong (Sun Temple). Until 50 years earlier, there had been a small temple where people would come to worship the sun god. The temple had long since disappeared, but the name remained. Now Taiyanggong was a farming village, producing vegetables for the city.

The office door was locked when we got there, and no one seemed to be around. We had to search out the person responsible for marriage registration. Finally, we found a middle-aged woman. I supposed it was rare for people outside the village to come here for marriage registration. She seemed a little annoyed to be disturbed.

"What are you here for?" she asked with a poker face, even though it was obvious. We explained that we'd like to register to get married. The woman gave a grumpy sigh, rolled her eyes, and sat down at the desk. It was plain that she didn't see us as two young people trying to celebrate a happy occasion, but as a major inconvenience and a pile of paperwork.

"How long have you known each other?" she asked, looking at me. It was a standard question for the marriage form, but I was annoyed by her unpleasantness on such a happy occasion. "Three days," I replied, curtly and innocently; the cynic in me was coming out. The woman stared at me, and then turned to Bin. "Do you really know this man?" she demanded. It took a while for my bride to convince her I was only joking.

We finally had our wedding ceremony on February 12, 1980. We just invited a few family members for dinner at my parents' apartment. The guests included Bin's mother, her only living immediate family member, and my parents, of course, as well as my sister and brother.

Although we were married, we did not have a place of our own to live. Your work unit assigned you to a home, and since there was a severe shortage at the time, newly married couples might wait years for one. We had to use a room in the apartment of my parents, or sometimes stay at Bin's mother's. Or we slept in my office—which I shared with others but had to myself at night—on a small mattress on top of two rows of chairs.

Bin wanted to have a new dress made after the wedding; I remember the dress she wanted was light green in color. The day she went to the tailor she had to get up at 4 a.m. and wait in line to take a number, and then wait again for her turn to have the appointment with the tailor. She asked me to go with her. I thought it was not worth it to get up so early for a dress, because I hadn't yet learned about what members of the opposite sex considered important.

Later that morning, Bin came back from the tailor's crying. She had waited for almost four hours in line, but when her turn came all the numbers were already drawn, and she left empty-handed. She was less angry at the tailor shop than with me for not having shared her pain by getting up early to go with her. In the end, she gave up the idea and never had a dress made. To this day, I still regret her disappointment and sadness, since I had played a role in it.

★ ★ ★

The faculty training program really helped improve our language proficiency. I began to teach English in the spring semester of 1980. My students were in their third year of studies, having been accepted after taking the nationwide standardized exams in 1978. They were an even better class than the cohort of 1977, when Deng restarted the examination system. They arrived already reading and speaking English. These students were bold, proactive, curious, and challenging. I quite enjoyed teaching them.

In the spring of 1980, a group of Americans arrived on campus. A San Francisco–based organization called the Asia Foundation came to recruit visiting scholars. The foundation received funding from public and private sources and provided support to programs to help developing countries in Asia. It was offering scholarships for three BIFT faculty members to study at US universities for a period of one year. This was the first time anyone at BIFT had had such an opportunity. All faculty members under the age of 45 were eligible and encouraged to apply, but the selection would be through a rigorous, comprehensive, and blind examination process, meaning that the test papers were identified by number and the examiners wouldn't know who took the test.

I had already been accepted into the UN translator program on a deferred basis. But that program wouldn't start until winter of the following year. The Asia Foundation visiting scholar program would start this autumn. The dean of the English Department, where I was teaching, encouraged me to apply. "You are going to America anyway so it doesn't matter if you do well or poorly on the exams," he told me. "You might as well give it a try."

But this time, I was competing not only against my peers but also with many of my own professors. I didn't think I could outcompete my professors, but since there was nothing to lose, I decided there was no harm in trying.

The tests were rigorous, covering a wide range of both English and Chinese languages, essays, and history. The blind nature of the tests allowed me to level the playing field somewhat in my own way. I knew that those who administered the tests would be biased in favor of those mid-aged scholars who had been educated before the Cultural Revolution, because the education quality had been much higher then. After all, this was a process of selecting visiting scholars to the United States. In my essays, I wrote in a style and a voice that would give the reader the impression I was one of those mid-aged scholars.

The result was announced: I came in first. I was surprised, but of course happily. Maybe my trick worked, but still I hadn't expected to do better than my own professors, many of whom I knew were far better educated than me. I knew I was just more experienced than they were in taking tests. For the past three years, they had been busy giving exams without taking any themselves, whereas I had been busy taking them.

I was much happier with this result than with that of the UN exam because I didn't disappoint myself this time. By then my father had returned from his African post. I hurried to my father's office to tell him the good news, as I knew this would make him happy.

"Oh." That was all he said, but I could tell he was pleased.

Suddenly, I had two opportunities to go to the United States. All roads were leading to Rome. All I had to do was pick one.

By the rules of that time, a graduate of the UN interpreter-training program would be deemed as having obtained a graduate degree. That was a big deal for me. I was still, like the rest of my cohort, a worker-peasant-soldier student, considered to be of lesser quality than those who were accepted into college through the formal entrance examination. Accordingly, my pay was less than that of college graduates before the Cultural Revolution. The UN job would pay tens of thousands of dollars per year, an astronomical sum compared to my 49 yuan a month teacher's salary, or just $379 a year. At the time Bin was earning 56 yuan a month. To this day, she enjoys telling friends that I married her for her money.

Most important, the UN job would allow me to take my spouse with me to the States.

The Asia Foundation program, on the other hand, would only pay a stipend of about $250 per month. I could only stay in the United States for one year. And I could only go there alone, leaving my bride behind. But I would finally get a chance to study in a US university, which was something I had dreamed of doing. It was hard to say goodbye to a lot of money the UN job promised, not to mention my new wife.

Eventually, I chose the Asia Foundation. My friends at BIFT told me that I exchanged a watermelon for a sesame seed. In any case, the die was cast. On August 8, 1980, I received the formal notice to go to the United States as a visiting scholar.

The president of BIFT would decide which university I was going to attend. "There are three universities on the list provided by the

American sponsor," the president said, opening a letter written on finer, thicker paper than I had ever seen. "We can send one person to each. Since you did so well on the exam, you will go to the best one."

I thanked him and waited anxiously to hear my destination.

"The first on the list is called Stanford." The president paused. "Stanford. I've never heard of it. It must be an obscure school. You know there are thousands of universities in America."

I nodded in agreement.

"Another is called the University of California at Berkeley. We have all heard about California. The University of California must be pretty good, but this one apparently is a branch school."

At that time, because of the surging demand for higher education after the Cultural Revolution, several Chinese universities in Beijing had set up branch schools that accepted applicants who otherwise could not qualify for regular universities. A branch school to us meant second rate. I would not want to go there.

"The final one on the list is the University of San Francisco." The president beamed. "San Francisco. I have heard so much about San Francisco. Have you heard of San Francisco?"

"Yes, certainly," I replied. Who had not heard of San Francisco, the Old Gold Mountain, as it is known in Chinese?

"This one must be the best of the three." He folded the letter. "You will go to the University of San Francisco."

I smiled and thanked him profusely. I was so grateful and so excited.

Chapter 20

Old Gold Mountain

As the relationship between the United States and China warmed up, the tension between the United States and the Soviet Union reached another high after the Soviet invasion of Afghanistan in 1979. In retaliation, the United States boycotted the Moscow Summer Olympics in 1980.

Americans were gripped by the Iran hostage crisis that had started in November 1979 when 66 American embassy staff members and their families were held hostage in the wake of the Iranian Revolution, which overthrew the Shah. President Jimmy Carter authorized an ill-fated attempt in April 1980 to rescue the hostages that resulted in the deaths of eight servicemen due to mishaps with their aircraft on the ground at their own base after the mission was called off. The incident dealt a serious blow to the credibility of the Carter administration and contributed to his defeat in the subsequent presidential election. The hostages were finally released before the next president took office in January 1981.

In the United States, 1980 was an election year. Ronald Reagan, a former actor and the governor of California, challenged Jimmy Carter and won. Reagan was good-looking, confident, and charismatic. Carter had been so ensnared in international crises that he looked tired and distressed during the campaign, appearing more often on TV with a frown rather than the broad smiles that bared his piano-key-like teeth, his former trademark.

345

In China, Deng Xiaoping was now firmly in control of the country. Zhao Ziyang, a reformist, replaced Hua Guofeng to become the premier. Zhao, under Deng, had initiated broad-scoped and large-scale economic reforms and continued to adopt market-oriented policies. The doors of China were opening wider in trade, investments, and international exchange of students.

In January 1981, Jiang Qing and the rest of the Gang of Four were put on trial; Mao's wife, ever defiant, received a suspended death penalty and the others were sentenced to jail terms. The trial itself was a farce. But it marked a clear break from the arbitrary persecution of political opponents that had been the hallmark of Mao's rule. It also seemed to have closed the final chapter on the Cultural Revolution.

★ ★ ★

The name "San Francisco" translated into Chinese literally means "Old Gold Mountain." It must have originated from the time of the California Gold Rush (1848–1855), a time also of significant Chinese immigration to the United States. Thousands of Chinese workers built the first transcontinental railroad in the United States, completing it on May 10, 1869.

I arrived in San Francisco on August 28, 1980, along with three other BIFT faculty members, and was picked up at the airport by Andy Andrews, the Asia Foundation's Director of Programs. Andy was in his forties, with close-cropped dark hair and a salt-and-pepper beard. His high forehead and prominent nose gave him an intense look, but he smiled warmly and greeted me as I approached.

"I knew you were our new scholar from China," he said. "I could tell from your suit and haircut." I must have stuck out like a sore thumb.

Andy drove me in his Buick to downtown San Francisco. The scenery along the highway from the airport was beautiful. On the right I caught glimpses of the blue water of San Francisco Bay, and on the left were rolling hills covered in yellowing late-summer grass.

Andy took me to lunch in San Francisco's Chinatown. The food was excellent. Andy was surprised when I told him the Chinese food in this restaurant was tastier, with a broader range of fresh ingredients, than what we had at home; China was still working its way through shortages. The only things not Chinese were the fortune cookies, the likes of which I had never seen. Yet Americans loved them and seemed to think they were authentically Chinese. Still, I thought they were clever, a small splash of entertainment to end a meal. I remember my fortune read, "Confucius likes mini-skirts." I was sure he did and laughed inwardly.

Doggy bags were a surprise, too. In China, no one would want to lose face by asking to take leftovers home. Americans have a clever way of getting around the face issue, by ostensibly implying that the leftovers are for their dogs. In the United States, I also learned later, children were told to eat all their food, and become members of the "clean plate club," because children in China were starving.

After lunch, Andy dropped me off at my hotel on Post Street. I wanted to take a shower, but I couldn't figure out how the faucet worked. It took me a while to examine and experiment with the knob under the shower before I managed to turn it on. After cleaning up, I turned on the television for news, but it seemed every channel was only broadcasting commercials. When I found a news broadcast, there was hardly any international news.

One thing that surprised me was that Americans had not been receiving the same news that I had for years. I thought that in San Francisco Voice of America would be ubiquitous. But I couldn't get the VOA shortwave broadcasts anywhere. Where had those voices I'd been listening to all those years been coming from? Shortwave travels all around the world, allowing people to receive signals from anywhere in any country. In China, almost every radio sold in stores had short-wave bands, which could travel long distances and without which a radio would be virtually useless in China's vast rural areas. In the United States, it was almost impossible to find a shortwave radio. Americans did not seem to need news from outside their own hometowns, and therefore AM/FM radios were sufficient.

The day after I arrived, Andy drove me to the Asia Foundation office on Geary Street to meet with Dr. Haydn Williams, its president. Square-jawed and patrician, Dr. Williams had served in the State Department and the Pentagon under presidents Eisenhower and Kennedy and as President Nixon's ambassador-level representative to the talks deciding the fate of Micronesia. I thought he looked straight out of central casting for the role of a US diplomat.

He welcomed me to the States and said how pleased he was to meet me, one of the first Chinese visitors sponsored by the Asia Foundation. He wished me an enjoyable stay and asked me not to hesitate to contact him if I needed any help. He asked me for my first impressions of America. I told him everything looked wonderful, the people were very friendly, and I had even managed to take a shower. I was so looking forward to learning more.

Then Andy and I went to his office and he asked me what I would like to study. I was surprised to be offered a choice, and I couldn't tell if he was being polite. I told him it didn't matter what I would study as long as I studied something. He paused for a few moments and then said, "China doesn't have a legal system. It would be good if you would study law." I had already heard before leaving Beijing that I might be assigned to study law in the United States. I had no idea what it entailed but law sounded exotic.

My future course of study seemingly decided, Andy drove me to the University of San Francisco (USF). The hilly streets made me carsick, and at one point, Andy had to stop the Buick to let me out so I could get some air and settle my stomach. It would take a few months for me to get used to riding in a car through San Francisco's roller-coaster streets.

USF is a Catholic school, established by the Jesuits in 1855, riding on the growth of the post-1848 California Gold Rush. The most prominent building on campus is St. Ignatius Church, whose twin spires can be seen for miles across the city; it sits at the corner of Fulton and Parker Streets. A few years before I arrived, the school had expanded by acquiring a second campus nearby, a former women's college high on top of a hill, called Lone Mountain. It was an imposing complex of buildings with red-tile roofs, set at the top of an elaborate series of stone staircases with gardens on all sides and shaded by tall pines. This was where I would be living during my year at USF.

At the heart of the Lone Mountain campus was a large, windowless chapel at the top of yet another set of imposing stairs. It seemed to be unused except on Sundays. I was given a room to myself in the chapel building, in what I assumed had been housing for the clergy. It was a luxury to have a room of my own, but I was quite far from the four-story dorm building where the rest of the students lived.

My first night there was very quiet. Nobody else seemed to inhabit my particular part of the campus. Once I wandered into the church to look around, but I found the vast emptiness somewhat intimidating when the lights were out. Even though I was afraid of nothing after the Gobi, the eerie walk back to my room gave me goose bumps. The darkness, the silence, and the unfamiliar setting made me feel like a stranger in a strange land and deeply lonely. I felt the name of the place, Lone Mountain, was quite fitting.

After having been so attentively taken care of by Andy upon arrival, I was surprised to be left to myself. I was already late for school, as the semester had started more than a week ago. What's more, my first day on campus turned out to be the Friday before the long Labor Day weekend, so the campus remained largely deserted. Labor Day was another surprise. I had always known it to fall on the first day of May. I had no idea Americans celebrated the day in September.

I was sure to be in for a lonely weekend on Lone Mountain. Fortunately, there were some students from Taiwan on campus who also didn't have anywhere to go. A few of them came to check me out, because they had never met anyone from the Communist mainland. I tried my best not to appear menacing. I did not know if they were surprised or disappointed, but they said I didn't look much like a Communist bandit, which was the term of endearment Taiwan had reserved for Mainland Chinese. Soon we got along quite well. A couple of them offered to tour me around the campus and to pick up a few needed items in the bookstore.

My new Taiwanese friends assumed that since I was fresh off the boat from China, I couldn't speak English, and they offered to help me translate. At the bookstore, I asked the shop assistant some questions about the things I wanted to pick up. One of the Taiwanese women, Xu Wen, who spoke English more fluently than others in the group, exclaimed: "Wowsai! Your English is so good." For some reason, still unbeknownst to me, Americans used the expression "Wow," but my Taiwanese friends all said "Wowsai." I had no idea where that expression came from. I took delight in surprising them, as they must have thought a country bumpkin like me had to learn English from scratch. They had no idea that I had almost become a one-eyed UN interpreter.

I got along handsomely with the Taiwanese students; we spoke the same Chinese language. I was also amused by their curiosity and ignorance about the mainland. They were interested in whatever I said. Clearly, they did not expect me to know much about world affairs and history, especially modern Chinese history. But when comparing notes, I found they themselves knew little. After having spent some time with me, one of them, Wu Shoumin, asked me with a concerned look on his face, "Are there many young people like you on the mainland?" I knew he was worried about the potential conflict between Taiwan and the mainland, as they were theoretically still at war with each other.

"Yes," I replied, "I am one of the dumber ones. The brighter ones were sent to better schools."

Andy invited me, as well as a couple of the other BIFT faculty who were studying in the Bay Area, to his house for Labor Day. He stopped by USF in his Buick to pick me up. With him was Guo Yujin, the wife of the BIFT vice president, who had traveled with us. Andy took us to his home where he and his wife, Eve, entertained us. It was a tidy house with a backyard pool near the top of one of the Bay Area's many hills. It was probably not large or even remarkable by California standards, but it looked so to me. Everything was modern. I was amazed at the many time-saving appliances: a toaster, a vacuum cleaner, a refrigerator, a washer and dryer, and of course a color television. I wondered how many decades it would take China to attain this living standard. But what impressed me most were the animals around their property. There were deer, wild rabbits, squirrels, and many kinds of birds, moving around seemingly oblivious to us. I love animals, and I found their movements and activities engaging. I was glad that Americans did not want to capture and eat them; in China, I was sure, they would all become food.

After the Labor Day weekend, the campus filled with students. Now two weeks into the fall semester, I needed to get on with it. I had come to the United States with the objective of obtaining a formal academic degree, since I was one of the "worker-peasant-soldier students" who were not considered to have received a formal education. Now that I was apparently studying law, I visited USF's School of Law to find out what I needed to do to get my degree.

There I met with the associate dean, April Cassou, a lively, bespectacled woman with brown hair. In addition to being the associate dean, she also taught a course in legal research and writing, which she encouraged me to take, as these were required skills for being a lawyer.

I asked her how I would go about obtaining a degree. My question surprised her, as her answer surprised me. She didn't expect me to say that I was planning to get a degree, she said. Then she gently told me that getting a degree was simply not possible.

First, as with most law schools in the United States, a juris doctor (JD) at USF would take three years; my program would allow me to stay for only one year. Second, as a visiting scholar, I could audit or sit in on any classes on campus; but to formally receive academic credits I would need to be enrolled in a degree program, which required payment of tuition and fees.

Tuition? What was that? I had never heard of that term or the concept. In China, you might not get a chance to go to college. But once you were in, everything was paid for and education was free. The idea that I could be denied a formal education for lack of money was shocking to me. Of course, I didn't have any money other than my monthly stipend from the Asia Foundation, which was barely enough to pay my living expenses. For the first time in my life, I realized that money mattered. I was quite distressed by this discovery. Getting my degree was the whole point of coming to the United States with the Asia Foundation.

Later in the week, I met with another law professor, Jack Garvey, who told me the same thing. He was offering a course on legal contracts and was happy for me to take his class, but he didn't think I could get a degree either. He suggested, however, that I go across the street to speak with the business school. They had a two-year program, which conferred the degree of master's of business administration. That would do, I thought. If it took most people two years to get an MBA, I might be able to do it in one by doubling my efforts. Professor Garvey was doubtful, but he agreed to connect me with a professor at the business school who might be able to help.

Professor Garvey introduced me to Professor Bill Murray, who was a solidly built man about my height, with a beard and twinkling eyes. He smoked a pipe, but more often than not just held the unlit pipe in his mouth or in his hand. He listened as I explained my case, and then said he would be happy to help. We would put together a program, he told me, and then we would go talk with the dean about it. He also invited me to sit in on his class that evening. My hopes were up again.

Professor Murray taught a class in managerial finance. He spoke without notes. He did not refer to the textbook even once during his lecture, though he frequently cited statistics to illustrate the point he was making. He peppered his lecture with humor. This was the first business class I had ever taken in my life. But to my surprise, I understood most of what he said, and I quite enjoyed it. For me, finance was easier to understand than the lectures at law school, at first because the issues in finance did not require much context to appreciate.

After class, I asked Professor Murray how he could possibly remember all the data points and statistics he had effortlessly reeled off without consulting notes throughout the lecture. "Oh, I just made them up," he said, winking. I took an immediate liking to him.

Professor Murray, together with Mrs. Cassou and Professor Garvey, put together a tailor-made program for me that included courses at both the law school and the business school. My program was unique, since law classes were not a requirement at the business school. I wanted to do both, as I had an interest in both subjects. Also, studying law fit the program the Asia Foundation had in mind for me. Academically, if I took and passed all these courses, I would qualify for an MBA degree. I feel certain my professors went out of their way to help me because I was the school's first student from China. Professor Murray also gave me a number of textbooks in statistics and other subjects to study on my own, in order to build the requisite basics.

After the program design was complete, Professor Murray took me to see Dr. Bernie Martin, the dean of the business school. He was very friendly and said he would support the program that had been worked out for me.

Feeling quite encouraged, I visited Andy at the Asia Foundation, to tell him my plan. He admitted he was a little surprised that barely a week after landing in America, I had made so much progress toward setting up a degree program for myself. Nonetheless, he said that if USF would waive tuition and fees for me, the Asia Foundation would have no problem with what I chose to do.

But tuition was the issue. There was no money. Professors Cassou, Murray, Garvey, and the dean's office had all tried to find a source of funds to help cover my tuition, to no avail. At that time, I didn't appreciate how unlikely the school would be to waive my tuition, or, because

I was an unknown quantity, how unlikely any other party would be to step up to help me financially. I had not demonstrated any qualifications or the ability to complete a degree program. I had not gone through the normal application process that other students had, and even though I was nominally a visiting scholar, I came from a background vastly different from the other USF students. There was really no way for them to tell if I would be able to successfully complete the requirements of a degree program, so why should anyone risk wasting their money on me?

Having exhausted all the possibilities of finding a way to cover the tuition for a degree program, I decided that I would take all the courses and sit for all the exams anyway, so that at least at the end of the program I could tell myself that I had learned as much as other MBA students. I thought ultimately the knowledge would count regardless of whether I received a degree. After all, it was just a piece of paper.

My first few weeks of classes were difficult to say the least. I could understand almost all the words spoken by the professors, but for some classes, especially at law school, I had no context for what they meant. It was not the language, but the concepts that were unfamiliar. It was difficult for me to participate in class discussions, which were common in US colleges. In China, teachers would teach and students would listen and take notes. Students almost never asked questions, and teachers did not call upon them. But here in the United States, "participation" could count for 20 percent or more of your grade. I had no idea how to participate, and I was also fearful I would ask a stupid question or say something wrong that would insult others accidentally.

The hardest class for me was marketing, because most of the analyses were qualitative, as opposed to quantitative. It was also the subject where my completely different background as a product of China proved to be the greatest handicap. One time, a professor caught me off guard in class by asking me why McDonald's was so popular. At that time, I didn't yet know McDonald's was a restaurant chain, so I guessed: "Maybe he is very handsome?" The entire class burst out in laughter, and I sank into my chair.

While marketing was somewhat puzzling, law school was even tougher for me. For Professor Garvey's class on contracts, the reading material was a thick book, more than a thousand pages long, titled *Contracts, Cases and Comment*. I was surprised to find that it was not a textbook, but a collection of legal cases and rulings by judges, and some of them had lived hundreds of years ago in England. At first there seemed not to be a common thread from one case to another. Without any framework of reference for what a contract looked like, I couldn't figure out the relevance of a particular case, even after reading it carefully. In class, Professor Garvey would start out by asking, "Folks, what are the issues?" when he referred to a case. Initially, I thought to myself, "I read the case and I know how the judge ruled. What does he mean by 'issues?' How do you identify issues from reading a story?"

In the United States, contracts were deeply ingrained in the culture. One had to sign contracts all the time: for a student loan, a credit card, an insurance policy, housing rental, and other matters. By contrast, the culture in China at the time was definitely not contractually based. First. there was almost no commercial activity, and second, the Party settled all disputes.

It was confusing. Why couldn't there be a simple textbook to explain what a contract was? Instead, the cases illustrated all the different elements of a contract, like offers, acceptances, considerations, damages, and remedies. It was not until midsemester that I figured out, generally, how a contract works. It is like a puzzle with, say, 20 pieces. Each one means nothing on its own. But once you have put 10 pieces together, the picture emerges. That was how it felt. I suddenly came to the realization that there was a logic connecting all the different elements and concepts. Then I could enjoy reading all the old cases and analyzing how the judges had made their decisions. That still didn't mean I found it easy, but I was glad I took Professor Garvey's class.

A few weeks after classes started, I arranged to move to the dormitory wing on Lone Mountain. I had had enough of my lonely single room by the chapel. Doubles were cheaper, and my stipend wasn't enough for me to afford the luxury of living alone; besides, I was feeling isolated. I was assigned a room on the fourth floor, Room 406, with an American law student named Charlie.

Dorm life was fun. Most rooms were shared by two people. Male and female students occupied different floors. There was a common shower room and bathroom on each floor. There were two cafeterias, one on Lone Mountain and a bigger one on the main campus. It was the first time I saw people eating raw, uncooked vegetables, which they called salad. Raw vegetables in China would not have been particularly hygienic. They were also tasteless, but the dressing made them more tolerable. I soon got used to them.

I loved the meat, however, and I loved that it was so plentiful that you could eat until you were full. It took me a little longer to like cheese. I was first exposed to it when Professor Garvey invited me to his home in Marin County for dinner. Before dinner, Mrs. Garvey brought out plates of hors d'oeuvres, including different types of cheese cut into small pieces. They smelled like spoiled food, somewhat stinky. Knowing it was something completely new to me, she prodded me to give it a try, as Professor Garvey watched, smiling. I tried not to breathe and took a bite. It tasted like rubber. I had no idea why Americans liked this stuff. But after a while, cheese also became one of my favorite foods.

★ ★ ★

I experienced my first Halloween with Mrs. Cassou and her husband, Phil, at their home in Marin County. I didn't have any idea what to expect—I'd never heard of this holiday before. Why Americans celebrate ghosts is still beyond me. It was a Friday evening, and I arrived to see their doorstep decorated with pumpkins with faces carved into them and candles inside. Phil Cassou was an executive at IBM and a sports car enthusiast. Over dinner, he talked to me about fixing cars. I noticed that Americans used the word "fix" often. Everything could be fixed: fix a dinner, fix a salad, fix a schedule, fix a car, and so on. I had thought that "to fix" meant to make something stationary, but of course it made no sense to make a dinner or a car stationary. When Americans talked about "fixing," they meant getting something done.

Later, Phil took me out for a ride around the neighborhood in his new red Corvette. He also owned a Jaguar with 12 cylinders. I didn't quite know what 12 cylinders really meant, but I knew it was more powerful than all the horses I had ever ridden combined.

The guests arrived in strange costumes, dressed as firemen, gypsies, and princesses. A couple living in the neighborhood were friends of the Cassous. The husband, whose name was Bill, worked for the chemical division of Chevron, which made pesticides and herbicides. When I told Bill I used to be a farmer and worked with pesticides, he invited me to visit his company in the future.

Costumed children came to the door from time to time. They yelled "trick or treat," and our hosts would give each of them a handful of candy. This, too, was completely new and strange to me.

The dinner was delicious. Aside from cars, the upcoming presidential election dominated the conversation. I had watched the televised debate between Ronald Reagan and President Jimmy Carter earlier that week, and my impression was that Reagan looked more natural and relaxed. He seemed to enjoy himself, smiling and rebutting his opponent as if he were a teacher reproaching a student: "There you go again," he would say. President Carter, on the other hand, seemed often to be defensive and somewhat awkward. Someone at the table was dismissive of them both and called them "a pair of losers."

For dessert, there was pumpkin pie. Mrs. Cassou asked me if I had ever tasted pumpkins. I had to tell her I used to grow the stuff in the Gobi. In fact, we had to eat it day in and day out, so much so that the sight of pumpkins repulsed me. But I had never thought they could be made into such delicious pies. I could not get enough of the dessert that evening. I found out that US pumpkins were very different from the types I had grown in the Gobi, much more solid and starchy.

The next week, Ronald Reagan was elected president of the United States in a landslide. I was impressed with Jimmy Carter's concession speech. I thought he was very gracious after losing. I gave him much credit for having normalized diplomatic relations with China. Without him, I wouldn't have been in the United States. Admittedly, another president might have done it too, but who knew? Politics in China had taught me that leaders could not always be counted upon.

★ ★ ★

By the middle of my first semester at USF, I had become something of a celebrity on campus. Many people were curious to talk with me because none of them had ever met anyone from Red China. For a while, they took turns to pop in to visit with me, stopping by my dorm room for a chat or joining me at my lunch table in the cafeteria. I felt almost like a panda.

A couple of weeks after the election, a couple invited me to visit their home in Marin. I had been introduced to them by a woman named

Julie, an American who had recently returned from China bearing a letter from a friend of mine. Julie asked if I would be interested in meeting her friends. They were musicians, Julie said, and had never met anyone from China.

Their living room was filled with musical instruments and equipment. Their names were Pete and Jeannette Sears. Pete told me he was a member of a rock band called Jefferson Starship. Jeannette, I found out later, had written lyrics for some of the group's best-known songs. I had certainly heard of and read about rock-and-roll music, but I had never actually listened to it. We sat in their cluttered living room, and Pete and Jeannette played me some of their records. I was shocked that music could sound so much like loud noises. After a few songs, they asked me if I liked it. "Not really," I said politely.

They must have thought I was an idiot, at least as far as music was concerned, and they would have been right. But they nonetheless gave me copies of three records by their band: *Red Octopus, Freedom at Point Zero*, and *Earth*. Pete autographed each of them: "To Shan, best wishes, Pete Sears."

Back in the dorm, when Charlie, my roommate, saw those records, his eyes lit up. "Where did you get those?" he asked. I told him that the musicians had just given them to me. He didn't know what I did to deserve them. Charlie had a record player in our room, and he immediately pulled my new records out of their sleeves one by one and started playing them, very loudly, which attracted other residents to come to listen. One person pulled me aside and whispered to me that these autographed records were very valuable, especially in mint condition, and therefore I shouldn't let Charlie play them. But it was too late and I didn't know how to not let him do it.

Since I had so much catching up to do and I wanted to compress two years of work into one year, I spent almost all my time on campus studying except when people invited me to their homes. I soon learned that it was quite difficult to get around without a car. I could go downtown by bus, although I preferred to walk. But going anywhere else outside the city was impossible. One of my friends among the Taiwanese students, Chen Yizhou, had a car. He drove a Ford Pinto, a model that had been recalled a few years earlier due to its propensity to catch fire in rear-end collisions. But it was a great privilege to own a car as a student, no matter what kind. He would take some of us out occasionally, on trips outside the city or down to Fisherman's Wharf, a tourist spot on the city's northern waterfront.

Yizhou had a special and unique talent. Fisherman's Wharf was full of carnival games of all types, where you could win prizes by throwing a ball into a hole, shooting a basketball into a small basket, or throwing a ring over some bottles. Yizhou somehow mastered the game of Skee-Ball, where you try to throw a fist-sized ball into a series of tiny holes and hoops. He was like a sharpshooter. Every time he visited those parlors, he would come back with giant stuffed toys. He won so many that sometimes the operators had to ask him to leave. His room was filled with stuffed animals and toys of all kinds and he gave them away to his friends. He gave me a white bear that was half as big as I was. I kept it and eventually sent it home to Beijing.

Living in San Francisco was the first time I'd ever had to deal with violent urban crime. In Beijing, robberies were unheard of. But in the Bay Area, muggings seemed to be a fact of life. One night, as I was leaving our dorm to take a walk, a man whose face and body were covered with blood came staggering toward me. There was so much blood on his face I couldn't tell who it was, although I vaguely recognized the clothes he was wearing. The sight was so shocking I could hardly bear to look at his battered face. Many people rushed over to help him and someone called the police and an ambulance. It was not until he spoke that I realized it was a student from Taiwan named Chen Junda.

Junda and his father had gone out shopping in downtown San Francisco. They took a bus back to Lone Mountain, but they overshot the university by two stops. As they were walking back to campus, three men followed them. Just as they reached the stairs at the bottom of the hill, the men jumped them. One of them put a gun to Junda's head and another held his father by the neck. His father had the presence of mind to immediately hand over all the money in his pocket, $1,500 and some 20,000 Japanese yen. I had no idea why he was carrying so much cash with him. But the money probably saved their lives. The robber punched him, twice, and let him go. Junda himself struggled to get free. The robbers punched and kicked him repeatedly, broke his glasses, and cut his face in multiple places. Then the three men fled with the money.

The police came and asked some questions. It took a while for the ambulance to arrive to take him to the hospital. I saw him the next day. His face remained swollen and black-and-blue, and his eyes still could not open. It seemed there was never any follow-up by the police, as we never heard from them again. When I told my roommate Charlie about the incident, he told me that he had been mugged three times in the previous year, including once at gunpoint. I had known of the crime problems in the United States, but this was the first time I had witnessed it and heard about it from those I knew. I walked that path leading to the Lone Mountain stairs almost every day to and from the main campus. I never did it again at night after that incident. Junda dropped out of his program and moved to a university in Arizona.

Not long after that incident, I read in the newspaper someone advertising to provide a reward of $5,000 for anyone catching the perpetrator who cut off the tail of his cat. I didn't know what the punishment would be if the perpetrator was caught. Nor could I understand why anyone in his right mind would do such a terrible thing. My eyes wide open, I was seeing another side to the United States that I hadn't anticipated.

★ ★ ★

Since I arrived late for the semester, it took me awhile to catch up and then keep up with all my classes. But when I finally came to grips with the workload, I began to enjoy the courses. I continued to think classes in law were harder than in the business school. But my objective was clear. I was determined to do well on my exams so that I could finish the program for an MBA regardless of whether I would eventually be able to get a degree.

I became impressed with the common law system adopted by England and the United States. There was a great respect for precedents and history. A ruling by a court a few hundred years back could still be relevant and applicable today, when similar issues came before the court. Laws could be amended by the legislature, new laws could be written, and all laws, including the constitution, were subject to amendments and interpretation. But rarely would they change suddenly or arbitrarily. I believe that this tradition reduced uncertainty in the legal environment and social systems. They helped make a contract-based market economy possible.

China, in contrast, had operated without a sound and independent legal system. Mao used to say that he was a "monk holding an umbrella": *wu fa wu tian*, or "no hair and no sky." The pronunciation of "law" and "hair" in Chinese is the same. The expression means "without regard to any laws or any kind of constraints." The Cultural Revolution was the best demonstration of this arbitrariness. Mao's word was the law, like that of the emperors who had preceded him. Even now that the chaos of the Mao era had ended, laws, policies, and rules were subject to change, sometimes arbitrarily or quite suddenly. There was a common expression in China at that time: "*ji hua* (a plan) cannot catch up with *bian hua* (change)." The resulting uncertainty and risk necessarily led to greater social costs.

But keeping track of all these cases and precedents, especially in the age before computers were widely used, was a daunting challenge. How does one find all the relevant cases in a vast library? The answer, which I learned through Mrs. Cassou's class on legal research and writing, was a system known as Shepard's Citations, which was an indexing system. To "Shepardize" is to look at a particular legal issue in the index book, which would lead the researcher to find all the past cases related to the issue to know how the courts had ruled and whether the rulings had been subsequently overturned, reaffirmed, questioned, or cited by subsequent jurists.

I thought the system of Shepardizing was ingenious. It allowed the researcher to find relevant cases and the written opinions of judges going back hundreds of years with efficiency and speed. I wondered how the US legal system worked before Mr. Shepard came up with his books in the late nineteenth century.

I also learned from Mrs. Cassou's class that lawyers were trained not to write as intelligibly as they could; I found some legal documents so verbose that a whole paragraph consisted of just one run-on sentence. By the time you reached the object of the sentence, you had already forgotten what the subject was, or worse; you had to read several times to get it. It was not only foreign students who were frustrated by this. I remember reading something written by Jimmy Carter suggesting that lawyers should write in a way that a layman could understand. I couldn't agree with him more.

I took my final exams for that semester in mid-December, just before the campus shut down for the winter break. All the students were expected to move out of the dorms; my Asia Foundation fellowship didn't allow me to go back to Beijing, so I had to find another place to live.

Luckily, I was invited to spend the holiday with Sandy and Connie Calhoun, to whom I had been introduced by Dr. Williams of the Asia Foundation.

In his fifties, Sandy was tall and slim. He almost always wore a witty smile on his face. He liked to joke and as he was doing so, his eyes twinkled behind his glasses. Connie, also in her fifties, reminded me of my mother, gentle and kind. They had a big, beautiful home in the Pacific Heights neighborhood of San Francisco. From their dining room on the second floor, one could see the Golden Gate Bridge. At night, when the fog rolled into San Francisco Bay, I could hear the foghorn. It initially kept me awake but I soon got used to it.

Sandy Calhoun was a partner at a law firm, Graham & James.

I knew that Sandy and his family had a long relationship with Asia, both through business and culturally. Sandy's father had been a banker in Manila, where he met Sandy's mother, who was teaching math at the University of the Philippines. Then they were transferred to Shanghai, where, in the 1920s and 1930s, he worked for First National City Bank, known in Chinese as *huaqi yinhang*, or Colorful Flag Bank, the predecessor to Citibank. Sandy spent his childhood in Shanghai, but he told me he only remembered swear words in Shanghainese.

When the Japanese invaded China, his father went to work for the bank in Manila. He was captured and spent much of Sandy's high school years—while Sandy was at school in New England—in a Japanese prison camp.

After graduating from high school in 1943, Sandy joined the army, which shipped him out for Japan just as the war was ending, and he stayed for two years attached to General MacArthur's headquarters. He returned to the United States, to Harvard, where he majored in Far Eastern history.

He started his legal career with a San Francisco law firm specializing in maritime law. From there he built his business, living in and earning a license to practice law in Japan. Many of his clients were Asian and he had a deep appreciation for Asian art.

Given Sandy's ties with pre-1949 China it was not surprising that, as China opened up, he helped rebuild old connections that had been severed by war and the revolution. In 1979, Sandy, as a member of the National Committee on US-China Relations, hosted visiting Chinese delegations and, as a result, met a group that included representatives from BIFT. It was Sandy who had introduced these officials from BIFT to Dr. Williams at the Asia Foundation.

The Calhouns had four young children, three boys and a girl. At the dinner table, the whole family would often talk about politics. I was quite intrigued to watch the children arguing among themselves and with their parents. They made me feel at home. Connie was doing graduate studies in mycology. Once I accompanied her into a forest not far from San Francisco to help her collect mushrooms; there had been reports of a murder in that area and she wanted my escort.

Shortly before Christmas, Sandy took me to visit his mother, who had been a banker in Asia as well as a member of the Shanghai Municipal Council, the de facto governing body of the city when it was divided up into foreign settlements. She had attended the wedding of Chiang Kai-shek. I quite enjoyed talking with her about Old China.

On Christmas Eve, I went with the Calhouns to St. Luke's Church for mass, my first time to a Christian religious service. The church was packed, but everyone was quiet and solemn. All the priests wore white robes over their black suits. A choir was singing beautifully, accompanied by a big organ. There were seven flickering red lights hanging above the stage and there were five candles burning on one side. There were two big candles on the altar, burning bright. The preacher gave a sermon and told a story of how people were able to find a lost boy by joining hands with his mother. Then a few people walked along the aisles to collect money. This was followed by Holy Communion, in which the congregants were invited to "join us at the Lord's table."

I participated in the whole process except the Lord's table, which was only for the baptized.

★ ★ ★

I received my grades once classes resumed after winter break. Other than marketing, I received all A's at the business school. Professor

Murray told me that I had placed first in his class. I was most concerned about how I did at the law school, especially Professor Garvey's class on contracts, because it was so hard. Unlike at the business school, the law school professors posted grades next to the social security numbers of the students. I thought this was brilliant because it allowed you to know your own grade and how you stacked up against others, without disclosing the names of the students. I got a B + in contracts, but I was surprised to see that of 65 students in the class, only 3 received an A– and 4 received a B +. None received an A. I felt that my effort had paid off. My roommate, Charlie, also took this class. Throughout the semester, I had pestered him with questions, such as what an "arm's-length transaction" was, or what "malfeasance" meant. When I told him my grade, he looked both incredulous and somewhat upset, which told me that he didn't do as well as I did. From then on, I didn't dare bother him with questions.

When I returned to my dorm in January 1981, I noticed that my bed was already occupied. There were a few books placed on the bookshelf at the head of the bed. Among them were Japanese-English and Japanese-Chinese dictionaries. I was curious who would be using a Japanese-Chinese dictionary. I waited for this student to return, as now I had nowhere to put my own belongings. Soon he returned: medium height, dark hair, smiling face. He looked Japanese, probably because I was expecting a Japanese student. To my great surprise, he spoke fluent Mandarin Chinese with a hint of a Shandong accent, similar to that of my parents.

He introduced himself as Arai. Japanese names are usually written in *kanji*, or Chinese characters. The characters of his name are transliterated as *huangjing* and the name means "abandoned well" in Chinese. Even though he was Japanese, he told me that his Chinese was better than his Japanese and his Japanese better than his English.

Arai's story was a fascinating one. His father was a military doctor in the Japanese imperial army. After Japan surrendered in 1945, his parents decided to stay in China to work among the Chinese. They continued to work in China after the Communist takeover in 1949.

Arai was born and grew up in Shandong, where he attended local schools. I asked him if he got along with his classmates or other Chinese children, considering the hatred for the Japanese among the Chinese

populace because of the Japanese brutality during the war. He said he
did, that occasionally some children would taunt him by calling him
"Little Jap."

Like the United States, Japan did not recognize Beijing as the legitimate government of China for more than two decades. Nixon's visit to
China in 1972 took Japan by surprise. After the US president's historic
trip, Japan quickly moved to change its policy and soon normalized
diplomatic relations with China. After normalization, all Japanese who
lived in China were given a chance to return to Japan. Arai's parents
returned in 1974, apparently for their children's education.

Eventually, the school figured out that they had made a mistake
in assigning us both to the same bed. He was given another room
elsewhere, but we remained good friends.

I received an even bigger surprise when I went to see my law school
dean, Mrs. Cassou. She and her husband, Phil, had been trying to find
a solution to my tuition problem. They had helped me apply for a
scholarship from Chevron, the company their neighbor Bill worked for.
That didn't work out. But now, she said, she had some good news for
me: the school had found a private donor to help cover my tuition. I
was overjoyed by this news. I realized that my performance during the
last semester must have helped her convince my unknown benefactors
that they wouldn't be wasting their money. I wanted to know who the
donors were, but she said the donor preferred to remain anonymous. I
was overwhelmed by this generosity from a stranger.

What's more, Mrs. Cassou had already spoken to Bernie Martin,
the dean of the business school, and he had agreed that the donor could
cover the tuition requirement for my degree program. I was so grateful
to her for working so hard on my behalf and for having resolved this
money issue after I had given up all hope.

But there were still two obstacles. First, I did not have enough time
left under my fellowship to get all the credits I would need for my
degree. I would need another semester in order to graduate. The Asia
Foundation had to approve the extension of my program. The second,
which I knew would be more difficult, was to get approval from my
institution back in Beijing.

I had been talking with Andy Andrews about my degree program
for a long time. Now that the tuition issue was resolved, I hoped to get

the Asia Foundation's support. I went down to their offices on Geary Street to give Andy the good news. But he was not as enthusiastic as I was. The foundation was unlikely to help me out, he told me. But he would try and he asked me to be patient.

I was determined to pursue my degree program regardless of whether the foundation agreed because Mrs. Cassou had gone to great lengths to resolve my tuition problems. My business school professors had designed a study program just for me. Now that a degree was within my reach, getting permission was not going to stand in my way.

I had never cared to respect authorities on the basis of their authority alone, and I believed that authorities should be defied if they stood in the way of what I considered to be right. Growing up in China, I never had much of a choice, as people by and large had to do what the Party told them to do, and there was no point ramming your head against a rock. But this was the United States, which its citizens always said was a free country. Here, I knew I would be able to do what I wanted. I would make every effort to win over the Asia Foundation and BIFT, but as far as I was concerned, my course was set.

I came to the realization that there was a big difference between China and the United States. China was, more or less, a land of equal pay but unequal access to opportunities. The United States was, more or less, a land of equal opportunities but vastly different pay. Growing up in China, I knew almost everyone was equally poor, but to get what was considered a coveted job, you either had to be lucky or you needed to have the right parents or connections. In the United States, it seemed opportunities were available to all: if there was a will, there was a way to get almost anywhere in society, although lack of money did sometimes pose an obstacle. China was a society where survival didn't depend on fitness, whereas in the United States, the fittest had a much better chance to succeed.

Even then, China was changing. The college entrance examination system was the first step toward providing equal opportunities to all who aspired.

I finally figured out why the Asia Foundation officials were reluctant to give me their blessing for my degree program: They were concerned about creating a problem between the foundation and BIFT. Otherwise, they were supportive of my new plans. Andy was prepared to write a letter to the authorities at BIFT to plead on my behalf. I gave Andy some advice. I suggested that he not ask for BIFT to give its consent, but to simply inform them of the good news that I had performed well and had received financial support to complete a degree program. I explained that if the foundation asked BIFT for its consent, it gave it a choice of saying yes or no. What if they said no? I suggested to Andy: "Why don't you write to simply congratulate them for the achievement I have made?" That way, I reasoned, it would be hard for them to say no.

Andy took my advice and carefully composed a letter to Beijing. He showed me the letter in which he heaped much praise on me but was careful to reserve most of the flattery for BIFT. Two weeks later, I went back to the Asia Foundation. It had a warehouse of donated books that were free for me to pick through. As I was selecting books, a call was patched through from Andy's office. He said he received a cable from BIFT in response to the letter he had sent. "What does it say?" I asked anxiously. He paused for a moment. I could hardly bear the suspense. Then he said, "It only says 'Thank you very much.'" I was elated. That was exactly what I had expected them to say. Who could say no to a congratulatory cable?

The second semester was a lot easier for me than the first, even though I was taking more courses. I had begun to get the hang of it. I settled into a daily routine of going to classes and reading class materials. I spent practically every day moving between classrooms, the library, and my dorm.

On March 30, 1981, as I was reading in the library, my friend from Taiwan, Xu Wen, walked in. When she saw me, she walked over and whispered to me, "President Reagan was shot!" What? I was shocked by the news. I rushed out of the library to find a TV and see what had happened. The news report confirmed it: There had been an assassination attempt. President Reagan and three other people, including his press secretary, James Brady, had been wounded. It was not clear at that moment if the president would survive. I thought this was a great crisis for the United States. But when I looked around, it seemed everyone was rather calm. People were going about doing what they were doing. There was no sense of crisis. I went to the law school to find Mrs. Cassou. She was just about to go to the church on campus to pray for President Reagan. I went with her. It was the first time I had stepped into this church. There were a few people gathered, apparently also praying for the president.

Fortunately, Reagan's wound was not fatal. It was reported that he was alert enough to joke to his wife, Nancy, "Honey, I forgot to duck." Eventually the president made a full recovery. Later it was reported that the assassin did this to impress an actress he had a crush on. This was so bizarre I figured it had to be made up.

One day in April 1981, Mrs. Cassou informed me that the anonymous donor who provided the funding for my MBA wanted to have dinner with me. I was so grateful to this mysterious benefactor, but I was also nervous to finally meet him. At about 6:30 p.m. on April 15, I went to the parish house where the priests who taught at USF lived. I met up with Bob Glavin and Father Callahan, both faculty members. They were to take me to the restaurant and represent the university at the dinner. We were dining at the Blue Fox, one of the finest restaurants in town, I was told. It was located in an alley off Montgomery Street.

The décor of the restaurant was impressive, with gold-leaf walls, chandeliers, and red carpeting. I was the only guest there without a suit and tie, which was apparently required by the restaurant, but I was wearing my Mao suit because Mrs. Cassou had earlier advised me that my "national costume" would do. I brought with me a Chinese landscape painting as a gift for my benefactor. I sat down with Bob and Father Callahan, nervously awaiting the arrival of this mysterious person.

Just then a waiter came over to announce that guests of ours had arrived. Bob hurried out to meet them. I tensed up in anticipation. Then I saw a lady walk in, followed by a gentleman: April and Phil Cassou. I felt a huge sense of relief. It would be nice to have some friendly faces with me when I finally met my benefactor.

Then it dawned on me: the Cassous *were* my benefactors. I was taken aback, completely at a loss for words. Mrs. Cassou wore a dark green evening dress with a shiny sequin border and beautiful shiny jewelry. She was absolutely beautiful and dazzling. She looked at me mischievously, satisfied that her surprise was complete. Her husband, Phil, also looked his best in a tuxedo and a butterfly tie. He also enjoyed seeing my state of shock. I had prepared to give a brief report of my work to the mysterious donor but now those words were not needed. All I could blurt out was: "I . . . I don't know what to say . . . It had never occurred to me it was you. I am so grateful you would do this for me."

I was flabbergasted by their overwhelming generosity to a total stranger, who only a few months ago had come from a country on the other side of the planet. Mrs. Cassou explained that she didn't think it was fair for someone to be denied a formal education just for lack of money, which was the reason they had decided to step in. They had waited so long to reveal their identity probably to make sure I would succeed academically. They really made a bet on me; I was glad I didn't fail them, and I would not. That evening was the most memorable dinner of my life, although I have no recollection of the food I ate.

Many years later I had the opportunity to reciprocate some of that generosity, but in a way the Cassous would approve. In the 1990s April and Phil Cassou and I established the Cassou-Shan Scholarship to provide financial assistance for students at USF. For my contribution, USF presented me with a souvenir. It was a thick red brick, at least a third thicker than the bricks I used to make in the Gobi, but it was quite pale, almost whitish; I assumed the maker mixed clay with a high proportion of white sand. Embossed in the center of the brick was a cross. The plaque on the stand read:

Foundation Brick
Old St. Ignatius College
Hayes and Van Ness 1880–1906
In appreciation for your generosity to the University of San Francisco

It was explained to me that St. Ignatius College was the predecessor of the university. In the 1880s, when a new school building was constructed at the corner of Hayes Street and Van Ness Avenue, the contract was first awarded to Chinese workers. But this was a time of anti-immigrant sentiment in the United States. Shortly after the workers broke ground, Congress passed the Chinese Exclusion Act of 1882, which remains the only law ever passed that prohibited a specific ethnic group from immigrating to the United States. White workers held protests against St. Ignatius, and eventually the contract was split in two, with one part given to whites and the other to the Chinese laborers. To distinguish themselves from Chinese workers, the white workers carved a cross on each brick they made. My brick had a cross on it.

The college was destroyed in the Great San Francisco Earthquake of 1906, but a few of the foundation bricks from the ruins were kept, and ultimately were given out to benefactors of the university as a token of the school's appreciation. The irony of this brick was not lost on me. In the 1880s it was designed as an explicit symbol of discrimination against the Chinese. A century later, in the 1980s, the university, its faculty, and its alumni had generously helped me, a Chinese student. Now this brick was given to this Chinese for my modest contribution to the university. History sometimes makes ironic turns.

★ ★ ★

To complete my MBA before the end of 1981, I decided to take classes during the summer as well. For my summer semester midterm exams, I received full marks in the finance course Professor Murray was teaching, whereas the class average was 64. I wrote four essays for the class. On three of them, he marked "Excellent," and on the fourth one, he gave me a full mark and remarked: "You are now a certified capitalistic scholar."

After one of the classes, Professor Murray took me aside and asked me if I would like to get into a PhD program. The idea had never occurred to me. "You know how difficult it was for me to get the funding for my MBA," I said. "Where will I get the money to pursue a PhD program? Besides, I have a wife at home in Beijing whom I haven't seen for a year. How do I support her, even if I can bring her here?"

He replied, "Money shouldn't be a problem," without explaining any further.

I was skeptical, but I was also intrigued by the idea and decided to give it a try. Again, my philosophy in life is always: no harm in trying. Following the advice of Professor Murray, I began to prepare to take the usual standardized tests. I gave no thought to which schools I would apply to because I knew I could count on Professor Murray to point me in the right direction.

After the summer term concluded, the Asia Foundation bought me an air ticket to travel to the East Coast for a 12-day visit. This was part of the visiting scholar program. The idea was to provide me with a more complete exposure to American society. I was going to New York City and Washington, DC.

The Cassous had moved to Greenwich, Connecticut, over the summer, after IBM transferred Phil to the East Coast. I would be staying with them for a couple of days, and Mrs. Cassou offered to take me to New York City.

The Cassous' house was modest by Greenwich standards, but it was quite handsome and comfortable. The rest of the houses in their neighborhood were some of the largest and most stunning homes I had ever laid my eyes on. Each house looked unique, but all had big lawns and tall trees. Obviously, there was a lot of wealth concentrated in this town. After I arrived, Mrs. Cassou took me for a walk around the neighborhood to look at the big houses. At one point, my shoelace came loose. I saw a low rock on the lawn in front of a big house, just a couple of steps off the sidewalk. I walked over and sat down on the rock to tie my shoes. "Shan, get back on the sidewalk!" Mrs. Cassou said. The lawn was private property, she explained, and I was trespassing.

I was impressed by her sense of respect for private property. This stood in sharp contrast with China, where there was practically no private property in big cities at that time, although tall walls surrounded every residential compound and every work unit to prevent unrelated people from getting in. There were walls in Beijing everywhere, and the biggest and the tallest were the walls surrounding Zhongnanhai, where the central government was located. Here in the United States, there were few walls, and there were open lawns in front of private homes. Yet people were accustomed to respecting private property. I thought it was ironic that walls were necessary in Beijing, where there was practically no private property, but not necessary in Greenwich, where every property was private.

Mrs. Cassou and I took the Metro-North train to Grand Central Terminal. "New York City can be dangerous," she warned me. "Try to avoid eye contact with people." We first went to visit the United Nations headquarters and joined a tour to see the various function halls, including the Security Council Chamber and the domed General Assembly Hall. This was the place where I would have worked if I had chosen to join the UN interpreter program. In fact, the program's director, professor Zhang Zailiang, was still writing me to urge me to join the program after I finished my studies in the United States. I was touched by his persistence and grateful that he took me seriously, but

I also knew it was unlikely I would join his program. The next class of UN translators would start in September, and so many people had already moved heaven and earth to help me get a degree that I couldn't just quit and go back to Beijing now. Besides, I was going to get my MBA. My life seemed to be heading down a different path, even toward a PhD. Looking back now, I am glad I didn't get into the first UN program. My life would have been completely different.

I sent my wife a postcard from the UN post office in the building. It was a photograph of UN headquarters as seen from the East River. It looked pretty. But I wrote, "New York City is very dirty, chaotic and noisy, the difference between heaven and earth from San Francisco." I also wrote, "The fall is coming. I will be able to go home by the end of the year!"

We took a cruise on the Hudson River around Manhattan. As we looked down from the upper deck, we saw a group of foreign tourists on the lower deck eating lunch and throwing their food wrappers into the river. I could hear someone standing near me say in a low voice, "Go back to your own country!" I also felt outraged by these tourists littering the beautiful river.

The cruise took two or three hours and covered about 30 miles. I was impressed to learn from the guide that there were 20 bridges on the river, and we were also told there were 16 tunnels under the river. Parts of Manhattan looked modern and nice, and other parts were dilapidated and run-down, with broken windows and dirty walls. It reminded me of the run-down factory buildings I often saw in China. I also noticed the trees in New York City were similar to those in Beijing, probably because the climate in both cities is similar. For example, there are willow trees in both New York and Beijing, but not in San Francisco.

We returned to New York City the next day and took the subway to Wall Street. New York's subways were horrible, with graffiti covering the inside and outside of every car of the train. I've seen pictures of gorgeously colored murals on the sides of New York subway cars, but the ones I saw in real life were not even artful. As we stood on the train holding onto the overhead bar, a panhandler in dirty clothes walked through the car with an open box in his hand, begging for money. His eyes seemed closed but he was walking without bumping into anything or anyone. I asked Mrs. Cassou in a whisper if he was blind. Ever a lawyer, she said, "Allegedly blind."

We visited the New York Stock Exchange. From the visitors' gallery, I could watch the frenzied activity below through a thick glass wall. It seemed that the brokers were running around like mad, and they frequently tossed pieces of paper into the air and let them drop to the floor. The floor was covered in scrap paper. I couldn't hear their voices; the sound was just a low humming noise through the thick glass. But from the frenzied waves of their hands and the shapes of their mouths, I could tell many were shouting. It felt like looking into a zoo full of hyperactive animals. This was supposed to be the center and pinnacle of American finance. I was studying finance, but I couldn't imagine I would want to work in such a place.

Later we visited Liberty Island and took pictures at the Statue of Liberty. We also visited the famed Fifth Avenue, although we did not go into any of the shops. My lasting impression of New York back in 1981 was of the sharp contrast everywhere, between modern and old, between rich and poor, and between order and chaos. I was struck by how dirty some places were, with trash everywhere, and how polluted the air was. New York City in general was dirty and noisy—old, dilapidated, and run-down in some places and yet beautiful, luxurious, and modern on streets like Fifth Avenue.

During my trip I was also able to spend some time with my old English teacher, Tom O'Neill, and his French wife, Monique, who had taught us at BIFT. Tom and Monique had returned to the United States and lived in Fort Lee, New Jersey, about 45 minutes' drive from Greenwich. Tom went on to get a PhD from McGill University in Canada. He would later become a successful retail executive, serving as CEO of Harry Winston jewelers and later as president of the clothing companies Burberry and Clarks.

While staying with Tom and Monique in Fort Lee, I called on an older gentleman by the name of Ralph Henry. He was one of the tourists I guided when I worked as an intern at the Beijing Travel Service in 1979. He'd given me his phone number, but I don't think he ever expected me to call him. He was mightily surprised to hear from me. After dinner, Tom and Monique drove me to Ralph's place. He gave us a slide show of the pictures he had taken on his China tour back in 1979.

Tom and Monique took me back to Manhattan, where we visited the New York Public Library. I was impressed by its size and fast service. We also went to a bookstore, the largest I had ever seen. I bought a Chinese atlas there for $5.38 even though the list price was $75. We visited the Metropolitan Museum of Art. It had a vast collection, and the museum's layout was excellent and well organized. There were numerous treasures from all over the world: antiquities, sculpture, paintings, clothing, furniture, architecture of different styles, artifacts from Egypt, China, Europe, America, ancient Rome, ancient Greece, Medieval and Renaissance Europe. Everything.

After saying goodbye to my friends in New York, I took a train to Washington, DC. A young man named Ken Bowman, from the National Council for U.S.-China Trade, met me at the train station. After visiting with some of the council members, I went to take a tour of FBI headquarters, where I was fascinated by the firearms demonstration. Washington was neat, clean, and grand, just as a capital should be, with all its monuments—a real contrast to New York City. I was impressed by all the museums, libraries, and government buildings in Washington, and by the fact that the admission to all of them was free, and there were free guided tours as well.

The council people took me to visit the White House, the Washington Monument, the Lincoln Memorial, the Jefferson Memorial, the National Cathedral, the Chinese Embassy, and the East Wing of the National Gallery of Art, designed by I. M. Pei. There was a special exhibition of Rodin sculptures. I also visited Capitol Hill.

The next day, I visited the Smithsonian Institution's Air and Space Museum, where I watched the movie *Fly* on a giant 100-by-100-foot screen. I also visited the Middle Wing of the National Gallery of Art, had lunch with the director of the Southeast Asia collection of the Smithsonian, and toured the Library of Congress and the Supreme Court.

I packed so much into those two days in Washington, DC. It was a great exposure to US institutions and a great learning experience. Now I realized why the Asia Foundation arranged for me to take this trip to the East Coast. I only had seen a small corner of the country before this trip.

I flew back to San Francisco just before the fall semester began.

★ ★ ★

One big challenge for me for my last semester at USF was, again, money. The private donation from the Cassous covered my tuition and fees, but the financial support from the Asia Foundation for my living expenses ended with the conclusion of my East Coast visit. I needed to find a way to support myself.

Sandy and Connie Calhoun, who had hosted me over the winter break, invited me to live with them. I was grateful for the opportunity to save a bit of money and felt very warm toward the family. But more importantly, Sandy helped me get a job.

By then, I had completed a year's worth of studies at law school. Graham & James, the law firm where Sandy Calhoun was a senior partner (later merged into Squire, Sanders & Dempsey), offered me a job as an intern. The firm was located in Embarcadero Center. I was excited about this job, not only for the money but also for the experience. And the salary was good. The firm offered to pay me $1,200 per month. It later raised it to $1,300, presumably because the partners there found me useful. I was pleased with the pay. It was enough to cover my living expenses with plenty to spare. Since I was planning to go back home at the end of the year, I was hoping to bring some gifts for my family and friends.

The second week of work at Graham & James, on September 15, 1981, Sandy Calhoun invited me to visit the mayor's office with him. He had been appointed the Commissioner of East Asia Arts of San Francisco, and asked me to attend his swearing-in ceremony.

The mayor of San Francisco was a 48-year-old Democrat named Dianne Feinstein. Mayor Feinstein had been head of the city's Board of Supervisors until November 1978, when her predecessor, George Moscone, and her colleague on the Board of Supervisors, Harvey Milk, were assassinated by Dan White, a disgruntled rival politician. Feinstein served out the rest of Moscone's term and won reelection in her own right the following year. I was impressed by how young she looked. She had a large porcelain statue of an old Chinese sage in her office. She told me it was a statue of Confucius. I wasn't so sure because the statue was quite colorful, and Confucius was usually presented as a rather dull, colorless old scholar. She explained, however, that a museum curator told her it was Confucius. I was impressed with her interest in Chinese art and history. Under her leadership, San Francisco had established a sister-city relationship with Shanghai. She told me that she was going there for a visit the following Monday.

I found the work at Graham & James interesting. I had a room to myself with a phone and a desk, and I was delighted to find I could use all the office facilities, including the library. I had never worked in an office before. Mr. Calhoun had a British secretary named Della. Della was cool and reserved and spoke with a distinct British accent. Mr. Calhoun received a copy of *Reader's Digest* at the office every month, but he never read it. Many years ago, he said, he'd gotten a deal to pay for a lifetime subscription. Since then he had received a copy every month even though he had long ago stopped reading it. I had loved *Reader's Digest* ever since I began studying English back in Beijing. I was happy to put his free copy to good use. Even after I finished working at Graham & James, Della would make a point of mailing the magazine to me every month.

I was placed under the mentorship of a partner named Bob Patterson, helping the lawyers with their legal research. I was requested to fill in a time sheet for all the work I did; the time sheet was the basis to bill clients. I was quite certain my work earned enough for the firm to cover my pay, for which I felt happy.

In 1981, the computer revolution was just beginning to change the way office work was done. One day at law school, Professor Garvey showed me a clipped newspaper article with a photograph of a machine called a "personal computer," which IBM had just produced. "Look at what they have come up with," he said excitedly to me. "With a machine like this, it will make writing so much easier."

At Graham & James, I discovered there was already an electronic service for legal research. It was called Lexis Nexis, and would print out all the relevant cases when a keyword was typed in. But the service was expensive, it required the approval of a partner to use it, and was used only if it was difficult to locate the right materials through Shepardizing.

One day, a partner named Norman Laboe gave me an assignment. One of his clients wanted to sue the San Francisco city government for condemning and seizing a property of his, purportedly for the purpose of building some public works. But the city eventually abandoned the project and sold the property for a profit. The client did not think this was fair and wanted to either recover the property or the profit the government had made.

The case fell under the doctrine of "eminent domain," which is the power of government to take over private property for the purpose of public use. It seemed unfair to me that the government could condemn someone's private property and then turn around and sell it at a profit. Nonetheless, through my research, I discovered that our client did not have a case. The government only needed to prove that it had *intended* to build the public works as announced, and that the compensation given to our client was fair at the time the property was condemned. If the government later changed its mind and abandoned the project, it was under no obligation to give the property back to the previous owner or to pay the difference in price.

I wrote a memo to Norman to that effect. When I next went to the office, Bob Patterson shared with me a handwritten note Norman had sent him. It read: "Mr. Shan did a fantastic job on the question. The fact I don't like the answer is irrelevant. I am convinced that he came down on the legally correct side of the equation." Needless to say, I was delighted he thought my work was useful.

This particular case also quite intrigued me, in the same way that Mrs. Cassou's warning against trespassing on private property had when I was visiting her in Greenwich. Even though private property and ownership were regarded as sacred and were protected by law, the government had the power to take private properties for the good of the public, provided fair compensation was paid. In China, there was almost no real private property, but it was difficult to seize land from someone occupying it even though all the land was supposed to be state-owned. I was reminded of a wall that BIFT had been building before I left Beijing. There was a small tree growing where the wall was supposed to cut through. BIFT approached the farmer who claimed to own the tree, asking him to relocate it so that they could build the wall. But the farmer refused and the negotiation failed. Eventually, the wall had to zigzag to avoid the tree.

The experience also made me think back to what Andy Andrews had said when he tried to persuade me to study law, that China did not really have a legal system. It seemed that China still had a long way to go to build its system of laws as it moved in the direction of the market and private ownership.

Being a lawyer was a lot of hard work. I always had perfect eyesight. But reading all the fine print in legal documents day after day took a toll on my eyes. One evening, I walked out of the office and was about to cross the street. Then I noticed that I could not clearly read the street sign on the opposite side. It seemed blurry. I went to see an optometrist. She said, "Look, you have to accept the fact that you now need glasses." That was quite bad news for me, as I always thought myself lucky to have good vision. Fortunately, the glasses she prescribed for me made only minor corrections to my eyesight and, more often than not, I did not wear them.

At school, Professor Murray asked me to fill in three application forms for PhD programs: New York University, the University of Washington (in Seattle), and the University of California at Berkeley. I thought that money was an insurmountable obstacle, so I did not hold out much hope. I did not do any research about PhD programs in different universities or take the initiative to pick any specific degree programs. I just did what Professor Murray asked me to do.

Coincidentally, the Asia Foundation arranged for me to visit the University of Washington to give a presentation on China to a group of students and faculty members. The few Chinese students in the audience were all from Taiwan. At one point, one person in the audience asked me about the relationship between Taiwan and Mainland China. I said, "Well, Taiwan is part of China." I then realized that the statement could be a bit controversial for the Taiwanese students, as the Nationalist government in Taiwan claimed to be the legitimate government of the whole of China. So I continued without a pause, "or China is part of Taiwan." The audience laughed.

That visit went well. The business school tried to woo me to its PhD program and offered me a full scholarship. My application to UC Berkeley was received favorably as well. The lead professor there, Dick Holton, worked hard to get me all the financial support necessary, not only for myself but also for my wife. He introduced me to Captain Tsui, a private businessman and the owner of one of Oakland's Free Trade Zones. Captain Tsui agreed to provide Berkeley with funding in support of my program.

I was going to go back to Beijing after completing my MBA program at the end of 1981. The big challenge remained whether or not BIFT would allow me to return to the United States to pursue a PhD program. All my friends offered to help. Dr. Williams of the Asia

Foundation and Professor Bill Murray were going to visit Beijing soon. They both told me they would do their best to lobby BIFT authorities on my behalf, even before I returned to Beijing, to get the institute to allow me to come back to the States to pursue a PhD.

I completed my MBA program by Christmas 1981, after one year and three months in America. I spent my second Christmas and New Year in San Francisco. On January 9, 1982, I left San Francisco to fly to Hong Kong on my way back to Beijing.

I felt, however, as the opening line in a song made famous by Tony Bennett went, that "I left my heart in San Francisco."

Chapter 21

The People's Republic of Berkeley

Frederick F. Low was a Gold Rusher. Few people remember him today, but he held a few prominent positions in his life that link him to my story. Born in Maine in 1828, he was a self-taught man. He came to California hoping to make a fortune and struck gold within a few months, unearthing about $1,500 worth of it. His gold haul was worth more than $5 million in today's money ($100 in 1850 = $3,412.56 in 2017), a handsome amount. He was elected to the US Congress in 1862 as a representative of California, a year after the outbreak of the US Civil War; a year after that, he was elected governor of the state and served until 1867. Under his governorship two great California institutions were established: Yosemite National Park and the University of California.

Even fewer people know that two years after he left the governor's office, he became the US ambassador to China. His title, quite grandly, was Envoy Extraordinary and Minister Plenipotentiary to the Great Qing Empire; more simply, he was the United States Minister to China. By then China's fortunes were on the decline and the country was greatly weakened by the corrupt rule of the later Qing emperors, a defeat in both Opium Wars at the hands of Britain, and the invasion of foreign powers. It is unclear whether Low, as the US ambassador, ever set foot on China's soil.

Frederick Low is remembered mainly as the founder of the University of California. He had set in motion the establishment of the great educational and research institution it is today. Its first major campus was established at Berkeley, across the bay from San Francisco, in 1868, although by then Frederick Low had been succeeded by Henry H. Haight as governor.

Today, the University of California has 10 campuses across the great state, with more than a quarter million students and more than 20,000 faculty members. The UC system is recognized as one of the finest university systems in the world. In particular, its oldest campus, Berkeley, has consistently ranked among the top universities in the United States. The UC system has produced 187 Nobel laureates and counting, more than 50 percent of the total for the entire United States (which has a total of 371 laureates, including recipients of the nonacademic Nobel Peace Prize). Berkeley alone has had 104 Nobel laureates, four times as many as Russia, which garnered just 26 even including the former Soviet Union. Berkeley is truly a first-rate research institution with a reputation for academic excellence.

Known for its liberalism and tolerance in both academics and politics, Berkeley has also been a hotbed of political activism. Berkeley was ground zero for the hippie movement and the antiwar movement during the 1960s and 1970s. Berkeley has a rebellious spirit probably unrivaled anywhere else in the world among institutions of higher learning.

★ ★ ★

After finishing my studies at the University of San Francisco, I went back to Beijing in January 1982 to rejoin the faculty at the Beijing Institute of Foreign Trade. China was going through much change due to Deng Xiaoping's policies of market-oriented reforms and opening up to the outside world. Now private businesses in the form of proprietorships were encouraged. Deng said of the new policy: "Let some people get rich first." The first foreign-owned hotel, managed by Holiday Inn, had just opened in Beijing.

At BIFT, a new Department of Management was established to teach business in the Western style. I was asked to offer a course in

Western mainstream economics to train new faculty members for the Department of Management. The trainees had been carefully selected from among the best of the most recent graduates from the Department of English. The textbook I used for the course was *Economics* by Richard G. Lipsey and Peter O. Steiner, copies of which had been shipped to me by the Asia Foundation. Armed only with some basic concepts of economics picked up in my MBA program at USF, I had to train myself first before I lectured my trainees. I taught my class in English. My students, who were smart, highly motivated, and eager to learn, kept me constantly on my toes. They had now had so much exposure to visiting faculty members from foreign countries that they were as proactive as US students in asking questions, making points, and challenging the teacher. I found it stimulating to teach this class, but I also felt compelled to read up to stay ahead of them.

The subject matter of my course was, I admit, quite dry, and I did my best to liven it up with examples of practical applications of economics in current events. I often used articles from the newly expanded collection of publications in the school's library and reading room, including *BusinessWeek* and the *Wall Street Journal*, although the copies were somewhat outdated. The expanded collection of foreign publications reflected a new level of openness, which I found refreshing and encouraging.

Between March and April 1982, I received acceptance letters with full scholarships from the PhD programs of all three universities to which Professor Murray of USF had asked me to apply. I was worried I might not be able to receive the necessary permission from my institute to return to the United States to further my studies. After all, I had just come back to China. Professor Murray and others intensively lobbied the leaders of BIFT on my behalf. As luck would have it, Xu Shiwei, BIFT's vice president in charge of academic affairs, was visiting San Francisco. The senior members of the Asia Foundation, including Dr. Williams, L. Z. Yuan, and Andy Andrews, strongly impressed upon him that my enrollment in a doctorate program would help further the relationship between the foundation and BIFT. The lobbying worked. Mr. Xu sent a cable from San Francisco to instruct the personnel department of BIFT to process my papers for my return to the States.

★ ★ ★

On August 21, 1982, I flew back to San Francisco. It felt almost like a homecoming. I was excited about starting my doctorate program at UC Berkeley. But I also felt deep regret that I had to leave my wife behind yet again, and there was no telling when we would see each other next. The separation was painful. But being among the first Chinese students from the PRC, if not *the* first, to earn a PhD in United States was an opportunity that neither Bin nor I ever considered turning down.

Our marriage so far had been punctuated by separations. After just six months I'd left for America the first time, and we were apart for more than a year. Now, after less than a year together in Beijing, I was off again. Communication was difficult then. Like most people in China at that time, Bin didn't have ready access to a telephone, nor could I afford to call her; overseas calls were prohibitively expensive. We relied on letters to keep in touch through what would be a period of intense joy and sadness.

After I arrived in Berkeley, I rented a room in a small house owned by Jean Radford, a kindly woman who was a professional cellist. Situated on El Camino Real in Berkeley, it was biking distance to campus. My room cost $200 a month, thanks to Berkeley's rent control policy, which was good for tenants but not so popular with landlords. Because of the restrictions on raising rent, I'd heard of landlords in the area who did not improve their rental properties. But Jean's home was comfortable and well maintained.

On the first day of class, I rode the roughly two miles to campus on a borrowed bicycle. While crossing Sproul Plaza, the heart of UC Berkeley, I saw a huge red banner in front of the school bookstore. It read:

FOR ALL THINGS REACTIONARY, IF YOU DON'T HIT THEM, THEY WON'T FALL DOWN. THIS IS LIKE SWEEPING THE FLOOR: WHERE THE BROOM DOES NOT REACH, THE DUST WILL NOT CLEAN ITSELF. —MAO ZEDONG

I stopped and stared, mouth agape. Wow, I thought, this was like the Cultural Revolution all over again. Since his death, Mao's quotations had largely disappeared from public places in China. The last place I expected to see them reemerge was the United States.

This quotation from Chairman Mao, I soon found, along with policies like rent control, was why some people jokingly referred to the town as "the People's Republic of Berkeley." The city was a bastion of liberalism and radicalism in the 1960s and 1970s, known for the hippie counterculture and the anti–Vietnam War movement. In the campus bookstore, a portrait of Karl Marx stared down from the wall, along with one of Albert Einstein.

On Telegraph Avenue, which I took every day to classes, an earnest American man kept trying to sell me a copy of Mao's Little Red Book. He was not at all happy with the path of economic reform China was taking. "China has changed color," he would yell at me. "Down with the revisionists! Down with Deng Xiaoping!"

Finally, after a few weeks of haranguing, I'd had enough. "You know that little red book of yours?" I stopped to say. "You don't need to sell it to me because I've memorized it." He snorted. "I don't believe you."

"Would you like me to recite it?" I asked. I was bluffing—I couldn't recite the whole thing—but I did know quite few passages by heart. I could even sing them, since during the Cultural Revolution, many of Mao's quotations were made into songs.

"The force at the core leading our cause is the Chinese Communist Party," I began. "The theoretical basis guiding our thinking is Marxism-Leninism. If there is to be a revolution, there must be a revolutionary party . . ."

"Okay, okay, okay," the young man said hastily. Still, he wanted to lecture me on how Deng Xiaoping betrayed the revolution, and why Jiang Qing was a great woman and a true Marxist. There was no point in arguing with him. I simply said, "You would know better if you were sent to the Gobi for a few years."

"Eh?" He was puzzled.

I didn't explain and went on my way. But he stopped harassing me.

The first professor I went to meet with on campus, on September 15, was Professor Dick Holton. He was in his midfifties and wore a pair of dark-rimmed eyeglasses. Soft spoken, he came across as both kind and patient. He had served as the dean of the Haas School of Business, as Berkeley's business school is known. I had corresponded with him in connection with my admission, and he was a great help in securing my financial support at Berkeley. I considered him to be my faculty sponsor. He was happy to see me now that I had finally made it to Berkeley, as he knew how difficult it was for a Chinese student to navigate the process of coming to the United States.

Then I went to meet with the faculty adviser I'd been assigned, Professor Janet Yellen. Her sunlit office was modest in size and well organized. She greeted me warmly and introduced me to her husband, Dr. George Akerlof, who happened to be in the room. He was a professor in the Economics Department. She appeared to be in her midthirties and he in his early forties. They were both friendly and casual in their manners and in their dress, she in her red sweater and he in his green one. I immediately felt relaxed and comfortable.

Professor Yellen had known that my background was different from a typical doctoral student. She was still quite surprised when I told her I had never taken a formal course in mathematics in my life beyond elementary school, although I had studied some math on my own. She was somewhat incredulous. She must have wondered how on earth this guy had managed to get into a doctorate program at UC Berkeley. If she had such doubts, she did not articulate them. But both she and her husband thought the courses would be challenging for me, as they put it rather mildly, in view of my educational background (or lack thereof).

The doctoral program required a concentration in another branch of social sciences, like economics, psychology, or political science. I chose economics, which required a lot of mathematics and statistics. I knew I was ill prepared, but I was confident I would be able to do it by working hard, as I had done at USF.

I wanted to take Econ 201A, a graduate-level course in microeconomics, in my first quarter. Professors Yellen and Akerlof both strongly advised me against it, suggesting the level of difficulty would be "insurmountable." The right thing to do, they said, was to first take Econ 291A, *Math Tools for Economics*, the prerequisite course for 201A. I was hesitant. I couldn't tell if they doubted my abilities, or if the course was truly that difficult.

I found some senior-class doctoral students and borrowed their homework and final papers for Econ 201A, to get a feel for how difficult this course was. Even though I couldn't understand much of it, I felt I could grasp the concepts. I decided to take Econ 291A and Econ 201A concurrently, as well as some other courses in math and economics. Drs. Yellen and Akerlof were not convinced I could handle the course load. She counseled me to only take the required math classes, fearing I might get distracted and bogged down, but she let me make my own decision.

Dr. Akerlof taught one of the classes I took; he turned out to be a funny, genial lecturer and an absolute perfectionist. Copies of his lecture notes were kept on file at the university library for student reference. While reading them to catch up on a missed class, I was astonished to find he meticulously wrote down every single word of his lecture, including what he would do in class. It was like reading the script of a show. A discussion on market barriers to entry, for example, would go something like this:

> *Why do companies like Coca-Cola spend such huge sums on advertising? It's not as if people don't know what they make. The answer is that the advertising deters competitors from entering the market. Advertising is a contest to see who can burn the most money. (Take $10 bill from pocket and show to students.)*

Dr. Akerlof was well known for his influential paper, published in 1970, titled "The Market for Lemons: Quality Uncertainty and the Market Mechanism." The paper explained that "information asymmetry" was the underlying cause for the differentials in the perceived value of the same product between sellers and buyers. Among other applications, his analysis helped lay the theoretical foundation for the insurance industry to price its products. This and his other contributions to economic theory would win him the Nobel Prize in 2001.

It turned out that he and Professor Yellen were right about Econ 201A. After two weeks, I was devoting two-thirds of my time to this one course and only one-third to all my other subjects. Eventually, as an economist might put it, I conceded that Econ 201A was not an efficient use of my time and dropped it.

Another academic challenge for me that semester was linear algebra, a required course for doctoral students. Without any training in the basics, I plunged in and struggled. But I noticed that I wasn't alone. Several other PhD students were having a hard time, too, including a few from Taiwan who I knew were strong in mathematics. Our textbook, *Linear Algebra and Its Applications*, was a beast, at more than 400 pages long. I read each chapter repeatedly and did all the exercises to drill myself on the concepts, theorems, and formulas. By the end of the quarter, I counted that I'd read the thing cover to cover seven times. An A + for the course was the hard-won reward.

Thankfully, the straightforward logic of calculus I found to be a bit easier. Berkeley offered a self-paced calculus program, which allowed you to take Calculus A and B in two quarters. I had completed Calculus A halfway through the first quarter and sat for the exam, which was supervised by a teaching assistant from South Africa. I ripped through the test at a fast pace, finishing long before the other students, and gave it to the TA. She flicked through it quickly and then put the test booklet down.

"You cheated," she said, staring at me.

"What do you mean, I cheated?" I said, thinking this was a joking conversation opener.

"It's not possible to have finished so quickly and get every answer correct. You must have cheated," she said scornfully.

I felt somewhat insulted that she would accuse me of such a thing. But I was also a little amused that she didn't believe anyone could do it—when I clearly just had.

"Okay, fine," I said. "Why don't you give me another exam? Just for me this time. I will do it right in front of you." She rolled her eyes, searched in her pile of papers, took out a sheet, and handed it over to me. "You have half an hour," she said.

I sat in front of her and set to work. She was reading but glanced up from her book from time to time, to check on me and to see how the others were doing. I finished the second exam before some of the students turned in the original. Seeing my work was genuine, the TA apologized and gave me an A.

I had worked hard. I got straight As that quarter, if I remember correctly, but honestly, some of it was a blur. I would have enjoyed studying in a more leisurely manner, but I didn't have that luxury, as I had so much ground to make up.

My studies were not the only focus for me that fall. Both Bin and I had been making every effort for her to join me. We had the all-clear from Berkeley, as Bin was included in my stipend. The problem was that we needed the approval from BIFT.

I wrote letters to Bin frequently and eagerly anticipated hers. On November 15, 1982, a letter from Bin arrived. In it, she told me that she was about four months pregnant. At first, Bin and I had not wanted to have a child until we were settled down in one place. But when I was home in 1982, we decided to try, partly hoping a grandchild would be good for my mother-in-law. Her health had started to decline even though she was only 46 years old then. She appeared open and carefree in front of others, but the loss of her husband and Bin's two younger sisters in the tragic earthquake had taken its toll on her, despite her brave nature. We hoped a new baby in the family would bring Bin's mother some new joy and help improve her health.

★ ★ ★

Bin and I were elated about the pregnancy and redoubled our efforts to be together. In spite of our petitions, there was still no telling when she would receive the permission to travel to the United States to join me. Allowing spouses to travel abroad was as yet unprecedented and there was no clear policy in this regard. The relevant authorities we had petitioned probably did not wish to take the risk of setting a precedent.

Just before Christmas, I met up with an acquaintance visiting San Francisco from Beijing. He brought me a package from Bin, containing a cassette tape of her talking to me, updating me on her life and the goings-on at home. She also included a pair of elegant blue pants that she'd made in a sewing and tailoring class. I donned them immediately with some excitement, finding they fit me perfectly. It was raining that day, and by the time I got home, I was soaked. Looking down, I noticed my shoes had turned completely blue. When I removed my wet pants, I was amused to find that even my legs were dyed blue, and the pants had lost most of their color. It was no surprise that the dye from the hand-sewn pants had run, but neither Bin nor I expected it would wash out almost clean after one rain.

Bin and I changed tactics to get her to Berkeley. Since there was as yet no policy in China to permit students studying abroad to bring their spouses, we decided there was little point in being crusaders for change. Our best chance for Bin to join me was for her to come to the States in her own right, as a student, not a spouse.

Her specialty was Russian, a subject she had studied since elementary school and for which she earned an undergraduate degree. We felt she excelled in the subject and had a good chance of winning a scholarship. I was pleasantly surprised to discover that UC Berkeley had a Department of Slavic Languages and Literature. I dropped by and discussed Bin's case. It was certainly unique: The professor I spoke with said she had never heard of a Chinese student interested in studying Russian in the United States. But she was warm and encouraging, urging her to go ahead and apply to the graduate program. Bin and I shared a laugh in our letters about the irony of coming to America only to study Russian, but getting her on a plane was all that mattered.

We set to work feverishly to apply for the program. Bin gathered her transcripts and a copy of her diploma, taking the required exams to complete her application while pregnant and taking care of her mother as well. Our hopes were up, but we sensed there would be many hurdles before our dream of living together became a reality. At the Asia Foundation, I discussed our plans with L. Z. Yuan, a spry 73-year-old who had been born in Shanghai in the last years of the Qing dynasty. Educated in American schools, he became a war correspondent for the United Press Syndicate after the Japanese invasion and later was the founding editor of Hong Kong's first Asian-owned English-language paper, the *Hong Kong Tiger Standard*. Although he had officially retired from the Asia Foundation in 1977, L. Z. had returned to manage the foundation's China program.

He took our case under his wing and assured me that if Berkeley's Slavic languages department accepted her, the Asia Foundation would write a support letter for Bin to get a student visa.

Bin and I received great news on March 2, 1983: She had been accepted, with a scholarship, by Berkeley's Slavic languages department. We were overjoyed. L. Z. Yuan, who was traveling to Beijing, brought with him both the visa form and the admission letter from Berkeley and delivered them to Bin personally. We are both grateful to this day for his kindness to us.

But just as we thought things were looking up, Bin's mother began to experience severe bouts of muscle weakness and could not function on her own. She needed Bin's help and Bin would not leave her mother alone. There were no other close relatives. So it seemed that our dream of Bin coming to the United States would have to wait, at least until her mother recovered. I felt helpless to do anything to ease the burden Bin carried of caring for her mother, even as she was on the verge of giving birth to our son.

On April 20, 1983, I received a letter from my father informing me that Bin had given birth to a boy on April 13. Our son weighed 8.7 pounds and had been delivered by caesarean section in the same Army General Hospital where her mother was being treated in a different ward. One consolation for Bin was the knowledge that her mother received the best care possible. This was the hospital where Bin's mother had worked as a dentist and Bin's father had worked as a doctor. Bin visited her mother every day.

When I first found out Bin was pregnant, I'd suggested the name Bo if the baby were a boy, which in Chinese means "doctorate," in recognition of my recent good fortune. My father considered that somewhat vain, however, and suggested using a different Chinese character that is also pronounced *bo* but means "fight." Bin didn't like "fight," as she thought it evoked the image of a fighting rooster. So we named him Bo, settling on the pacifist character. My mother, ever considerate, suggested we nickname him LeiLei. The character for *lei* is made up of three characters for *shi*, which is also the character for Bin's family name. So, our son would have my family name, but his nickname would contain six of Bin's family names. It seemed more than fair. I was overjoyed at my son's birth, but I knew it would be a long time before I could see him and his mother.

My landlady congratulated me and offered me some wine to celebrate. I called Mrs. Cassou and some other friends to report the good news. I happened to reach the Cassous on their eighth wedding anniversary. I knew they had been trying to have a child. I privately wished that my good luck would rub off on these lovely people who had helped me so much.

Happiest of all, I think, was my mother-in-law. To finally have a grandchild after losing so many members of her family cheered her up immensely, but it was not enough to save her. Two months later, in June 1983, she succumbed to her illness, at the young age of 47.

Even beyond the grief of her mother's death, Bin's life in Beijing was hard. Not only was she taking care of a newborn, she was also working in the administrative office at BIFT. Bin would leave our son with my parents during the day, and then commute for 45 minutes by bus to her job on campus. It was exhausting, emotionally and physically.

I stepped up my efforts to help Bin get all the necessary approvals and papers to travel to the United States. Now there was the added complexity of our newborn son. Naturally, Bin wanted to bring him with her. But I thought that was unrealistic. It was hard enough for her to come. I thought we had to take it one step at a time, and the priority was to get her over first. My parents would take care of our son until we could manage.

By then, Bin's acceptance by Berkeley's Slavic language department had expired. So she had to go through the application process again, and petition authorities in Beijing for necessary approvals. As with our previous efforts, we had no idea if any of this was going to work. It was nearing midsummer of 1983. Bin and I had been apart, for the second time, for nearly a year. We had been apart more than we'd been together.

I enlisted the help of my US friends to speed up the process to get Bin over. Again, thanks to the help of L. Z. Yuan, the Asia Foundation issued papers for Bin to obtain a student visa. Dr. Haydn Williams of the Asia Foundation and Professor Dick Holton of UC Berkeley both wrote letters to the president of BIFT, lobbying him to let Bin join me.

Meanwhile, my life in Berkeley went on. Americans like to say that theirs is a free country. I had discovered that you could not be free in America without a car. That spring, I bought my first car. It was a used beige-colored Opel that cost $1,900. The day I was to pick it up, the woman I was buying it from called to say that, despite our agreement, she had sold it to a dealer. I had no idea that someone could just walk away from a deal. I called my friend Bob Meyer, a lawyer I knew at Graham & James, to ask for his help. I don't know what Bob said to the seller, but I was able to pick up the car at the dealership the next day. I was so excited about my newly found freedom that I immediately began to drive everywhere, even though I had yet to obtain my driver's license.

Later that term, Professor Yellen suggested that I find a summer job to supplement my income. I interviewed with two banks, the First National Bank of Chicago and Chase Manhattan. Eventually I chose First Chicago because I liked the person in charge there, Rand Sparling. Rand was a man of his word. When he said he would call me at 5 p.m., the phone rang promptly at 5. First Chicago placed me in the trade finance department in its San Francisco office and paid me $500 per week. I was reporting to Ken Petrilla, the head of the department. Ken was kind to me, as were the two young women who worked for him.

After some discussion, Ken tasked me with a study of the trade flow between Asia and the West Coast of the United States. This job was perfect for me, as it allowed me to get some experience working in a bank, earn some additional income, and use my training in business and economics to do something that was both satisfying and useful.

When classes started again in the fall, I moved out of Jean's house and into Berkeley's International House, an on-campus residence for students known as I-House. Every quarter it awarded free room and board to one student selected on the basis of both merit and need. I qualified based on grades, and I was also demonstrably poor. My coming from China probably also appealed to the selection committee.

Berkeley's I-House was the second of an international network of residential dormitories that John D. Rockefeller Jr. had funded. It was the brainchild of a young YMCA official, Harry Edmonds, who came up with the idea after encountering a Chinese student on the steps of the Columbia University library. After Edmonds wished him a polite "Good morning," the Chinese student was overcome with emotion, saying that he had been in New York City for three weeks and that those were the first words anyone had spoken to him. Edmonds and his wife realized they needed to do something to help foster better interactions between US students and their foreign classmates. The first International House opened in New York City near Columbia University in 1924.

Berkeley's I-House, which opened in 1930, was built on the university's fraternity and sorority row. It began, at a time when the university didn't allow coeducational living and people of different races generally didn't mix, as a deliberate attempt to promote integration and to draw foreign students. I-House was a grand building, five-plus stories topped with a distinctive dome. It had its own dining hall and a 24-hour library, and it was bustling with social activity at all times.

If John D. Rockefeller Jr. had meant to foster communication between Americans and foreigners, Berkeley's I-House was a screaming success. We all had our own rooms, yet I still found the collegial buzz of the students quite noisy and potentially distracting. One had to be disciplined, so as not to be lured by all the parties, activities, and gatherings. One time, I found myself sitting in a circle on the floor of someone's dorm room. Someone lit a cigarette and passed it around. Each person took a deep inhale of the smoke. But it did not smell like tobacco. I was naïve enough not to know it was marijuana until a few moments later. I politely declined a toke, but sat there chatting. I expected the joint would have some noticeable effect on my friends, but it didn't seem to me anyone behaved any differently after smoking it.

I also became a teaching assistant that quarter. On Professor Yellen's recommendation, I interviewed with Professor David Teece, who taught BA188, Introduction to International Business. I got the job but soon nearly lived to regret it as more than 100 students were on the roster. I taught four sessions, one day a week, plus office hours. The salary of $9 per hour didn't compensate me for the many hours of preparation required. Nor did I anticipate that many of my students also lived at I-House and, once they discovered me there, would drop by my room endlessly to ask questions. Despite this, it was a rewarding experience. I enjoyed teaching, and especially interacting with the students.

Once I had enough mathematics and economics under my belt, I retook Econ 201A, the microeconomics course I had earlier dropped after two weeks. This time, the class wasn't difficult to understand, and in fact I enjoyed it.

Fall turned to winter, and my semester-long residence at I-House came to an end. Although there was still no certainty that Bin would join me, I applied, and was accepted, for an apartment at Albany Student Village, housing for married graduate students. The new apartment was in the town of Albany, right near the San Francisco Bay, about three miles from campus. With its streets lined with two-story apartment buildings made of wood, it looked like an army barracks. My apartment, on an upper floor, felt extravagant to me. It had two bedrooms, a small kitchen connected to a modest-sized living-dining area, and a bath-room: This was the most spacious and luxurious home I'd ever lived in. I knew Bin would love it, if only she could get here.

Just before Christmas 1983, Bin and I got a break we sorely needed. Captain Nelson Tsui, a businessman who had made his fortune in shipping, offered to pay my airfare to Beijing for Christmas vacation. I had been away for 16 months, and I was desperate to see Bin and meet our son for the first time.

I left for Beijing on the cheapest flight I could find, transiting through Hong Kong, which was tense from negotiations between Britain and

China over its return to Chinese rule, and arrived to find Beijing in a deep freeze. The temperature was −15° C (~5° F). The steel gray sky was forbidding, and the air, as usual, badly polluted. Chimneys belched black coal smoke from the furnaces keeping the city warm. I could feel and smell the soot in the air. Most residents walked or biked around wearing white surgical masks, as did I. These both made breathing easier and kept the face warm in the freezing cold.

Underneath the soot, economic activity was visible. For the first time, Beijing had supermarkets and telephone booths. Perhaps my favorite sign of progress was that, due to the increased number of cars on the roads, the government banned honking, so Beijing was much quieter than it had been when I left.

These economic green shoots were sprouting thanks to the efforts of Deng Xiaoping and his left and right hands, Party Secretary Hu Yaobang and Premier Zhao Ziyang. One of Deng's major contributions to China was the abolishment of lifetime tenure of senior government officials. Deng himself never assumed the highest titles in the Party or the government, even though they were his for the taking. In 1983, he suggested the establishment of the Advisory Committee of the Party Central Committee. Essentially this was made up of retired senior government officials, and it became a gracious way for them to retire. Deng himself became chairman of this advisory committee, setting an example for others.

This was a major step away from Maoist policies and cleared the way for a more regular transfer of power. Hu and Zhao now were implementing Deng's vision, helping to streamline the bureaucracy and introducing more market elements into the Chinese economy. The reforms that took root in these years would underlie much of China's future growth. Unfortunately, the one that didn't last was the ban on honking. Beijing would soon be back to its noisy self.

The time I spent with Bin and LeiLei that winter was better than anything I could have imagined. For Bin and me, seeing each other again was so satisfying that we simply stayed inside, enjoying being together. We had so much to talk about. I was floored when I saw LeiLei, who was only eight months old. I felt an immediate bond. Despite my misgivings, it took him only a few minutes to warm up to me and soon we were playing together as naturally as if I'd been there all along. It was still freezing cold outside, so apart from visiting with a few close friends and relatives, we didn't do much. But those moments were priceless, more than enough to warm our hearts and celebrate as a family.

I made an exception to spending time with my family for a visit to BIFT, noting with satisfaction the progress my former students, who would be future BIFT faculty, had made in their studies.

I was asked to give a lecture while there, on a subject of my choice. I spoke about the benefits of international trade and the need for developing countries to industrialize.

The lecture went over quite well and was well attended. By this point BIFT not only had foreign professors of languages, but also foreign professors of other subjects, such as economics. A visiting US professor named Vin Hawink liked my lecture so much that he personally gave me $400 to help me out financially. He wouldn't take no for an answer when I said I couldn't accept his gift. Instead, I gave the money to the school to help the next student going abroad.

My winter break was over quickly, and I left Beijing on January 17, 1984. Soon after returning to San Francisco, I learned from Berkeley's Chinese Student Association that a delegation from the Chinese Ministry of Education was visiting, and there was a party at the Chinese consulate. So I went. That night, I learned an astonishing thing. The delegation announced a new policy regarding Chinese citizens studying overseas. The spouses of graduate students studying abroad would now be granted approval to join them, assuming the spouse was also accepted at a university and had proof of sufficient financial support. This was a major step in China's policy regarding Chinese students abroad. It fit Bin's and my own situation perfectly. The path seemed clear for Bin to join me: All she needed was an acceptance letter from a US university, a passport, and a visa from the US consulate.

I was so excited I tried to call Bin to tell her the good news. She had no phone at home, so I had to call her workplace. I asked the operator to place a person-to-person call, a concept that seems so antiquated now. On a person-to-person call, the rate per minute was higher than for placing a regular call, but the caller would not be charged if the person they were calling couldn't be reached. The operator told me that it would take five to six hours to get through to Beijing.

I gave up and wrote Bin a letter. "Now all is ready but the start of the East Wind," I wrote. It was an old expression, referring to a historic battle on China's Yangtze River. "Please don't delay. We need to seize the day, even the minute and the second. I know how Beijing people do things, including ourselves: never in a hurry, and always taking our time. We can't do it that way. You must come as soon as possible. Now that the door is open, there will be a rush and if you are late, you have to wait in line and then there will be further delay. Please hurry!"

I thought it was an extraordinary thing for Deng to open the door for so many Chinese students to study abroad. In one form or another, every country in the Communist world had a barrier preventing its people from traveling abroad—an Iron Curtain or something similar. The gap in living standards between China and the developed world was much greater than that between, for example, East and West Germany. It seemed obvious that many Chinese students who went to study abroad would not return. Deng's open-door policy seemed almost certain to lead to a brain drain, just as China's economic development needed more smart young people than ever. When Deng had told Jimmy Carter he would send 10 million Chinese to the United States, everyone thought he was joking. But Deng was resolved to make this bold move. In order for China to become a member of the international community, Chinese people had to be able to study and travel abroad. Eventually Deng's decision paid off, although it took decades.

To wait for Berkeley's Slavic languages department to readmit Bin would take too long. I went back to USF for help. My old friends at the business school, including Professor Murray and others, helped Bin apply for the MBA program. She was quickly accepted. L. Z. Yuan also informed me that the Asia Foundation would issue her the necessary visa forms.

Things moved quickly after that. At the end of January 1984, I received a letter from Bin saying that she expected to leave by May 1, although she still hadn't received all the papers. Finally, on March 12, I received a phone call from China. It was a collect call. I knew immediately it was from Bin. Her voice came across loud and clear. She told me that BIFT's vice president had agreed to do everything possible to help her join me. She was planning to be in Berkeley by the end of June.

It was a busy and overloaded academic term for me at Berkeley. I had a full course load and was continuing as a TA for Professor Teece's class. I found out that I had already taken enough courses in economics to qualify for a master's degree short of a comprehensive exam. Professor Yellen advised me that I didn't even need to take the exam—instead I could just take another course, Econ 201B. Since taking a class was more appealing than preparing for an exam on old materials, I chose the class. But it was one more thing to do, on top of my other responsibilities.

The workload and preparing for Bin's arrival must have put too much pressure on me. One night I was jolted awake by a sharp pain in my chest. I was worried and took myself to the university clinic the next day. A cardiologist told me that my blood pressure was high: 145/110, indicating early stages of hypertension. After a slew of tests, the doctors eventually found nothing else wrong. They advised me to take it easy and get more sleep. They were right. After a few nights' rest, the problem was gone.

★ ★ ★

On March 23, 1984, Dick Habor, a Berkeley administrator from the business school, called to inform me that I had been elected by my students as the best teaching assistant, and that I would receive an award for Excellence in Teaching during the University's spring banquet. It was the annual Earl F. Cheit Award, Dick explained, named after dean emeritus "Budd" Cheit, and given to the business school's best teachers. (Professor Cheit worked at Berkeley for more than three decades and helped build the business school into a major institution; he eventually became a good friend of mine.) Only one teaching assistant was chosen to receive it, voted on by students and based on three criteria: excellence in teaching, genuine interest in the students, and attention to their personal development. I was quite surprised and did not know what I did to deserve this honor. But I was grateful that all my efforts to help my students were not lost on them. All those late-night visits by my dorm mates at I-House the previous quarter must have counted for something.

Dick invited my family to the award ceremony. But of course, I did not have any family with me. In the end, Mrs. Calhoun and a few other friends joined me. After the award was presented, I was asked to say a few words. I remembered how my parents had always wanted me to get a good education, and how proud they would have been at this moment. In addition to thanking everyone, I said I was happy for my parents. But I was so embarrassed to be honored in front of so many people that it was difficult for me to find words to express myself. The audience must have been wondering how someone who spoke so incoherently could be a good teaching assistant.

Just before the end of the spring quarter, Bin's paperwork came though; she was ready to fly to the United States. I bought her an air ticket, Beijing to San Francisco, for $475, which Sandy Calhoun's secretary and my friend Della kindly put in the Graham & James inter-office mail pouch for delivery to Beijing. On the same day, we heard from Berkeley's Department of Slavic Languages and Literature that Bin had been readmitted to its program. I had kept her application current even while we pursued acceptance at the USF business school. Now, when she arrived, Bin would have the choice to study Russian or business.

On a warm and sunny June 30, 1984, Bin arrived in San Francisco, just shy of two years since I had left Beijing for Berkeley. We were together at last. Bin loved ice cream, and I wanted to surprise her with the variety of American ice cream flavors. After I picked her up at the San Francisco airport, I drove her to Fisherman's Wharf and bought her the largest bowl of ice cream I could find. In China, ice cream usually came in one flavor, milk, and a serving was the size of a golf ball. That day, Bin's was a rich, dark chocolate and the American portion was about the size of a grapefruit. Too much of a good thing really can be too much. She loved it but she couldn't finish it and possibly made herself a little sick from such sweet, rich food so soon after a long plane journey. She steered clear of ice cream for many years.

The apartment in the Student Village was a hit with Bin. We finally had a home of our own. As we settled in, I enjoyed seeing the United States through Bin's eyes. She was so impressed with the abundance of everything in the supermarket that she wrote to a friend back in China that here in the US she'd seen communism—the utopian ideal of which was defined by Marx and characterized by the abundance in the supply of everything.

That July, the 1984 Summer Olympics were held in Los Angeles. China participated in the Games for the first time since 1952. We bought a secondhand TV and friends joined us to watch. China had never won any medal in Olympic history but won 15 gold that summer. It was exciting for us to watch this strong showing, which was doubtless helped by the Soviets, as well as other East Bloc competitors, having boycotted the games in retaliation for the US boycott of the 1980 Moscow Summer Olympics.

Xu Haifeng, a Chinese sharpshooter, won the first gold medal of the Games, for the 50-meter pistol event. Chinese gymnast Li Ning captured the world's attention with his beautifully articulated moves, winning six medals in all: three gold, two silver, and a bronze. But the most mesmerizing, for us, was the fast-paced, nail-bitingly suspenseful women's volleyball championship match between China and the United States, which China won, 3–0. Our friend, Li Yue, was so excited she was jumping up and down in front of the TV, shouting instructions at the players like a coach from the sidelines. We had to calm her down for fear our downstairs neighbors would complain of the noise.

Bin and I were given two tickets to the closing banquet for the Chinese athletes. The banquet was held in a large hall in Los Angeles, attended by hundreds of Chinese from all over the United States. As soon as the athletes entered, the event descended into chaos. Li Ning, the incredible gymnast, and the members of China's women volleyball team were mobbed. All night, the event's moderators attempted to restore order in vain; the athletes spent the dinner surrounded by swarms of picture-taking, autograph-seeking fans.

We drove down the Pacific Coast Highway to Los Angeles and back in a rented car, because mine was too rickety to make the journey. I remember at one point, driving through a storm, enjoying the serenity inside the car with Bin, the windshield wipers rhythmically beating time as we sped along next to the ocean. My mind wandered to the Gobi, with its choking sandstorms and days of bitter cold. I felt deeply appreciative of my life's journey in that moment, triggered by something that I now take for granted, the simple act of traveling in the comfort of a car with my wife, protected from the weather. I think one always appreciates most the things that are difficult to get, those things that once seemed impossible to attain.

★ ★ ★

That fall, Bin had to choose between continuing her Russian studies at Berkeley and working toward her MBA at USF. She chose the latter because she had studied Russian since she was small, but she had never met with a Russian to speak the language. She settled into the routine of class but was haunted at the thought that we had left our son, now over a year old, with my parents in China.

In the summer of 1985, I went back to Beijing with Bin to see our son and to visit with our family. Bin spent the whole summer running around the city trying to persuade the relevant authorities to let us bring our son to the United States. I was not hopeful about our chances of success, but she would not give up, and spent day after day tirelessly working at it.

LeiLei, now two years old, was a handful, and proving difficult for my parents to take care of alone. At that time, they were also caring for my sister's daughter, as my brother-in-law lived and worked in Shanghai and had been unable to get a permit to move to Beijing. I was worried that the two kids would wear out their grandparents completely. One time, our son fell and fractured a bone in his leg. Another time, he fell down horsing around in my parents' small apartment and split open his chin, requiring stitches.

These accidents worried Bin to death. She was determined to find a way to bring LeiLei to California with her, or she would not leave Beijing—even though her own semester at USF was about to begin. At the end of July 1985, I flew back to San Francisco by myself. Bin stayed in Beijing and continued her campaign.

I spent the next several weeks by myself in Berkeley, feeling down and wondering if Bin would return in time for the start of the semester. Just before the new academic year began, I received another collect call from China. I was incredulous when Bin told me she had succeeded in securing all the necessary papers for our son to travel to the United States. They would be arriving by the end of August. If there's a will, there's a way, I thought. And Bin's will had won out.

Bin and LeiLei arrived in San Francisco at the end of August. Bin and I had been married in 1980, and now, after five years, our family was finally together. It was our happiest moment. Money was tight, but we loved being in the Bay Area; Bin and I never tired of taking LeiLei to the zoo and Golden Gate Park. The Albany Student Village operated a university-sponsored kindergarten, with free admission for residents. We would drop LeiLei off in the morning and pick him up after school in the afternoon. He soon fit in, even though he arrived not speaking a word of English.

Albany Village also had a swap shop where residents traded clothes and items they no longer needed, exchanging them for others. Bin volunteered as a manager. It was unpaid, but throughout the rest of our stay at Berkeley, she did not have to buy a single piece of clothing for any of us or toys for LeiLei. Everything we had was secondhand, sent over to the swap shop by departing students.

It was a frugal life, but we felt privileged to have made it work. We were the envy of many other Chinese students, as we were the first to have our whole family living together. This soon changed, as China relaxed its passport issuance rules, and more student families reunited in the United States. But then the US consulates in China began to tighten their visa issuances. We were lucky to be among the first ones to squeeze through the door of opportunity.

★ ★ ★

Meanwhile, I worked steadily toward my doctorate. My thesis was on the collaborative relationship between established pharmaceutical companies and biotech start-ups. It was an empirical analysis of what determined these relationships. Biotechnology was a relatively new realm of medicine. Tackling as it did new areas like recombinant DNA and gene sequencing, biotech was risky and not well understood by the established pharmaceutical companies, so funding was often provided by venture capital.

Companies like Genentech and Amgen were launching all kinds of innovative new drugs. The ecosystem that allowed this to happen was, I thought, a uniquely American one, where venture capitalists would fund biotech start-ups' work to develop new therapies, and then the start-ups would license the technology to large pharmaceutical firms that could afford the many years and hundreds of millions of dollars it took to go through the FDA approval process and to bring a new drug to market.

At the beginning of 1986, when I was still about a year away from finishing my doctoral thesis, a representative from the World Bank came to Berkeley to meet with me. He was looking for candidates for the bank's Young Professionals Program, a special recruiting program to bring in talented young professionals and future senior managers. The program was highly selective and only accepted 25 people a year, he told me, chosen from among those who had recently earned graduate degrees. He said that since China had recently become a member of the World Bank, they were keen to recruit more Chinese nationals. I told him that my intention after getting my PhD was to pursue a career in teaching. But he was persistent and encouraged me to apply. "The YP program only accepts the best talent," he said. "You may find the World Bank interesting. If you don't, you can always quit."

Soon I received an invitation to interview at World Bank headquarters in Washington, DC. I arrived on January 28, 1986. My interview was scheduled for the following day. I visited the home of a friend, and no sooner had I walked in the door than we saw the news flashing across his TV screen that the space shuttle *Challenger* had exploded during its ascent, killing all the crew members. It was such a tragedy. One of the shuttle's crew, Christa McAuliffe, had been a schoolteacher. I shuddered at the thought of her students, sitting in front of a TV eagerly hoping to watch their teacher's historic mission, and instead seeing a tragedy unfold.

The next day, with that gloomy thought in mind, I arrived at the headquarters of the World Bank on Pennsylvania Avenue. I interviewed with a number of officers. The last person I spoke with looked to be the most senior of the half-dozen or so people who had spoken with me. He asked me what I hoped to be doing in 10 years. Growing up in China, I always did what I was assigned to do, and I had never planned for my own future. I captured opportunities that came my way, but I was not used to the idea of making plans for myself. "I have no idea what I'll be doing in 10 years," I told him. "I don't think so far into the future."

"Well, what about five years?" he asked.

I had to repeat my answer.

That clearly wasn't the answer he was looking for. He prodded me: "Come on, you must have an ambition. Everyone does."

I realized that he would not let me off the hook easily. I long ago learned from experience that it was useless to think about a future over which I had no control. To me, the future had always been unpredict-able. Why torture myself with dreams? My philosophy in life was to be always prepared, to capture whatever opportunity came my way.

"My ambition knows no bound," I said.

"That's a *good* answer." He appeared much more pleased. "But what's your next career objective?" He just wouldn't let it go.

Amused, I said, 'My next objective is to take over your position so that I can ask people the same questions as you are asking me now."

He laughed and didn't push me further.

The World Bank offered me a position in the YP Program. I still hoped to get a teaching job. But I was scheduled to finish my PhD pro-gram in December and I had yet to search for one. Even if I found one, it likely would not begin until the following September, the start of the next academic year. I decided to take the job at the World Bank while I looked for a job at a university. After all, as my recruiter told me, if I didn't like it I could just quit.

Chapter 22

Ivy League Professor

The term "Ivy League" epitomizes academic excellence and social elitism. The schools that make up this group—Brown, Columbia, Cornell, Dartmouth, Harvard, Princeton, Yale, and the University of Pennsylvania—are regarded as the most prestigious of US colleges and universities. But they are not the only top schools in the United States, and they are not necessarily the best: Stanford, UC Berkeley, and MIT are also considered among the finest institutions in the world.

Today, the Ivy League is really little more than a collegiate athletic association. But the reason it survives as an institution has as much to do with the proximity of its members' locations and the commonality in their history as it does with their reputation for academic excellence. These Ivy League schools are all situated on the East Coast; seven of the eight were founded before the American Revolution. Their academic reputations were built over generations.

Harvard is the oldest college in the United States, founded in 1636. It and three other colleges established in the English colonies—William and Mary, Yale, and Princeton—were all created to educate the clergy. Benjamin Franklin founded the first true liberal arts university for common folks, the University of Pennsylvania, in 1740 in Philadelphia, the city that would become the center of the American Revolution.

Joseph Wharton was a native of Philadelphia. Born to a Quaker family in 1826, he started his career as an apprentice accountant and learned bookkeeping and other key aspects of running a business. He became a successful industrialist, with interests in mining and steelmaking, among other areas. He gave $100,000 (nearly $2.5 million in today's dollars) to the University of Pennsylvania to found the first business school in the United States, which he called the School of Finance and Economy. Today, it is known simply as the Wharton School of the University of Pennsylvania. Joseph Wharton's intention was, in his own words, for the school to "instill a sense of the coming strife [in business life]: of the immense swings upward or downward that await the competent or the incompetent soldier," or in other words, to understand and navigate through business cycles, to keep a clear mind through the difficult challenges all leaders face.

★ ★ ★

I completed my PhD in December 1986 and started working at the World Bank in January. The Bank had offered to pay for our travel to Washington, DC, where I would be working. We had a choice: travel by rail in first class, or by air in coach. The rail journey would take us across the continental United States, and we could get off and on the train if we wished to stop at some places. A comfortable train journey across America appealed to our sense of adventure.

We boarded the train for the East Coast at Oakland Train Station on December 29, 1986. Our first-class sleeper cabin was big enough for the whole family, with its own shower. Over the next several days we enjoyed the endless and changing scenery as we traveled across the country. Our son loved it, jumping up and down on the sleeper bed when he wasn't staring out the window and pointing out interesting things passing by. We got off train twice, in Denver and Chicago, to visit friends. Denver was sunny and warm, just like the Bay Area. But Chicago, true to its reputation, was wind-whipped and freezing cold. Still, it impressed us as a great city, with its soaring buildings. Lake Michigan seemed so vast that Lake Wuliangsu in the Gobi looked like a small pond in comparison. Bin and I had not been so relaxed and carefree since she had arrived in the United States. As we had the private cabin all to ourselves, we found ourselves singing aloud whenever we felt like it, joyfully. What a great way to see the country, I thought to myself.

Our family settled into an apartment in Arlington, Virginia, across the Potomac from Washington, DC, and a 15- to 20-minute drive from World Bank headquarters on Pennsylvania Avenue. The compound where we lived had a kindergarten where we enrolled our son. The suburbs of Washington were a nice place to live, with so many attractions in the vicinity including parks, museums, and monuments, which our family visited on weekends. Even Foggy Bottom, where my office was located, wasn't so bad. Although it was deserted after office hours, it offered some of the best Chinese restaurants in town. We loved the Maryland blue crabs from Chesapeake Bay, where we would go occasionally to buy them fresh off the boat.

The World Bank was founded at the Bretton Woods conference in 1944, as part of the new world financial order conceived by John Maynard Keynes and others. As an institution, it started off providing reconstruction assistance to countries recovering from World War II and grew to become a major source of capital for the developing world. By the time I joined, the bank was making billions of dollars' worth of loans to developing nations, financed by its 170-member countries. The YP Program rotated its members through several different assignments at the bank, allowing them to get broad experience with the bank's operations. I was placed in the investment department, where I would be trading Canadian government bonds. In addition to loaning capital around the world, the bank also invested, conservatively, to maintain the level of funds in its treasury. The World Bank was only allowed to invest in triple-A rated government bonds. They set me up with a phone and a computer, and I was allowed to begin trading for the bank under the guidance and supervision of my senior colleagues. Every day, I bought and sold bonds with my Canadian counterparts.

I enjoyed bond trading, which involved analyzing how interest rates might move in response to macroeconomic factors. There was one Toronto-based trader who would call me every morning and ask, "How's the weather in the nation's capital?" His cheerful greetings brightened my day.

We tracked trades using paper tickets, which would be sent along for record keeping and processing, but prices were agreed upon and confirmed over the phone. A verbal agreement between traders was binding. There was no cancellation, even if one made a mistake. One day, the cheerful Canadian trader offered to buy a certain number of bonds at a price that looked extremely attractive to me. I quickly agreed to the trade. I later realized my friend in Toronto might have made a mistake and quoted me an incorrect price. Since the word of a trader was as good as a contract, the transaction went through. But that was the last I heard from this cheerful trader.

While I learned a lot from the job and from my colleagues on the trading desk, I was still interested in teaching, which, after all, was why most people entered PhD programs. David Teece, who had been the chair of my thesis committee, wrote letters to a number of US business schools to recommend me for a position. Teaching jobs typically started in September, at the beginning of the academic year. So I had several months to go, and in the meantime the job at the World Bank provided me with both good work experience and needed income.

A couple of months after I'd started working at the World Bank, I received invitations to interview at the Wharton School at the University of Pennsylvania, the Sloan School of Management at MIT, and some other business schools. I was quite pleased, but I also thought I stood no chance. These were among the top business schools in the world. I figured the invitations had much more to do with Professor Teece's reputation and academic standing than my own. I thought I would simply take this as a good exercise, and I appreciated the opportunity to meet with the best in the field.

I arrived in Philadelphia on a Sunday night in February 1987, just ahead of a major snowstorm. The next morning, the entire city was blanketed with several inches of heavy snow. When I arrived at the university campus, it was quiet and empty; there was no one in sight, and the paths had not been plowed. I trudged through deep snow and eventually found Penn's famous Locust Walk, a wide footpath lined with its namesake locust trees, their branches weighted down with snow. On one side of Locust Walk stood Steinberg Hall–Dietrich Hall, Wharton's main building. It seemed deserted. As I walked in, however, I noticed a light on in one of the offices.

I knocked on the door and pushed it open when invited. A tall man with a mustache and a pair of glasses was seated at his desk. He gave me a broad smile. I excused myself and told him I was here for a job interview.

"*Ni hao*," he greeted me in good Chinese.

I was surprised. I did not expect the first person I saw on this campus to speak Chinese. He told me his name was Jeff Sheehan and he was the associate dean in charge of international relations. He said that the university was closed due to the snowstorm; but he lived nearby and he had too much work to do, so he came to the office anyway. He said the Wharton School had many alumni in Asia, including Chinese in Hong Kong and Taiwan, and he had frequent interactions with them, which explained his Chinese.

He made a phone call to one of the faculty members of the management department. As we were chatting, Bruce Kogut came in. He was another Wharton professor who lived within walking distance. Bruce was about my age, with lively blue eyes; he greeted me warmly and offered to take me to lunch. We had a pleasant chat through which I learned about the faculty, the management department (the one considering me as a candidate), and a few things about the city of Philadelphia. The interview itself would have to be rescheduled, however, so after lunch I returned to Washington by train.

The following week was my interview with MIT. I arrived in Boston on March 1, and the following morning, a cold, windy Monday, I went to visit the campus. My impression of MIT was of a lot of concrete and not much else; perhaps in the summertime, I thought, it would be greener. It certainly felt like an engineering school, as the buildings were tall with sharp and precise edges. I met with Professor Don Lessard, a tall, dark-haired Stanford PhD who taught international business management and who had been responsible for arranging my invitation to Boston. I also met with a number of other faculty members and gave a seminar in the afternoon on my thesis research. I was prepared for the audience to tear apart my presentation, but they were surprisingly polite. Afterward, I thought I'd handled their questions well. I was certainly familiar with the subject.

The next day, I was in Philadelphia again. The drill at Wharton was similar to the one at MIT. I visited with a number of faculty members and gave a seminar in the afternoon. The presentation went a bit better as I had already been through it once at MIT, and answered many similar questions.

Professor Russ Root of Wharton called me the very next day, on March 3, to offer me a job as an assistant professor. I was delighted. I called Bin immediately to share the good news with her. A week later, following another trip to Boston where I met with several more faculty members, Professor Don Lessard and Professor Al Silk, the business school's deputy dean, called and offered me a job as an assistant professor at MIT.

By then I had received a few other offers as well, but I knew my choice would come down to those two schools. I still knew little about either, and even less about the cities of Philadelphia and Boston. But to me, it was more of a decision to choose where to work than where to live. I thought our family would grow to like any American city, as we did San Francisco, Berkeley, and Washington, DC. I was wrong, but I would not know until much later.

I decided to visit both schools again. I went to Philadelphia on March 15. The weather was beautiful. After visiting the campus, I walked around the city, admiring the rowing crews racing on the Schuylkill River and the museums by the riverside. I found it all quite pleasant.

Then I went from Philadelphia to Boston, where it was much colder. The next day, March 17, was Saint Patrick's Day. It was the first time I'd heard of the Irish day of celebrations. I attended a lunch at MIT's Faculty Club. In keeping with the Saint Patrick's Day tradition, everything was green: green tablecloths, green napkins, green décor on the walls. If you want to etch a special event into memory, it helps to use a dramatic color scheme. To this day, I still remember how it looked: green everywhere in that sun-filled dining room.

Among other faculty members, Don also brought me to visit with Professor Franco Modigliani in his office. He won the Nobel Prize in 1985 for his life-cycle theory of savings, among other things. I met with Professor Lester Thurow, Sloan's incoming dean. I had heard Professor Thurow speak once, back in California, and found him to be an impressive, powerful, and eloquent lecturer. Someone told me that he also had the nickname "Less Thorough," which I suppose was how academics pulled each other's legs.

The Wharton School had its own share of Nobel laureates. Professor Laurence Klein received his Nobel Prize in 1980 for his work creating computer models to forecast economic trends.

As I was visiting the two universities, the offer packages were also sweetened. Both schools offered me an endowed position, or "term chair." An assistant professorship came without tenure, and therefore the chair was only for the term of the appointment. But it did come with supplemental pay, which I greatly appreciated.

In all, I was overwhelmed by how the faculty members of the two schools went out of their way to recruit me. It was humbling, and in fact a little terrifying. I knew I didn't deserve all this attention, and I was fearful that no matter which institution I picked, I would end up disappointing them and embarrassing myself. I also knew I would feel bad about having to turn either one down.

I was beginning to appreciate why US institutions of higher learning were able to attract the best talent from all over the world. Many non-Americans had received the Nobel Prize for the work they had done in US institutions. In 1980s, 35 percent of US Nobel laureates were foreign-born. It was not, I realized, because the United States was such a rich country—Japan and Europe were no less rich. It was because of the equality and respect you felt, and the competition for talent in the US system. Later in my career, when I was considering a teaching position in Europe, a few European professors told me that as an Asian I could never hope to make it in European academia. I never felt there was any limit how far a foreigner could go in any profession in America.

I was keenly aware of the pervasive racial issues in the United States. Perhaps I was not completely in touch with these things, but honestly I don't remember a single racist incident directed against me in all the years we lived in the United States. By and large, I found Americans to be open, tolerant, and friendly. In almost every top-rated US university, the faculty was made up of a large variety of races, religions, and ethnicities: Jews, Indians, Chinese, and Europeans. Indians and Chinese were particularly disproportionally represented in physical sciences and engineering. The student populations at these schools were the same. It was in the United States where I first felt not only that the man makes the system, but that the system also makes the man. A good system unleashes the potential in people, whereas a bad system suppresses it.

Years later, I was walking on the street in Beijing with Jamie Gates, an American colleague. It was a Sunday, but at a construction site we passed, the builders were hard at work. He asked me, "Why do the Chinese work so hard?" I think the Chinese have always been an industrious people, but China as a country only began to grow after the system changed.

Of course, none of this helped me make up my mind between Wharton and MIT. Professor David Teece suggested that I go to Wharton: it was bigger and had more resources, as well as a robust international exchange program that I might find interesting. "Besides," he said, "it's an Ivy League university."

"Why does that make a difference?" I asked. I did notice that the walls of some buildings at Penn were covered by ivy, whereas MIT's walls were generally bare. But aside from their vegetation, traditions, and history, I knew that there wasn't much difference in terms of quality. MIT and Stanford were considered among the best schools in the world, even if they weren't in the Ivy League.

Sloan was a smaller school with a couple of dozen faculty members, whereas Wharton had probably about three or four times as many. Wharton was also better off financially, I was told, with its own funding sources and endowments, while Sloan was dependent on MIT's budget. These resources were important, not only because they allowed the school to give faculty members slightly better pay, but also because they allowed for more research grants. In the "publish or perish" world of academia, the availability of financial resources for research was critically important.

In 1983, Wharton had made history by becoming the only major US business school to appoint a dean from outside academia. A decade earlier, at age 37, Russell "Russ" Palmer had become the youngest person to lead a "Big Eight" accounting firm when he took over as managing partner of Touche Ross (now known as Deloitte). Dean Palmer did not have an academic background or an advanced degree, but he was an accomplished and successful businessman and a proven leader. Among other achievements during his tenure, he successfully raised tens of millions of dollars in endowment money for Wharton, an accomplishment envied by other leading schools—several of which subsequently also gave their top jobs to business leaders. That kind of practical thinking appealed to me.

Still, it was a difficult decision. One day in late March I rang up Professor Janet Yellen in Berkeley to ask for her advice but her husband, George Akerlof, picked up the phone. George, who had received his PhD from MIT, was emphatic. "Nobody turns down MIT," he said.

Then Professor Yellen came on the line. Her advice was a bit more balanced. She carefully analyzed the pros and cons of both institutions. And I took careful note of what she said. But after the call, weighing all the pros and cons, I still didn't know what to do.

Faced with conflicting advice, I decided to put my academic training to work to help me reach a decision. Using a methodology known as decision tree analysis, I decided I would sketch out a chart showing all the possible outcomes of each choice and weigh them according to the probability and benefits of each one.

By then I'd become good friends with Bruce Kogut, the Wharton professor who took me to lunch on that snowy day when I'd first visited. Bruce had a PhD from MIT so he knew both institutions well, although he'd never pressured me to choose one over the other.

I told him that I was thinking of creating a decision tree to help make my choice. Bruce laughed and asked if I was familiar with another business professor, a man who had made important contributions to the methodology of decision tree analysis. This success had led to job offers from a number of top institutions. Like me, he could not decide which university to pick so he went to his dean to ask for advice.

The dean said, "You're the one who came up with this methodology of decision tree analysis. Why don't you apply it to your own case?"

"Come on," the professor said, exasperated. "This is serious."

I laughed. So much for decision tree analysis.

In the end, on March 20, 1987, Bin and I decided to toss a coin. It landed on Wharton.

★ ★ ★

We settled in the town of Cherry Hill, New Jersey, across the Delaware River from Philadelphia. I commuted to work on the days when I had classes to teach. The town was primarily known as the home of the Cherry Hill Shopping Center, said to be the first indoor, air-conditioned shopping mall on the East Coast when it was built in the 1960s. It was still the only big mall for miles around. Other than that, though, Cherry Hill was a typical New Jersey town, filled with suburban houses along tree-lined streets. We bought, for about $160,000, a four-bedroom, two-story house with a two-car garage on Greenvale Road. It seemed a bit pricey, but the real estate agent told us to simply accept the asking price. "The housing prices here have been going up for the last 20 years," he said. "They will continue to go up."

Maybe it was because of us, but home prices in that neighborhood stopped rising as soon as we moved in. Bin sold the place 10 years later, for about two-thirds of what we had paid.

We quickly became friends with many of our neighbors. Cherry Hill had a sizable Jewish population, and when we were invited to dinner at the homes of our Jewish friends, the food was overabundant, and our hosts would not stop serving until they were assured we were beyond stuffed. This of course is similar to the Chinese way of entertaining, except that a Chinese host would never believe you have had enough. I believe the famine and starvation endured by Jewish and Chinese people throughout their long histories must be imprinted on our DNA, and therefore the highest respect for a guest is to feed him so much he can go for a long time without food.

We joined the Jewish Community Center on Springdale Road, which had a big indoor swimming pool and other facilities. We went there often with our son to swim. The day I signed up for our membership, the lady in the office stared at me with a puzzled look on her face. I put on my best smile and said gently, "What? You haven't met a Chinese Jew before?"

Like many top universities in the United States, Wharton was a research institution first, and an educational institution second. So much emphasis was placed on research, in fact, that only a professor's publications counted toward his or her academic advancement. As for teaching, one was required only to do enough to get by. Harvard, I found, was a notable exception to this rule; Harvard Business School was the only major institution to produce case studies in a systematic way for teaching purposes, which it then sold to other schools. Professors did write case studies at Wharton, but these did not really count toward their career accomplishments.

Of course, most professors did take teaching seriously. But the teaching load was quite light: usually one class per semester, never more than two. The rest of the time was devoted to research. If a professor could find grant money from somewhere, he could effectively "buy out" of his classes for a semester and concentrate on research alone. This was the advantage of a well-endowed school with a large body of faculty members.

Between the teaching and the research, I felt being an assistant professor at Wharton was not too different from being a doctoral student at Berkeley. The difference was that now I had access to far more resources, as well as my own research assistants and a tremendous amount of freedom and flexibility. Other than a relatively light teaching schedule, a Wharton professor had complete control over his own time—not to mention the summer and winter breaks, which added up to four or five months a year. A young professor could be easily distracted without strong self-discipline; there were so many interesting things competing for your attention.

★ ★ ★

The campus of the University of Pennsylvania was in West Philadelphia, across the Schuylkill River from the city center. The Schuylkill was quite scenic, with trees lining both sides of the river and a long row of boathouses on the east bank leading up to the magnificent Philadelphia Museum of Art. Rowing was a popular sport; when the weather was good, sleek rowing shells slid smoothly along the calm river, propelled by the rhythmic movements of their rowers.

Just northeast of the airport, near the site of the former Philadelphia Navy Yard, the Schuylkill merged into the heavy flowing Delaware River, which separated Pennsylvania from New Jersey. Crossing the Delaware were two bridges named after a pair of the area's most famous native sons, Benjamin Franklin and Walt Whitman (who was born on the New Jersey side, in Camden). The commute across either of these bridges between my home in Cherry Hill and Penn's campus only took about 20 minutes, usually without much traffic.

The campus was quite pretty, with tree-lined paths zigzagging across its green and well-tended quads. I soon realized, though, that the surrounding neighborhood of West Philly was considerably rougher. Just a few blocks from campus, the university buildings gave way to dilapidated row houses. Crime rate was high. Few faculty members chose to live near the school, preferring instead to settle in New Jersey or in the city's affluent northwest suburbs, an area known as the Main Line. While homes in Cherry Hill were generally modest and similar in style, the Main Line offered homes of many different styles and eras, with big lawns and mature trees. It was also known for its schools, including a number of good colleges such as Bryn Mawr. I preferred Cherry Hill mainly because of the commute: whereas I had a choice of two highways to take me between the town and campus, commuters from the Main Line had to drive through the city, which took considerably longer.

In comparison with San Francisco and Washington, DC, the greater Philadelphia area offered limited attractions for weekend recreation. Our favorite was the astounding Longwood Gardens, about 30 miles west of the Penn campus. Known also as Du Pont Garden, it was the legacy of Pierre Samuel du Pont, an industrialist and business executive, who in his lifetime served as president of both General Motors and of the chemical company that bore his family's name. Longwood covered more than 1,000 acres (4 square kilometers) with gardens, woodlands, meadows, water fountains, ponds, outbuildings, and greenhouses, some of which housed exotic plants and horticulture. It was hard to imagine an individual could have accumulated such immense wealth not only to build this spectacular garden, but to also have enough left over for it to be maintained in perpetuity.

In comparison with UC Berkeley, I found Penn to be somewhat sleepy. There were almost no major campus-wide events at Penn, other than football games, and little interaction between the university departments. At Berkeley, all professors wore casual clothes, even jeans, when teaching classes. At Penn, almost every professor wore a suit and tie. While hardly a week went by without some prominent figure from academia, politics, and culture giving speeches or holding events at Berkeley, I never attended one such event in all my years at Penn. This was probably because Philadelphia was somewhat out of the way for travelers, especially foreigners; a stop on the Amtrak flashing by between New York and Washington. San Francisco was a gateway to the United States and a cultural center of the West Coast; Boston, with its large number of colleges and research institutions, was one of the world's major centers for academics. New York, of course, was New York. I wondered, had I accepted the offer from MIT, if my family would have enjoyed living in Boston more.

I taught classes at both the undergraduate and graduate levels. The students came from diverse ethnic backgrounds, and there were also a fair number of foreign students. Penn being an Ivy League university and Wharton being one of the top business schools in the country, just getting in was already a big accomplishment; only the best and the brightest were admitted. Looking at what they had to go through to be accepted, I told my students that I might qualify as a professor, but I was not sure if I would have been able to get in as a student. And I was not kidding.

Teaching was not hard for me, and I found that my experience as a TA at Berkeley served me well in my new job. Teaching these students was fun but hard work. A lecture might take only an hour to deliver, but it often required hours of preparation to make it a good one. While professors gave grades to students, students also rated professors, at least implicitly, by choosing whether or not to sign up for their classes.

I had learned so much from my students, especially the graduate students who on average had had five to six years of work experience after college. It was humbling to deliver lectures to these students on the topic of management, which was my specialty, even as I had not had a single day of experience in managing a business. The job of a professor was to broaden his or her students' scope of knowledge and to teach them the tools, methodologies, and ways of thinking that would enable them to make better business decisions. It is like the job of a coach for an athlete. Almost no coach can beat the athletes on his team in their chosen sport. But he can help them excel.

Nonetheless, in retrospect, lack of real business experience can be a handicap to a business professor. Many years later, after I had left academics for a career in finance, I was invited to speak with a group of MBA students from Columbia University. One of the more successful investments I had led had been turned into a Harvard Business School case study. Some of the students had studied the case and had several questions for me about the deal. They told me the explanation their professor had given them as to why and how the deal had come together. But the explanation made no sense. I knew, because it was my deal. I had to tell the students, "Don't always believe what your professors tell you."

Foreign students typically were not as active as their US peers in participating in class discussions, but they brought perspectives that allowed all to think more broadly about the issues and about how cultural differences mattered when doing business in the international market. In the late 1980s, the rise of the Japanese economy and the Japanese way of doing things were big topics at business schools. The concept of firms having to specialize and build "core competencies" to compete effectively became the established wisdom in management circles. But as American firms specialized and honed their core competencies, the highly diversified Japanese and Korean conglomerates were making significant inroads in the US market. Brands such as Toyota, Hitachi, and Sony became household names, often outcompeting the established US brands. In view of this evidence, should a firm specialize or diversify? To get into a discussion of this question would require more space than I have here, but it is just one of the examples of why it's so necessary to understand business practices in the context of different markets.

The Wharton School had a policy of allowing professors to take their students to dine in the university's Faculty Club from time to time. Sometimes, students took their professors out to lunch. I always enjoyed conversations in these intimate and casual settings, exchanging stories and sharing a joke or two with my students. I still remember one I heard from one of my female students when a group of us were talking about the differences between international airlines during lunch. After we'd generally agreed that Lufthansa, the German flag carrier, offered some the most exceptional service, the student told us a joke about a Lufthansa plane that had experienced a mechanical failure and had to make a crash landing in the ocean. As the plane began to sink slowly beneath the waves, an announcement by the head stewardess came through the speaker. The student imitated the announcement in English with a thick German accent:

"For those of you who know how to swim, please exit the rear door. For those of you who don't, thank you very much for flying Lufthansa!"

When I was teaching a course in international business, I had a few students on an exchange program from West Point, the famous United

States Military Academy. I enjoyed chatting with them over a meal and found them as intellectual and curious as any other Wharton students. They came across as deferential and humble, which pleasantly surprised me, maybe because I had expected them to be macho and direct. I didn't know what relevance an education in international business management had to their careers in the military, but I was impressed that the education for these elite cadets was so broad.

Then as now, top business schools competed for the best students. It was a big deal for a school to be ranked as the number one business school in the United States in *BusinessWeek* or *U.S. News & World Report*, as Wharton was from time to time. I personally don't believe there is a marked difference in the quality of teaching and learning among the top-ranked schools, as the teaching methods and materials are all similar. But brand names matter to employers, as do rankings. For that reason, I think there are two major purposes for a student to go to a top business school in addition to learning: to get labeled (by the brand name of the school) and to network (as the friends they make will help them in their future careers).

Most of my time was spent on research. I became a faculty member without having published any prior research papers. Navigating the process of getting published in academic journals was a new experience for me. My colleagues, especially my fellow assistant professors, were generous in dispensing advice and in helping review my manuscripts. In most cases, an academic publication would subject a submitted paper to peer review; I never liked this process because it could take months or even years for a paper to be accepted or, even more frustratingly, rejected. Sometimes one of the three reviewers would request that a paper be reworked repeatedly, even though the other two reviewers had endorsed it. Peer review, however, is probably the only way to ensure the quality of published papers. At the same time, I also felt that to some extent getting academic papers published was like a game one had to learn to play: You had to choose the right journals to submit your work, and certain topics and certain ways of writing would give you a better chance that the editor would send the paper to reviewers who would appreciate your work.

★ ★ ★

Just as I'd settled into a routine at Wharton and our family life in Cherry Hill, Bin and I received a surprise that threatened to derail our comfortable life. On Thursday, September 15, 1988, shortly after the fall semester had started, I received a letter from the Immigration and Naturalization Service ordering my family and me to leave the country.

The notice was not clear about the reason. In fact, the whole thing was puzzling because we all had valid visas. At the advice of my colleagues, I engaged a law firm to find out what happened. The lawyer advised me that the INS notice bore the identification number of my wife, Bin, suggesting the problem had to do with her. It turned out that when the Asia Foundation had helped her obtain a visa, it issued a form usually reserved for individuals who obtained financing from their own governments to study in the United States. Such individuals had to go back to their country of origin for two years after their studies were completed. Bin's trip to the United States was clearly not funded by the government. She could have obtained a student visa form from the University of San Francisco just as easily; none of us knew the implications of the form issued by the Asia Foundation, whose staff had probably just checked the wrong box.

The notice from the INS threw our life into disarray. After discussing with our lawyers, I wrote to the INS to explain that Bin's visit to the United States was privately sponsored and financed, as the code letter "P" indicating "private," for her program clearly showed. For weeks, there was no response. With this uncertainty hanging over our heads it was impossible for me to plan my work and research or for our family to plan our life. It had been a long time since I had had to face such bureaucratic arbitrariness, and I had almost forgotten what it felt like. It was like pleading with someone who was holding a gun to my head, and I had no idea if he would step away or pull the trigger. The suspense was so agonizing I sometimes thought it might be better if he just pulled the trigger and got it over with.

The school was supportive. Dean Russ Palmer and the associate dean, Jeff Sheehan, launched a multipronged effort to help us, using Wharton's connections in Washington, DC, and other places. Via Russ's introductions I spoke with a number of DC policymakers about my case. It was unbelievable how many friends of Wharton, who were strangers to me, stepped forward. I received a call from Carl Covitz, the deputy secretary of Housing and Urban Development, who asked me how he could be of help. He patiently listened to the nuances of our problems and said he had friends in both the Department of Justice (of which the INS is a part) and the Department of Education, and he would be happy to talk with them about my case. I was quite touched. If an American got into a similar problem in China, I thought, I could not imagine a vice minister would pick up the phone to call and offer help.

The law firm I had engaged was not being much help. So I called Bob Patterson, my old mentor at Graham & James, and within half an hour he connected me with a colleague named Brian McGill in his firm's DC office. Brian specialized in immigration law. He was experienced and responsive. He advised me to wait until he had done all the research and analysis of our case before asking anyone to help. I felt I was in good hands.

I had to drop everything to fight this battle with the INS. Bruce Kogut and other faculty members stepped in to teach my classes from time to time. In late October, I told the students in my class about the problem, and that I could be kicked out of the country at practically any moment. I had to inform them because I might not be able to finish teaching the class. I was moved by my students, many of whom offered to help me, although none had any idea how. One student came to my office with an unusual proposition: She offered to marry me, so that I could stay in the country. I told her I was happily married and in fact our family was facing this crisis, not just myself. I knew she made the offer to help me at the expense of complicating her own life. I was so touched and thanked her profusely.

About a month after we received that fateful letter, Dean Palmer invited me to speak at a luncheon for Wharton's board of overseers and board of advisers. Russ must have told some of them about my plight. After the lunch, one of the board members came up to me. It was Jon M. Huntsman, head of Huntsman Chemicals, the largest company in Utah. Huntsman was a Wharton alumnus and a major benefactor. By the time of his death in 2018, he had given some $50 million to the school. In 2002 Wharton's new main building, Huntsman Hall, was named in his honor.

Jon invited me to give a speech at a conference organized by his company the following January. He also offered to help with my problems with the INS, through some friends of his in the US Senate. I accepted the speaking invitation, but I thought I wouldn't want to trouble him with my personal problems unless I had exhausted all other means. But Jon insisted on helping and asked me to send copies of our files to him.

Huntsman was a man of his word. A few weeks later I received a phone call from his son, Jon Huntsman Jr., who surprised me with his impressively fluent Chinese. Jon Jr. had graduated from Penn, where he'd studied the language. He had worked in the White House as an assistant to President Ronald Reagan—"carrying his bags," Jon Jr. joked—and had stayed for two months at the State Guest House in Beijing, where he was responsible for the logistics of Reagan's presidential visit in 1984. His father, he told me, had put him in charge of helping with my case.

A few colleagues at Wharton suggested I might obtain the support of some US government agencies on the basis of my research. At the time I had been examining biotechnology and pharmaceutical companies, an extension of my doctoral thesis work at Berkeley. My colleagues and my lawyer, Brian McGill, recommended that we approach the Department of Commerce and the Congressional Office of Technology Assessment, or OTA.

The OTA was created in the early 1970s essentially as a research institute for the legislative branch; its role was to provide members of Congress with analyses of complex scientific and technical issues. It was governed by a 12-member board made up of senators and representatives from both parties. I asked Brian McGill to check in the Congressional Directory which lawmakers currently sat on OTA's board. Today, if one wished to find that information—and if the OTA hadn't been defunded in the 1990s—one could simply Google it. But in 1988 it required tracking down a physical copy of the directory, of which few were readily available outside Washington, DC.

A senior member of the OTA board, Brian discovered, was Utah senator Orrin Hatch. I called Jon Huntsman Jr. to let him know and ask him about our plan to approach the OTA regarding my case. Jon said his father knew Hatch well, and in fact the senator and I would be speaking at the same conference in January. This was a fantastic coincidence. Jon asked me to send my background and some research papers to him to be forwarded to the senator.

I was very impressed with Jon Huntsman Jr. He was only 28 years old but he sounded much more mature. He had extensive knowledge of American politics and international affairs and was so lucid in his discussion of various issues. I wrote in my journal on November 7, 1988: "I spoke with Huntsman Jr. He pays great attention to politics and is thoroughly familiar with the backgrounds of various political figures. He says if Bush is elected, he may be appointed Assistant Deputy Secretary of State. It seems to me that this man will very likely become the US ambassador to China one day."

Thirty years later, I was proven right. Jon Huntsman Jr. was appointed ambassador to China by President Barack Obama in 2009, after serving as the Republican governor of Utah. It is quite unusual for a Democratic president to appoint a member of the other party to such an important post, which showed how extraordinary he is, to be a leading US politician and an expert on China at the same time.

Meanwhile a Wharton colleague, Professor Ian MacMillan, connected me with a friend at the Department of Commerce. I wrote letter upon letter to various agencies and individuals to plead our case. It was autumn 1988, an election year, and as November loomed Vice President George H. W. Bush held a solid lead over his challenger, Massachusetts governor Michael Dukakis. I wished that Bush would win the election, not because I had any political leanings but because I worried that all the powerful people whom Wharton had enlisted to help me would be kicked out of office if he and the Republicans lost. Happily, Bush did not disappoint me. Orrin Hatch was handily reelected as well.

I was surprised and grateful to get so much help from so many people in my fight to stay in the Unites States. But there is a Chinese saying: "A clever rabbit always has three holes to his nest." I needed a backup plan, in case the order from INS proved irreversible and my family was kicked out of the country. I hadn't entertained the idea of returning to China, as I knew I could only develop my academic career in the West. With some of my colleagues agreeing to cover my classes, I traveled to France to visit INSEAD, the Institut Européen d'Administration des Affaires, located in Fontainebleau, just outside Paris. It was reputed to be the best business school in Europe and one of the best in the world.

INSEAD was a very international school, drawing students from every corner of the globe. Most classes were taught in English, and I was told I did not have to know any French to function perfectly well there. I liked the school and its faculty, its beautiful campus, its proximity to the many attractions of Paris. But even though teaching required no French, I felt that it would be difficult for our family to live there without speaking the language. Sometime after my visit, INSEAD made me an offer to join its faculty. But I decided I would only consider it if I was forced to leave the United States.

Through the help of my friends at Wharton, the Department of Commerce issued a letter to the INS to recommend that Bin and I and our son be granted permanent visas, which came as a tremendous relief. But just as we thought the issue was resolved, we received a registered letter from the INS on December 1, 1988. The letter informed us that we would have to leave the country "voluntarily" by a certain date. Of course, this notice was anything but voluntary. It reminded me of the time when I had to "volunteer" to go to the Gobi Desert.

Fortunately, the INS was not known for its competence. Just as they had mixed up Bin's visa status in the first place, the service had made a mistake on the new letter: the date by which we had to leave the country was left blank. I supposed if we simply ignored the letter, we could stay in the United States legally forever. Brian McGill immediately wrote back to the INS to request an extension as our case was still being processed.

We finally received word that our visa problem had been resolved at the end of February 1989. But our troubles weren't quite over yet. The INS had somehow lost our file, and it was only recovered following the intercession of Senator Orrin Hatch and his distinguished colleague, Senator Jake Garn of Utah, thanks to the help of both Huntsmans— Sr. and Jr. The INS might not be the most competent government bureaucracy, but it acted quite efficiently when the offices of two senators called. Thanks to all the twists and turns in our case, it was June 1989 before Bin, Bo, and I received our permanent visas.

★ ★ ★

In May 1989, there were almost daily news reports about student demonstrations in Beijing. Tens of thousands of students had taken over Tiananmen Square, waving banners, making speeches, and singing patriotic songs. The crowds were so great that the leadership had to change the venue for the welcome ceremony for Mikhail Gorbachev, the first state visit by a Soviet leader in 30 years. Citizens from all walks of life were coming out in support of the students. There seemed to be widespread discontent.

The demonstrations had been triggered by the death of Hu Yaobang, the former Party general secretary. I had strong memories of him. As a young teen in Beijing in 1966, I had witnessed his "struggle session" on the balcony of his apartment, where he was forced to stand bent over while being denounced by Red Guards not much older than I was.

Hu was ultimately rehabilitated and supported the return of Deng Xiaoping to power. He became the general secretary of the Party in 1981 and held the top position until 1987, when he was removed after clashing with the old guard on the Politburo, including Deng himself.

Hu was seen as a reformist—a "bourgeois liberal," as Party conservatives labeled him before his 1987 ouster—but was widely respected. He was open-minded about freedom of expression and advocated bringing more democratic elements into the system. In 1986, for example, he became the first to propose abolishing lifetime tenure for senior leaders.

Hu's reputation for integrity and for his liberal-leaning mind stood in sharp contrast to what was increasingly being seen as widespread corruption among government officials, not to mention an unpopular recent crackdown on political dissent and "spiritual pollution" (i.e., Western liberal ideas). Thus his untimely death on April 15, following a heart attack he had suffered during a meeting of the Politburo, triggered a massive outpouring of grief.

The memorials to Hu Yaobang soon turned into political demonstrations. Article after article and poster after poster appeared on university walls, demanding more freedom, greater democracy, and an end to official corruption. These demands were perceived by the conservatives in the leadership as representing the very bourgeois liberalism that Hu's tolerance had engendered. When these demands were ignored, protests and demonstrations followed. University students were at the forefront of the protest movement.

At no time since I first arrived in the United States had I seen the media cover China so intensively. We followed the news of what was going on in Beijing every day, watching as more and more people went to Tiananmen Square to protest. By mid-May, some of the students in Tiananmen Square had gone on a hunger strike. Now even official newspapers such as the *People's Daily* began to report the protests and to print articles sympathizing with the student movement.

In the early morning of May 20, the government declared martial law in Beijing. Troops moved into the city. Tensions in Beijing were so high that it was nerve-wracking, even for us on the other side of the world. My wife and I were gripped by the news reports coming out of China, and every day we were worried what would happen next. It seemed that neither the students nor the government were going to back down from the confrontation.

If the students had wanted their protest to reach the widest possible international audience, they could not have timed it better. Every major US TV network and newspaper had sent correspondents to cover Gorbachev's historic visit to Beijing. There was probably more news media in Beijing than when Nixon visited. But Gorbachev's visit had been completely overshadowed by the protests. We were transfixed as live coverage of Tiananmen Square filled the airwaves every day. The same day the government declared martial law, it also ordered all foreign networks to terminate their broadcasts from Beijing. We watched as CBS anchorman Dan Rather argued with Chinese officials on live television as they attempted to shut down the network's makeshift studio in a Beijing hotel. He managed to stay on the air for nearly half an hour before the plug was pulled. In all, though, these attempts to black out the news were quite futile; there were probably thousands of foreign journalists in Beijing. Live reports, photos, and videos continued to pour out of the city.

For days, the stalemate dragged on. The students continued to occupy the square, while troops called in to enforce martial law ringed the city center, although for some reason they seemed to be restrained from marching into the square. On television, we could see convoys of armored personnel carriers.

I was interviewed a couple of times about my take on the situation in Beijing. When journalists contacted me, I explained the economic reasons for the discontent. But I offered no prediction what would happen next. I was hoping for a speedy resolution and for some meaningful changes. The uncompromising position taken by the government disappointed me. As troops gathered outside Beijing, the big question in everyone's mind was whether or not the troops would shoot their way into the city, and if there would be bloodshed.

On June 3, 1989, a television camera crew came to our home in Cherry Hill to interview me. They focused the shot on our front lawn. The TV reporter asked me a few questions about how to make sense of what was happening in Beijing, then he asked, "Do you think the troops will open fire on the protesters?"

I replied without hesitation, "No. It won't happen."

"Why are you so certain?" he asked.

"There are three reasons," I began. "First, it isn't necessary. It seems this is already at the tail end of the protests, and there are not many people left in Tiananmen Square. Second, it is unthinkable the troops will shoot ordinary citizens. Third . . . "

At this point, someone handed a note to the reporter. He took a brief look at it and handed it to me while I was still on camera. It read: "The troops opened fire."

I was completely shocked. I had not even finished my sentence before my prediction was shattered by reality. With this breaking news, the interview stopped and we all rushed inside to turn on the television. The coverage on the screen did not show troops, just people running in the streets, but gunshots could clearly be heard. I could not believe it had come to this. I felt so sad and angry.

The reporter wanted to get my reaction to the shootings in Beijing. I had just proved myself wrong with my prediction. Now I said, "I was giving you a rational analysis just now. What is happening there isn't rational. I don't know how to explain it."

It was June 4, 1989, Beijing time. Throughout the day and into the night, we followed the events on television. We heard gunshots and people shouting; we saw images of the wounded or dead being rushed away, tanks being set on fire, soldiers holding their guns as they marched into Tiananmen Square, and students, hand in hand, being herded out by the advancing troops as fire burned around them. By the next morning, the television footage showed tanks rolling down the main street in front of Tiananmen.

In the wake of June 4, the global response was immediate. Western countries including the United States imposed sanctions on China, while leaders worldwide expressed their shock and outrage. What worried me most was that the tragic events in Beijing would set back China's reforms, now that the staunch reformers such as Hu Yaobang and Zhao Ziyang were gone. Zhao, who had succeeded Hu as the Party's general secretary, was removed from his position and put under house arrest, because he was opposed to the crackdown. Where was China headed? Would it go back to the old system? I hoped fervently that would not be the case.

★ ★ ★

At Wharton, I founded an academic journal, *China Economic Review* (*CER*). I did so because of my interest in China and my association with the US-based Chinese Economists Society, even though *CER* was a sideline undertaking for me and the work didn't earn me any credit with the university. I signed a contract with Herb Johnson of JAI Press, a well-known publishing house for academic works, and invited a number of well-known economists to be members of the editorial board, including my Wharton colleague the Nobel laureate Lawrence Klein; Gregory Chow of Princeton; Ezra Vogel and Dwight Perkins of Harvard; Nicholas Lardy and Kenneth Lieberthal of the University of Michigan; and Yang Xiaokai of Monash University in Australia.

I also invited Nobel laureate Milton Friedman, then at the Hoover Institution at Stanford. He declined, but he sent a very nice letter wishing me success.

The first issue was published in the spring of 1989. I had invited all the members of the editorial board to submit papers for publication and received a gratifying response, particularly as such prominent academics would usually prefer to publish in established journals and not some unknown start-up. There was one problem. Dr. Chow had submitted an account of his experiences teaching economics and studying economic reforms in China. Chow is a renowned expert in the field of econometrics, and his firsthand involvement in China's economic reforms and his interactions with the Chinese premier Zhao Ziyang made an interesting read. But this was a short memoir of his experiences, not a research paper. I wrote to him to explain that *CER* was an academic journal and therefore his paper was not suitable.

Dr. Chow did not like my decision. He suggested that I was legally obligated to publish his piece because I had invited his submission. I explained to him that I made clear in my invitation we would only accept academic papers, which his was not. I was concerned about setting a precedent with our inaugural issue, that we would only publish articles based on academic research. He requested that I send his paper for review anyway, as he was convinced independent referees would support him.

Indeed, I had declined to publish the paper before sending it around for peer review, as I thought it was obvious that it was not an academic piece; but his request was fair, and I had to oblige. Given Dr. Chow's stature, I had to find some heavyweights in the field of economics to review his paper. I sent his paper to two Nobel laureates, Lawrence Klein and Milton Friedman. I left Dr. Chow's name uncovered, explaining that while this generally violated the rules of peer review and because it was an account of his personal experiences, it would be fairly clear who the author was anyway.

Within a couple of weeks, I received letters from both of them. The decision was unanimous: Dr. Chow's submission, while interesting, should not be published in *CER* because it was not a research paper. These were world-renowned economists, and I was sure they were very busy. I was gratified that both were willing to spend the time to help this young publication.

I covered up the reviewers' names and sent their letters to Dr. Chow, informing him that both were economists of great standing. But I also came up with an idea. I suggested we publish his paper, not in the main body of the journal, but in a special section at the end of the issue titled "Reflections." I thought it was a good solution that satisfied Dr. Chow and allowed me to keep the academic standards of the journal intact.

★ ★ ★

In March 1990, I went with a group of Wharton Executive MBA students to Spain and Germany as part of their foreign immersion program. The EMBA program was an intensive study course for experienced executives. I and the other faculty members were taking them to visit a few companies in Europe, to learn a bit about the European market and to understand how these companies were preparing for the European Union to become effective in 1992.

The program concluded in Munich and students went their separate ways. I joined three other Wharton faculty members for a trip to Berlin. The city's famous wall separating East and West had fallen just four months earlier, in November 1989, and I was eager to see what the city looked like in the aftermath of such an historic event.

West Berlin, where we arrived on March 17, was like a different country from Munich. It was much more lively, colorful, crowded, and noisy. It felt like New York City at Christmas time. My colleague Skip Rosoff and I and another colleague, Isik Inselbag, walked for an hour and a half from our hotel to reach the Brandenburg Gate, the massive eighteenth-century monument that straddled East and West Berlin. On that bright day, many people were walking on the wide boulevard leading to Brandenburg, as there were almost no motor vehicles. Originally, the boulevard extended through the gate into East Berlin, but the Berlin Wall had cut it off. Just by the boulevard on the West Berlin side was an enormous memorial to the Soviet Red Army soldiers who had died in the war, presumably in the final conquest of Berlin. We could only look at the monument from a distance as it was ringed off and guarded by Russian soldiers.

We arrived at the Berlin Wall to find throngs of people, both in front of the wall and on the wall. The barrier at this section was made of two parallel walls, with a no-man's-land in between. The Brandenburg Gate lay between these two walls, unreachable by either the East Berliners or the West Berliners, until the walls were breached. When we saw it, scaffolding covered the gate, which was obviously under much-needed repair. We learned that between 1961 and 1989, more than 4,000 people had been shot to death trying to scale the walls to flee East Berlin.

The decision by East Germany to lift its border control in November 1989 prompted thousands of East and West Germans to take hammers and pickaxes to the Berlin Wall in a joyous attempt to erase the barrier that divided them. But on the day of our visit much of the wall still stood. It was covered with colorful graffiti and defaced with chisel marks. Many people were busy chiseling at the wall from the side and on top. We climbed onto the wall ourselves and took pictures. On either side of the Brandenburg Gate, there were gaping holes in both the eastern and western walls so that people could cross through the holes. East German soldiers stood idly by without stopping anyone, so we decided to climb through the hole in the wall to visit East Berlin.

The East Berlin side was even more crowded and festive. The sky was blue and the sun was bright. It was warm spring weather even though it was still March. We were told the high temperature was rare at this time of the year. As we walked around, I was impressed with the grand buildings lining wide boulevards. Indeed, all the historic buildings were on the east side of Berlin. East Berlin's government office buildings, in contrast, were similar to the Soviet-style ones in China. They were tall and heavy, appearing formidable and monolithic.

We came to an impressive-looking white stone building by a river. This was the Pergamon Museum, named after an ancient temple complex in what is now Turkey. It housed several gigantic ancient architectural structures, including the Ishtar Gate of Babylon and the towering Market Gate of Miletus, all of which had been taken from the Middle East and Turkey and reconstructed inside the museum.

The centerpiece of the museum and its namesake was the second-century BC Pergamon Altar, standing 35 meters (~115 feet) wide and 33 meters (~110 feet) deep. The massive marble structure had formed part of the acropolis of the ancient Greek city of Pergamon; its front stairway alone was almost 20 meters (~66 feet) wide. On the side of the structure around the altar was a 113-meter-long (~370 feet) frieze depicting the struggle of the gods and the giants. It was absolutely amazing to see such a large building inside a building. It was clear that all the antiquities were well preserved and the museum itself looked and felt modern and could rival the best in the West. It was quite a miracle it all had survived the intensive bombing and gunfire the city had sustained before the German surrender in 1945. For nearly 40 years it had been a hidden treasure, unseen by people outside East Germany.

The museum was located on an island in the Spree River, which was probably scenic at one time but was now badly polluted. Pollution, I understood, was a major problem in East Germany. Outside the museum, a crowd was busy exchanging money. The official exchange rate between East and West German marks was one to one. On the black market, however, a West German mark was worth as much as four and a half East German marks—even though in many places, such as the Pergamon Museum, the price was the same regardless of which mark you used. The three of us were Wharton professors, and we could not miss such a good arbitrage opportunity. We bought a bunch of East German marks at the black-market rate.

We had a good lunch in a nice restaurant. I was surprised by the quality of the food and particularly by the good service. Even though it was state-owned, the services in the restaurant were much better than what one would have found in state-owned restaurants in China. I didn't know the reason for it and put it down to the fastidious German culture. We paid for our lunch with our new East German marks; it cost the three of us the equivalent of only about US$3. Prices in East Berlin were like those in pre-reform China.

Over lunch, we struck up a conversation with an East Berlin couple. We found them to be hopeful and optimistic about the future. They wished for reunification as soon as possible. Even though there was a big gap in the standard of living between the two sides of Berlin, people on both sides longed for reunification. I thought Berlin would become a world-class city after it became reunified. The couple also talked about the general resentment toward official corruption in East Germany, much of which was exposed only after the fall of the Berlin Wall. But listening to them, it seemed the officials of East Germany just had many privileges and better living conditions, not as outrageous as the corruption I heard about in China.

While East Germany was no doubt a less developed part of the city than the western side, I was surprised to see how many cars there were on the street. It seemed that car ownership was common in East Germany, which was probably the wealthiest of the Soviet-bloc countries. But the cars in East Berlin all looked the same: small, boxy, and shoddily built. Most were either light beige or light green. Catching sight of an East German car parked next to a Mercedes-Benz, Skip could not resist pointing out the obvious contrast in quality. He asked me to take a picture of him standing between the two cars, stretching out his arms to point at each of them as if to say, "Look at the difference."

We wandered around until evening came. We came upon what looked like a fancy and expensive restaurant. With the stack of East German marks in our pockets, we felt quite rich. We walked in and sat down for dinner. The decor inside the restaurant showed it was quite high-end, with a grand piano in the corner.

We ordered steak and wine, followed by some good dessert. Again, the service was good. We quite enjoyed the meal while listening to the live piano music. When the bill came, it was equivalent to about US$15. Based on my experience in China, I knew this was not going to last, nor would the East German marks in our pockets, so we might as well spend them when we could.

It was probably about 10 p.m. when we finished dinner. We walked back to the Brandenburg Gate, intending to return to West Berlin the way we had come. But when we arrived, we discovered the crowd had disappeared and bright spotlights illuminated the wall. A tall East German soldier with a submachine gun slung across his shoulder now guarded the hole we had passed through.

We went up to him and explained that we wanted to go back to out hotel on the other side, and that we had come through this hole earlier in the day. For an East German soldier, he spoke good English. He politely refused our request and told us we had to go to Checkpoint Charlie for crossing. The checkpoint was about 2 kilometers (~1.2 miles) away, it was out of our way, and it was already getting quite late. So I was trying my best to negotiate with him to let us through. He would not budge. As we talked, we shifted our positions so that I was standing right in front of the big hole and West Berlin was only one step away from where I stood. At that point, I said to the soldier, half-jokingly: "What if I give a dash across?"

He stared at me, and with a serious and straight face he replied in a polite and subdued voice, "Then I'll be obliged to shoot you, sir." He didn't appear to be kidding.

We took a long walk to Checkpoint Charlie only to find that we couldn't get through without our passports, which we hadn't brought because we didn't expect to cross the border when we left the hotel. It took us more than an hour of further negotiation before the guards finally let us through.

The next day, Skip and I went back to East Berlin through Checkpoint Charlie. This time, the crossing took more than an hour. It was so much easier through the hole in the Berlin Wall. We were lucky, as it was a historic day, the day of the first free parliamentary election in East Germany since 1932 (when Hitler lost the presidential election but was soon appointed chancellor). We followed the crowds in the direction of a tall television tower rising into the sky. A young man caught up with us and offered to walk with us. We were happy to have an English-speaking local guide. He told us that he was a resident of West Berlin. He also said he could easily tell who in the crowds around us was an East Berliner and who a West Berliner. We asked him how he knew, as they were all German and they all looked more or less the same to us. The difference, he said, was in the clothing and in the shoes. It reminded me of the day I had first arrived in America, when Andy Andrews could immediately tell I was from Mainland China by my haircut.

In the square around the television tower a band was playing on a large makeshift stage. Here and there, some people were speaking on a high stand—politicians doing some last-minute campaigning, I supposed. So many people, including many foreign journalists, had swarmed East Berlin to cover this historic election. Children were running around with colorful balloons. It was another beautiful sunny day, and most people just walked around to enjoy the festivities and the sun. We mingled with the crowd and soaked in the excitement and happy atmosphere.

The voting ended at 6 p.m. By 7 p.m., preliminary results were already out. East Germany's Christian Democratic Union won the general elections with 47 percent of the seats in Parliament. The Communist Party won only 15 percent of the seats. The stage was set for German reunification, which was achieved later that year. When I returned to Berlin a couple of years later, the wall was already gone. I did bring home a few pieces of concrete taken from the wall as mementos. But I soon read that the wall materials contained asbestos, so Bin threw them away, ignoring my protests.

★ ★ ★

In addition to my regular classes, I did a fair amount of executive education organized by Wharton. These programs took me to different parts of the United States and abroad, often in summertime, because Wharton has a large network of alumni in many countries, and they were willing to help fund these programs. In fact, my family only took summer vacations when they traveled with me on these trips.

In the summer of 1990, Wharton held an executive training program in Shanghai on the campus of Shanghai Jiaotong University, one of the best in China. It was the first program of its kind in China. I served as the program director. The participants, about 50 of them, were relatively young officials drawn from different levels of the Shanghai government and state-owned companies. The level of their English proficiency varied, but by and large they were able to follow the classes in English. For a period of two weeks, Wharton professors took turns giving lectures on various subjects related to management, marketing, finance, and international business.

Many of the participants in the Shanghai program went on to become high-ranking officials in the Chinese government. One early star was Chen Liangyu, who became the city's top leader and a member of the Party's Politburo. Unfortunately, he fell from grace in 2007 and was sentenced to 18 years in jail for corruption. Another one was Hua Jianmin, the CEO of Shenergy, a state-owned power company. He became secretary general of the State Council and eventually vice chairman of the People's Congress. Meng Jianzhu was the head of a suburban county government who rose through the ranks to become China's minister of public security and a member of the Politburo.

The social unrest of 1989 had taken a toll on China's economic growth. In both 1987 and 1988, the real economy grew at more than 11 percent. In 1989, it grew only 4.2 percent, followed by an even tamer growth of 3.9 percent in 1990. Economic reforms seemed to have slowed down, and in some cases to have halted or reversed. Many were concerned that China might go back to the pre-reform old system.

I judged that in spite of the recent setback and slowdown, China's reforms had become irreversible. This had been borne out by my observations on the ground during my visits to Beijing and Shanghai. In the United States I gave speeches on a number of occasions, including at Wharton and elsewhere, to explain my reasoning. China's population was much better off now than it was in pre-reform days, and any policy to reverse that would meet with insurmountable resistance. When people were making a dollar a month, as I had been doing in the Gobi, nobody cared much how the politics changed; whatever happened, we could not be much worse off and there was nothing to lose. But people were now making $50 a month; going back to the old days of $1 per month was unacceptable. Such a change would create so much chaos and instability that no government would be able to roll back the wheels of history.

In 1992, Deng Xiaoping was also concerned about the slowdown or reversal of reforms. Even though he was already 88 years old, he embarked upon what the official press called a "southern tour." He traveled to Shanghai, Guangzhou, and Shenzhen, three cities that had become the most open and market-oriented over the previous half-decade. During his visit, he declared, "Development is the hard truth," suggesting that any debate about socialism or capitalism was irrelevant and no policy was good if it did not produce growth. He also said, "Whoever isn't in favor of reforms must step down."

His very act of the southern tour and his pro-reform remarks resonated strongly with the population and rekindled another wave of enthusiasm for reforms; it also silenced those officials who still questioned whether reform policies were socialist or capitalist. It was clever and practical of him to set aside that ideological debate to focus on efforts to promote growth. And it worked. After his southern tour, investment surged. In 1992, the real economy grew an astonishing 14.2 percent. If there was any doubt about China's resolve to continue with market-oriented reforms, it dissipated. China was entering another round of rapid growth.

A joke I heard in China captured Deng's pragmatism well: Three cars came to a crossroads, driven, respectively, by Mao; Josip Broz Tito, the former Yugoslav leader who split with Joseph Stalin to lead his country into a market economy; and Deng Xiaoping. Mao took the road on the left. Tito took the road on the right. Deng signaled to turn left but took the road on the right.

My visits to China convinced me that it was moving into a new phase, one that represented the opportunity of a lifetime for millions of Chinese. I wanted to find a way to capture these opportunities and also to help in this process. The training programs I had taught, the seminars I had led—these all helped. But I wanted to do more. I was thinking of going back to China.

I knew, however, that returning to China would mean that I would have to leave too much behind. Life in the United States was comfortable. Bin had a good job at the corporate office of AT&T. Our son, Bo, now 10 years old, was an American kid who loved his friends at school and in the neighborhood. The year before we had welcomed our daughter, LeeAnn, who was born in New Jersey, and who was now taking her very first steps. We wanted the best for our children. Going back to China would mean I would leave academia to plunge into the world of business, in which I had never tried my hand, and our family would have to uproot itself and face new challenges. It was the toughest decision I had ever faced in my life. At this stage in my career, I knew it was now or never: Once I made a decision, there would be no turning back. And while Bin said she would be supportive whichever road we took, I knew I would be making a decision for my family that would forever alter their lives as well.

★ ★ ★

By 1992, I had been teaching at Wharton for six years. I had published my fair share of research papers, although I knew they were not enough to earn me a tenured position. But I found I didn't much care. I could have concentrated more on my research instead of traveling almost every summer to different countries for teaching and consulting. I allowed myself to be pulled into these excursions, away from my research work, because I found them interesting and rewarding, whereas academic research was getting quite tedious and dreary. Increasingly, I felt that my research was of trivial significance and did not provide any profound insight anyway. I could not imagine myself holed up in an ivory tower forever when the outside world seemed so exciting and enticing. Besides, I told myself, I had preached for too long; I needed an opportunity to practice what I had preached.

My life had taken many twists and turns so far. Now I was looking for another change. I thought I would make an attractive candidate to big US firms with ambitions in China, because of my familiarity with US businesses, my knowledge of China, and my stature as an academic in business education. I opened myself up to opportunities.

Soon, I received job offers from some of the most venerable names in the US corporate world, from firms that were increasingly looking for ways to capitalize on the fast-growing Chinese market and on its potential. I was somewhat surprised by the generosity of these offers. I had long known that Wharton graduates, especially those working on

Wall Street, earned more than their professors. But I had no idea how much more until that moment. Professional athletes are also paid vastly more than their coaches. However, there is a difference. While sports coaches cannot really compete as professional athletes do, there is no reason for business professors not to be able to do the same work they teach their students to do.

In the spring of 1993 I took a job with JP Morgan, the banking institution as storied as Wall Street itself. Soon I shipped out, together with my family, to the then-British colony of Hong Kong, to start a new career in banking. My responsibility would be to help the firm develop its business in China.

Epilogue

In 2005, 30 years after leaving, I returned to the Gobi.

My life took me a long way from the desert. I had since earned a PhD at UC Berkeley, taught at the Wharton School, and worked as a managing director of JP Morgan. Then, in 2005, I became a managing partner of Newbridge Capital, the Asia offshoot of Texas Pacific Group (now called TPG), a major private equity investment firm based in San Francisco. When in the Gobi, I often did not know where and when my next meal would be. At Newbridge I was dabbling in the dispensing of hundreds of millions of dollars in investments and corporate acquisitions. How I got into playing high-stakes money games is, perhaps, another story worth telling.

In 2005 I was also serving as an independent director on the board of China Unicom, one of China's largest mobile telecommunications companies.

Unicom's management had arranged for all of its independent directors to take an "inspection tour" in a province of their choice to learn more about the company's operations at the grassroots level. I chose Inner Mongolia, which I hadn't seen since I left in September 1975.

On Saturday, July 9, 2005, I flew from Hong Kong to Beijing, then to Baotou, the second-largest city in Inner Mongolia. I thought I could use the weekend to go back to see Urat Farm. The flight from Beijing to Baotou took little more than an hour. What a sharp contrast from 36 years ago, when the journey took more than 30 hours under so much less comfortable circumstances.

I was met at the airport by a team from China Unicom, who presented me with a bouquet of flowers. They drove me to Weixin Golf Club, a resort about halfway between Baotou and Urat Qianqi. I arrived just before sundown. I was surprised: a golf course surrounded by modern-looking villas had sprouted in the middle of the Gobi Desert. My hosts told me proudly that Weixin had more sand traps than any other golf course in the world. I didn't tell them that in my time the toughest thing to find was not sand but rather a way to grow grass in the Gobi. As we got out of our vehicles, I saw wild rabbits eating grass and running around by the roadside. They were lucky to live in modern times. In my time, they would have been all caught and eaten.

I was given a luxury villa all to myself. It was the sort of place you would find in resorts in the Caribbean Islands or in the Maldives where the wealthy go on holiday. The front driveway of my villa alone could fit several cars. How times had changed. During our hungry years there, who could have imagined anything like this would ever exist in the Gobi?

The team from China Unicom and I had dinner at the clubhouse of the resort. The main course was a roasted whole lamb. I joked with my hosts that I would have stayed in the Gobi if life had been so good in my time.

The next day, we left the resort and drove first to Urat Qianqi and then to Batou, the former headquarters of my regiment, almost 80 kilometers (~50 miles) away. Batou was where I had received my medical training 35 years earlier. Almost nothing was recognizable. The regiment headquarters building remained, but it was empty and dilapidated, apparently no longer in use though not yet demolished. But there were many modern-looking multistory buildings with tinted glass windows reflecting the sun.

After a tour of Batou, which had been turned into a lakeside tourist attraction, my hosts and I went into one of the restaurants. There had not been a single restaurant in Batou 30 years ago. Now there were several. But I didn't eat. I was anxious to go and find my old farm, but I didn't want to go back with so many people in tow. So I snuck out of the restaurant with a driver, and we got into his white four-wheel-drive SUV. I took the wheel while he sat on the passenger side.

I had to stop the vehicle several times to ask people if anyone knew where former Company No. 5 of Regiment No. 19 was located. Someone who used to be with Company No. 4 pointed us in the right direction. After a few minutes of driving, the paved roads of Batou gave way to gravel and dirt tracks. Soon, the road disappeared entirely. Now I was really back in the Gobi. All around me was sand, gravel, thorns, and dunes, stretching to the horizon. The sky was blue with a few white clouds. I saw a whirlwind here and there moving across the dunes and then dissipating. All the familiar sights.

After about an hour of driving through the Gobi, I stopped at a small village. A few people were sitting in the shade of a tree. A woman told me this was where the subheadquarters of our regiment had been. The site of our company's old barracks was just a few minutes' drive to the east. Remarkably, the small shop where I used to buy canned pork was still there; it looked exactly as it had 30 years earlier.

I asked the woman if there were still any Construction Army Corps soldiers left here. She told me that yes, there was one married couple. She led me to an iron gate. I opened the gate and walked into a rather dirty yard where I saw a well-dressed young woman in her twenties who looked more like a city girl than a farmer's daughter in the Gobi. Her mother had been with the Construction Army Corps. Just then, a woman came out of the house. As soon as she saw me, she called out my name in a loud voice: "Shan Weijian!" I was so surprised that she immediately recognized me after 30 years. She looked familiar, but I couldn't recall her name.

It was Li Yongzhi. The young lady who had greeted me at the gate was her 24-year-old daughter, Wang Hui. Yongzhi took me to her home in the back of the yard. Their living quarters were quite small, no more than 50 square meters (~400 to 500 square feet) combined. There was a foyer just inside the door where a piglet snuffled quietly in a box. The couple's bedroom was on the right side and their daughter's bedroom was on the left. That was about it. The place was quite dirty and run-down, not much different from what I had been familiar with in the old days.

As I stepped into the room to the right, a man greeted me. I recognized him as Wang Shuangxi, whom we had all called Er Xi (meaning "double happiness"). He was reclining on a *kang* by the window. He excused himself for not being able to get up; he had broken his leg riding a motorcycle not long ago and had been bedridden since then. Both of them were happy to see me, as I them.

Er Xi was Company No. 5's stableman, taking care of our horses and driving horse-pulled carts. He was a good horseman and could mount a barebacked horse by jumping on from behind, which I had never seen anyone else be capable of doing. I asked him why he was riding a motorcycle, not a horse. He told me that keeping and raising horses was largely banned because their grazing would further destroy what little vegetation remained in the Gobi. Only camels were still allowed because they were considered somewhat endangered. Motorcycles were much more convenient. They did not need to be fed or taken care of and they traveled much faster. But I could see from his accident that riding a motorcycle in the sandy desert could be a challenge, too.

They offered me some tea and an ice bar from their freezer before telling me their story. Er Xi and Yongzhi were the only people left of our company. They now made a living by raising pigs and selling piglets. They had about 40 pigs in the pens in their gated yard, guarded by two big ferocious-looking dogs.

Er Xi said that they had made about 60,000 yuan the previous year (about US$7,500). Yongzhi told me that they also continued to collect a pension from the government for their service in the Construction Army Corps. In addition to raising pigs, she had also taught at the village school, although now the school was shut down for lack of students.

I could imagine that no young people, if they had a choice, would want to stay in this place. Yes, life here had immensely improved from 30 years ago. But it was still in the middle of the Gobi with not much to do other than limited farming under improved but still harsh conditions. Wang Hui, their daughter, was now working in Beijing, where she stayed with Yongzhi's parents. She was home temporarily to care for her father. Little wonder that she aspired to a life away from the Gobi.

Yongzhi and her daughter took me to the site where the barracks of Company No. 5 had been. This was where I spent six years of my youth. There used to be rows of mud-brick houses that we had built with our own hands. But now all of them were gone, so completely that there was no trace left. They had just disappeared into the soil of the Gobi. The small baked-brick house of the blacksmith's shop remained, as did the building that housed the company office and the medical clinic where I worked as a barefoot doctor. They now looked terribly shabby.

Gone also was the company's water well. There was no longer any farmland by the site of our former barracks, although we had toiled for years to cultivate the land. The water of the nearby lake flooded it, and now reeds grew there. We had spent so much of our youth battling with nature to turn this land into arable farms. Eventually nature prevailed and took it all back.

We drove to the kiln where I had spent so many days and nights making bricks. Now it was just a tall mound of earth, but it was still the highest vantage point within sight. Surprisingly, it was surrounded by farmland, where some kind of green vegetable was growing in tidy rows. The farm seemed to have shrunk back to the size of its former self, before the hundreds of Construction Army Corps soldiers arrived. All our efforts for so many years to reclaim farmland from the Gobi had come to naught.

As I looked around, all the memories of our life here more than 30 years ago flooded back. It was here we had buried our youth. It was here we had grown from teenagers to adults. It was here we had learned the harsh realities of life. It was here we had seen our hopes turn into despair. And it was also here so many of my friends had been denied a future, wasting their best years when they should have been in school. What for?

I waved good-bye to Yongzhi and her daughter and hopped back into the SUV. We turned around to return to Batou. Still, there was no road and as I drove, the terrain around us looked the same, endless in every direction. Soon I got lost. Then I noticed a power transmission line on top of tall poles stretching as far as the eye could see. I figured the power line would lead me to Batou, the only place around that a power station could possibly be located. As I drove in parallel with the transmission line, I saw a group of people standing with their motor-cycles by one of the poles. I stopped the SUV to ask for directions.

A slim, bare-chested, dark-skinned man who looked to be in his late forties or early fifties approached me. As I rolled down the window I saw his face chiseled by weather although his chest and arms were muscled. He looked like any other local peasant. But barely had he started to speak when I recognized him. He was the boy who was jailed for the crime of "lying on top for a moment."

"Er Gou!" I cried.

He tensed up. A stranger calling him by his nickname, "Second Dog," must have shocked, indeed frightened him. I hurriedly told him my name. He relaxed and apologized for not immediately recognizing me. I would not have expected him to remember me; we were never close. He, of course, became notorious after his arrest and public sentencing.

I couldn't believe that, 30 years later, in the middle of a desert where it was hard to find a soul for miles, I had come across not just an old-timer I had known but also none other than Er Gou. Both of us were incredulous at this almost-impossible coincidence. I wanted to know what had happened to him after all these years. I was sure his curiosity about me was equally strong. He invited me to his home. I followed his motorcycle as he led the way.

Er Gou lived in a nice-looking whitewashed concrete house near Lake Wuliangsu. But inside, his home was a mess. There were dirty dishes in his bedroom and watermelon skins piled up high on the desk next to his bed.

We sat down and he told me his story.

After being sentenced, Er Gou served four years in jail. By the time he was released, around 1978, the Construction Army Corps had been disbanded and all the educated youths had returned to the cities they had come from. He went back to Beijing as well. But because of his criminal record, nobody would give him a job. He just stayed with his parents, loafing around without much to do.

In 1979, Deng Xiaoping, who had returned to power the previous year, launched a campaign to "severely crack down on crimes." Er Gou was picked up by the police for no other reason than his prior criminal record and sent to a forced-labor camp in Tacheng, in Xinjiang Province. Tacheng was on the very western edge of China, right on the border with Kazakhstan. The Chinese government had been exiling criminals there since the Qing dynasty, because it was farthest from the civilized center than anywhere else in the country.

Er Gou was in that labor camp for five years. But he did not entirely waste his time there. By the end of it, he received a college degree through correspondence courses.

But even a college degree couldn't help Er Gou find a job back in Beijing upon his release, because of his prior record. Although he had always denied the charges, his conviction three decades earlier had condemned him to a life in and out of jail, forced labor, and eventually back to the Gobi. He married a local woman and had a daughter. His wife and daughter were now in Beijing, living with his parents, because, I think, the daughter could get a much better education there. I did not think his wife and daughter would want to return to the Gobi. So he lived by himself.

Even though he and I now lived in completely different worlds— and he was unlikely to be able to imagine the world in which I now lived—I felt no distance between us as we reminisced about the old times. He wanted me to stay for dinner, to eat fish from the lake, but I told him I had to go back to Batou before dark because there were people waiting for me there. He offered to take me back to our old "battlefields," where we had spent winters cutting reeds on the lake.

He first took me to the village of Nanchang, where we had spent a couple of winters. At one time, I stayed in the home of a local peasant, but I could find no traces of his house. The living quarters for our platoon were gone but the row of mud-brick shacks for the second platoon and the sixth platoon were still there, although crumbling.

I could drive the SUV no further because the trail became too narrow and full of potholes. I left the SUV with the driver and hopped onto the back of his motorcycle. Er Gou negotiated his way slowly forward until we came upon a higher ground on which stood the ruins of a few rows of old mud huts. "This is Fanshengedan," he told me.

Fanshengedan was the cluster of mud huts where we had lived in the winter of 1971–1972 while cutting reeds. There was nothing recognizable, absolutely nothing. Standing there and looking out, I saw sand dunes all around us, and waves of reeds in the distance.

All was gone, except the crumbling ruins, a fading but potent reminder of what this place meant to my life and to the lives of so many friends.

Index